System i
Disaster Recovery Planning

System i
Disaster Recovery Planning

Richard Dolewski

MC Press Online, LP
Lewisville, TX 75077

System i Disaster Recovery Planning
Richard Dolewski

First Edition

First Printing—March 2008

MC Press offers excellent discounts on this book when ordered in quantity for bulk purchases or special sales, which may include custom covers and content particular to your business, training goals, marketing focus, and branding interest.

For information regarding permissions or special orders, please contact:
    MC Press
    Corporate Offices
    125 N. Woodland Trail
    Lewisville, TX 75077 USA

For information regarding sales and/or customer service, please contact:
    MC Press
    P.O. Box 4300
    Big Sandy, TX 75755-4300 USA

ISBN: 1-58347-067-0

To my home and iSeries family

I could not have done this piece of work without the support of my wife Maria, who kept faith in me throughout. Thank you to my children Cassandra, Alexander, Nicholas, and Matthew for supporting my need to stay focused in lieu of throwing the ball around while promising that I would be finished "soon." Their curiosity about the book was never ending... "who would read it" and "would it help someone in a disaster?" As was their ultimate question, "what page are you on now?" I love you all for your support. And boys, yes, I am now finished.

Finally, the dream of writing a book would never have been possible without the encouragement and support from my MTS colleagues, TUG board members, special clients, and fellow iSeries professionals. You guys pushed me onto the presentation stage 10 years ago, supported the growth of my business, and allowed me to share my experience with every one of you.

This book is dedicated to all of you for making this dream happen.

Happy reading.

Richard

Contents

1

Building a Disaster Recovery
Plan—The Need

Disasters can strike any time, anywhere. Years of organizational success can be lost in minutes. Suppose you had to piece your organization together if it were to all go away tomorrow. It is a difficult task and a big job. You need a starting point, an ending point, and a roadmap to show you the way to systems recovery. You need a disaster recovery plan in place and staff dedicated to making the plan actually happen. The difference between losing your business and surviving in business depends on how well you're prepared for the unexpected. If a disaster struck today, how would your company do? Organizations must not only protect mission-critical data, but also put disaster recovery plans into place to prevent and support the recovery of any business outages.

Why is it that many organizations today still do not have a disaster recovery plan? Here are some typical excuses I have heard:

- There's not enough time.
- We're downsizing.

- My résumé is offsite.
- It will never happen to me!
- It's not in this year's budget.
- I just do not know where to start.

Do any of these sound familiar? If you have used any one or even all of these excuses and still don't have a comprehensive written and tested disaster recovery plan, you are not alone. A great amount of creative energy is spent formulating excuses instead of developing a plan. Even if you have a disaster recovery plan, are you really prepared? It is equally important to regularly test the plan to ensure that your business can be recovered as documented. Survival in business depends on how well you're prepared and trained for the unexpected. It is safe to say that disasters come without warning. A disaster will not happen during a convenient time to meet personal or work schedules.

The need for disaster recovery planning has been recognized by industry as an essential tool for business survival. Don't kid yourself—disasters do occur. The very survival of a business is in question when that business does not have a current, documented, and implemented recovery strategy. Insurance can help fund recovery, but it cannot service or replace your valued customers.

A fully documented and tested disaster recovery plan keeps bad things from happening to good companies. Disaster recovery (*DR*) means being aware of the threat and supporting the resumption of your business following any man-made or natural disasters. A disaster recovery plan not only protects your organization's most vital asset—your corporate information—it also helps create awareness within your organization. In addition, a DR plan helps you refine your infrastructure processes. Incorporating DR methodology into all IT integration strategies is forward thinking.

Most companies depend on their Information Technology (IT) to remain in business. Planning helps eliminate the need to gamble the livelihood of your business in hopes that a disaster will never strike your organization.

The success of your company can be attributed to years and years of hard work and risks that you successfully managed. Companies simply do *not* financially recover from a disaster when there is no fully documented and tested plan integrated into the business. Disaster recovery planning helps mitigate risks associated with the failure of the IT services on which your business depends. The most important goal is to enable your company to remain in business. If a disaster strikes, your company has everything to lose: critical data, profits, and information. All of these are critical assets in any company.

> *After 14 days without access to IT systems, 43 percent of businesses will not reopen; 29 percent of those that do reopen will close for good within two years.*

U.S. Bureau of Labor

The Need

What happens if the power goes out in your home? You grab a flashlight or light a candle, and look out the window to see if the neighbors' homes are dark. If they are, this is probably a widespread outage rather than just a circuit breaker in your basement. In that case, you know that your lights will come back on when the utility company restores power. You can view your company's computer processing as just another utility, like power and water. It is a utility that supports your business; it's not the business itself.

For over 15 years, I have had the opportunity to study disasters first-hand. The one thing they all have in common is that no one ever believes it will ever happen to them. You will have a halt in your business activity . . . a halt in your flow of information. How quickly you recover will determine if it is business as usual. If the business is worth the investment in the first place, it's probably worth protecting and recovering.

Some companies take for granted that a disaster will never strike. Rather than developing proactive solutions for such an event, importance usually falls on other corporate IT deliverables. Does your company have a comprehensive disaster recovery plan (*DRP*) that would allow it to continue to function in the event of a disaster?

Recent events around the country have kept us all on our toes. You just cannot pick up a newspaper or watch the news without hearing some bad news that requires some form of disaster-recovery planning response. Hurricanes Katrina and Rita in 2005, and Ivan and Francis in 2004. The great power outage in the American and Canadian northeast. The events of September 11, 2001. There are more everyday disasters, too, such as rotating power shortages or brown-outs. Finally, do not forget hardware failures. (Yes, the System i does break down!) All of these can have major impacts on today's business needs.

The underlying philosophy of disaster recovery planning needs to be deeply rooted in your organization's desire to protect the viability of its business, public image, and information assets. Your sales and marketing teams work extremely hard to build your corporate image and acquire new customers. New customers can be very difficult to get. Statistics show that it takes much more effort to gain a new customer than to maintain a customer. And once customers are lost, it is nearly impossible to get them back. So customer satisfaction is paramount. Trying to get new customers or convincing the old ones to hang around in a disaster is an uphill struggle if your corporate image has been damaged.

What Is a Disaster?

The textbook definition of a disaster is "a sudden, unplanned event that causes great damage and loss to an organization." The time factor determines whether the interruption in IT service delivery is an inconvenience or a disaster.

The time factor varies from organization to organization, of course. What does the face of disaster look like? What types of disasters should you consider? The list in Figure 1.1 is by no means complete, but it should give you an appreciation of the types of disaster you might wish to evaluate.

Act of God • Air Conditioning (HVAC) Failure • Arson • Avian Flu • Blackout • Blizzard • Bomb Threat • Brownout • Brush Fire • Building Fire • Chemical Spill • Civil Unrest • Communications Failure • Computer Crime • Disgruntled Employee • Disk Array Failure • Earthquake • Explosion • Flood • Hardware Failure• Heat • Human Error • Hurricane • Ice Storm • Labor Dispute • Lightning Strike • LPAR Failure • Malicious Activity • Mud Slide • Plane Crash • Power Outage • Sabotage • SARS • Sewage Backup • Software Failure • Sprinkler Failure • Tornado • Train Derailment • Vandalism • Virus • Water • Wild Fire

Figure 1.1: Disasters, A to Z.

My own definition of a disaster is quite simple: "A disaster is anything that stops your business from functioning and that cannot be corrected within an acceptable amount of time." Disasters are defined and quantified in relation to time. Time is important from the standpoint of when an interruption occurs and how long the interruptions lasts. The bottom line is that a disaster is defined as any interruption of mission-critical business processes for an unacceptable period of time.

This time-related definition reflects the very nature of a disaster and avoids the problems that frequently arise by only applying categorical adjectives to a disaster. We all tend to get caught up in categories and types of disasters instead of the impact they can potentially inflict. A category that constitutes a disaster for Company A might not be a disaster for Company B. For this reason, you need to take a holistic approach to examining what constitutes a disaster and examine the business and regulatory impacts to your specific organization. Whether it is a hardware failure of the RAID5 disk array or the loss of power due to a weather-related event like an ice storm, anything that could severely impact your own company is a type of disaster.

What Is Disaster Recovery?

Disaster recovery is your IT response to a sudden, unplanned event that will enable your organization to continue critical business functions until normal IT-related services can resume. Disaster recovery must address the continuation of critical business operations. A *major* incorrect assumption made in our industry is that disaster recovery can be fully realized by simply prearranging for hardware replacement with your business partner or channel distributor. Write one check and you have a DR plan. Call the supplier and they will come running with all the hardware you require at time of need. Will they? Even if they will, is disaster recovery only about hardware? The obvious answer is NO!

What Is Your Level of Disaster Preparedness?

Most of us initially think our chances of being hit by a disaster are remote. Unfortunately, this view might not change until after the fact—like buying a home alarm system after you have been robbed. While threats of a major disaster from a storm, earthquake, or flood are always present, it is more likely that your IT department would experience an extended communications outage, technology failure, or loss of power. Most organizations are ill-prepared to manage any sort of emergency. Time and money spent on a disaster recovery plan is a good business investment. Planning and preparation before a disaster can minimize the loss of revenue and help ensure an effective, timely recovery.

Suppose you get a phone call in the middle of night. (We all know those types of calls can only bring bad news!) The IT person at the other end of the call states that there has been a terrible accident in the manufacturing plant. The fire marshal has cut power to the building, and things do not look good. Your centralized data center is there, which supports national manufacturing plants, sales offices, and distribution centers.

Quick—what would you do?

If your answer takes longer than 10 seconds to formulate or includes more than "make one telephone call," you've got a problem. If you simply do not know the answer, or if you answer "Maybe I'd do this . . . ," you have a serious problem. It might be some comfort to know that, unfortunately, you have plenty of company. Despite the increasing dependence on the integration of technology into nearly every aspect of business, most corporations remain unprepared to recover IT infrastructure supporting critical business functions in a disaster. By remaining unprepared, you are putting your successful enterprise at risk.

Organizations fall into one of four levels of disaster preparedness, compared in Figure 1.2 to popular movies. Which level of preparedness best represents your organization? This question is vital to knowing the organizational culture in the eyes of senior management.

How prepared are you?

- Understand and are ready
  ✓ *Top Gun*

- Understand and are not ready
  ✓ *Sleepless in Seattle*

- Understand but don't want a disaster recovery plan
  ✓ *Dumb and Dumber*

- Don't understand. Why bother?!
  ✓ *Clueless or Armageddon*

Figure 1.2: Levels of organizational disaster-recovery preparedness.

If you don't know what level you're at, there's a relatively quick and easy way to find out. Ask yourself what are your organization's key business functions and which server infrastructures support these functions. Now assume that you were no longer able to use the systems because of an unplanned event— one hour, 12 hours, one day, two days, more? Then, estimate the financial impact this loss would have on your business based on how long your systems would be out. Determining your level of disaster preparedness may be a sobering exercise, when you consider lost sales, lost revenues, penalties from regulatory agencies, SLA-driven fines, and worst of all, damage to your public image! Obviously, quite a bit is at stake.

Questions for Preparedness

Here are some questions to help you assess your level of preparedness:

- Is your IT department positioned to respond in a disaster situation?
- What appropriate steps are currently in place to resume IT services?
- Is IT positioned to continue critical business functions during a disaster?
- Which daily business functions could IT afford to lose without suffering potential financial loss or disruption of expected services?
- Is IT positioned to respond to its business expectations, needs, and commitments in an acceptable manner despite a serious disruption?
- Is the IT management team trained in the discipline of crisis management?
- Who will make decisions during the disruption, and how will those decisions be communicated through the IT department?
- Is there a vital-records program in place that will allow the organization to retrieve and restore information following a major loss?
- Is there a contracted commercial or internal solution in place to test and train for disaster preparedness?

Effects of a Disaster

The effects of a disaster include the following:

- Business momentum
- Competitive edge
- Cash flow
- Human elements

In a disaster, one of the first things you will notice is a halt to your business momentum. It's not business as usual. The key is to minimize that and have a quick response so you can make your organization viable. A halt to your business momentum for an extended period of time could lose you any competitive edge that you hold in the marketplace. If it's a day or two, your customers will roll with you. If it's for an extended time, they will go elsewhere. So, if you are out for an extended period of time, it will start to effect your cash flow at a time when your company needs it most. If you experience a halt, you are going to need cash to control the problem. If you cannot send out your invoices to collect your accounts receivable, for example, you are effecting the thing that hurts the most: the bottom line.

Shock is another important effect of a disaster. Even your most competent staff, the person who's cool day-in and day-out, can experience shock. That's one of the reasons to document your course of action and develop task lists to keep people on track.

Information Technology Dependence

It is not necessarily the size of the disaster, but the likelihood of its occurrence and it potential effect on your IT installation, that you should weigh when evaluating and maintaining a disaster recovery plan.

Today, IT has become a strategic part of everyone's business. If the IT systems go down, it's very likely your business will not be able to continue its day-to-day operations. Disaster recovery planning is all about being able to mange the impact of disasters. More precisely, it must be about the ability to meet your organization's commitments, maintaining reliability, consistency, and dependability. A properly managed disaster recovery response can be a differentiating factor in this highly competitive business world. Most importantly, it supports your organization's commitment to shareholders, employees, customers, and suppliers.

It was not all that long ago that most companies were only open for business from nine to five, and just Monday to Friday. Having a system unavailable did not prevent a sale from happening. Customer transactions were usually conducted in person or over the phone, with details transferred from paper via a data-entry department, usually overnight. If a disaster shut down computing services for a few days, you could simply continue working in a manual business mode. In other words, it was business as usual.

Today we are faced with new realities. Employees, customers, and suppliers are all interrelated. With a global economy and the use of electronic commerce, we are in a 24/7 business operation. There is no end to a business day. We are always open for business! Why? Because our customers say so! Systems are no longer isolated; they interact with other systems to complete a transaction, regardless of hardware platform. The realities of today's business underscore the importance of protecting the data in computing systems. Table 1.1 summarizes how IT evolved.

Table 1.1: IT Evolution	
1990s	**Today**
IT supported the back office only.	IT is integrated with the business.
Services expectations were low.	Service delivery expectations are high.
Downtime was available.	There is no tolerance for unplanned downtime.
There was no competitive advantage.	IT can serve as both a source of competitive advantage as well as competitive disadvantage.
IT was contained and proprietary	IT provides wireless, high-speed, on-demand, client/server infrastructure solutions.
IT was purely reactive, with limited or no disaster recovery planning.	Disaster recovery is planned for and tested.
There was no ROI for disaster recovery planning.	Systems and high availability implementations exist and support a return on investment.

Key business initiatives such as Enterprise Resource Planning (ERP), supply chain management, customer relationship management, email, and e-business have all made continuous access to information crucial to an organization. Gone are the days when you can simply reenter lost transactions from paper.

Chances are, you don't have a paper trail anymore! This means business can no longer function without information technology. To successfully manage business continuity during a disaster and restore normal operations, organizations require a proper disaster recovery plan.

Plan for All Types of Disasters

When considering any type of disaster scenario, you need to identify the types of potential disasters that could face your organization. Examine where your primary data center is located. Consider local weather and other factors that could relate to business interruption. It makes sense to look at weather and seismic events, as they will differ significantly from one geographic area to another. Let's take a look at a few possible natural disasters you might need to consider:

- Earthquakes
- Floods
- Storms
  - » Hurricanes
  - » Tornadoes
  - » Electrical storms
  - » Blizzards
- Fires

Depending on where you are located, you will have a higher or lower probability of encountering many of these natural disasters. For example, southern California has a higher occurrence of earthquakes and wildfires than you might find in Kansas. On the flip side, there is a higher occurrence of intense storms in Kansas. So, the situation you may face to support a disaster will depend on where you are geographically located.

In 2006, FEMA (the Federal Emergency Management Agency) recorded over 100 weather-related disasters in the continental United States. This implies that weather-related disasters produced over 100 chances for unplanned downtime in your data center. This is a staggering number when you consider the magnitude of what constitutes a FEMA-recorded weather disaster. These FEMA-identified disasters, in turn, had a direct impact on thousands of companies within the affected regions. This should give everyone cause for concern. Consider what would have been the financial impact on your organization if you were affected by one of these disasters. The scenarios that threaten system loss are more prevalent than ever, and the business impact is far greater.

Many companies attempt to perform risk assessments that include all possible disaster situations, determining for each the likelihood that it will happen to any particular geographically dispersed data center. For example, coastal regions usually prepare for hurricanes or tsunamis. In the U.S., parts of Texas, Oklahoma, and Kansas have so many tornadoes each year that they're called "Tornado Alley." Other parts of the country are more susceptible to earthquakes. Do not dismiss any particular type of disaster with a "that will never happen to me" statement. Murphy's Law will find you. The disaster you do not prepare for is the one that will strike. Isn't that the way it typically works out?

In addition to natural disasters, there are also man-made disasters, whether intentional (such as arson) or accidental. For example, a complete data loss (RAID5 card failure) or hardware failure can be caused by an interrupted supply of power because a construction crew accidentally cut power lines or other feeds to the data center. Another common occurrence is water damage, whether from broken pipes or something as simple as a washroom overflow that remained undiscovered for hours or days. Take some time and effort to consider all of the possible types of disasters and make sure your disaster recovery plans take each of them into account. Any of them can have a profound effect on your ability to do business. You must first learn how to handle the crisis at hand, and then recover from the disaster.

Reasons for Planning

Disaster recovery planning can be defined as planning to ensure continued availability of essential services. It prepares an organization to respond to an interruption of essential business functions and provides the guidelines to fully recover these services. A proper disaster recovery plan ensures the availability of necessary resources, including personnel, information, equipment, financial arrangements, services, and accommodations. A disaster recovery plan is no good unless it is realistic, current, tested, and well-known by those who must implement it. Disaster recovery planning is an integral part of any effective business strategy. When a disaster strikes, the last thing you need to do is waste valuable time fumbling through an inadequate recovery plan.

A good disaster recovery plan ensures business survival during a prolonged interruption of computing services. Like a good insurance policy, a complete disaster recovery plan will be effective if all the risks are carefully and realistically assessed. You might have heard disaster recovery planning described as *business continuity planning* (*BCP*). The BCP focuses on restarting and resuming an organization's business processes, such as payroll or order processing, after a disaster. The BCP commences after recovery of IT processing, which is supported by a disaster recovery plan. Sometimes, the terms *contingency plan* and *disaster recovery plan* are used interchangeably. However, disaster recovery planning is by far the most recognizable concept in our industry, and the one referred to throughout this book.

The main reason for planning is that it gives your organization a significantly better chance of recovering from a catastrophic event than an organization that simply ignores or defers building a disaster recovery plan. By having trained recovery-team members implement preplanned strategies, you remove significant risk from your organization. Advance arrangements that support IT systems recovery in the wake of a disaster will give your organization a place to go when a disaster strikes, and a place to train for a disaster. Disaster recovery planning involves knowing what to do beyond a disaster. It includes getting over the original crisis and getting the business back online, knowing how to recover or rebuild all your IT-critical infrastructure components, and bringing your data center back into a position where it can support the business. To do that, you have to have a disaster recovery plan and know how to follow it.

Audit Requirements

For many years, IT staffers viewed the role of auditors as coming in to "shoot the wounded" or get them fired. To say that auditors are sticklers for detail and picky about the most trivial things can be an understatement. However, with the auditors comes some reality. That's why an audit of your disaster preparedness readiness is an essential early step toward the goal of an efficient and workable disaster recovery plan. More than that, the audit is protection for the company's shareholders. For you, a DR plan is like car insurance . . . no, it's house insurance . . . no, life insurance . . . maybe all three.

Executives have come to realize they can learn a lot from an audit, even if the results are anything from a slap on the wrist to a major citation for non-compliance. The audit process has evolved into a collaboration, rather than a confrontation. (Well, many are still evolving . . . .) To protect your company, auditors will review your current disaster preparedness state. They will assess whether it meets acceptable IBM-compliance and industry-recovery practices. Finally, auditors will verify whether mission-critical applications and data are adequately protected. In that way, auditors can help justify your disaster recovery program.

An auditor who points to the absence of a written and properly tested disaster recovery plan is doing his or her job properly. An auditor's primary role is to point out the potential risk to your organization. Absence of a disaster recovery plan identifies a serious exposure to the timely recovery of information assets for your organization, as well as threatening your organization's compliance with legal data-retention mandates. In many industries, disaster recovery planning is required by law, and company compliance is rigidly enforced.

Regulatory Compliance and Disaster Recovery Planning

Regulatory compliance adds a layer of risk and complexity within your IT department. New federal regulations and compliance rules require organizations to ensure currency, accessibility, and retention of their data to pre-determined levels. Being directly affected by a disaster is not an acceptable excuse for regulatory forgiveness. Lawsuits, corporate audits, and Securities and Exchange Commission (SEC) fines are quickly becoming a harsh reality check for organizations that cannot meet these very high standards. For example, organizations that retain medical information are subject to the Health Insurance Portability and Accountability Act (HIPAA). Financial organizations conducting business in the United States must comply with the SEC 17a-4 rule requirements, and publicly traded industries of all types are accountable to Sarbanes-Oxley (SOX) stipulations. SOX compliance has become front and center in organizations today. Similarly, anyone doing business with corporations in Canada will be very familiar with the Personal Information Protection & Electronic Documents Act (PIPEDA), which mandates strict controls of access and retention for any form of personal information.

Each country in the world either has or is in the process of developing similar regulatory regulations. The risks of noncompliance are serious. They can include fines that are often in the hundreds of thousands or even millions of dollars. These regulatory bodies are very strict and command authority. Worst-case examples have identified prosecution of key corporate officers and organizations being forced to close their doors.

The Securities and Exchange Commission

The SEC has regulations that mandate the offsite storage and protection of backup data. If an organization does not meet compliance regulations, the SEC will impose fines, or even keep delinquent companies from doing business on financial exchanges.

The SEC rules imply very strict backup and recovery procedures, documented recovery plans, testing, and displaying the ability to restore

15

all your data to a consistent and useable state. Your backup and recovery program design will come under scrutiny. Every aspect, including executing, signoff, bonded offsite storage, retention, and testing, will get reviewed.

HIPAA

If you're in the healthcare arena, you've been affected by the Health Insurance Portability and Accountability Act of 1996. While this legislation is aimed more at the protection of privacy than the protection of data, the mandates of HIPAA include segments that deal with disaster recovery. HIPAA requires that organizations falling under its regulations take "reasonable" measures to provide DR solutions. HIPAA doesn't spell out what these measures are, but it does note that failure to adequately recover from a disaster could lead to noncompliance. Failure to comply inevitably exposes officers of the organization to repercussions, such as fines or jail time. Since these organizations must provide disaster recovery as part of their HIPAA compliance, the finance department is no longer able to yank the DR budget without coming up with a stellar reason.

Now, the Good News

Believe it or not, there is some good news here! Your organization can use the existence of regulations to gain funding and create projects to meet or exceed your current disaster recovery and high-availability implementations. This is all about the ability to recovery your systems and system information to the state they were in pre-disaster.

Understanding program compliance and obtaining funding can help you achieve the necessary standards for disaster recovery. There is plenty of information on the Web to support this position. However, you can start by just asking your auditor. After all, he or she is the individual representing the regularity body in the first place.

Let's Get Started

The disaster recovery planning process begins well in advance of any disaster occurring. As I have stated several times already, no business should risk operating without a disaster plan. Now it is time to start building a disaster recovery plan.

Feeling overwhelmed? You probably should be, at least initially. It's a big job, but it is certainly not an insurmountable job. The disaster recovery plan is best broken down into several phases that you deal with one at a time. Don't let the challenge of starting paralyze you.

During a disaster, you want to focus on critical things, like recovering the System i. Let's start planning, however, by focusing on the routine things you can resolve easily . . . the things that happen when the sun is shining, it's a nice relaxed atmosphere at work, and you have a lot of options available. Take the time today to document what your course of action might be. Don't wait until you have six inches of water under your feet before you make these decisions.

Phase 1 of Disaster Recovery Planning

As shown in Figure 1.3, phase 1 of disaster recovery planning is used to obtain an understanding of the existing and projected computing environment of the organization. This enables the project team to define the scope of the project and the associated work program, develop project schedules, and identify and address any issues that could affect the delivery and success of the project.

Figure 1.3: Phase 1 of disaster recovery planning.

All of the required policies will be developed to support the recovery program design. An awareness program will be initiated to educate management and senior individuals, who will be required to participate in the initial planning methodology used to develop a disaster recovery plan.

Phase 1 includes the following:

- Obtain commitment from senior management to sponsor, support, finance, and participate in the recovery effort.
- Provide management with a comprehensive overview of the resource effort required to develop and maintain an effective disaster recovery plan.
- Define the scope and recovery requirements from the perspective of the business.
- Select project teams that represent the needs of your organization.
- Develop a contingency-plan format that is understandable, easy to use, and easy to maintain.
- Define how the disaster recovery planning methodology will be integrated into ongoing IT integrations, change control, and business changes to keep the plan viable.

Disaster Recovery Plan Accountability

The Chief Financial Officer (CFO) and Chief Information Officer (CIO) can be your biggest allies. Who better than these folks can fully understand the ramifications of their decision to support disaster recovery planning? The question they should ask themselves is "Should this organization spend the money on disaster recovery, or leave the business exposed?"

Be prepared to answer all the required questions when you get these senior corporate officials involved. This is not a matter of visiting the corner office and getting a signature. Making a successful pitch will require getting the CFO and CIO on board. At the same time, do not take them for granted.

Today's business is all about the bottom line. The CFO understands cash flow, and because disaster recovery does not contribute directly to the profits of the company, he or she might be a hard sell. After all, disaster recovery is a non-operating expense. However, emphasize that this non-operating expense could save your company from catastrophe should a disaster occur. On the positive side, these senior company officials do understand that the value received from disaster recovery planning is exactly equal to the potential losses avoided. This financial exposure can be enormous. Believe me, they are *fully* aware of this.

A key factor in the success of developing your disaster recovery plan will be holding someone on the executive management team accountable. It could be the CIO or CFO, or possibly both. For smaller organizations, it will be the IT director or manager. It will be necessary for the entire organization to know that the disaster recovery planning requirement is deemed an essential project by senior management. This level of authority will provide you with enough visibility in the organization. The company backing will give you all the required access to key staff throughout the project because everyone in the organization has the same objective of completing the disaster recovery plan on time. Executive support, particularly in the form of an executive sponsor, is necessary for developing a truly robust disaster recovery process.

The executive sponsor has several other responsibilities:

1. Select an owner for the disaster recovery plan, who is often referred to as the *disaster recovery coordinator*.
2. Get the support of other managers to ensure that participants are properly chosen and committed to the DR plan. These other managers may be direct reports, peers within IT or outside of IT, or consultants.
3. Demonstrate ongoing support by requesting and reviewing frequent progress reports, offering suggestions for improvement, questioning unclear elements of the plan, and resolving issues as any challenges occur.

Without this level of management support, having a successful project delivery within the agreed-upon timelines will be difficult. Although the probability of a major disaster is remote, the consequences of an occurrence could be catastrophic in terms of financial impact and public image. Senior management will appreciate the implications of any such occurrence. Therefore, it should assign ongoing responsibility for recovery planning to an employee dedicated to this essential service. With the management team knowing this process will get done, a DR plan just might help them sleep better at night.

Defining Your DR Plan Objectives

The primary objective of recovery planning is to enable an organization to survive a disaster and to continue normal business operations. In order to survive, your company must ensure that critical operations can continue normal processing. The old saying of "business as usual" applies. Throughout the recovery effort, the plan establishes clear lines of authority and prioritizes work efforts.

As you document your disaster recovery plan, it is important to understand the goals of your organization if a major system interruption were to occur. Aligning your information technology deliverables with the requirements and objectives of your business is imperative to obtain a common recovery goal. Internal politics can complicate recovery efforts. Differing opinions about what information and supporting technology is important can paralyze your DR planning initiatives at the outset. It is imperative that everyone is onboard with the common goals of the business.

Management must make a decision to undertake a project that satisfies the following objectives:

- Agree on delivery objectives between IT and the business
- Identify the DR planning scope: what's in, what's not
- Minimize the gap between requirements and deliverables

- Define acceptable risks
- Illustrate disaster scenarios
- Provide a high-level needs overview
- Develop a documented plan approach
- Document the authority of team members in the plan
- Clearly communicate the commitment of the planning project internally
- Set the timing of all plan deliverables

Disasters come in many forms and will create numerous business-interruption challenges. All companies insist on immediate recovery. That is the way business works. Everything is critical to the success of your organization. Without a clear strategy linked directly to the organization's recovery objectives, disaster recovery planning can become a frustrating and expensive effort. The goal for companies with no business tolerance for downtime is to achieve a state of business continuity, where critical systems and networks are continuously available, no matter what happens.

At the end of the day, your disaster recovery plan has to be three things:

- Complete
- Comprehensive
- Current

By complete, I mean the plan must be detailed enough so that *any* System i professional would be able to recover your servers based on the information supplied. The plan must spell out each and every step so that it can be followed like a recovery roadmap. That means no implying or reading between the lines. It's a common mistake to rely on specific individuals during a disaster, because they might simply be unavailable. The plan must be able to stand on its own.

The plan must be comprehensive so that it covers all critical business aspects. It covers all the company's technological hardware platforms, business processes, and network recovery elements required to meet business objectives. Both technical recovery and management aspects are clearly outlined. Use the classic "who, what, where, when, how" approach:

- Who will execute recovery actions?
- What is needed to continue, resume, recover, or restore business functions?
- What actions need to be performed at what time?
- When must business functions and operations resume?
- When do you put the hotsite on Alert or Declare?
- Where do you go to resume corporate, business, and operational functions?
- How are the procedures for continuity, resumption, recovery, or restoration detailed?

Ensure your plan is current. In the changing environment of the computer industry, it is inevitable that a disaster recovery plan will become outdated and unusable unless someone keeps it up to date. Changes that will likely affect the plan fall into several categories:

- Hardware
- Software
- Facilities
- Procedures
- Personnel

As changes occur in any of these areas, they must be incorporated into the body of the plan, and distributed as required.

Staff Commitment

Organizations that have tried to develop a DR plan without dedicating the required resources to the effort have been largely unsuccessful. Some organizations, after spending time and money developing DR plans, have failed in maintaining their ongoing recovery capability. This is mostly due to a lack of commitment to keep their plans current. I cannot stress enough that it is essential that management is committed to the development, implementation, and maintenance of this DR plan, and that required resources are freed up as required.

Many times, I hear customers telling me that they have a plan. So I ask them to show it to me, and the first thing I read on the cover page is "Last revision date October 2002." An outdated plan is worse than no plan at all. Management is walking around thinking that a disaster recovery plan is in place. You need to commit people to making the plans current. As your business evolves, so should your DR plan. You need a system in place to keep up with the changes going on in your environment.

Some plans get their start because of a close call. For example, a bad storm passes through your city and rips the roof off the building across the street from your company. The next day, management comes running to you and states, "We must have a disaster recovery plan right away! It's high priority; read some books, go get some education, source some consulting. Go ahead and work on it . . . part time."

You need to at least initially work on writing a DR plan full time. Blocking off the third Friday of every month to work on the plan is not acceptable. You will certainly waste valuable time getting back on track every time you open the document. I know your plate is full, and that you are wearing many hats. A key factor in the successful development and implementation of disaster recovery plan, however, is the dedication of a full-time staff resource. Initially, you or someone who works for you should be dedicated the project. Once the plan is in place, it can be maintained part-time. If you do not maintain the plan, it will become a project all over again.

Disaster recovery plans are living documents. Both the information technology components and the business environments are constantly changing and becoming more integrated and complex. Disaster recovery plans must keep pace with these changes. Continuous testing/exercising of the DRP is essential if your organization wants to ensure that recovery capability is maintained in such an environment. The organization also must ensure that staff with recovery responsibilities are prepared to execute the plan. Since disaster recovery planning is a very complex and labor-intensive process, it requires redirection of valuable technical staff and business resources. This must be clearly stated and provisioned for up-front.

Initial DR Project Planning Team

The size of the planning team will depend on the organization's requirements and resources. Usually, involving a group of people is best because of the following:

- It encourages participation and gets more people invested in the process.
- It increases the amount of time participants are able to contribute.
- It enhances the visibility of the planning process.
- It provides for a broad business and IT perspective on the issues.

The composition of the project team will vary depending on the number of System i5 servers, hardware platforms, scope, and business units the DR plan will support. In some cases, managers of specific business units may be selected because of business-needs knowledge. The managers represented on the various teams may recommend other senior individuals in their areas to represent them or to join specific teams where their expertise will be required for the development of the plan.

Personnel and Teams

The suggested personnel include the following:

- Disaster recovery coordinator
- System i5, iSeries, or AS/400 support staff

- Network and communications staff
- Voice communications staff
- Applications teams
- Business leaders
- Subject matter experts from the business

The specific types of teams required are based on the number of systems and platforms within the scope of the DRP. The size of each team and specific team titles will depend on the nature of the organization. Here are some typical team names:

- Executive Sponsor
- Senior Management Team
- Damage Assessment Team
- Systems Software Team
- IT Recovery Team
- Server Recovery Team
- LAN/WAN Recovery Team
- Database Recovery Team
- Application Team
- Hardware Salvage Team
- Site Restoration/Salvage Team
- Media Relations Team
- Legal Affairs Team
- Human Resources Team
- Procurement Team (for equipment and supplies)

Personnel should be chosen to staff these teams based on their skills and knowledge. Ideally, teams would be staffed with the people responsible for IT systems support under normal operating conditions. Teams should be sufficient in size to remain viable if some members are unavailable to respond. In other words, teams of one will not suffice. All team members should be familiar with the goals and procedures of other teams to facilitate cross-team coordination of recovery efforts. Each team is led by a team leader who directs overall team tasks and responsibilities and is the liaison to the IT management team.

Establish Authority

Authority must be demonstrated by senior management authorizing the planning team to take the steps necessary to develop a plan. The team should initially be led by the disaster recovery coordinator until formal recovery teams are established. Then, the leadership will be driven by the IT recovery-management team leader, working extensively with the DR coordinator.

The key to success is establishing a clear line of authority between group members and the group leader. While team members must respect the chain of command, it should not be so rigid as to prevent the free flow of ideas. Throw out the corporate organizational chart, however. The authority of a DR plan is unique.

Phase 2: Definitions and Risk Mitigation

Your organization must define all levels of associated risk and levels of business acceptance for mitigation of any perceived risks. Financial impacts to the business and alignment of IT deliverables are clearly defined in this phase, as shown in Figure 1.4. Timelines will be modified as risk and associated business impacts become more clearly defined.

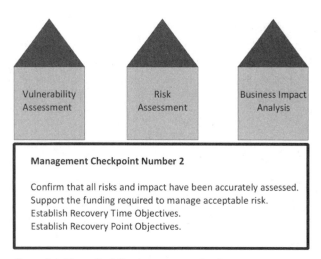

Figure 1.4: Phase 2 of disaster recovery planning.

Conduct a Vulnerability Assessment

Key activities of the vulnerability assessment include the following:

- Document and review the business environment.
- Review resource inventories.
- Review backup procedures.
- Review third-party capabilities.
- Identify risk avoidance/mitigation steps.

Traditionally, a vulnerability assessment includes all potential vulnerabilities in the information technology infrastructure. A DR plan is based on technology components and their underlying business processes. With today's businesses relying on technology, a vulnerability assessment is fundamental to a successful disaster recovery plan.

Don't take your installed IT infrastructure for granted. Assuming that all major components of every server computer room are properly managed, fully functional, and tested regularly is a common mistake made in this industry. In an evaluation of your computing facility's design, it's crucial to look for all possible points of failure. Therefore, it is critical to perform a site vulnerability assessment to examine the current operating environment. A strategic requirement for every company is to investigate all system-level components, infrastructure, environment, and backup process, and determine the capabilities to recover all critical systems.

During the vulnerability assessment, examine the following:

- Temperature and humidity
- Electrical power, static electricity, grounding
- Uninterruptible power supply (UPS), backup UPS batteries
- Generator
- Water detection
- Smoke detection
- Fire suppression
- Facility monitoring
- Earthquake/tornado safeguards
- Controlled physical access
- Equipment redundancy
- LPAR system level and hardware-level dependencies
- Disk protection

Conduct a Risk Assessment

To effectively determine the specific risks to an IT system, a risk assessment of the IT data center is required. A thorough risk assessment should identify the system vulnerabilities, threat, and current controls, and attempt to determine the risk based on the likelihood and threat impact. In the past, the words "risk assessment" might have only referred to the process of identifying and minimizing the exposures to certain threats that an organization might experience. The very important next step is to assess the vulnerability of your primary data center. IT systems are vulnerable to a variety of disruptions, ranging from short-term power outages or disk drive failures to long outages via such things as server loss or fire. These disruptions could come from a variety of sources, from natural disasters to malicious activities.

While many risks may be minimized or eliminated through technical management or operational solutions as part of the DR team's risk-assessment effort, it is virtually impossible to completely eliminate all risks. In many cases, critical resources might reside outside the organization's control (such as hydro or communications). Thus, the organization might be unable to ensure their availability. What is the probability and potential impact of each type of acceptable disaster recovery scenario?

Risks can vary over time, and new risks might replace old ones as a System i5 and supporting IT infrastructure evolves. Therefore, the risk-management process must by ongoing and dynamic. Here are some other factors to consider:

- **Historical—What types of disaster-related scenarios have occurred in your geographic area, or at this office facility?**
- Fires
- Severe weather
- Hazardous material spills
- Transportation accidents
- Earthquakes
- Hurricanes
- Tornadoes
- Terrorism
- Utility outages

- **Geographic—What can happen as a result of the facility's location?**
- Proximity to flood plains, seismic faults, and dams
- Proximity to companies that produce, store, use, or transport hazardous materials

- Proximity to major transportation routes and airports
- Proximity to nuclear power plants

- **Technological—What could result from a process or system failure?**
- Telecommunications failure
- Computer system failure
- Power failure
- Heating/cooling system failure
- Emergency notification system failure

- **Human error—What emergencies can be caused by employee error?**
- Poor maintenance
- Carelessness
- Wrongful misconduct

- **Regulatory—What emergencies are you regulated to deal with?**

Business Impact Analysis (BIA)

Key activities of the BIA include the following:

- Analyze business functions.
- Review business applications and interdependencies.
- Evaluate business resources for criticality.
- Evaluate potential interruptions.
- Interview key individuals.
- Identify critical business activities/technologies.
- Assess the financial impact and supporting recovery.
- Establish recovery points and recovery time objectives.

A BIA outlines the consequences of an interruption to the business and other interdependent applications. It serves as a benchmark for funding decisions and strategy development. The BIA must be conducted to support all major business functions. It enables the DR project team to identify critical servers, critical supporting infrastructure, financial impacts, and levels of availability acceptance. This information will help assess the economic impact of incidents and disasters that could result in a denial of access to critical servers.

A BIA summary spreadsheet or report should be compiled to identify critical service functions and the timeframes in which they all must be recovered after any extended interruption. The BIA report should then be used as a basis for identifying systems and resources required to support the critical services provided by IT. The next phase of the BIA provides an overview of all of the different types of supported disasters and their associated probability.

Justifications for recovery spending dollars will be derived from the assigned cost to each type of disaster, for each critical server. Such costs can come from a number of factors areas starting with the potential loss of business. Some of the cost criteria used are public image, customer confidence, market share, and regulatory and financial penalties. The critical functions, their recovery priorities, and their interdependencies must be established so that the recovery time objective (*RTO*) can be set. Simply stated, while your servers are down, you are not taking orders, manufacturing products, or delivering any level of service.

Downtime Costs

If the information that a company uses to generate revenue is unavailable, revenue is lost. However, just how much revenue a company ultimately loses depends on a number of factors, including the type of business, the type of data that is unavailable, and how long the data is unavailable.

Downtime can also equal lost opportunity. Although more difficult to quantify, this might have equally lasting consequences for future revenue. A long-time customer might be more willing to excuse downtime than a first-time customer.

The cost of downtime to any organization depends on your type of business and geographic location. To estimate downtime costs to your company, review the per-hour costs to your organization in the following categories:

- Lost productivity—The number of hours of downtime per year multiplied by the number of employees at their hourly wage. Include overtime to make up for extended system outages.

- Lost revenue—The direct loss of business during the period of the System i5 interruption.

- Additional expenses—The cost of additional employees to assist with changes in business process, the cost of additional or replacement equipment, staff overtime during the interruption, travel costs to perform the recovery, and sourcing of hardware/facilities.

- Financial performance—The impact to corporate cash flow, loss of discounts for on-time vendor payments, penalties, and decreases in market valuation.

The scope of any disaster-recovery solution system should be driven by the ability to make available to the business all the critical systems and IT infrastructure required to conduct normal production activities. Talk to your business executives and ensure they are fully aware of what IT can deliver. Don't be afraid to ask the difficult questions before you document your disaster recovery plan. Disaster recovery is a combination of how long you wait to bring your business back up after a failure, and how much data the company or the business is willing to lose in the process. This all equates to a balancing act of how much system availability you are willing to pay for, and what return on investment management is looking for.

Business-impact objectives must include the following:

- Agreement on delivery objectives between IT and the business
- Prioritization of required business processes (ranking your critical servers)
- Minimizing the gap between requirements and deliverables
- Defining the acceptable length of downtime (*RTO, Recovery Time Objective*)
- Reducing the potential loss of data (*RPO, Recovery Point Objective*)
- Determining the cost of disaster recovery (*ROI, Return on Investment*)
- Reducing the complexity of recovery effort
- Setting recovery strategies
- Defining a mission statement for recovery
- Setting the scope for the recovery process

Phase 3: Server Criticality and Recovery Strategies

A hierarchy of all critical business-service offerings and infrastructure to support these applications must be determined, as shown in Figure 1.5. It's a reality that all applications and all servers are not equal in the level of importance to your business. Always consider assigning a priority to your various applications. Some are more critical to your organization's business recovery than others. Some are real-time, some are transactional, and some are simply archival . . . and then there is always email. Specifications detailing the minimum requirements for your mission-critical servers are an integral part of any DR plan.

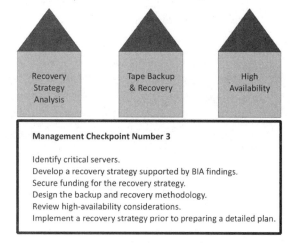

Figure 1.5: Phase 3 of disaster recovery planning.

Recovery Strategy Analysis

Tape Backup & Recovery

High Availability

Management Checkpoint Number 3

Identify critical servers.
Develop a recovery strategy supported by BIA findings.
Secure funding for the recovery strategy.
Design the backup and recovery methodology.
Review high-availability considerations.
Implement a recovery strategy prior to preparing a detailed plan.

Recovery Strategies

Key activities of determining recovery strategies include the following:

- Develop/approve interruption and service levels
- Develop strategies for critical activities
- Develop strategies to recover crucial activities
- Compare costs of all strategies
- Develop IT installation projects
- Provide recommendations

Deliverables include the following:

- Avoidance strategy
- Mitigation strategies report
- Cost-benefit analysis report
- Recovery strategy report
- List of critical resource requirements
- Options/recommendations report/matrix
- List of recommended spin-off projects
- Overall recommendations

Recovery strategies provide a means to restore IT systems quickly and effectively following a service disruption. The strategies should address the acceptable downtime as identified in the BIA. Several alternatives should be considered when developing the strategy, including cost, allowable downtime, security, and integration with larger, organization-level contingency plans. The selected recovery strategy should address the potential impacts identified in the BIA and should be integrated into the system architecture during the design and implementation phases of the system lifecycle.

Several recovery strategies can be employed for iSeries/400 and System i5 recovery. The most reliable and cost-effective strategy is either a vendor-supported, commercial *hotsite* or an internal hotsite located in another place within the same organization. Under the HIPAA and many other regulatory guidelines, a backup and recovery strategy for information technology, or a clear public statement of acceptability of risk needs to be in place.

Traditional tape-recovery-based DR plans provide 24- to 48-hour disaster recovery for mission-critical applications. With technology linked closer than ever to business processes and with costs of outages escalating, many organizations are seeking shorter recovery times for critical applications. Use of *high-availability* or *clustering* techniques is increasing, especially for ERP and e-business applications. Enabling organizations to achieve recovery time objectives and recovery point objectives is now calculated in minutes and hours, rather than days.

For high-availability implementations, the recovery point is always what was last transmitted and received by the backup server. Any changes that haven't been completely transmitted will be lost. One factor to consider is your line capacity. Insufficient bandwidth can cause latency and a backlog of transactions on the source system. The use of object journaling with synchronous replication for logical copies can help ensure that changes to critical data are transmitted as they occur. If multiple techniques are used by the logical copy operation, delays can result in lost changes for objects that aren't journaled. With 24x7 systems availability requirements, a hotsite solution might not be good enough.

From a transaction perspective, the recovery point is the same for all solutions and depends on the application's use of techniques such as commitment control to ensure transaction integrity. If commitment control is used, the recovery point includes only those transactions that were completed, and, for logical copies, only those transactions that were successfully transmitted, received, and accepted on the backup server. Without commitment control, the recovery point might include changes from partial or incomplete transactions, which then must be manually reconciled before you restart your applications following an outage.

The shift from the emphasis on data recoverability to continuous application availability is natural and logical. The traditional approach for deploying high availability has been to replicate data from one system to another, with the primary objective being the data's recoverability. A common goal for IT departments is now to achieve 100 % availability against *any* business disruptions, and produce an ROI for your business. A supporting argument for ROI is the consideration for planned outages. Mitigating both planned and unplanned downtime can start out being fairly straightforward, but can quickly become very complex.

Reducing Costs

When data is not protected properly, businesses can rack up a lengthy list of hard costs (such as fines levied on an organization) and soft costs (such as missed business opportunities or damaged reputation). An effective data-protection strategy is able to minimize these costs by ensuring that data is available to authorized users who need it, when they need it, and according to business objectives.

Cost Justification

Once you begin the process of selecting data-protection systems, you need to justify the cost of each purchase. To be successful in doing so, you must have completed the steps mentioned previously in this section:

1. Define your RTOs, RPOs, backup windows, and consistency group requirements.
2. Determine what to protect for each critical system.
3. Determine the cost of each outage.
4. Plan for all types of disasters.

Once you have accomplished this, justifying the cost of each data-protection system should be a relatively easy thing to do. You simply need to state your required RTOs and RPOs, what you're protecting against, and what a system to protect against those things costs. If any part of the system is not authorized by senior management, you simply need to explain how that affects your ability to meet these requirements.

The technology requirements for a successful recovery must include hardware and software equivalents to production. Careful research during this phase will ensure that the recovery solution will meet the stated objectives. The business needs dictate the recovery strategies and recovery time objectives. The recovery time requirements of interdependent applications must be taken into consideration. Two key components to any recovery program design are strategies to back up and restore vital records.

Backup and Recoverability

Everyone should be aware of the importance of backing up critical data. As a System i5 administrator, you need to bring all your key processes and procedures together through a backup solution that is reliable and recoverable. Data is the backbone of today's organizations. When data is lost or damaged or simply unavailable, it completely halts your business. Adequate backups protect against permanent loss of data. However, the time it takes to rebuild and recover from a disaster can itself be a catastrophic business consequence if all is not in place.

A traditional disaster recovery plan focuses on the technology recovery. All companies have some form of data backup methodology in place—or should have. Unfortunately, everyone assumes their IT department's current data backup solution is capable of supporting key business functions even when a disaster strikes. Nothing can be further from the truth. You need to ensure that all critical servers are being backed up on a reliable and consistent schedule. Many backup systems are either partially or completely broken. Even a good backup success rate of 95% means that 5% of the data center isn't backed up on any given night. This process, although it seems obvious, is often not exercised to completion in many IT shops. Assigning backup responsibilities to an administrator is not enough. Sometimes, the root of a DR problem is much simpler. A company might have DR plans with realistic RTOs and RPOs, but if its backup system didn't work just prior to the disaster, the DR plan won't work.

An effective recovery strategy must always be designed first, followed by a backup strategy implementation. Typically, these tasks are performed in the opposite order. Usually, we recover from what we are given—that is, from last night's backup tapes—and then try to bridge the gaps. In other words, reverse engineering. Ensure your recovery point objectives are examined from both a midweek and weekend failure, as this will almost certainly present different backup program designs.

It is imperative that your disaster recovery plan specifies, in detail, when backups are executed, the complete contents of your backup, the frequency of your backups, and your vaulting procedures, with supporting documentation all included. In addition, an effective disaster recovery plan should detail all the steps to support the process for restoring this data within the specified timeframes by the business.

Create vital records and provide offsite storage. A critical component in plan development is the selection of backup and restoration software capable of storing and successfully retrieving data. Without this, there is no business continuity program. Backup scheduling must include an offsite storage location.

Once the data is carefully backed up, it must be accessible in the event that the facility is not accessible. There are bonded, commercial storage vendors to provide security and offsite data storage. Data is usually retrieved for daily restores as well as disaster recovery testing.

Systems Availability and High Availability

The common goal of companies today is to accept no tolerance for downtime in their business. Information and server access is something we just cannot afford to lose. Systems availability is not just about system failures. It includes both planned and un-planned events. This is important to the business because the business is always open. Your customers say so! Somewhere in your enterprise you are manufacturing or shipping goods, or a customer is buying, and you are probably settling financial terms as well. As dependence on systems increases, so does the cost of not having access to it. Disasters will happen, but you also have to back up your systems, clean the database up, and keep software maintenance up to speed with IBM compliance and warranty support guidelines.

In the past, high-availability (HA) solutions were reserved mostly for large enterprises. They were the only ones who could afford the total cost of high availability. A significant shift has recently occurred in the System i5 disaster-recovery world, making high availability much easier to use and dramatically less expensive. A combination of lower hardware investment from IBM, a huge market shift in the cost of data communications, and the HA software providers have significantly reduced software costs. The timing could not be better for the industry, helping balance the impact costs identified in the business impact analysis. This decreasing cost of high availability and the increasing cost of downtime is giving small- and medium-sized companies the financially motivated incentive to re-evaluate today's high-availability solutions.

High systems availability is not just having a second iSeries/400 server handy. It's about designing a solution that's all-encompassing. It includes networks, high-availability software, and a managed and monitored solution. And of course it needs to be fully tested. Business disasters happen any time, anywhere. They do not need to be catastrophic to cause serious and permanent damage to your business.

Pressures to meet customer needs include the following:

- The requirement to support both internal and external Service Level Agreements (SLAs)
- Just-in-time supply-chain requirements and penalties
- Pressure to guarantee service commitments from bigger suppliers
- New service-delivery-related penalties that leave no room for any downtime
- Rigid government and industry controls

SLAs define the requirements and metrics. The entire business defines the availability requirements.

Phase 4: Develop the Plan

Once you get into the planning stage of your disaster preparation (shown in Figure 1.6), you'll be able to make an informed decision about which is right for your organization. During the plan-development stage, you will evaluate your required activities, your critical applications, and your overall recovery steps. This will help identify all required steps. During this phase, the detailed disaster recovery plan components are defined, and plan documentation begins. This phase also includes the implementation of changes to user procedures, upgrading of existing IT operating procedures required to support disaster recovery strategies, vendor contract negotiations (with suppliers of recovery services) and the definition of recovery teams, their roles and responsibilities. Recovery standards are also developed during this phase.

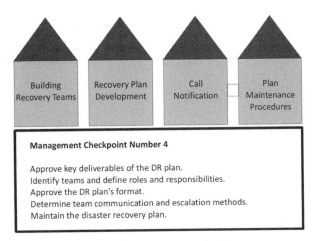

Figure 1.6: Phase 4 of disaster recovery planning.

Key activities include the following:

- Develop response plans for critical applications/technologies
- Develop assessment requirements
- Develop mitigation requirements
- Identify operational requirements
- Document restoration procedures
- Document team procedures
- Assist in the development of hotsite requirements
- Assist in the development of a hotsite vendor RFP
- Assist in the selection of a hotsite vendor
- Assist in vendor negotiations

Deliverables include the following:

- Disaster recovery plan
- Response plan
- Team roles and responsibilities
- Crises communications
- Recovery team procedures

A critical step in plan development is actually building the plan. Full cooperation from all of the teams is necessary to create a viable disaster recovery plan. This is where the majority of the work will be performed.

Plan Maintenance

Maintenance of the disaster recovery plan is critical to the success of an actual recovery in a disaster. To be effective, the plan must be maintained in a ready state that accurately reflects system requirements, procedures, organizational structure, and policies. IT systems undergo frequent changes because of changing business needs, technology upgrades, or new policies. Therefore, it is essential that the DR plan be reviewed and updated regularly, as part of the organization's change-management process, to ensure new information is documented and contingency measures are revised as required. The DR plan must clearly step through a recovery roadmap and be able to reflect changes to the server environments that are deemed mission-critical. It is mandatory that existing change-management processes are all-encompassing, to take DR plan maintenance into account.

Key activities include the following:

- Develop plan update procedures
- Develop a testing strategy
- Develop training material
- Develop a task-responsibility matrix

Deliverables include the following:

- Recovery plan update procedures
- Training materials
- Recovery plan testing strategies

Having a maintainable DR plan is a key element to success. Careful consideration must be given to the layout and format of the written plan to ensure that it can be easily maintained. Having a scattered approach will lead to a neglected disaster recovery plan because of built-in complexities.

Phase 5: Validate the Recovery Plan

Phase 5, recovery plan validation, is illustrated in Figure 1.7.

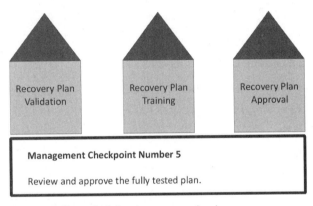

Figure 1.7: Phase 5 of disaster recovery planning.

Key activities of recovery plan validation include the following:

- Plan the test
- Conduct the test
- Evaluate the test
- Schedule any additional future tests
- Revise the recovery plan

Deliverables include the following:

- Test plan
- Test log and documentation

- Test evaluation
- Action plans
- Revised recovery plan

Key activities of recovery plan training include the following:

- Conduct team training
- Conduct staff awareness training
- Evaluate training

Deliverables include the following:

- Trained recovery team members
- Trained staff
- Updated training materials

Testing Your DR Plan

Once the DR plans are developed, initial tests of the plans are conducted, and any necessary modifications to the plans are made based on an analysis of the results. Specific activities of this phase include the following:

- Defining the objectives
- Identifying test team participants
- Structuring the test
- Conducting the test
- Analyzing test results
- Modifying the plans as appropriate

Disaster recovery testing is an essential part of developing an effective disaster recovery strategy. Testing will identify where a company's DR plan falls short and can assist you in finding ways to better prepare your recovery teams. The worst way to test a disaster recovery plan is to wait for an actual incident to occur. A disaster is not conducive to gathering data without stress, emotion, or irrational thinking. Using an untested DR plan during a real disaster is ill advised.

Disaster recovery testing is more than just going through the steps. It requires a post-mortem analysis of every test to identify where a plan has failed and where it can be improved. Testing is an exercise involving testing objectives, scenarios, evaluation, and remediation. Learn how to make such tests effective, and you'll be well positioned to ensure your organization's survival in a calamity. Many companies have disaster recovery plans, and they might have realistic technically compliant requirements. However, because testing a disaster recovery plan is extremely time-consuming and costly, they aren't usually tested often enough. Think about how much a data center changes in a year. It's only when you test your disaster recovery plan that you find the gaps.

A great approach to testing is to involve the end users for user acceptance. Every user should create a test script designed to validate the accuracy and performance of their specific applications in a recovered environment. The test script should give a clear indication of whether or not they can do business as usual, as stated in their recovery requirements.

Disaster recovery plans should be tested at least once a year. Progressive companies test two or three times annually. The DR coordinator should maintain a checklist during the test to record all events and timelines. A post-mortem after each test should also be conducted with the intent to review the lessons learned. Discuss how the test was executed to identify what went well, what needs to be improved, and what enhancements or efficiencies could be added to improve future tests. The recovery team members should provide comments regarding lessons learned and improvements and modifications they would like to see as a result of the test. A user sign-off sheet should be provided for this purpose and must be signed off by a manager of the business. Arrange a briefing for the senior management to obtain written approval. All plans must be tested on a regular basis in order to be contingency compliant.

Key activities of the approval process include the following:

- Develop a DRP presentation
- Publish a recovery plan
- Distribute the plan

Deliverables include the following:

- Management approval

Distributing the Plan

The disaster recovery plan should be distributed to every member of the disaster recovery teams assigned specific roles and responsibilities in the plan. The plan can be distributed electronically, or on stored media. The choice of media will be determined by your organization's distribution, encryption, and corporate polices for a confidential document of this sort. You might simply place the final plan in three-ring binders and number all copies and pages. This approach is perfectly valid.

Each individual who receives a copy of the plan, in whatever format, should be required to sign a document accepting all privacy policies associated with this document.

Summary

Like it or not, DR planning is a fact of life for IT managers today. Too much has happened in the past few years for any company to simply ignore the need. If it weren't for CNN, most people would probably never think about disasters. IT staff tend to focus on day-to-day issues, such as system performance and systems availability. Backups get far more attention than disaster recovery in most companies. Whether you are a Fortune 500 company or a mom-and-pop shop, everyone will experience the need for operational data recoveries. As the frequency of natural and man-made disasters has increased over the last few years, the need for complete disaster recovery plans is being scrutinized and is today undergoing much more testing and refinement.

Twenty years of experience in disaster recovery have proved the point over and over again that companies recover successfully only when they have a DR plan and test regularly. It is an easy three-step process:

1. Align IT with the business to build a plan
2. Document the plan
3. Test the plan

It is imperative that both you and your business executives understand the dependence on information technology today. In today's time-sensitive, mission-critical economy, every organization should have a documented and tested disaster recovery plan. When building your DR solution, making a management commitment to building a recovery strategy will protect your company against the greatest risk of all: complacency. Today's computing environments face rapid business and technological changes. Investing in disaster recovery keeps bad things from happening to good companies.

2

Vulnerability Assessment & Risk Analysis

One of the goals of every disaster recovery plan is to minimize your organization's risk and loss potential in a disaster. That means following the old Boy Scout motto, "Always be prepared." This is accomplished by evaluating your IT support infrastructure capabilities, reviewing the levels of acceptable risk, and examining the procedures for handling any unplanned interruption of critical business functions. Evaluating your data center vulnerabilities is an important initial step of disaster recovery planning. Companies with mission-critical data centers and a near-zero tolerance for downtime must maintain precise disaster recovery and prevention measures. With so many possible single points of failure within a data center, every disaster recovery planner should examine all potential single points of failure and associated risk factors.

Building a strong program based on mitigation of known vulnerabilities has changed from a simple operational process to a DR planning necessity for businesses to recover successfully in a disaster. This assessment enables the identification of significant risks that might increase with the possibility of a disaster or complicate the recovery effort in the event of a disaster. Disaster prevention is undertaken to establish and implement all IT capabilities for avoiding a disaster long before the actual incident occurs. Finding preventative solutions for disasters is money well spent. An important part of this phase is the acquisition and implementation of solutions for preventing avoidable disasters in advance. The implementation of all recommendations will minimize both the probabilities and consequences of any such occurrence.

The ability to provide computing services within the data center may be partially or totally lost for a variety of reasons. A severe fire, for instance, may partially or totally damage all equipment and/or tape backup media. Disruptions to your processing ability may take many other forms. They may be security related, due to an equipment failure, or the result of sabotage by a disgruntled employee. The goal of risk analysis is to provide the company with a prevention capability that will reduce the risk of unplanned downtime and the exposure of employees to health and safety hazards.

Performing a vulnerability assessment of your data center can go a long way toward disaster avoidance. Reviewing the site will give you a sense of comfort, knowing that all potential single points of failure are addressed. Unlike other disaster recovery planning expenditures, these capabilities can offer numerous side benefits, and thus will aid you in cost justification to your senior management team. Consider that insurance companies tend to give a reduced annual premium for nearly any preventive measure implemented by your company. Simply stated, insurance companies calculate policy premiums on the basis of the perceived risk of your organization. Eliminate all the reasons they can justify a higher premium.

Site Vulnerability Assessment

A very common mistake in this industry is to assume that all servers housed in the data center facility are properly managed, fully functional, and tested regularly. You might take your installed IT infrastructure for granted. I have done the same. However, in an evaluation of your computing facility's design, it is crucial to look for all single points of failure. Therefore, it is highly recommended to perform a site vulnerability assessment to examine the current server operating conditions and evaluate the environment in detail. A strategic requirement for every IT shop is to investigate all system-level components, infrastructure, and backup processes, and determine the capabilities to restore and rebuild all critical systems.

Conduct interviews with staff to review the current management practices performed by the IT technical support group and building infrastructure support staff. This will allow you to gain a complete understanding of procedures currently in place for the data center. The primary purpose is to identify any current system inefficiencies that may exist and provide solutions based on the findings. It is always preferred to identify gaps in advance before they present themselves in the most inopportune time.

This is a systematic approach towards reducing the frequency of outages by eliminating all single points of failure, and reducing the duration of outages by configuring hardware and software for the fastest possible recovery.

When performing the assessment, these are the major components to investigate for completeness:

- Temperature and humidity
- Electrical power, static electricity, and grounding
- An uninterruptible power supply (UPS) and backup UPS batteries
- A generator
- Water detection
- Smoke detection
- Fire suppression
- Facility monitoring
- Earthquake/tornado safeguards
- Controlled physical access

Temperature and Humidity

If a failure occurred with the air conditioning unit (HVAC), the temperature in most computer rooms would increase significantly and surprisingly quickly. Never underestimate heat distribution when no cooling is available. Walk behind a blade center, for example, and it will blow you away . . . literally. Considering the size of the room and heat distribution over a period of time, some significant long-term damage could occur to the computer equipment. Many times the damage might not be immediate. Instead, it might appear over time, well after the initial event has been resolved. Humidity can cause just as much damage to computer equipment as can high temperatures.

Real-World Example

I once had a client whose air conditioning system pushed out a factor of 86% humidity into the server room. The HVAC would simply not shut off. The room was both very cold and humid. There was literally water beaded on the top of the iSeries 5094 disk towers. Needless to say, several server and disk issues resulted from this.

Keep your air conditioning controlled via an electronic thermostat set to 68.5 degrees Fahrenheit. Humidity should also be managed by the same method, and set to 35%. Both temperature and humidity-level settings should be made based on the size of the computer room and number of supported servers.

Air quality controls are often overlooked in a site assessment. However, the impact can be quite substantial. Consider where your air flow is coming in for your computer room. Is it filtered or coming in directly from the plant, or worse?

Real-World Example

A while back, I was enjoying BBQ at a local restaurant. Wood-smoked ribs . . . the city's best! The food was great, but downwind some 1,000 yards was the central data center for a major manufacturing company. You could smell

---

those tasty ribs in the computer room. After constant environmental-related failures, the company finally installed a dual air-cleaning filtration system for the computer room. Problems solved. Take a look (or smell) around, and you might be surprised. The cause of your problems might just be your favorite local food establishment!

Insufficient maintenance of the facility's air-conditioning units might cause downtime, too. The risk of failure rises as data centers attempt to save money by trimming maintenance schedules. How often is the maintenance of HVAC scheduled? Ask to see the maintenance records. There should be a log book stored in a common place and available for review. Examine these. Are there any maintenance activities still outstanding because someone simply forgot to follow up? Always review the maintenance logs and ask the technician about any concerns. In the event of a failure in the air conditioning, are there sufficient spare parts onsite to fix a variety of common or most likely problems? In terms of air conditioning units, does your building use chilled water or air-cooled units? Air-cooled units are less efficient and will drive up operating costs.

Temperature and humidity levels should be monitored constantly and electronically, 24/7. Temperature and humidify sensors can feed back information electronically to the enunciator panel, and alarms can be triggered to notify staff on a timely basis. It is still a good practice to use recording chart equipment, which in turn should be reviewed regularly. Most of today's air conditioning units also contain electronic sensors for various error conditions. The key is to have procedures in place so that when a temperature or humidity alarm is triggered on the weekend or overnight, procedures are in place to avoid a major catastrophe.

Consider what you might do in the event of an air conditioning failure. Here are some suggestions:

- Shut down non-essential equipment. (Identify non-essential hardware in advance with colored labels.)

- Have air-handling devices onsite.
- Open all doors to create an air flow.
- Lift ceiling tiles to allow hot air to escape.
- Evacuate all personnel from the room to eliminate body heat. Standing around watching the temperature rise makes no sense.

Portable Cooling Systems

Cooling is not just for the comfort of your System i5 system administrators or other staff in the computer room. Proper temperature controls are essential in computer rooms, network racks, and electrical and telephone switching rooms. Purchase portable A/C units as backups to your primary HVAC system.

Consider the following when selecting portable A/C units:

- Vendors with a large selection of units for varied load capacity requirements
- Availability
- Vendors that can support your needs locally
- Reputation for performance and service reliability
- Technical assistance programs for operation repair assistance, and parts availability
- Units that are quick and easy to install, maintain, and repair
- Standard components and replacement parts that are easy to find and readily available
- Quiet units that don't disrupt the workplace atmosphere
- Air distribution that does not produce a wind tunnel
- Units that help reduce cooling costs
- Units requiring minimal floor space
- Environmental and safety features
- Warranty and extended-warranty availability

Make sure portable cooling equipment is really what you need. Accommodating your cooling system needs of tomorrow may be worth the investment today. Do your homework now, not when your computer room is 95 degrees.

Electrical Power Supply

A conditioned electrical power source provides a continuous power stream at the proper voltage, and phasing to your computer room. Power conditioning maintains the quality of the electricity for greater reliability of your servers. It involves filtering out stray magnetic and electrical fields that can induce unwanted inductance and unwanted capacitance, and surge-suppression to prevent severe voltage spikes. To further ensure power into your facility, select two separate demarcation points for hydro power into your building.

Here are questions to consider about your power supply:

- What is the present electrical load capacity in your facility?
- Are you maxed out? Future capacity might not come cheap!
- What capability does the facility have to support itself if power from the main power grid becomes unavailable?
- What considerations do you make for static electricity and space heaters?

Static electricity can affect the operation of sensitive equipment. Static electricity builds up in conductive materials, such as carpeting, clothing, and other non—insulating fibers. Antistatic devices can be installed directly on your server racks to minimize this condition. Instruct your server-maintenance staff in techniques for properly grounding themselves to eliminate any potential server outages, let alone possible injury due to short circuits. Installing carpeted tiles in a computer room might look elegant, even trendy, but it causes a high risk of static shocks to the equipment and everyone you come in contact with. This type of flooring is definitely not recommended for a computer room.

Remove space heaters. They cause fluctuations in your power supply and discharge air-borne contaminants that can affect the electronics of the server equipment. Other personal electrical devices in the computer room, such as water kettles and water coolers, are just plain dumb!

UPS

A UPS is a critical component of the computer room's power-support system. The UPS, sometimes referred to as the battery backup, is a device that maintains a continuous supply of electrical power to all your connected equipment. The UPS equipment is placed between the outside flow of power (your primary power source) from your regulated commercial power utility and the computer room hardware. The UPS provides a dual purpose. First, it provides protection from power irregularities, such as spikes or brown-outs. These fluctuations in power can cause costly damage to computer equipment. The second role of the UPS is to act as a bridge, supplying interim power between the time when external power is lost and your alternate power source (like a diesel generator) kicks in.

UPS system batteries supply power in lieu of power from your utility for only a predetermined period of time. Typically, this is long enough for the power to be restored (in a short outage) or for the backup generator to be brought online for a prolonged outage. A UPS provides protection from a momentary power interruption only. The amount of time it can supply electricity depends on the battery capacity of the UPS and the number of servers or other piece of equipment connected to it.

There are several common power problems that UPS units correct:

- Power failure—The total loss of utility power
- Power sag (drop)—A short-term under-voltage
- Power surge (spike)—A quick burst of over-voltage

- Under-voltage (brownout) —Low-line voltages for an extended period of time
- Over-voltage—Increased voltages for an extended period of time
- Frequency—A variation of the power waveform
- Harmonic distortion—A power frequency superimposed on the power waveform

Inspect the batteries for compliance and ensure that periodic testing is performed to guarantee that power reserves will be available when needed. A UPS is sized and selected to support the total load represented by the server hardware, lighting, and any other equipment it must support during a power failure. Deciding which unit to purchase is determined by the amount of runtime the unit is required to provide when the power fails. This number will vary with the load amount that is plugged into the UPS. For example, a unit might run a single computer for 30 minutes, but run two servers for much less time. Larger units typically can provide more runtime for the same load than smaller units, but that is not always the case. Some UPS units are designed to provide extended runtime or have the ability to have external battery packs connected.

Replacing Batteries

To provide the desired protection, UPS units must be properly maintained. Sealed lead or acid batteries have a useful lifetime of only three to five years. In determining when to replace batteries, remember that while batteries might be completely bad after four years, they lose their ability to hold a charge gradually over that time. If a UPS started with one hour of runtime for the connected load, after one year, it might only provide 52 minutes. After two years, it might only provide 45 minutes, etc. In other words, the batteries will be most productive in the first year of life, and less in each successive year.

Disposing of UPS Batteries

Many UPS solutions contain lead-acid batteries, which can be detrimental to our environment. In the United States and Canada, it is illegal to dispose of lead-acid batteries in a landfill. They must be properly recycled. Sealed lead-acid batteries are recycled in the same manner as car batteries. This means that any auto shop that accepts used car batteries for recycling will also accept sealed lead-acid batteries.

Air Conditioning the UPS Room

Air conditioning is a prerequisite for proper UPS operation in a contained room. Ensure you have proper ventilation to allow hot air to escape. Temperature levels should be monitored constantly and electronically, 24/7. Temperature sensors could feed back information electronically to the enunciator panel, and alarms can be triggered to notify staff on a timely basis. Often, a special chiller unit will be installed in the UPS room to provide optimal operating temperatures.

I have, on countless occasions, found that opening the door to a UPS battery room was like walking into the Mojave Desert in August. A tropical 120 degrees plus. This is not a good sign. Supply ample air conditioning and ventilation to prevent a temperature-related shutdown. The issue is larger than shutting down this room due to high temperature readings. The primary concern is that raw, unconditioned power is allowed to reach the computer room. This could cause damage to your servers.

Here's what to look for when buying a UPS:

- Products listed with UL in the United States, CSA in Canada
- A scalable battery-management system to increase battery life and runtime
- Adjustable option switches that allow users to tailor voltage-transfer levels to site specifications

- Customizable paging methods, such as paging and email notification
- Site wiring-fault indicators and front-panel indicators, including "low battery," "replace battery," and a load meter
- Communications that fit user applications, such as RS232 interfaces
- Output voltage regulation
- The ability to correct for surges and sags
- Flexible output connection types
- Unattended shutdown software and a bypass system switch
- Magnetic isolation
- Optional runtime availability
- Sine-wave output on battery
- Vendors with engineering capabilities to meet special needs
- Vendors equipped to respond in crisis situations and offering 24-hour field service

Here are key questions to ask potential vendors:

- What's the unit's run time? Voltage range?
- Are visual and audible alarms included?
- What are the battery-management capabilities?
- What noise-filtering technology is employed?
- Is the UPS compatible with power-management software?
- Has the unit met IEEE 587 or IEC 664 test requirements for surge suppression?
- Does the unit include modem and network protection, to safeguard from surges coming through phone lines or network data lines?
- Will you repair or replace equipment damaged due to a UPS malfunction?
- What are the specifics of the warranty and extended warranty?

RS232 Interface for the UPS

All your servers have an interface that communicates with your UPS and should be connected. This provides your systems with an intelligent front-end interface that can be built into the server shutdown scripts for a warm, clean shutdown. This is important during periods when no staff are on site.

Most servers are set up with default power-management settings that will shut down the servers "hard" upon a power outage, or power down with a very unreasonable delay. This is not a recommended shutdown approach. A detection service or sleeper program/script should be written to monitor the messages generated for loss of power from your UPS. Even if you have an alternate power source installed, such as a diesel generator, you must have the assurance that the generator has fired up and is supplying the desired clean power. Another element sometimes overlooked is whether UPS batteries are kept fully charged. We all keep investing in and growing our server infrastructure. It also makes sense to understand your present load running in the computer room, whether the UPS can support the load, and the length of time the batteries will function.

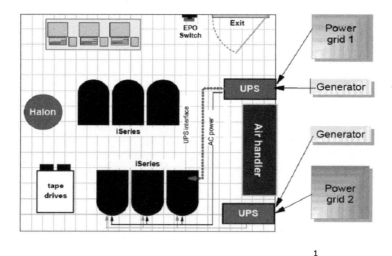

1

Figure 2.1: Highly redundant power configuration.

Diesel and Natural-Gas Generators

You must always ask yourself , what capability does your facility have to support itself if power from the main utility grid goes down? The alternative usually is to invest in an emergency-power generator solution. We have all witnessed the importance of power and the potential for future power disruptions. The cost justification has become quite simple for a generator:

No power = No systems = Closed for business

Emergency generators provide power in the event of a prolonged interruption of utility power. Generators must be sized according to the load they are expected to support and the length of time they are expected to support that load. Many people assume that a generator does not provide protection from a momentary power interruption or spike, as this is the role of a UPS. The UPS provides enough standby power to allow the generator to properly come online to service your equipment. Generators can be switched into service either manually through human intervention or automatically via an automatic transfer switch.

In a highly redundant power supply configuration such as in Figure 2.1, there must be at least two generators and two UPSs, each one with the capacity to generate enough electricity at full load to power the entire computer room and potentially critical locations throughout your office facility. The real question is, how often are the generators tested? Are the backup generators tested under full load to simulate real power demands for several hours? Put into place a regular testing schedule for the diesel generators to ensure that staff members are trained in the operation and that the generators work when you need them most, which is during a power outage. It is a little embarrassing to walk out with a flashlight to try and play mechanic when the lights go out. Consider the capacity of the fuel tanks and how long the equipment will stay up with current workload. When are the diesel tanks filled up, and at what interval? Do you wait until the fuel tanks go down to 25% capacity and then call the supplier and wait for a refill, or do you simply top the tank up on a scheduled interval? Is there a formal contract in place with a documented Service Level Agreement to obtain fuel during a regional crisis?

Here are some considerations for generators:

- How many backup generators exist? Fully redundant solutions call for at least two generators, each one with the capacity to generate enough electricity at full load to power the facility.
- Are there redundancies built into the facility's electrical switches that power the computer room?
- How often are backup generators tested?
- Are the backup generators tested under full load to simulate real power demands for several hours?
- What expertise does the IT team have?
- Is service support available 24/7, 365 days per year?

Assuming that your generator's fuel supply will outlast the disaster itself, most diesel-powered generators only have a two to three day supply of fuel in their tanks. Often, during a disaster, areas become inaccessible to fuel trucks for longer periods of time than that, and alternate plans need to be drawn up for that eventuality. In a recent regional disaster, one organization trucked in fuel from companies well over 700 miles away due to high local demand. It's all about supply and demand, and the fuel companies do run out of supply in regional disasters.

Water Detection

The facts speak for themselves: water is the number-one disaster potential affecting data centers today. Flooding can result from a number of sources, including weather-related events, plumbing issues, water leakage (especially in a shared building), cooling systems, washrooms, sewers, and fire sprinklers. The very obvious result from water into a data center is short-circuiting the live running servers. Water, electricity, and computer hardware are a bad mix. However, even if you shut down the servers, damage to sensitive equipment is still realized in many cases in water disasters.

There are a number of methods for water detection. Most use an array of sensors placed strategically within the protected area. Some intelligent sensor models can pinpoint the exact alarm sensor that is triggered.

Water and smoke detection are common environmental safeguards in today's data centers. Water is important, as many computer rooms have raised-floor designs. How would you know if you had water underneath the computer room's raised floor, unless you lifted the floor tiles to visually check every hour? Install a water-detection trough with multiple water sensors that feed back information to the enunciator panel, which in turn is monitored by a qualified service. A water drainage pipe with a shutoff valve is also invaluable.

It should be understood that flood detectors can do very little for you in the event of massive flooding caused by inclement weather. Early warning is all you can expect in a major situation. Minor leaks are quickly identified before they cause major damage. Water can find its way in through the most obscure methods, so ensure water sensors tell you before your servers do. Service providers that supply solutions such as pumping out flooded rooms can become overwhelmed with the demands of a disaster. The disaster recovery coordinator should also source out-of-state, alternate providers beforehand.

With the use of a water-chilled air conditioner, water sensors must be installed under the raised floor to protect against the possibility of a leak from the A/C unit or any other water source. Set up a trough around water chillers to isolate the spread of water. The physical location of a data center can also be problematic. A basement-level computer room might be safe and secure from the outside, but it might also be more exposed to water leaks or floods.

Real-World Example: Ignoring the Obvious Based on Folklore

I came across a primary data center where the computer room had a "raised floor" that was at the same level as the ground floor (see Figure 2.2). I must have glanced back and fourth five times. In fact, they had a sunken computer room. Yes, for real!

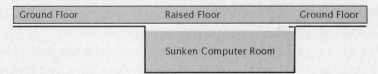

Figure 2.2: A "raised" sunken computer room.

I brought this to the attention of the IT manager, emphasizing the potential risk for water damage. I pointed out that they had a flat roof that collected rain, and an outside door no more than 20 yards away from the computer room. I just did not like the chances there. The IT manager shrugged and assured me it could not happen in our lifetime, "Have you never heard of the 100-year flood?" I had not.

He explained that a flood back in 1972 made a real mess of things, but another was not likely to happen for another hundred years. It made no sense, but everyone in this company believed the same thing. Even a local firefighter talked about how thankful he was that another flood would not happen in his lifetime! How could I argue? I had to let it go.

A year or so later, a wicked storm passed over the town. The guard at the main gate noticed Internet access was down when he was unable to obtain his NFL scores online. He tried his email . . . that was also down. So, he called the help desk. Quickly, it was discovered that all systems were down. Guess what? The in-famous "100-year" flood had visited early, in the form of 8 inches of water. Luckily for them, they had four pumps and a shopvac handy, and got the water out before permanent serious damage occurred. (Just what every IT department has, right?! But after all, they were a steel mill and had these types of supplies available.)

Lesson learned . . . I hope! Actually, I doubt it. Happen again in their lifetime, what are the chances?

> ### Real-World Example: The High Rise
>
> A client had a computer room on the 44th floor of a downtown office tower. They had a weekend incident that was reported by building security. Four inches of water had accumulated under the raised floor, and the circuit breakers were triggered, shutting down power to the computer room. There was some minor damage, but the power-distribution panel did its job to prevent a complete catastrophe. The issue was caused by an executive shower room on the 52nd floor.
>
> Water is tricky. In this case, 12 floors were passed by, but not the computer room. Guess what? There were no water sensors under the floor.

Fire Suppression

Is your computer room a fire hazard? Is it a storeroom of paper, cardboard, toners, and miscellaneous computer hardware piled to the ceiling? This is often the case because server racks conveniently conceal an inventory stockpile. Careful consideration should be given to what is being stored behind the row of server cabinets. Investigate what level of fire suppression you have in place. Automatic water sprinklers are the first line of defense against a fire. A sprinkler system not only detects a fire, but also automatically transmits an alarm to the local fire department or central monitoring station. A sprinkler system is on duty 24 hours a day, 365 days a year.

Here are some basic fire facts:

- The temperature at which a fire begins to damage computer equipment is 180 degrees Fahrenheit. In comparison, paper burns at 400 degrees.
- Tape media such as LTO begins to deteriorate at 130 degrees.
- Smoke introduces tremendous amounts of contamination into the computer room. The effects usually appear well after the event.

- Water combined with burning cable sheeting emits a poisonous gas.

- Most computer rooms are not built to code. You need more than an easily accessible exit. Storing old PC units in front of an emergency exit door is a poor strategy, let alone life-threatening.

- Storing a vault in the computer room to keep valuable backup tape media is a bad idea. Even if it remains accessible, if the heat does not destroy your tapes, the smoke will.

The computer room should have multiple smoke detectors installed. The smoke detectors should always be unobstructed and should be arranged in two cross-zones. Bidirectional zones combine both opposite ceiling detection and floor sensors. All zones are wired back to the computer room's enunciator panel and to the building panels for monitoring by an external agency and fire department. A floor-plan schematic should always be made available to display fire-suppression equipment under any raised floors adjacent to the door of the computer room. Ensure fire detection and suppression is supplied with a dependable supply of electricity. Should there be an extended power outage, the fire-detection system would not be online to respond to a potential fire situation.

Regular tests *must* take place by placing the enunciator panel on bypass (always document it) as you test each of the zone fire sensors. The computer room should also be equipped with fire extinguishers. Finally, staff training is imperative to ensure that procedures are understood and followed.

Sprinkler Fire-Suppression Systems

Each sprinkler head is closed independently by heat-sensitive seals. These seals prevent water flow until a pre-specified temperature is exceeded at each individual sprinkler head. The seal melts, and the sprinkler head is activated. Each sprinkler head activates independently when the predetermined heat level is reached. The intention of this is to limit the total number of sprinklers that operate simultaneously without a need, thereby providing the maximum water supply available from the water source to the point of the fire's origin.

Consider the water damage in your computer room from a sprinkler system versus that from the fire department. An activated sprinkler will do less water damage than a fire department's hose. That hose will stream water at around 250 gallons per minute, whereas an activated sprinkler head generally discharges water at around 23 gallons per minute. In addition, the sprinkler will activate immediately upon fire detection, whereas a fire department takes an average of 10-15 minutes to reach a reported fire incident. This delay can result in substantial damage from the fire before the fire department arrives. Also, the fire will be much larger, therefore requiring much more water to extinguish.

There are three sprinkler suppression types:

- *Wet pipe systems* are installed more often than the other types by a wide margin in our industry. They have the highest reliability, as they are simple, with the only operating component being the automatic sprinkler. A water supply provides pressure to the piping, and all of the piping is filled with water adjacent to the sprinklers. The water is held back by the automatic sprinklers. When one or more of the automatic sprinklers is exposed to sufficient heat, the heat-sensitive seal melts, allowing water flow from that sprinkler. Each sprinkler operates individually.

- *Dry pipe systems* can only be used (by regulation) in spaces in which the room temperature might be cold enough to freeze the water in a wet pipe system. Dry pipe systems are most often used in unheated buildings, in refrigerated coolers, and in computer rooms. Dry pipe systems are the second most common sprinkler type. Water is not present in the piping until the system operates. The piping is pressurized with air at a "maintenance" pressure valve, which is relatively low compared with the water supply pressure. To prevent the larger water supply pressure from forcing water into the piping, the design of the dry pipe valve (a special type of check valve) intentionally includes a larger valve clapper area exposed to the maintenance air pressure, as compared to the water pressure. When one or more of the automatic sprinklers is exposed to sufficient heat, it operates, allowing the maintenance air to vent from that sprinkler. Each sprinkler operates individually. As the air pressure in the piping drops, the pressure differential across the dry pipe valve changes, allowing water to enter the piping system. Water flow from sprinklers needed to control the fire is delayed until the air is vented from the sprinklers. For this reason, dry pipe systems are usually not as effective as wet pipe systems in fire control during the initial stages of the fire.

- *Pre-action sprinkler systems* are specialized for use in locations where accidental activation is undesired, such as in computer rooms. Pre-action systems are hybrids of wet and dry systems. The operation of these systems is similar to dry systems, except that pre-action systems require that a preceding and supervised event (typically, the activation of a heat or smoke detector) take place prior to the action of introducing water into the system's piping due to opening of the pre-action valve (which is a mechanically latched valve). Once the fire is detected by the fire alarm system, the system is essentially converted from a dry system into a wet system. Or, if an automatic sprinkler operated prior to the fire being detected by the fire alarm system, water will be allowed into the piping, and will discharge water from the sprinkler. This system works hand-in-hand with a bidirectional smoke-detection system.

Facility Monitoring

Facility monitoring systems and their alarms should be visible enough to be seen and audible to be heard from almost any area in the computer room, even when noisy pieces of equipment, such as printers, are running. A strobe light is an example of this type of alarm. It just makes sense to automate the monitoring of computer rooms, to ensure stability. However, it's easy to get a dulled sense of security if you do not test the monitoring systems. The mistake of relying solely on monitoring systems can become fatal if sensors, alarms, or enunciator panels fail during a disaster. Outage reports should point to the frequency and duration of service interruptions caused by facilities. From there, it should be easy to analyze trends, repeat incidents, and root causes.

An affordable facility-monitoring solution today is to install wireless IP-based cameras. Any camera in a zone can become activated when motion is detected in the computer room. All events are recorded to a CD drive or video system. This type of tracking system provides strong enforcement and controls. Electronic recording of these activities in addition to automated monitoring provides peace of mind.

Certified companies that offer facility monitoring typically offer higher levels of service and reliability because they are mandated to follow certain guidelines and policies.

Physical Security

Before examining the inside of a computer room, consider the outside access and the surrounding perimeter of your office building. Let's start by asking the following types of questions about the outside:

- Are there glass windows with a clear view of the data center?
- Are there glass-break alarms?
- Does the facility stand alone, or does it share a building with other tenants?
- Do other tenants pose any kind of threat to security?
- Are there frequent shipments of products? Of hazardous materials?
- Is the site surrounded by fences, berms, or shrubs that pose easy access points to and from the site perimeter?
- Is the parking gated, with access controls and guards at the main checkpoint?
- Are the security guards professionals employed by a security firm, or are they part-time college kids getting paid to do their homework at the security desk?
- Are the security guards present 24 hours, seven days a week?
- Are there adequate security cameras covering the perimeter and entrances?
- Is activity on these cameras being recorded and made available for recall?

- How long are video surveillance data kept? What are the audit requirements?
- Does the building have managed and controlled door-access systems?

A completely secure computer room is vital to every organization. Maintaining the security of the computer room is also a demanding task. Computer-room security is necessary so that only authorized personnel can enter the computing facility. Many organizations employ a host of software and hardware controls to prevent authorized access to the computer room. Physical access controls are intended to keep unauthorized personal out . . . period.

How accommodating is your physical security? Check the following:

- Open-door policy
- Entry points
- Cipher locks
- IP cameras

I am often fascinated by the open-door policy of some computer installations. The computer room's door is often simply unlocked throughout the business day. Some organizations like to believe they do not have to worry about "that type of issue" because they know all their employees by name, and even their kids and their pets. That's great, but there is trust, and then there is too much assumed trust. Would you trust all your staff with a key to your own home?

Cipher locks are another sign of false security. These six-digit keypads force you to key in a numeric code to open the door. It's supposed to work by keeping unauthorized people out, but everyone seems to forget the code, so you have to make it easy. How about 1–2–3, or 2–4–1 (like two-for-one pizza), or 4–5–6? With a combination of these three sequences, you will get into half the rooms protected by cipher locks. It makes no sense.

All computer room access must be controlled by a door-management system. Each entry and exit must be recorded and archived. No buddy system here;

everyone must swipe in and out separately. There is no room for leaving the door unlocked throughout the business day. Limiting physical access to the computer room reduces the chance of accidents and potential malicious damage that could leave your systems disabled for days. Door-management systems allow you control during off-hour and holiday periods. Are there adequate security cameras covering all the entrances? How is activity on these cameras being recorded, and how long is the video surveillance data archived?

Earthquake/Tornado/Hurricane Safeguards

If the location of your computer room is prone to natural events, equipment should be anchored and secured. You should include emergency preparedness for earthquakes and other natural or man-made disasters as a basic part of general safety training for all personnel working inside a computer room. Your staff should be knowledgeable about emergency power offs, evacuation procedures, first-aid assistance, and emergency telephone numbers.

Alternate Installation Device

You will need to use the alternate installation device in addition to your primary installation device (i.e., TAP01) in any recovery scenario that requires replacing Licensed Internal Code or a complete system restore. You will execute your recovery procedures by initially using the primary installation device CD and performing an IPL D. This device can be a tape drive or an optical CD/DVD-ROM. When you use an alternate IPL device, the system will load a small portion of the Licensed Internal Code during an IPL-type D and then continue the installation by using the media specified in the alternate installation device screen.

It is critical to ensure you are fully aware of how to define an alternate installation device when there is no pressure to perform this operation. To set up an alternate installation device, you need to ensure that you define it on a system bus, and you must enable the device. You should record and keep the logical address of the system bus and of the system card at which the alternate installation device is attached. This should be documented in the "System Information" section of your disaster recovery plan. If you have the device set up on a different bus and you do not have this information available, you will not be able to complete a system recovery.

> **Note:** Tape devices attached by a fiber channel interface will need to be set up as alternate installation devices. If you use an alternate installation device, you need to ensure that you set up the device and that you enable it. You also need to have the CD-ROM, DVD-ROM, or tape media that contains the Licensed Internal Code and your save media. The CD is labeled I_BASE_01. You must ensure you use the correct CD for the current version you are running on the iSeries or System i5.

During the next maintenance window, this functionality should be tested to ensure the alternate works properly. There is no risk to your production system in testing this functionality in advance, unless of course you proceed to load a new system. Ensure that the installation device has the correct firmware levels and is functional at time of need. This can easily be accessed with a manual IPL to "D" using the LIC CD and assigning a new alternate IPL device through dedicated service tools.

The License Internal Code CD

The IBM LIC CD serves a critical function toward building an iSeries/400 system. The location of this CD should be clearly stated and made available for a system recovery. Without the LIC CD, recovery is not possible. After every operating system upgrade, ensure that the CD labeled I_BASE_ is safely stored in your hot box.

What happens if your system fails and you cannot locate your LIC CD? Can you use a LIC CD from another system or another company that has an iSeries/400? The answer is yes. The LIC CD is not unique to your specific model of iSeries/400. The only consideration is that you use the same operating-system release-level LIC in a recovery as the SAVSYS.

Media Tape Condition

The condition of tape media can play a vital role in the success or failure of your backup strategy. Always make sure that your tapes are in good working order. Imagine having to tell your boss that an entire week's worth of company data has been lost because of a $30 tape!

Always verify the quality of the data saved and examine all system error-log reports to ensure the tape is readable when you need it most. The System i5 does not come out and send a message to the QSYSOPR message queue telling you to replace a tape. You must run BRMS reports and error logs, and review their contents. You should then decide if a specific tape volume needs to be replaced. Seeing numerous permanent write errors on any tape volume is a reason to replace it. This, of course, is well under the system-stated level of acceptability, but for $30, the risk just isn't worth it.

Vulnerability Assessment Summary

Performing a vulnerability assessment of your data center can go a long way towards disaster avoidance. Addressing all potential single points of failure that support IT service delivery is a very important initial step towards risk mitigation. Correct environmental and physical controls will further ensure data center availability. Additionally, ensure your insurance provider receives full supporting documentation of every mitigating improvement that is made to your facility. Consider that insurance companies tend to give credit in the form of a reduced annual premium for many preventive measures implemented by your company.

The installation of a fire detection and suppression system plus a generator, in addition to a documented and tested disaster recovery plan, may reduce annual premium payments for business liability insurance. Simply stated, insurance companies calculate policy premiums on the basis of the perceived risk of your organization. Eliminate all the reasons for which they can justify a higher premium.

Performing a Risk Analysis

After assessing vulnerability, your organization next needs to investigate the requirements for developing a risk-mitigation roadmap. How do you ensure disaster recovery and maintain business continuity, should a disaster of any type strike? The risk of not having anything formally documented is too high. Today, most departments depend on dedicated computer access to perform their functions exclusively. To write a disaster recovery plan, your recovery planning team must understand the business and associated processes, computing technology, local and wide area networks, and expected levels of service. To achieve this level of understanding, a project must be started by preparing a risk analysis followed by a business impact analysis that includes at least the top potential disaster scenarios. The risk analysis should always include the worst-case scenario of completely damaged facilities and loss of computer room, as well as weather-related scenarios, geographic situations, and the current computer implementation design (vulnerability review).

Consider the following when reviewing levels of risk and probability in your organization:

Physical and technological threats and hazards:

- Fire
- Flood, burst pipes, and water damage
- Proximity to bodies of water
- Accidents and/or explosions
- Hazardous/toxic spills, contamination, and access denial
- Operational/equipment/mechanical failures
- Power outages or failures, and cable cuts

- History of utility company in providing uninterrupted power services
- Proximity to power sources
- Programming, system errors, and computer viruses
- Transportation mishaps via aircraft, rail, road, and boat
- Environmental systems and air conditioning failures
- Building collapse or outage
- Security system failure
- Communications systems failure
- Geographic location (topography)
- Airport flight paths
- Proximity to major highways or rail systems that transport hazardous waste and combustible products
- Proximity to nuclear power plants
- Hurricanes, tornados, and other severe weather conditions specific to your location

Political threats and hazards:

- Political disasters
- Terrorism
- Riots
- Civil disturbances and disorders
- Strikes
- Vandalism and theft
- Sabotage
- Disgruntled employees or intruders
- Human error
- Bomb threats
- Cable cuts
- Epidemics/pandemics
- Fraud and embezzlement

The Difference between a Risk Analysis and a Business Impact Analysis

The exact nature, potential, and consequences of a disaster are difficult to determine. It is beneficial to perform a comprehensive risk assessment of all potential threats that can realistically occur in your organization. It is important to be very realistic about this process. If your company is not subject to hurricanes or tornados, do not spend time evaluating and examining these types of events. Focus on the history within your company, and the geographic location of your company. Also introduce new issues like lack of consistent power or the new propane plant down the street. This is where you will measure the associated risks. There are some terminology and definition differences related to risk analysis and vulnerability assessment versus a business impact analysis (BIA). Consider the following definitions:

- A risk analysis involves identifying the most probable threats to your organization and analyzing the related vulnerabilities to your organization from these threats. The process involves measuring and assessing risk and developing strategies to mitigate or simply accept the risk. This may also include transferring the risk to another vendor or supplier.

- The vulnerability assessment involves evaluating existing physical and environmental computer-room process controls, and assessing their adequacy relative to a potential threat to your organization.

- A business impact analysis involves identifying the critical business functions within the organization and determining the financial impact of not performing these business functions beyond the maximum acceptable outage. Consider the financial impact of lost revenue, fines, and lost sales, and the intangible impact of not meeting customer obligations.

Every business depends heavily on computing technology. Disruption of service for even a few days *will* cause severe financial loss and potentially threaten the long-term survival of your company. The continued operation of an organization depends on management's awareness of potential disasters, its ability to mitigate all risks, and to minimize disruptions of mission-critical functions.

The Risk Analysis Process

The primary objective of the DR planning project is to protect the organization if all or part of its computer services are rendered unusable. The analysis should provide for the worst case, like the loss of the primary computing facility. However, other risk probabilities causing downtime or worse should be considered. A general relational rating system of "high" and "medium" can be used to identify and rank threats relevant to your company. Low-rated events are simply identified, as they are not in the scope.

The risk analysis has several purposes:

- Identify the various risks to an organization.
- Identify the requirements of an organization to resume or continue business functions.
- Identify the impact on the organization, both functionally and financially, of an occurrence of the risks.
- Identify the cost to the organization of establishing effective controls to reduce the risks.

The risks of a business outage include the following:

- Loss of control over the revenue stream
- Loss of business unit functionality
- Decreased customer service
- Decreased customer confidence
- Losses in product development, manufacturing, and delivery
- Loss of control over the enterprise

In an ideal list of scenarios for risk management, a prioritization process is followed whereby the risks with the greatest loss and greatest probability are handled first, and risks with the lowest probability and cost are handled later or not at all.

Documenting the rationale for arriving at decisions strengthens accountability and demonstrates due diligence. The common risk-management process and related activities are shown in Figure 2.3 and discussed in the following pages.

Figure 2.3: There are eight major steps in risk management.

Step 1: Identifying Issues

Identifying issues involves the following:

- Define the problems or opportunities, scope, context, and associated risk.
- Define personnel resources, expertise, tools, and techniques.
- Perform a stakeholder analysis (determine risk tolerances, stakeholder position, and maybe even attitudes).

Here are four basic questions to ask at this step:
1. What could go wrong? (Threat/event)
2. How often can it happen? (Frequency)
3. What will be the consequences? (Impact)
4. How certain are the answers above? (Confidence)

Identify all the threats, as this will include events or situations that could cause financial or operational impact to the organization. These are measured in probabilities, such as "this risk may occur one time in 10 years." Each threat has a duration of time during which the business would not be able to function normally, if at all.

Step 2: Assessing Key Risk Areas

Analyze the results of computer-room vulnerabilities and determine the types or categories of risk to be addressed. This may reveal significant organization-wide issues, and IT related issues. Consider whether your computing facility is supporting a centralized or decentralized computing model. Does the level of risk increase of decrease?

Once all the risks have been identified, they must then be assessed as to their potential severity of loss and to the probability of occurrence. These quantities are not always simple to measure, as in the case of a power failure causing the data center to shut down. Therefore, in the assessment process, it is critical to make the best educated guesses possible to properly prioritize the risk.

The downtime cost variable is expressed in $/hour. Understanding downtime dollars per hour is the most important key to understanding your availability requirements. With labor costs, lost productivity, and lost revenue, the cost of downtime continues to rise. Meanwhile, the cost of computing is falling.

Step 3: Measuring Likelihood and Impact

Determine the exposure level to your organization and the frequency of occurrence. This must be expressed as likelihood and impact of associated assessed risks. The fundamental difficulty in risk assessment is determining the rate of occurrence, since statistical information is not always readily available on all kinds of past incidents. The Web is a handy tool to review such things as weather-related data for the past 10 years in a specific city. Newspapers also cover major events, and the local library is another resource.

In ranking all relevant risks to your organization, classify them into three categories: high, medium, and low. It is always easier to group levels of risk into bigger buckets. Consider your organization's risk tolerance, using existing or new criteria and available information. Involve the business to understand what and how much risk it can accept. Some things to review during this process are the facility infrastructure, computer and communication recovery, and business function processes and components to help identify the kinds of risks and controls in place. During this phase, additional controls might be recommended to mitigate the effects of a particular risk.

Step 4: Risk Avoidance

One possible example of risk avoidance is never performing an operating system upgrade on the System i5. If you do not change the OS level, there is no new risk. On the other hand, after several years, when IBM no longer supports the operating system, not changing would bring on a different kind of risk.

Avoidance might initially seem an answer to all risks. However, avoiding risks also means losing out on the potential gain that accepting the risks might have allowed. Running a business to avoid the risk of loss also avoids the possibility of earning profits. Avoiding putting your System i5 on the Web because of the perceived security risk means losing potential new market share! Manage the risk and install the required firewall protection and DMZs. Consider risk versus reward and managed risk for managed gains.

Step 5: Developing Solutions

During the solutions-development step, identify and analyze all available mitigation options and costs. These options should identify ways to minimize the threat of any associated risk. Try to maximize this opportunity, and base solutions on revenues lost for the duration of the incident, penalties incurred, and competitive advantages. The risk reduction involves methods that reduce the severity of the loss. Examples would include sprinklers designed to put out a fire to reduce the risk of loss by fire. This method might actually cause a greater loss by water damage, and therefore might not be suitable. Halon or Argon fire-suppression systems will mitigate the risk of water damage on your server infrastructure, but the cost might be prohibitive.

Step 6: Selecting a Strategy

Choose a strategy, applying your decision and criteria to obtain results. Present a defined risk and problem as an opportunity. Where appropriate, apply the precautionary approach/principle as a means of managing risks of serious or irreversible damage.

Mitigating factors in selecting a risk strategy solution include protection devices, safeguards, and procedures that, if put into place, will reduce the effects of the risk. They do not reduce the actual threat; they only reduce the impact of the threat. Examples of mitigating factors might include UPSs and generators for replacement power, sprinkler systems to control the spread of fire, and access card readers to control physical access to the computer room.

Step 7: Implementing the Strategy

Once a strategy for risk mitigation has been selected, obtain vendor quotations for the solution, and obtain executive commitment and financial approvals. Develop an implementation plan to mitigate the stated risk. There is nothing worse than going through the previous six steps and stopping there. As Murphy's Law will have it, the specific identified risk will greet your organization front and center.

Step 8: Monitoring and Evaluation

During the monitoring and evaluation step, you perform three key activities:

- Improve the decision-making/risk-management process.

- Using effective criteria, report on performance and results.
- Show how the monies invested for risk mitigation have paid off.

Organizations might vary in the execution of all nine basic steps and supporting tasks. However, ensure your DR planning team is suited to achieving a common understanding and implementing consistent, efficient, and effective risk-management techniques. A focused and integrated approach recognizes that all decisions involve management of risk, whether in routine i5 operations or for major initiatives involving significant resources and planning efforts.

While each organization will find its own way to integrate risk management into the existing decision-making matrix, here are factors that may be considered:

- Aligning risk management with objectives at all levels of the organization
- Introducing risk-management components into existing strategic technology planning and iSeries administrative processes
- Communicating acceptable levels of risk

The integration of risk management into decision-making is supported by a corporate disaster-recovery planning philosophy and culture that encourages everyone to manage risks.

Real-World Example

When you evaluate the aspects of risk management, there is a quantitative side (how much will it cost me) of not addressing the risk. This justifies to the business the cost to address the need. Let's examine the statement of risk. It includes the following quantitative attributes:

- Assigning values, such as dollars, to something
- Identifying the cost of a particular effect, incident, or phenomenon
- ALE—Annualized Loss Exposure
- Risk = Frequency multiplied by exposure (R=f*e)

The client had no alternate power source. When suggested that the business should invest in a diesel generator, the CEO snapped back, "It's not in the budget, and we really do not have the need. After all, we have a UPS that should last some 60 minutes and most power glitches are well resolved in that time."

I initially questioned the 60 minutes, but decided to let it go. The UPS was never tested, and the load increased with every server added to the computer room floor.

In the summer of 2006, the client experienced several severe lightning storms, causing power outages. Then, when winter arrived, a freak snow and ice storm caused the power to go out for eight hours. Two key issues came to light—or, more correctly, were evident in the dark. First, the UPS supplied interim power for only 18 minutes, rather than the perceived 60 minutes. The initial deployment of the UPS was for 60 minutes, but the organization had significantly added to the IT server infrastructure. It did not keep up with growth or measured utilized capacity. Second, at the 19 minute mark, there was a hard down of the systems. Ouch !! Can you say, "Reclaim storage or hard drive failure"?

We looked at the risk going forward, and what we should do to mitigate this type of occurrence from affecting the business. The client was only concerned about supporting two departments in a power failure: customer service and the sales order desk.

The annual loss exposure formula can be expressed as follows:

$R = f*e$

Where

R = Risk
f = Frequency
e = Exposure

Consider the example of a power failure where the frequency is five times a year, with an uncontrolled loss of $50,000 in the sales department and $10,000 in customer service:

> **5 failures at $ 50,000 per outage exceeding 1 hour = $250,000**
> **5 failures at $10,000 per outage exceeding 1 hour = $50,000**
>
> **Total ALE=$ 300,000**
>
> So, the company had an opportunity to invest in a diesel generator to avoid the risk of $300,000 per year. The impact was far-reaching, as we did not include the dollars lost when all of the remotes were down because the primary data center was down.
>
> The organization purchased a diesel generator and had it installed and operational for $170,000. Now, it can keep the site up regardless of what the local power utility decides to throw at them. More importantly, the entire business, including remote offices, is no longer affected by outages. What is the value of this?
>
> I still smile every time I see a newscast and the power is out in that client's city. I know they are still in business. Would you be?

Transfer of Risk via Insurance

Transfer of risk via insurance means assigning risk to another party or vendor, typically by a formal contract. Insurance companies are one type of risk transfer that uses contracts. Adequate insurance coverage is a key consideration when developing a disaster recovery plan and performing a risk analysis. Having a disaster plan and testing it regularly might not, in itself, lower insurance rates in all circumstances. However, a good DR plan can reduce risks and address many of the underwriter's concerns, in addition to affecting the cost or availability of the insurance in the first place.

Insurance underwriters are selective these days with which organizations they wish to insure. After all, every insurance company wants to hedge its investment and not take extra risk. Most insurance companies specializing in business-interruption coverage can provide the organization with an estimate of the anticipated business-interruption costs. Most business-interruption insurance covers lost revenues following a disaster. With estimates of the insurance premium cost, and the perceived lost revenue as per the insurance company, your risk analysis can evaluate the type and amount of insurance required.

Summary

The risk analysis process is an important aspect of disaster recovery planning. The probability of a disaster occurring in an organization is highly uncertain.

Risk is unavoidable and present in virtually every situation we encounter. It is present in everything we do in our work and home lives. Every integration, every day, your business will encounter risk. What is commonly accepted is the uncertainty of outcomes of risk itself. Technological complexity breeds risk. This phenomenon reflects Murphy's Law, "If something can go wrong, it will go wrong."

The fact is, risk should not be regarded with defeatism, but with awareness and preparation. People in different positions within a company might have different comfort levels with risk. Eliminating all risk is neither possible nor desirable. Without taking risks, nobody would succeed, and there would be no advancement on technology or profits.

3

Conducting a Business Impact and Recoverability Analysis

The business impact analysis, or BIA, is probably the most important component of your entire disaster recovery project. This is the part of the project that defines and quantifies all the reasons why you are going through the trouble of producing a disaster recovery plan in the first place. The more factual, comprehensive, understandable, and informative your BIA is, the better your chances are for success in the disaster recovery planning project. If your BIA clearly communicates the inherent vulnerabilities of the System i5, iSeries, and other systems, you will win the endorsement, support, and funding of senior management. A BIA is a formal method of assessing risks and determining the potential economic loss that could occur as a result of these risks. Probably the most feared risk in IT, and the one viewed as most problematic by IT managers today, is the need to recover from a complete disruption of computing services . . . in other words, the loss of the data center or the loss of customer server data.

To support the criticality and associated financial burden of a critical system loss, all business functions must be identified and analyzed during a BIA project. Then, these business functions can be aligned with supporting IT infrastructure and ranked as either critical, essential, or desirable (nice to have). Each process is evaluated to determine the potential revenue loss that would be incurred in the event of any such disruption. The DR planning team should also expand the business impact analysis to review the legal and regulatory ramifications associated with no delivery of goods sold and the contractual requirements to determine the consequences of any prolonged business interruption. The result of the BIA will help design the DR planning roadmap by assisting the recovery team in developing procedures for recovering from various types of disasters. Recommendations will be identified during the BIA.

Management representing the business will need to understand the cost of not being able to use IT services. Jointly, the recovery team and management must anticipate capital spending requirements for any strategic solutions presented to mitigate some of the projected revenue loss. Typically, it makes sense to demonstrate a return on investment (ROI) when you identify specific technological solutions required to mitigate the risk and damage of a disaster.

A BIA is an information-gathering exercise designed to methodically identify:

- The business functions performed by an organization
- The resources (server applications) required to support each business function performed
- Interdependencies between business functions (the information flow)
- The impact(s) of not performing a specific business function
- The criticality of each process
- A Recovery Time Objective (RTO) for each business function
- A Recovery Point Objective (RPO) for the data that supports each business function

This process lays the foundation for selecting the required recovery strategy, recovery scope, and accepted timelines for disaster recovery. The benefits derived from performing such a comprehensive BIA include the following:

- Reduce legal liability.
- Minimize the potential revenue loss.
- Decrease exposures.
- Minimize the loss of data.
- Minimize the length of the outage.
- Reduce the probability of any disaster occurrence.
- Ensure an organized recovery of critical applications.
- Reduce the reliance on specific personnel.
- Ensure legal, statutory, and regulatory compliance.

Starting the Business Impact Analysis

The disaster recovery coordinator should be involved in the entire BIA process. The role of the DR coordinator is to manage the process, ensuring its effectiveness within the DR planning project. A time commitment and specific resources will be needed to develop the BIA. The following senior executives within your organization will need to participate:

- Chief financial officer
- Chief information officer
- Vice-president of operations
- Risk management officer
- Security officer
- Facilities manager
- Senior management from key business areas
- IT recovery team

The recovery team should define the scope of the analysis and be involved in setting priorities, reviewing the BIA findings, and making recommendations. From the DR planning team's perspective, the objective of a disaster recovery plan is to enhance the survivability of your organization in a disaster.

Tangible Costs

When information on the System i5 server is not available to users for any reason, you have downtime. Very often, this will cause the business to completely stop. When the business stops, it gets very expensive, very quickly! You must understand how important this analysis is to the survival of the company. Simply stated, information is the lifeblood of a company. It is crucial to know the server on which all critical information resides and the associated plan for its acceptable, timely recovery.

Calculating costs associated with downtime is much more difficult than it would first appear. Your business executives deal with everyday numbers associated with their specific line of business, and they can normally provide reasonably quick, reliable financial information. The total of all revenue information for all lines of business is considered the tangible cost of downtime. However, this is still a 50,000-foot view of the total impact, which makes it incomplete. There are other tangible and intangible costs to consider, as shown in Figure 3.1. These include lost revenue, brand reputation, the cost of wages for idled workers, interim (temporary) labor costs, lost inventory, marketing costs, bank fees, late penalties, SLA issues, lost customers, and legal costs.

Figure 3.1: Many tangible and intangible costs are associated with downtime.

Lost Revenue

The most obvious tangible cost of downtime is lost revenue. We can all relate to this effect on the company's bottom line. If your organization cannot process customer orders, it cannot conduct business. With 24/7 electronic commerce, this problem is magnified. Sales depend entirely on system availability.

Having 24/7 availability implies the following:

- 24/7 customer support
- 24/7 services
- 24/7 e-commerce
- 24/7 manufacturing
- Expanded Internet dependence (email)
- Realtime enterprise strategy/business Service Level Agreements
- Global marketplace; mobile workforce

One way to estimate the revenue lost due to a downtime event is to look at normal hourly sales and then multiply that figure by the number of hours of downtime. Be sure to consider peak selling periods, like the Christmas season in the retail industry. Some typical downtime costs are shown in Figure 3.2.

Average Cost per Hour of Downtime by Industry

Finance:	Brokerage Operations	$ 5.15 Million
Finance:	Credit Card Authorizations	$ 3.10 Million
Telecom		$ 2.00 Million
Manufacturing		$ 1.60 Million
Online Retail		$ 613,000
Communications:	Internet Provider	$ 90,000
Transportation		$ 89,500
Media:	Ticket Sales	$ 90,000
Transportation:	Package Shipping	$ 28,000

Source: The Meta Group & Contingency Planning Research

Figure 3.2: This will give you an idea of the impact of downtime in various industries.

Lost Productivity

Employees are not laid off when a major system is down for an hour or two. Some employees will be idle, but their salaries and wages will continue to be paid. Others might get sent home with full pay. Still others might be able to do some work, but their output will likely be of lesser value to the company's bottom line.

According to *Dunn & Bradstreet*, 59% of Fortune 500 companies experience a minimum of 1.7 hours of downtime a week. This includes all planned and unplanned outages. Assume a company has a total of 1,000 employees affected by this outage at an average hourly wage of $21. The downtime would cost the company $33,600 per week (1,000 x $21.00 x 1.6), or $1,747,200 per year. This, of course, excludes the cost of benefits. Companies are in business to make money. The value employees contribute is usually greater than the cost of employing them. Therefore, this method provides only a very conservative estimate of the labor cost of downtime.

An additional calculation is required for recovery labor. After a period of downtime, employees not only have to do their regular jobs of processing current data, but they must also reenter any data that was lost or not entered during the system outage. This means additional hours of work, frequently on an overtime basis. Secondly, there could be overtime pay in the plant to catch up on the order processing. Overtime is expensive labor.

Late Fees and Penalties

Some companies like those in Just in Time (JIT) industries are subject to severe penalties for not delivering product on time. This is particularly true in the automotive industry. The "Big Three" do not care about your particular system woes. Their expectation is "Just get me the inventory so I can make cars." The fines can be very substantial, your vendor rating could drop, or your company could even get removed as a supplier.

In JIT industries, you might also be rated by the number of failed electronic documentation slips (Advance Shipping Notices) supporting trucking or rail deliveries. Therefore, even if you manage to get the product to your customer's doors, if your system cannot produce customer-required RFID or shipping documents, the product gets turned away. That is extremely costly.

Legal Costs

Depending on the nature of the affected systems, the legal costs associated with downtime can be significant. Downtime could cause a significant drop in share price. Shareholders might even initiate a class-action suit if they believe that management and the board were negligent in protecting vital assets, like the company's private data.

In addition, your partners can and will turn on you. If two companies form a business partnership in which one company's ability to conduct business depends on the availability of the other's computer systems, depending on the legal structure of the partnership, the second company might be liable for profits lost by the first during any significant downtime event.

Intangible Costs

Understanding the tangible costs is just the beginning. It is equally important in any downtime calculation to identify and quantify the intangible costs, which are not always clearly understood. These include the long-term impact of damaged reputations and future lost business from defecting customers, among others. These intangible costs are real.

For example, a perishable-goods producer like a meat supplier might have to dispose of spoiled inventory, or a manufacturer might incur setup costs to restart a stopped assembly line when inventory feeds a secondary finished-good line. I have had clients give away product because they could not get it on trucks to reach store shelves in an acceptable amount of time.

It is impossible to list all the potential intangible costs, as many are specific to the affected company and its particular environment. However, here are some typical ones:

- Lost business opportunities
- Loss of employees and/or employee morale
- Decrease in stock value
- Loss of customer/partner goodwill
- Brand damage
- Driving business to competitor
- Bad publicity/press

Lost Opportunity

When customers and prospects are prevented from dealing with one company because of a network outage, some will not try again later. Instead, they will purchase the product from the competition. It's the dreaded online buyers! They double-click, wait, double-click. No response? They go surfing the Web for another solution. A company therefore loses not just the immediate purchase of a potential customer; it also loses all the purchases that potential customer would have made over the life of the business relationship. This can add up to millions when weighed against how many potential clients were turned away and how much they could have purchased from you over the next five or 10 years.

Remedial Expenses

Large companies spend millions of dollars building their brands and protecting their corporate images. Constant, repeated downtime will harm a company's image. The impact could be felt in consumer confidence, sales, share value, and reputation. If a major downtime event causes a loss in brand appeal and consumer confidence, an expensive corporate-image and marketing campaign might be necessary to repair the damage. What about replacing lost customers who will not return? Market share is everything, and it takes years to establish it, with lots of sales and marketing cost.

The impact to your company should be measured as operating impact, financial impact, and compliance both legal and regulatory. Your business might be forced to operate in a manual mode for a significant period of time following a major catastrophic computing failure. This will, of course, affect the efficiency of your business and have a downstream effect on profits.

Your business might experience serious financial losses as a result of the business interruption, and many of those losses might not be covered by insurance. If your financial systems are crippled by inaccessibility of information, your cash flow will suffer. If payroll systems are affected, employees might not even want to work!

Lost revenues, additional costs to recover, fines and penalties, lost good will, and delayed collection of funds will all add up in a disaster. Once you have determined the impact of an incident on a business function, you can determine the recommended recovery timeframe for the function.

Identifying Mission-Critical Functions

During the business impact analysis, the DR planning team needs to identify the critical functions within the business. These can be identified by listing all functions performed, determining the impact that an incident would have on a business function, and estimating the business loss for the duration of an outage. This process is often most effectively achieved by gathering information from key business leaders via questionnaires or interviews.

The mission-critical business functions include all information, processes, activities, equipment, and personnel needed to continue operations if information systems become unavailable. To determine the mission-critical functions of your organization, each department should consider all important functions performed within that department. Here are some questions to ask, to begin the process:

- If the system was not available, how could the department continue to function?
- What happens if the system is not available for more than a working day, or two, or three?
- Can your department resort to manual processes?
- What is the minimum amount of workstations you can function with?
- What procedures would be necessary to limit exposure during online systems downtime?
- What happens if the data is lost and the system is restored with data that is 24 hours old? Can data be re-created?
- What special forms and supplies are needed?
- Do you have any IT systems you use outside of the primary data center, such as bank-payment connection software or digital certificates on a local desktop?
- Is a particular time in the business cycle, such as month-end, more critical than others?
- What are your critical IT applications?

» Application name?

» Application priority?

» Special requirements?

» Maximum outage (hours, days)?

Viewing the BIA process in terms of the needs of your business clearly states its importance to the disaster recovery plan. What is the priority associated with software applications such as your ERP system, in terms of importance to the business? Be aware that these questions might not be easily answered and might spark considerable discussion and controversy.

Do not exclude secondary applications, such as EDI and email. You might be surprised to find these applications supporting significant portions of the business without any recovery procedures at all.

The Workshop Approach

Your choices for gathering information about mission-critical functions include one-on-one interviews, written questionnaires, workshops, or a combination of these approaches. The culture of your organization will determine the best way to obtain the desired information within acceptable timelines. I personally prefer a workshop to kick things off, with a questionnaire as a take away. (A sample questionnaire is available in appendix A.) While one-on-one interviews can be helpful, they generally lack business objectivity and are very time-consuming.

I recommend inviting a group of no more than 10 senior executives at a time to a "Business Impact Workshop." I prefer an interactive session, and trust me, I ensure it becomes interactive very quickly. I send out an initial agenda outlining the scope and purpose of the meeting. Then, I send a high-level questionnaire asking the participants to evaluate the following four statements:

1. All IT systems are down and will be out indefinitely. At which time (1 hour, 12 hours, 1 day, 2 days) are you completely unable to perform business functions?

2. The systems will be back on–line by the end of the day after being down for 12 hours. However, they will be returned to you with yesterday's data. How does this affect you ?

3. What services does IT provide your line of business?

4. What priority (immediate, critical, important, vital, or deferred) would you assign to each application you use?

The workshop typically runs 60 to 90 minutes. Your goal during that time is to educate the group on disaster recovery, business impact, business functions, and alternatives for system recovery. Emphasize the need to validate business functions supporting servers, applications, and the specific data requirements for those applications in all critical areas, as identified by the executives. Have someone provide support in the workshop for white boarding activities, taking notes, etc. (This could be the disaster recovery coordinator.) Consider electronically recording the meeting, if that is an acceptable practice in your company. It is important to engage all the senior management, as you will certainly discover many business functions that overlap, and the needs of one department might be greater than those of another. The combined organizational needs are what you are looking to define in the BIA.

The workshop produces the following results:

- Provides a collaborative and self-validating exercise
- Allows you to educate executives about disaster recovery
- Removes "analysis paralysis" because of combined initiatives
- Minimizes problems with anecdotal informational about impacts, as everyone is in the same room

The workshop decreases the concern from the executives that they are writing their business needs in stone, or that this is going on deaf ears. Inform them that IT is developing a best response to disaster to support their business requirements. They are simply providing educated opinions about the criticality of their business functions and their IT system needs, and nothing more. During this meeting, you're gathering information about what server applications support those critical business functions.

Produce meeting minutes. They will go a long way toward the project's success. Summarize the findings of the meeting back to the executive team for review, to ensure they clearly reflect management's thoughts and business needs. Most executives claim that their part of the business is extremely vital to the short-term viability of the company. This might be true, but it can be overstated. This is a common issue with BIAs, as every business leader states their access to systems and user data is critical to the survival of the business. The question to ask is whether they can then quantify this with supporting data.

The Interview Approach

Some organizations might be better suited to an informal interview process supported by a questionnaire, instead of a workshop. A list of questions should be developed in advance that you can use to conduct each interview. This makes for an organized approach and will keep the interviews on track. You do not need a comprehensive set of questions to occupy the entire interview period. Instead, a basic set of open-ended questions will enable you to informally learn enough about a department's critical business functions and use of IT-related services. A common set of questions will also provide the necessary consistency between interviews and ensure that you have the same base level of information to later draw from.

Here are some sample questions to ask (see the business impact analysis questionnaire in appendix A for more detail):

- All IT systems are down and will be out indefinitely. At which time (1 hour, 12 hours, 1 day, 2 days) are you completely unable to perform business functions?

99

- The systems will be back by the end of the day after being down for 12 hours. However, they will be returned to you with yesterday's data. How does this affect you ?
- What services does IT provide your line of business?
- What priority (immediate, critical, important, vital, or deferred) would you assign to each application you use?
- What does your business area do for the company?
- What services does IT provide your line of business?
- What systems and software do you need to run your department?
- What would happen if these systems were not available to you?
- Do you have any manual work-arounds?
- What would you do if you had no access to IT systems for x hours or y days?
- At what time do you send staff home during an outage? How many do you send?

It is important to take extensive notes. You will need to know exactly who said what at a later date. Encourage interviewees to respond in terms of direct impact, future impact, lost revenue over different time periods, amounts of services needed for a variety of disaster scenarios, staff impact, SLAs, penalties, etc.

Outage Impact

Once the mission-critical functions have been documented, it is important to determine the financial impact of an outage to these functions. Consider the impact in a complete computer loss and an outage that is 24 hours long with loss of customer data. Other considerations might include the timing of the disaster, such as the potential impact of a disaster at the end of the busiest sales month.

When analyzing critical systems, consider the following:

- Systems relied on to perform critical business functions, their interfaces, and their maximum acceptable outage time
- Dependencies between business functions
- Dependencies between departments
- Dependencies between systems
- Dependencies between applications

Answers to the following should also be carefully analyzed:

- How much revenue would your company lose if its systems were unable to accept orders? (Multiply the average hourly revenue by the number of hours needed to recover.)
- What is the cost of lost productivity? (Add the payroll, taxes, benefits, and overtime for recovery and multiply by the number of all employees from all the affected business units.)
- What is the value of IT employee productivity lost while trying to resolve the problem?
- How much inventory will be lost or spoiled?
- What fines, fees, and/or compensatory payments will you have to pay? (Consider breach of contract, regulatory fines, and late-shipment or late-payment fees.)
- What sales and marketing efforts will you have to initiate to recover revenues, lost customer loyalty, reputation, and/or goodwill?
- What is the impact of not processing in each of the following areas:
  » Customer service
  » Noncompliance with government regulations
  » Noncompliance with existing contracts
  » Increase in personnel requirements
  » Increased operating costs
  » Loss of financial management capability

» Loss of competitive edge

» Loss of goodwill

» Negative media coverage

» Loss of stockholder confidence

IT to Verify Business Data

One of IT's objectives during a BIA is to understand how every piece of software relates to every business unit and how it all relates to every server. The next step in the process is to speak with the System i5 or iSeries/400 administrators and other IT staff, again preferably in a collaborative work-shop instead of one-on-ones. This is to confirm what was communicated by the executive team to determine the following:

- Where does the application reside—data center and server name?
- How quickly could the application realistically be recovered today?
- Based on historical information, how many help desk calls are received?
- What priority would IT put on a particular application?
- Does this align with what the business said?

Once all of these lists are created for each business unit, it will become self-evident which applications, vendors, etc. are most critical. Determining what constitutes a mission-critical business unit will also affect your final product. Spreadsheets on business priority and application recovery objectives are used long-term as a part of your overall backup and recovery plan program.

Business Impact from Planned and Unplanned Outages

A complete BIA for IT identifies all the financial costs that affect your organization resulting from a system outage, whether planned or unplanned. Normally, the impact on your business is discussed only in the context of unplanned outages. Unplanned downtime is any unscheduled event from scenarios such as natural disasters, power loss, network connectivity failures, and hardware failures. Since these events cause great financial hardship to an organization, they are, of course, highly visible.

While the BIA tends to measure only unplanned downtime and its associated costs, system downtime can be both planned and unplanned, as shown in Figure 3.3. Do not limit the scope of your business impact analysis. Consider that the majority of System i5 outages that affect your ability to perform business functions are planned. Planned downtime occurs when you have a scheduled interruption of services. In other words, you get a blessing or approval from the business to take the System i5 services down to do required work. Here are some planned downtime examples:

- Backup window—incremental, daily, and full system
- IBM and third-party software upgrades
- IBM and third-party PTFs/Service Packs
- Application maintenance
- Database file maintenance (reorgs)
- Hardware upgrades

Identify all these outages and calculate the total hours in a year that are set aside for them. Examine the daily backup window, system or ERP application maintenance, or other related support needs for your organization. You will find these numbers for a year quite staggering. It's probably safe to say that you're already on a course to eliminate all planned downtime due to fundamental changes in your company's IT delivery model to the business. Use a thought process of identifying the cost for planned outages as a means of estimating the payback for an iSeries or System i5 high-availability solution. The most basic requirement for all high-availability solutions should start with the premise of eliminating planned downtime first, and then examine unplanned scenarios.

	Per Week	Per Year
Full Backups Weekly	3 hrs	156 hrs
Daily Backups	6 hrs	312 hrs
Software Installs		20 hrs
+ Housekeeping		24 hrs
= Planned Outages		512 hrs or 21.33 days/year

Figure 3.3: The planned downtime scorecard.

Ideally, you should discover and aim for the financial payback gained by eliminating all planned downtime to cover the cost for a solution to address unplanned downtime. Eliminating planned downtime can provide immediate payback to your business users, and it is easily measurable.

You already know exactly what constitutes all of the planned outages in your IT shop today. Eliminating planned downtime is immediate and measurable, but assigning a cost to an unplanned event that might never happen isn't so easy. Beyond lost revenues and productivity, the devastation caused by a critical application's loss for an extended time period might be so severe that it could permanently hurt your business. You must focus on worst-case scenarios because they go beyond the levels of acceptable business loss.

93% of all companies that experience significant data loss are out of business within five years.

Gartner Group, Inc.

Recovery Time Objective vs. Recovery Point Objective

The BIA identifies all of the critical business functions and their supporting IT components. This is required to determine the Recovery Time Objective

(RTO) and Recovery Point Objective (RPO). The RTO is how soon the business units need to have their required services (IT applications) up and running. The RPO is the most recent point in time to which systems can be restored back. The shorter the RTO and RPO, the more complex, leading-edge, business resilient, and of course expensive the recovery solution becomes.

Not that long ago, most companies were open for business eight hours per day, Monday to Friday. Having the old AS/400 unavailable did not prevent any customer sales from occurring, because these transactions were usually conducted in person or over the phone, perhaps even recorded on carbon-copy paper. All of the transactions' details were gathered up through the day, and entered overnight. If some form of disaster shut down the AS/400 and the rest of computing services for a few days, the organization just continued working manually. The paper simply piled up, and when the systems came back online, the transactions would be entered. In other words, it was business as usual during an IT outage.

Today, you are faced with new realities. Employees, customers, and your suppliers are all interrelated . . . a global economy where the use of the Internet mandates a 24/7 business model. There is no official start or end to the business day. You are open 24 hours a day, every day. Systems are no longer isolated. They all interact with other systems to complete transactions, regardless of the hardware platform. The realities of today's business underscore the importance of delivering computing services and protecting the data that is your greatest corporate asset.

The goal for companies with no business tolerance for downtime is to achieve a state of readiness, where all critical systems and networks are continuously available, no matter what happens. Disaster recovery is a combination of how long you wait to bring your business back up after a failure (the RTO), and how much data the company is willing to lose due to a failure (the RPO). Finally, how much system availability your business is willing to pay for leads to the ROI. The interrelationship among RPO, RTO, and ROI is shown in Figure 3.4.

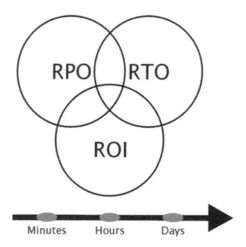

RTO: Recovery Time Objectives – *How long can your system be down?*
RPO: Recovery Point Objectives – *How much vital data can you afford to lose?*
ROI: Return on Investment Goals – *Planned vs. unplanned outages?*
– High availability vs. Conventional hotsite?

Figure 3.4: RPO, RTO, and ROI are intertwined in a business impact analysis.

The tolerance for RTO and RTP varies from industry to industry. Financial institutions, for example, require services back online in minutes, rather than hours. Even more critically, healthcare providers require emergency response immediately. Other industries can afford to be down 24 hours without access to IT. Organizations that cannot afford to lose more than a single minute's worth of transactional data must have strategies that include clustering or high availability, where online data is captured realtime in both the production and backup environments. Other organizations might find that tape backup programs supply ample data protection.

Recovery Time Objective (RTO)

As shown in Figure 3.5, the Recovery Time Objective (RTO) is the length of time required to recover from an unplanned outage as a result of a disaster. It includes the time required to resume normal operations for a specific application server or set of applications servers. The RTO is directly related to the BIA and is normally stated as a specific time value in minutes, hours, or days.

Time is of the essence when recovering your company's lost data. While the IT folks are busy recovering your company data, your customers may be contacting other suppliers. Just in Time manufacturing, distribution, and electronic commerce have put a premium on systems availability and access to corporate data.

Recovery Time Objective

RTO is the time within which business processes must be restored at acceptable levels of operational capability to minimize the impact of an outage.

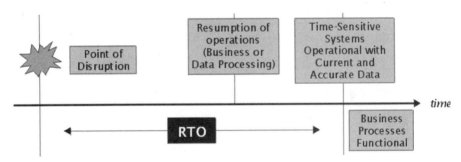

Figure 3.5: RTO is the length of time required to recover from a disaster.

The RTO is the acceptable time to recover all applications used in the business process, including recovery of applications, data, and end-user access to those applications within the maximum allowable downtime acceptable by the business. How long can your computer systems be made unavailable to support key business process? How long can you afford to be offline to your customers? Every business is unique, so the metrics for defining the RTO is different for each organization. You cannot answer these questions alone within the walls of IT. You must include the business directly, as they understand their business thresholds and service-level commitments to their customers.

To be cautious and save face, many organizations reactively set a 48-hour RTO as a place to start when defining initial DR recovery objectives, as shown in Figure 3.6. Aim for the quickest recovery your business can afford. When a disaster strikes your company, your competitors will jump at the chance to fill the void. An effective DR plan will ensure that you meet your RTO objectives. On the other hand, do not start with a 24-hour RTO without careful analysis. Twenty-four hours is not a lot of time to rebuild an entire server infrastructure.

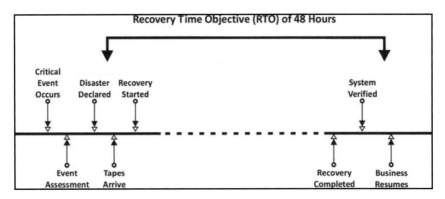

Figure 3.6: Many organizations typically start with a 48-hour RTO.

The system-restoration recovery timeline is the total length of time required to resume normal operations and application access after an unplanned outage occurs. The length of the recovery time depends on many factors. Table 3.1 walks through an example of typical recovery tasks in an outage. The total number of hours spent on these specific tasks will help determine the current capability to resume computing services after a system failure. This example is a single, stand-alone system with no LPAR considerations and includes 1.2 terabytes (TB) of disk utilizing a LTO3 tape drive.

Table 3.1: The Timeline to Rebuild a Sample System from Tape	
Recovery Tasks	**Time to Complete Task in hours**
Assess the disaster situation.	3 hours
Declare a disaster.	2 hours
Retrieve tapes from the offsite supplier.	1 howur
Transport key staff and backup tapes to the recovery site.	2 hours (Consider location of hotsite.)
Build the disk configuration.	4 hours
Restore LIC.	30 minutes
Restore OS/400 .	1.5 hours
Restore IBM programs.	30 minutes
Restore user data.	9 hours
Rebuild the IFS.	2 hours
Apply incremental data.	2 hours
Rebuild security.	30 minutes
Configure and redirect networks.	1 hour
Perform IPL.	30 minutes
Test and validate.	1 hour
Total Time	**30.5 hours**

With recovery at commercial hotsites, typically located out of state, you must plan for additional time to support the extended travel requirements. This typically will include airline travel to your destination. In accounting for travel arrangements for critical staff, do not assume everyone designated to travel has the personal funds to secure an airline ticket. Last-minute air travel can be really expensive.

Once you have determined how long your business can afford to be down, your RTO objectives will become obvious and accepted by the business. You will have to implement technological solutions to both manage the business expectations for downtime and observe your financial budget constraints. The shorter your RTO, the higher your financial investment will be towards an iSeries high availability, or System i5 clustering solution. Additional considerations would be required for site redundancy, as well. You will need to put the systems in another location to support your reduced RTO solution. It is very possible that you simply cannot afford the expenditure to meet your business RTO. In these situations, the business will have to accept the risk associated with a lesser IT deliverable.

Recovery Point Objective (RPO)

The point in time to which server data must be restored to resume back-to-normal processing of transactions without adversely affecting the organization is the Recovery Point Objective (RPO). Following any unplanned outage where data has been lost, you must ask yourself, "To what recovery point can I restore based on the most recent saved data?" How much data is actually lost, versus how much can your organization afford to lose? Never assume that, even if you can go back to last night's backup tapes, those backup tapes contain everything required to rebuild your iSeries/400 as of 24 hours ago.

Before you implement any type of backup solution, you need to consider what the impact of a system failure (complete loss of data) has on your business. In a situation where your iSeries/400 server has experienced some form of hardware or disk protection failure, you need to ask yourself "How re-creatable is the user data?" Keep in mind that most data transactions today are electronic and originate from many access points. What is the cost of lost data or missing transactions in your company? With a traditional tape backup strategy, every business transaction executed within the current day will be lost. For example, if your last backup finished at 2 a.m., and you had a disaster at 5 p.m. that same day, could you re-create the data entered during the business day? This implies you could lose from zero to 24 hours of business transactions. In a true 24/7 business model, that can be very significant.

Be careful about promising and delivering a 24-hour RPO. Careful consideration must be given for weekend activities, as shown in Figure 3.7. Many

IT departments are satisfied with this approach and have thus conceded the fact that 24 hours of data loss is completely acceptable to the organization for Monday to Friday processing. However, by including weekend business activities, the RPO exposure is increased three-fold over weekends. Ensure that this is agreeable at the executive level, as well as within your IT department!

The most important thing to consider in this definition is that RPO is the point in time where the recovery processing will return all your end users from the perspective of both the data and application processing. Loss of data can cost your company big money, or even close your business altogether. An increasingly common way to compare resiliency with server technologies is to look at the way each hardware technology handles resiliency. The RPO is the total acceptable data transaction loss when recovering from a disaster or system failure. IT shops that require an RPO of less then 24 hours or immediate recovery to the last completed transaction and its committed data require a much more data-resilient solution that would include one or several iSeries/400 solutions.

Sun	Mon	Tue	Wed	Thr	Fri	Sat
27	28	29	30	31	1	2
3	4	5	6	7	8	9
10	11	12	13	14	15	16
17	18	19	20	21	22	23
24	25	26	27	28	29	30

Increased exposure as tapes do not go offsite on weekends and holidays

Figure 3.7: RPO exposure.

Recovery point is the exact point in time you'll be returned to after all your recovery processing activities have been completed successfully. This is the point from which you'll resume normal business operations. A recovery point will differ with each recovery solution employed. For shared/switched devices (IASP, Integrated Auxiliary Storage Pools), the recovery point is always what was last written to disk. Transaction changes still resident in memory that haven't been written to disk will simply be lost. This means that it's vital to use journaling with these solutions, to help ensure that changes to critical data are captured on disk as they occur.

For high availability, the recovery point is always what was last transmitted and received by the backup iSeries server. Any changes that haven't been completely transmitted, and in some way acknowledged, will be lost. Another factor to consider is the total line capacity. Insufficient bandwidth can cause latency and a backlog of transactions on the source system. Too often the line between the target and source system is not dedicated; it is shared with the Internet solution (company wide!).

The use of object journaling with synchronous replication for logical copies can help ensure that changes to critical data are transmitted as they occur. However, this requires lots of bandwidth. Typical installations utilize asynchronous replication and forgo the system acknowledgement.

The 24-Hour RPO

What does a typical tape backup and recovery solution deliver? The solution delivers a minimum of minutes to a maximum of 24 hours of lost business transactions. The reason for this gap is that in every tape backup solution, the backup usually occurs only once per day. This means that the combined time that includes exposure to data loss and efforts to rebuild is always measured in days. Yikes!

In the example in Figure 3.8, the System i5 server goes down with an SRC indicator light at 5 p.m. on Tuesday afternoon. This is not a site loss, just a server failure only. Subject to IBM hardware availability and response to the Severity 1 call, the server will be repaired sometime late Tuesday evening or early Wednesday. The restoration process will immediately follow, and late in the day Wednesday, the user data will be as it was on Monday night's 2 a.m. backup. All of Tuesday's data is lost. If there were further issues with the full backup tape media, the data loss and restore effort would reach back through the entire previous week.

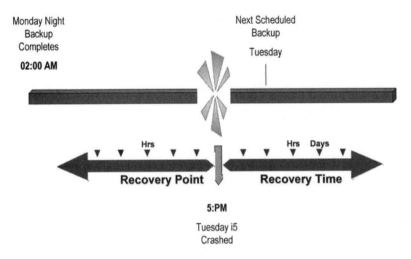

Figure 3.8: The real result of a 24-hour RPO.

Real-World Example: An Unacceptable 24-Hour RPO

I had a client that experienced a disaster in which the system was unavailable due to a multiple disk failure in their System i5. This meant a complete loss of data. The hardware repair effort took numerous attempts by the IBM hardware engineers, as the combination of failing disks, IOPs, IOA, and at the end the Raid card made it terribly difficult to troubleshoot. Many hours were lost in the hardware problem resolution. Then it was time to spend the 26 straight hours performing all recovery steps. Between formatting disk drives, restoring the key elements of the operating system, and recovering all user data from both weekly and daily tapes, the effort was fairly significant. Two terabytes signifi-cant! The total downtime was 36 hours.

The business was under great duress to ship all the product out. It had commitments to customers. The company had six warehouses scattered geographically within the continental U.S. Each was fully automated, with no means to operate manually. Union staff was sent home during the out-age . . . very costly. The data that was restored on the system following the failure was more than 24 hours old. The inventory and warehouse systems were as of a couple of days ago, including the day lost in bringing back the iSeries/400.

The arguments started between IT and business executives.

"How can we ship product out of our warehouses?," asked the VP of Logistics. "The information is totally unreliable. The system is feeding us product locations in the warehouse that do not contain the actual product. Has the product already shipped? Is the product sitting somewhere else in the warehouse on a pallet? Has the product been moved, or has the order been canceled altogether? Did we invoice already, were we about to, or do we invoice again to be safe?"

The situation was far worse than could have been imagined. The only course of action was to do a complete warehouse inventory position count and update the iSeries/400 with the quantities and locations on hand. This took 18 additional hours to complete, with lots of additional labor costs. The business had no choice; they could not operate with day-old information, as restored. The System i5 functionality was all intact, but the data told each user a different story. The aftermath was not pretty, as you can imagine. Nobody felt well enough informed from the business side as to what exactly IT was supposed to deliver. Secondly, nobody ever agreed to a 24-hour RPO of system data. This was simply unacceptable.

Do your business executives understand that everything your business sold, manufactured, serviced, etc. today will be lost if not captured by the nightly backup? I can assure you that many executives do not. This is a bad assumption many companies and IT make. Talk to your business executives, and ensure they are fully aware of what IT can deliver. An important lesson will be learned by all.

Every backup strategy must be examined closely to ensure both system and data are indeed recoverable. Many backup program designs are implemented and forgotten over time. An effective recovery strategy must always be designed first, followed by a backup strategy implementation. Typically, we perform this critical implementation task the other way. Usually, we are asked to recover from what we are given from last night's backup tapes, and then try to bridge both the system and user data gaps. In other words, we perform reverse engineering.

Ensure your RPO is examined from both a mid-week and weekend failure, as this will most certainly present different models. Can you bring back everything on a Wednesday system loss as you could from a weekend failure?

Shifting Focus for Return on Investment (ROI)

The shift from the emphasis on data recoverability to continuous application availability is natural and logical. Your investment must support both planned and unplanned outages. It is important to understand that data resiliency itself doesn't provide a high-availability solution. It will simply help ensure that the data is available in the event of an outage. The movement in IT to shift from recovery of data from tape with a 24- to 48-hour systems recoverability solution to high availability is strategic and logical. The traditional approach for deploying high availability has been to replicate data from one system to another, with the primary objective being data recoverability only—in other words, disaster recovery.

The goal for the high-availability solution has evolved toward eliminating or minimizing planned outage events that require the production System i5 to be made unavailable to the business. Now during any such planned outage, the IT staff switches the end users to the backup or target server after carefully quiescing the primary system. After ensuring that all of the data on the primary and backup servers is identical, meaning no latency in sending or applying journal transactions, production applications are started on the target server.

Unplanned events account for 10% of all System i5 downtime. Unscheduled or unplanned downtime can be due to the following:

- Power outage
- Human error or program failure
- Unprotected disk or multiple-disk failure
- Other hardware failure

Planned events account for 90% of downtime. This downtime is due to the following:

- Daily/weekly/monthly saves
- Software installation/upgrade (OS, application, or middleware)
- PTF installs
- Operating systems upgrades
- Hardware upgrades

The decision with ROI is whether to purchase and implement a solution based on a 10% ROI, or aim for 100%.

Return on investment is the critical measure in any investment decision. The expected benefits of the recovery solution under consideration must exceed that project's anticipated costs to justify the inherent risks. The BIA tends to measure all unplanned downtime and its costs. We focus on this because, as stated earlier in this chapter, it goes beyond the level of acceptable. The devastation caused by a critical application's loss for an extended time period might be so severe that it mortally wounds your business. However, eliminating planned downtime can be immediate and measurable. Ideally, you should discover and aim for payback gained by eliminating planned downtime that covers the cost for a solution that inherently addresses unplanned downtime.

The Process of the BIA

There are six main steps to conducting the business impact analysis.

1. Set the Objectives of the Business Impact Analysis

The basic objective of the BIA questionnaire is the collection and evaluation of specific business functional and process information from the business.

Identify:

- The most critical business units
- All business processes and their priorities
- The business impacts of an extended interruption
- The maximum length of the outage a business unit can sustain before it has a significant negative operational impact on the company
- The key computing systems used by the business unit and the impact of no access to these systems
- The critical IT applications used by the business unit
- Any recovery complexity of the business unit's critical processes
- The recovery time requirements of the critical business unit
- The recovery point requirements for the critical business unit
- The recovery strategy and priorities of the business unit's critical processes

2. Determine Critical IT Applications

The responses should identify the most critical applications that are required by the business units to keep the business functioning. During the definition of recovery strategies, IT will have the opportunity to implement supporting protective measures and recovery strategies to ensure that the business unit's critical applications will be available in a timely and cost-effective manner during an actual recovery effort.

3. Distribute the BIA Questionnaire

Each of the business units will be required to complete an electronic BIA questionnaire. Supply the date by which the completed questionnaires should be returned to you. (A sample BIA questionnaire is available in the appendix.)

4. Receive and Validate the BIA Responses

The responses to the BIA questionnaires provide IT with information that will influence the recovery strategy and disaster recovery plan. It is, therefore, extremely important that you do the following:

- Make sure you receive a completed BIA questionnaire from every participating business unit.
- Ensure that each BIA questionnaire is fully completed and that the responses make sense.
- Store and maintain the questionnaires in an electronic file for audit purposes.
- Use the responses during the recovery strategy and plan-development phases.

Check each questionnaire for completeness and validity:

- Review each questionnaire and make sure that each question has been answered.
- Make sure that each answer is complete (not just a yes/no answer)
- Do not be afraid to send the questions back to the participant.

5. Consolidate the Responses

When all of the questionnaires have been returned, all of the questions have been answered completely, and the answers make sense, it is time to consolidate the responses and prepare a summary of the critical IT applications. This should be prepared using the "Mission-Critical IT Applications Worksheet" in Table 3.2. Start building this applications summary by listing all of the business units that submitted valid BIA questionnaires. For each business unit, include the business unit name. Next, for each business unit entry, include the following information in the appropriate columns:

- Application name
- Application priority
- Maximum outage (days)

Table 3.2: Mission-Critical Applications Worksheet				
Date:		**Company Name:**		
Location	**Application Name**	**Application Priority**	**Maximum Outage (Days/Hours)**	**Maximum Data Loss (Days/Hours)**

These applications will be included in the final BIA presentation and report. The site's IT organization will be able to gain an early understanding of the critical business units' application requirements:

- The business unit's operational priority
- The business impacts of an extended interruption to the business unit's processes
- The maximum length of the outage a business unit can sustain before it has a significant negative operational impact on the company
- The vulnerability and recovery complexity of the business unit's critical processes
- The recovery timeframe requirements of the business unit
- The business unit's recovery strategy and plan development priorities

This information will be used in all of the early phases of the DR initiative. Review the findings to gain a business needs understanding of two key elements:

- The Recovery Time Objective (RTO) that defines the period of time in which a business unit must be able to resume its critical processes
- The Recovery Point Objective (RPO) that defines how much data the business can afford to lose

The business and the executive sponsor must agree with these RTOs and RPOs to help ensure the success of the BIA initiative.

6. Review the BIA Findings

You should now prepare a presentation of the BIA results for the executive sponsor and the participating business units' executives. Your basic goal is to get concurrence that the BIA results make sense and that there is a consensus agreement to proceed with the next phase of the disaster recovery planning project. Handouts of the presentation should be provided to all attendees.

Your presentation should cover the following:

- BIA phase summary
- Objectives
- BIA findings
- Prioritized critical business units by RTO and RPO
- Strategy/plan development schedules by RTO category
- Critical IT applications and potential issues
  - » Include a copy of the "Critical IT Application Worksheet" with an explanation of the contents.
- Vital assets and potential issues
- BIA phase action items

» Request approval of BIA findings from the business.

» Request approval to proceed with the next phase of the BCP initiative.

- Recovery strategy development phase

  » Objectives

  » Calendar timeframes

  » Roles and responsibilities

During this presentation, you need to get the business units and the executive sponsor to agree with the following:

- The prioritized list of critical business units and their RTOs
- The proposed recovery strategy and plan development dates
- Vital assets issues
- Other recommended action items
- Your request to proceed to the recovery strategy

Obtain a consensus of approvals from the executive sponsor and the business unit owners.

Summary

Performing a BIA will provide your organization with a complete, holistic view of how your company uses IT services to conduct its business. Critical application server definition and disaster recovery capabilities will identify the tangible and intangible revenue impacts on the business. The BIA will clearly state the inherent vulnerabilities that face your organization, their quantifiable impact, and the acceptance of an agreed-upon solution. IT alone cannot make recovery decisions. The BIA provides IT a recovery roadmap aligned with the business's needs and deliverables.

4

Critical Server Ranking

The servers are all down. The computer room is dark. What are your priorities? What do you do first? What is your next task, and what is after that? When, where and in which order do you start your server recovery? Everything is a business priority, but what is the most important priority? Quick, lock the doors before the stampede of self-proclaimed experts come charging into the computer room and start barking out orders! Otherwise, the person with the loudest bark will get his or her server back first. Of course, the computer room might not be recoverable at all in the short term. It might not be useable in the long term, either. You take a deep breath and say this is what you have been documenting and practicing for all these years. Now the situation is real. "This is not a drill. Repeat: this is not a drill."

When your computer room is no longer recognizable because of damage inflicted by a disaster, your goals are to know what happened, how it happened, where you stand, and what it will take to get things back on track. So, simply stop thinking and start following the disaster recovery plan. Step through the tasks and follow the order of server recovery importance determined by the plan, not by who yells the loudest.

Classifying Systems for Recovery Priority

When you walk into the computer room, you can be overwhelmed with rows and rows of servers. Numerous hardware platforms are powered on and ready to serve some business purpose. Typically, the servers will span several hardware generations. You need a planned roadmap to prioritize recovery of your complete critical server infrastructure. To get there, you need to understand the supporting business functions before any major event occurs.

Every server has some kind of purpose. The big question, do you need them all? Of course, in one sense, you do. Otherwise, they wouldn't be there in the first place. In a disaster, however, all the servers in your computer room are not equal in their importance to your business. That's why you must consider first what you need, then what you want, and finally what you do not need at all to run your business in a disaster. The IT recovery team should assign priorities to the servers as they relate to your business support priorities. There will be a mixed bag of opinions of course, but the Business Impact Analysis (BIA) discussed in chapter 3 will support those opinions one way or another.

Categorize the business functions and supporting servers as either *critical*, *essential*, *necessary*, or *optional*. Typically, you'll find a 30/30/20/20 breakdown. You'll find that 30% of all your servers are critical for business recovery, another 30% are essential, 20% are necessary but not required immediately, and the remaining 20% are optional or not required at all. This means you can focus on 60%, not 100%, of your servers.

Critical systems absolutely must be in place for any business process to continue at all. The business cannot proceed without these servers. They have a significant financial impact on the viability of the organization; you are simply closed for business without access to them. These are considered part of the *A-list* recovery strategy.

Essential systems must be in place to support day-to-day operations. They are typically integrated with critical systems. These systems play an integral role in delivering your business solutions. Extended loss of these servers will cause a long-term disruption to the business, and potentially inflict legal and financial ramifications. These are also on the A-list recovery strategy.

Necessary systems contribute to smooth business operations and provide handy tools for employees, but are not mandatory at the time of disaster. These might include business forecasting tools, reporting software, or improvement tools used by the business. Without these systems, there would be a high to moderate disruption to the business, minor legal or financial ramifications, or problems with access to other systems. These could be restored as a *B-list* recovery strategy.

Optional systems improve the working capabilities of your organization. These could include test systems, archived data, education servers, redundant target servers, and the company intranet.

Of course, this is not the only means of classifying server applications, but it does provide you with a baseline for your decision matrix. The DR planning team should worry less about the fine points of the definitions than about what you need to recover the servers in a disaster. The key is that the IT recovery team and the business must agree with the DR planning scope for classification of the servers and supporting business functions.

Mission-Critical Only, Please

By differentiating between critical/essential and necessary, the disaster recovery plan helps increase operational efficiency for both the server backups and recovery while reducing disaster prevention and recovery operating costs. Decreasing the amount of server redundancy and hotsite requirements positively impacts the business Recovery Time Objectives (RTOs) while reducing IT expense and infrastructure recovery costs. When classifying systems, the planning team will discover that some iSeries or System i5 servers will support more than one business process.

Critical/essential server applications are of great significance for business operations and profitability. This is why the organization depends on them. Without them, you have no product or service to sell. Critical applications either directly or indirectly support the business functions that have been identified as critical in the BIA. In the event of a disaster, you need to restore these applications on a priority basis.

When compiling the list of mission-critical applications, consider application interdependencies. For example, many ERP software solutions are considered modular in design, yet they must be completely intact (fully restored) to function correctly. You cannot break such applications down or only restore specific libraries or objects. You may choose not to use specific business functions, but the entire ERP software solution must be rebuilt to function normally.

Consider also the flow of information. Follow the flow of a transaction from order inception to product delivery. You might find that a server not considered critical by the BIA actually has a significant role in feeding information to a mission-critical application. To get this information, there needs to be input from the IT department in addition to the business defined needs.

Another part of the process is to save valuable restoration time on the System i5 hardware footprint for non-essential system ASP disk utilization. The iSeries or System i5 generally will be recovered as a whole, and non-critical libraries will be omitted to reduce restoration time. These omitted libraries and user directories could include the following:

- Performance data
- Audit journals
- Middleware application journal receivers
- Test libraries
- ERP walkthrough libraries

- Online education
- Developer working libraries
- User test environments
- Data archives
- Testing of new operating system partitions
- User Auxiliary Storage Pools (ASPs)
- Independent Auxiliary Storage Pools (IASPs)

After you have identified critical applications, you need to identify the hardware required to run them.

Rank Your Data Backup Priorities

Another important step in critical server definition is to identify your mission-critical data. An efficient disaster recovery plan supports backup, storage, and retrieval of data by differentiating the criticality of your server data infrastructure. Consider that the first step to recovering from a disaster is to identify which servers are performing which roles. The second is to determine where the data resides.

Data protection is usually classified based on criticality and the recovery window. Only you know your critical server requirements for backup and recovery. Unfortunately, many disaster recovery plans aren't based on the value of the data. Remember that data is the company's greatest asset. Important data must be protected from loss or damage caused by human or system error, hardware failure, or a complete site outage.

When framing the basis for your backup and recovery program design, you must maintain a clear distinction between these two objectives:

- Preventing data loss
- Recovering server and applications for business resumption after a disaster event

These objectives will drive different protection requirements for various types of data. Preventing data loss is performed by your day-to-day backup strategy. Being able to recover a specific library, object, user profile, or maybe recovering from a bad production day end, is paramount. Recovering from a disaster is a much higher level of backup complexity. The major difference is that you need to consider how you will recover the server infrastructure as well as the data. The prevention strategy typically takes care of data only. Some organizations still have the luxury of performing a full system option 21 save daily (saving the complete system) because they have a large enough backup window. This meets both protection and disaster-recovery requirements. (Techniques to support a full option 21 recovery capability daily are discussed in chapter 6.)

A comprehensive data-backup analysis by IT should be based on the mission-critical functional needs of the business. The data analysis is used to design the recovery strategy first. Yes, this means understanding the crucial applications recovery needs and building the backup CL program or BRMS group policy to support it. You might want to build the backups first and then try to cherry-pick your recovery solution, but this is backward re-engineering. You need to map out where the data resides in relation to the critical application, as it relates to the server supporting the application itself. The applications worksheet in Table 4.1 is an example of this. By going through this process, you will understand what data you need to back up, the backup frequency and recovery gaps, and the requirements for off-site storage. This process will also prompt you to document why you need this data and plan how to restore it in a timely basis to the same working order it was before the disaster.

Table 4.1: Applications Worksheet					
Application Name	**Server Name**	**Backup Location, Library name, User ASP**	**Backup Frequency**	**Acceptable Maximum Data Loss (Days/Hours)**	**Data Retention**
Payroll	PAY01	PAYPROD PAYBENFTS PAYHIST PAYTAX	Daily Weekly Monthly	24 hours	7 years
EDI	CITY01	EDI4XXDTA EDI4XXPGM EDI4XXORD	Daily Weekly Daily	24 hours	7 years
JDE - Sales	CITY01	JDESLS JDEWSE JDEPM JDEORDR JDEINV JDEMFG JDETRANS	High Availability	1 hour	13 months

Develop a recovery strategy to support the business requirements as determined by the worksheet in Table 4.1. During the BIA, you discovered which functions had the biggest impact. This list should be expanded to include IT system-level information, to help develop a backup and recovery program designed to support these needs.

Backups, and Recovery Time and Point Objectives

It has become a widely accepted fact that an increasing number of organizations have to manage and protect massive amounts of data on a daily basis. The amount of data stored in the Auxiliary System Pool is increasing at alarming rates, while the backup windows either stay the same or get smaller. The most common approach to protecting that data daily is through tape-based backup solutions. It is also a fact that, while most IT departments are comfortable with the success rate of their tape-based backups, most know they probably could not restore from those tapes within the business's Recovery Time Objective (RTO). Is this because of wishful thinking that nothing will go wrong, lack of funding, or trying to recover too much data outside of the disaster recovery scope?

You must first determine just what it is you are trying to protect and the level of protection you are trying to achieve. You need to align the recovery objectives with each server to determine the type of backup solution required to support the business RTO. This can include a host of data-protection strategies, involving tape, electronic vaulting, continuous data protection, and high systems availability. Even though the BIA phase is completed, you need to meet with the owners of the server application data to confirm two important factors for each and every system.

First, what is the RTO, the amount of time any system can remain unavailable? This time factor was agreed upon already and will be the basis for building the recovery strategy. With a typical tape-backup solution, the RTO is 24 to 48 hours. While this is still a readily acceptable standard in the industry, we are starting to see RTOs of less then 24 hours. In addition to preventing data loss, the IT recovery team must ensure that critical application servers are restored as quickly as possible after an outage, as specified in the RTO for each application. Where transactional integrity is paramount, high-availability solutions might be needed to recover data within minutes.

The second factor is the Recovery Point Objective (RPO). This is the measurement of how much data your organization can conceivably lose to a disaster without significantly affecting business. When evaluating a company's RPO, nearly everyone will first insist nothing short of an RPO of zero is acceptable. This gut response is not financially prudent, of course. There will always be some amount of data loss, but you need to see where it will happen and the impact. You will find that the majority of your data is protected (or should be) by the previous night's tape backup, but everything that the business executes today will be lost if a disaster happens before the nightly backup. The people who insisted on zero RPO might be shocked to realize that a 24-hour tape backup RPO has been in place forever.

The question is whether it is correct for your business to have a 24-hour RPO. If this is acceptable, then full protection against data loss by implementing high-availability solutions will be expensive overkill. For critical transaction-processing applications, on the other hand, an RPO of an hour might be too long. However, since very low RPO values are extremely expensive to achieve, it's important to ensure that the objectives are applied appropriately to specific data applications. Some tolerance by the business will go a long way to your recovery investments. By properly classifying your data, and assigning recovery objectives based on business needs, you should be able to meet the protection and recovery needs of the mission-critical server applications while reducing the disaster-recovery infrastructure costs for the less-demanding server applications. An RPO somewhere between zero and 48 hours will provide the recovery direction and delivery solution. Assemble an RTO and RPO spreadsheet like the one in Table 4.2 to clearly illustrate your backup and restoration commitments for every server.

Table 4.2: Sample RTO and RPO Chart			
Application Name	**Server Name**	**RTO Time**	**RPO Time**
Payroll	PAY01	24 hours	24–48 hours
EDI	CITY01	24 hours	24 hours
JDE—Sales	CITY01	1 hour	1 hour
JDE—Warehouse	CITY01	1 hour	1 hour
JDE—Manufacturing	CITY01	1 hour	1 hour
Email	MAIL	24 hours	24 hours
Fax server	FAX01	48 hours	24–48 hours

Take time to understand the business prioritization and valuation of each server application and its data. A good way to figure out an acceptable RPO and RTO is to calculate the cost of downtime. The formula for calculating this is:

Cost per application outage = (RTO + RPO) x (HR + LR) x time

Where:

- *RTO* = The time it takes to be back in operation
- *RPO* = The amount of data that can be lost
- *HR* = Lost worker productivity per hour of downtime
- *LR* = Lost revenue per hour of downtime.
- *time* = Length of outage in hours

Adjust the RTO and RPO values to match the acceptable cost per application outage. This is that application's RPO and RTO. This will provide the basis for your recovery requirements. If you choose the right solution and correct offsite combination, you know it will be there when you need it most. Therefore, you can recover within business expectations and timelines.

Critical Systems Definition, A-List

The purpose of an A and B (primary and secondary) list of critical systems is to identify to the business which computing services have been identified as mission-critical and will be recovered within the agreed amount of time (the RTO) as stated in the mission statement. It is a business reality that all server applications are not created equal; that's why you need to assign priorities to your various applications. Some are more critical to your company's business survival than others. Some are real-time, others are transactional, and some are for development. When a disaster strikes, be certain that the tasks and recovery strategies involve only getting the A-list servers back online first. The non-critical business systems will have a lower priority and are referred to as the B-list. This should be the recovery roadmap, and the recovery team's efforts should be first directed at these critical applications.

Being able to rapidly choose the server to be restored first after an outage is a must for running an efficient, effective IT recovery. To ensure your server administrators make these critical decisions both swiftly and accurately, you should develop a server triage policy. This policy should rank potential problems by level of importance. The ranking scheme should take into consideration the problems of business-critical systems, the number of systems affected by the problem, the number of end users affected by the problem, and how the problem is affecting end-user productivity.

The sample server listing in Table 4.3 should be used as a framework for your own server policy or to compare against your organization's existing

Table 4.3: Sample Critical Server List		
Server Name	**Function**	**Criticality**
iSeries/400 – PRD	**Enterprise Server**	**A – List**
UNI02PRD01	Warehouse Server	A - List
FPC0158	File/Print Cluster	A – List
DOM01	Lotus Domino Cluster	A – List
DC01	Primary Domain Controller	A – List
EXTWEB01	External Web Server	A – List
CITGATE	Citrix Secure Gateway Server	A – List
EMAIL	Exchange Server	A – List
SQL	Node 1 of SQL Cluster	A - List
COMM	Communications Server	A – List
DB2	Database Server	A – List
PRNITCL	Node 1 of Print Cluster	A – List
WHWARE01	VMWARE Node 1 - RFID Server	A – List
	VMWARE Node 2 - Security TAG	A – List
	VMWARE Node 3 - FAX	A – List
	VMWARE Node 4 - Key Tag Server	A – List
	VMWARE Node 5 - BAR CODE Server	A – List
	VMWARE Node 6 - Traffic Server	A - List
Blade Center	CIT01 - Citrx Presentation Server	A - List
	CIT02 - Citrix Presentation Server	A - List
	CIT03 - Citrx Presentation Server	A – List
BACK01	Backup Server	A - List

policy stated in the BIA. This policy document should be included in your disaster recovery plan. Although we have tried to make this sample as generic as possible, be aware that your organization's critical needs may differ from the example here. You should also consider special business events, such as busy or unique business time periods, when designing and implementing your server recovery policy.

Under normal operations, support will be given on a first-come, first-served basis and problems will be solved as soon as possible. However, a ranking scheme similar to Table 4.3 should be used to categorize all requests for server support. During a disaster, server recovery times will be longer.

Critical Systems Definition, B-List

The business must identify which computing services are non-mission-critical. These will be recovered some time after the initial RTO has been satisfied from the mission statement. These non-critical business systems are referred to as the "B-list," as shown in Table 4.4. Efforts should be first directed at critical applications on the A-list. There may or may not be hardware initially available at a hotsite or other facility. The procurement of this hardware may be required.

Table 4.4: Sample B-List Servers List	
Server Name	**Function**
L02	JDE—Development
FAX	Faxing Server
FORMS	Special Forms Overlay
EVAUL	Electronic Data Vault
DEV01	Development
DEV02	Development
DEV03	Development
TS13	Citrix Presentation Server

Table 4.4: Sample B-List Servers List (continued)	
Server Name	**Function**
TS14	Citrix Presentation Server
TS15	Citrix Presentation Server
SQL05	Staff Benefit Server
SQL06	Human Resources
SQL07	Human Resources
DB2	Data Warehouse 2
DB3	Data Warehouse 3

Is Email Mission-Critical?

The criticality of email can be a million-dollar question. Email represents the way you communicate with customers, partners, employees, and the rest of the global economy. However, email servers seem to get omitted from A-lists quite frequently. How could your business survive without email? Email has become a primary source for communications in every aspect of our business. Some might say, "No email? What a relief!" The reality, however, is that no email access can mean operating your company without a link to the outside world. Is this what you are trying to accomplish? Careful consideration must be given to this non-revenue-generating application when it is not available. Email might even be considered a high-availability application in your organization!

Hardware Requirements for Mission-Critical Servers

In the development of every disaster recovery plan, you must determine the minimum hardware requirements for your mission-critical servers. Some IT professionals will say, "Obviously, you want your mission-critical servers to run the exact same equipment. However, in an emergency, any equipment is better than none."

I hope you will not simply accept this statement at face value. Having available the minimum requirements based on whatever mission-critical applications are being run is important, I agree. However, will your business accept running the mission-critical business functions at, say, 50% less capacity or throughput? Probably not. In the BIA, you identified the financial impacts for your organizations of being down for an extended period of time. Working at half speed will further cripple your long-term business capabilities to ensure customer satisfaction. You chose to eliminate non-essential applications to reduce the hardware footprint, rather than provide less processing capabilities. The last thing you want is your sales order desk telling customers, "Be patient. We can only process half the orders right now because we had a disaster two weeks ago and we're still working things out."

It might be argued that the hardware required during recovery can be smaller because the production servers support a lot of applications that are not necessarily mission-critical. However, again you must consider—is this strictly a reduction in disk requirements, rather than CPU, cycles, memory, and other resources required to run these applications? Lastly, when using old hardware, you might end up not being technically compliant. You might be running on a System i5 that requires V5R3M5. However, the older AS/400 does not support the operating system version. This can be especially true for a Windows 2003 server going back to NT.

Summary

A lot of work goes into managing the ongoing requirements for mission-critical servers. Today, when access to mission-critical data is interrupted for whatever reason, you will have downtime. This usually means your business simply stops. When your business stops, it gets very expensive, very quickly. This is why critical server needs should be reviewed twice a year to ensure two things:

- Effective server processes are being carried out to support the needs.
- The servers identified as critical are still in alignment with the business.

Here are the elements required to support the critical server definition requirements:

- BIA and risk assessment
- Strategy for prioritization
- Change in prioritization based on different business cycles
- Application dependencies/interdependencies
- Application downtime considerations for planned and unplanned outages
- BRMS backup procedures
- Offsite storage for vital records
- Data retention policies
- RTOs and RPOs
- Hardware for critical server recovery
- Recovery and business management sign-off

The A- and B-list of critical servers represent the agreed recovery strategy as clearly and formerly identified by the Business Impact Analysis. Complete alignment between the business and the IT deliverables is necessary. When the RPOs and RTOs are kept up-to-date, the order in which servers are restored after a failure will not surprise anyone in the business. The A-list server chart becomes the basis for building and sourcing a recovery strategy for the company.

5

Building Recovery Strategy Requirements

The components of your Business Impact Analysis (BIA) and mission-critical server rankings will be used as the basis for developing and implementing a supporting recovery strategy.

Ensure the following information is absolutely clear:

- The critical business processes have all been identified.
- The recovery requirements for these critical processes are identified.
- The backup and recovery strategies reflect the assumed disaster recovery scenarios.
- The recovery strategies are scalable, flexible, and compliant.
- Everyone understands the assumptions on which the recovery strategies are based.
- Recovery Time Objectives (RTOs) are in place for the critical processes.
- Recovery Point Objectives (RPOs) are in place for the critical processes.

With the server priorities established for disaster recovery, the DR planning team now has a clear picture as to which systems need to be restored or replicated, in which time frames, and in which order for critical business processes to continue after a disaster. The team must develop the appropriate technology recovery strategies to meet the business objectives agreed to during the initial analysis of this project. The IT recovery team coordinates the technical recovery of the iSeries or System i5 and all other supporting hardware infrastructure. These have all been identified in the critical server definition phase and backed by the BIA. This information provides the recovery team the opportunity to implement supporting procedures and effectively plan for the data backup requirements, offsite tape media storage, recovery restoration procedures, system redundancy, network hardware and data communications infrastructure redundancy, and any other element necessary for an effective recovery.

The Disaster Recovery Challenge

How will you resume time-sensitive business operations with no warning and:

- At another (remote?) location/facility
- During a stressful recovery
- Using only information stored offsite (backups and documentation)
- Within a designated RTO
- Without some key personnel
- With the requirement that everything must work the first time

The IT recovery team ensures that all activities are completed in a timely manner to achieve the RTOs for the critical business functions as stated in the mission statement of the disaster recovery plan.

A disaster recovery strategy can be defined as the formal selection and implementation of the recovery solution(s) that your organization will use to support the actions for restoring mission-critical application servers following a significant disruption.

The recovery strategy has two primary goals:

1. Timely and cost-effective acquisition, implementation, and utilization of the required solution and resources in a disaster.

2. Enabling the business to perform the minimum essential processes within an approved RTO and with an approved RPO. The RTO and RPO define the maximum length of time that mission-critical applications can be unavailable and the maximum amount of acceptable loss of data.

Make sure that you understand the intent of an approved RTO. It is not expected that only the initial recovery activities should start within the timeframe. Rather, it is *demanded* that all of the agreed-upon recovered servers will be made available and ready to be used to perform the minimum essential processes within the timeframe. For example, if a business unit has an approved RTO of 48 hours, then all of its recovered server-related services should be installed, tested, online, and ready for use to perform their minimum essential processes by no later than hour 49.

Guidelines for Selecting Recovery Strategies

From an IT infrastructure stand-point, the challenge in selecting disaster recovery solutions is that there are a large variety of valid disaster recovery products available in the marketplace. The common problem is that there is a tendency to view the disaster recovery solutions as individual product technologies and piece together the total solution. Instead, a disaster recovery solution needs to be viewed as a complete, integrated, potentially multi-product solution.

By defining and selecting the appropriate recovery strategies in advance, you will reduce the complexity of the disaster recovery procedures and build in the efficiencies for a quicker implementation of the DR plan. With so many different recovery strategies available to support your plan, how do you select the appropriate one? Do you go bleeding edge, or make the entire data center redundant, or react as the situation presents itself? Spend nothing (because, after all, our team will have everything documented), or invest millions?

Your Recovery Strategy Should Be Flexible

The strategies selected for implementation should not be rigid or inflexible. A backup strategy built in advance of any recovery consideration is rigid. It would force you to recover your iSeries from a predetermined backup approach and would thus be very restrictive. For example, a SAVSTG backup strategy or full-system image save implies a full-system restore. No partial recovery is allowed. This is extreme, of course, but consider how granular your recovery capability is from the backups you implemented. How do you recover a specific object, user profile, subsystem description, complete application, or an entire server?

The recovery strategies should also allow for growth in the organization and changes in the number of supported iSeries servers or System i5 partitions. In addition, your strategies should be able to adjust to any increase in the amount of data that your organization maintains or keeps forever. In other words, as the business grows, the disaster recovery plan should be able to change with the growing needs, with the implementation of appropriate backup and restoration procedures to meet new demands.

Your Recovery Strategy Should Be Well-Planned

Every recovery strategy identified and implemented within the DR plan should be well-planned. In other words, all the required resources, such as personnel, recovery processes, and supporting technology that is required for recovery from a disaster should be identified when determining the recovery strategies. Define all the needs upfront, and detail them appropriately. Document the needs and provision for them. If you need the LIC CD-ROM, for example, ensure you know, in advance, the stored location of the CD, the version, and the process to use it in your recovery.

Your Recovery Strategy Should Be Comprehensive

The recovery strategies in the DR plan should address the most probable types of disasters likely to affect the organization. In addition, the strategies must ensure recovery from everything from minor day-to-day disasters, like accidental deletion or failure of a critical application, to disasters likely to cause maximum damage. In other words, the plan should address everything from disk or RAID failure to a complete site loss as a result of a hurricane. Document the assumptions and steps to facilitate such recoveries.

Your Recovery Strategy Must Meet the RPO & RTO

The correct selection of your recovery strategy is driven primarily by the ability to meet both the Recovery Point and Recovery Time Objectives and their stated expectations. Based on these business expectations and financial impacts, the strategy deployed might vary from a simple BRMS tape-backup solution to high availability, or maybe a combination of both.

Your Recovery Strategy Should Be Cost-Effective

When selecting a strategy or a combination of strategies, consider the reduction in the cost of recovery as a result and the increased value in ROI from any deployed strategy. Typically, a high-availability implementation requires some significant upfront costs in hardware, software, redundant site, capital, and implementation time. In addition to these one-time costs, you must consider ongoing costs, such as maintenance and monthly fees for alternate commercial or owned internal secondary computer rooms. This generally makes some organizations shy away from high availability (HA). However, HA can produce some very significant ROI when used correctly in an organization to obtain systems availability uptime. Keeping the systems available makes people listen.

The importance of each solution consideration will vary from one organization to another. The desired result of every organization is recovery of servers in a disaster. IT objectives must be in alignment with the business.

The most important consideration remains that the survival of the organization depends on the ability of IT to deliver an appropriate, timely response. The technology solution in place should support the recovery response needs. The documentation should provide repeatable restoration procedures to recover servers' infrastructure and data within stated recovery objectives. To identify recovery strategies, you should consider the immediate, short-term, and long-term outages caused by the occurrence of a disaster. The only question only that remains is whether the outage is an incident or a disaster. Strategies also differ on the basis of long-term and short-term recovery goals.

Market Trends

Figure 5.1 illustrates the changes in DR approaches over time. Companies today are seeing the need to effectively deliver a disaster recovery solution in a more proactive manner.

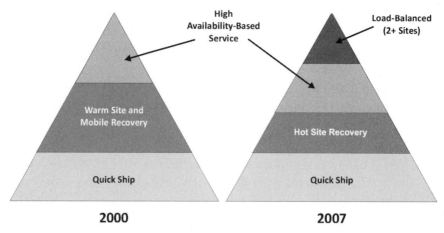

Figure 5.1: The trend in recovery strategies is toward hot sites and HA.

In 2000, most organizations were content with some form of quick-ship or drop-ship hardware solution, followed by a warm-site recovery strategy. High availability was only a consideration for 5-8% of major corporations. By 2007, the need to recover more quickly and consistently has become a higher priority in companies. There is far less reliance on drop-ship solutions and a greater trend to high availability, clustering, and even load-balancing applications across multiple sites. This now represents some 35% of organizations.

Traditional tape DR plans provide for 24- to 48-hour disaster recovery for mission-critical applications. With technology linked closer than ever to business processes, and with the costs of outages escalating, many organizations are seeking shorter recovery times for critical applications. Use of HA or clustering techniques is escalating, especially for ERP and e-business applications. RTOs and RPOs are now calculated in minutes and hours, rather than days.

With e-business 24/7 business requirements, even a hot-site solution might not be good enough. Many solutions now span across two or more physical sites, and downtime is totally unacceptable. With HA, if one of the data centers experiences a severe outage, the other site continues processing your mission-critical applications. Load balancing has also become more common. Transaction-heavy systems are located in two physical sites, and data is replicated between servers, typically either by mirroring or shadowing at the recovery site. *Shadowing* is performed at the transaction or data level, where *mirroring* replicates full databases and file systems by applying changes as they occur.

The shift from the emphasis on data recoverability to continuous application availability is natural and logical. The traditional approach for deploying HA has been to replicate data from one system to another, with the primary objective being the data's recoverability. This approach had limited focus on the recoverability of application end users. A common goal for IT departments today is to achieve a 99.999% availability for the business.

Recovery Strategies

The strategy to recover the entire computer center from disasters is aimed strictly at recovery of critical systems, information, and business functions supported by the computer center in the shortest possible timeframe. The higher the level of redundancy (RPO) and the quicker the recovery (RTO), the greater the cost of ownership, as shown in Figure 5.2.

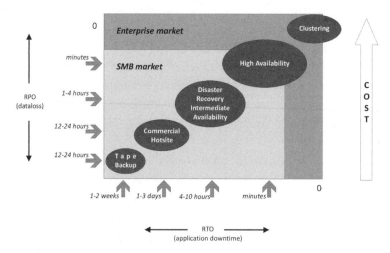

Figure 5.2: Recovery strategies.

The critical functions of an organization can be recovered in a matter of minutes to hours to as long as days.

The following decision factors can be used to determine which type of data recovery solution best meets your disaster recovery objectives.

RTO

There must be an overall Recovery Time Objective for the business and detailed RTOs for all servers. Each server has a defined RTO value, and this should be factored in the recovery strategy. A more resilient geographically dispersed solution (greater than a 500 miles away) using a mirrored system can reduce the RTO and guarantee uptime in a regional disaster.

RPO

The Recovery Point Objective determines the data-recovery point in time when the processing will return the end users after a restoration of the mission-critical servers. This will be when the last successful backup was run. The tape RPO is usually 24 hours. The smaller the RPO, the more expensive the solution will be. Each server has a defined RPO value, and this should be factored in the recovery strategy.

Planned Outages for Return on Investment

Identify the types of outages for which recovery must be provided. The primary categories include the following:

- Planned (i.e., backup window, software, or hardware maintenance)
- Unplanned (i.e., hardware failure or power failure)
- Disasters (i.e., computer room outage or regional disaster)

Cost

Cost identifies the financial impact of the recovery solution. The solution cost is typically predicated from the BIA. The tighter the RTO and RPO deliverables, the greater the increase in costs for your recovery solution.

Backup Tape Recovery

Several tape recovery strategies can be employed for recovery of your iSeries. All of these strategies are based on a methodology of a tape restore at some hot site with supporting equipment standing by. Under the HIPAA and SOX guidelines, a backup and recovery strategy for information technology needs to be in place, or a clear statement of the assumed risk if no specific guideline surrounding a recovery hot site solution is identified.

Data Backup Strategy

Back-up strategies reflect the critical nature of the data. A system outage should make you reflect on the methods used in backing up the data, and how long it would take to restore that data—if at all. Data protection is usually classified based on criticality and the recovery window. Envision the solution at four different levels of availability:

- Immediate failover
- Recovery within hours (no data lost)
- Recovery within a day (the current day's data lost; recovery at a hot-site)
- Source a solution at the time of the event

The primary gap with tape backup is that it occurs only once per day. This means that one must always measure data loss and recovery times in days. For example, suppose your iSseries/400 server failed (How likely is that?!) at 4:59 p.m. on Thursday afternoon. If IBM had all parts available for repair locally, the server could be rebuilt on Thursday night and the data restored. When users returned on Saturday morning, . . . wait a second . . . your office staff does not work on weekends. So, with a tape recovery solution, do not be surprised if it takes 18 to 24 hours to rebuild the server, subject to the amount of data. When the office staff comes back to work on Monday, their data will be as it was on Wednesday night's backup. Thursday's data was lost.

Maybe your organization keeps a spare old AS/400 around to ensure a server is available in case of disaster. You still have the same data loss, and you have the cost of running it in some outside facility. Shipping costs of tapes would also factor in. Are those tapes encrypted? For security's sake, I hope so!

When making your backup decisions, you must balance the cost of failure versus the cost of protecting against such a failure. Table 5.1 summarizes the pros and cons of several solutions, but only you know your requirements for backup and recovery. If you choose the right solution or combination, you know it will be there when you need it most. Therefore, you can recover!

Table 5.1: Pros and Cons of Various Backup Solutions		
Solution	**Pros**	**Cons**
Tape Backup		
	Easy to run	Media errors
	Easy to manage with BRMS	Interface errors
	Easy to automate with BRMS	Seldom validated
	High speed and high capacity reduced backup windows	Time to restore in a disaster
	Capacity of tapes reduces number of tapes	Loss of data because backup only runs once per day
	Virtual tape libraries (V5R4 solution)	Backups omitted in lieu of system access
IASP–Switched Disk		
	No special 3rd party software required; only Option 41 LICPGM switchable resources	Only protects against single server failure
	Easy to configure–iSeries Navigator	Complete systems cannot be saved on an IASP
	No out-of-sync or latency issues	Not a load-balancing solution
	Hardware solution	Local data center solution unless XSM is installed
	Easy to administer	
XSM		
	No special 3rd party software required; only Option 41 LICPGM switchable resources	High bandwidth required, upwards of 100 MB
	Easy to configure–iSeries Navigator	Distance limitations
	Easy to administer	

Table 5.1: Pros and Cons of Various Backup Solutions (continued)		
Solution	**Pros**	**Cons**
Data Vaulting or CDP		
	Every change to any piece of data backed up continually, using a snapshot process; no need to halt application I/O to create snapshot	Requires additional disk
	Roll-back capability to any point in time	Journal management
	No logging required	A double-write impact to disk performance
	No application changes required	

Replication

A replication solution is typically associated with two databases, in which transactions are collected from the production image of the database and replicated or "applied" to a duplicate database on a different disk-storage device. This level of redundancy supports a single disk failure, and recovery requires switching to your second disk storage device. IBM remote journaling would be the tool to use for this.

Data Center Recovery Solutions

When selecting your recovery solution, two major questions must be addressed:

1. Where will you go?

   » Recovery site

   » Internal alternative

   » Commercial hot-site

   » Hosted high availability (internal or commercial)

   » Location

   » Geographic separation

2. How will you connect?

   » Data connectivity alternatives

   » Solution to include connectivity to your recovery site

   » Multiple paths and pre-configured

   » Voice considerations

The strategies to recover a computer center from a disaster are discussed in the following pages.

Reciprocal Agreements

Some organizations are comfortable with sharing the costs of alternate processing capabilities with another organization by providing reciprocated services and cost sharing. First, you need to have an excellent working relationship with the partner organization. Second, testing is rarely performed, which means your plan is not validated. Third, the entrusted arrangement must work as well when both organizations are affected by the same disaster as when either party has a disaster. The bottom line is that most reciprocal arrangements do not work. When the going gets tough, each organization has selfish requirements and truly needs its business up first.

Next System i5 Off the Line from IBM Rochester

The "next box off the line" strategy involves stopping computer access and using some documented manual work-around until a new compatible system is installed and the network connections are completed. This strategy can be rarely employed in today's competitive environments. Is it feasible to do critical business functions manually? Probably not anymore. This requires a very strong and well-documented business continuity process. This is a DR plan, not business continuity.

If you're counting on a new-box solution for your disaster recovery, anticipate a minimal wait time of seven to 10 days, depending on the model type required. Can you just call up IBM Rochester and say, "I want that box that you have just manufactured for customer X because I have had a disaster?" My guess is no. In addition, you must ensure that your current solution is technologically compliant. This means that you must be ready to load your server operating system and data onto the new shipped server. So, you cannot be back a level in the IBM operating systems because the last level of complexity you need to add is to perform OS migration in addition to a system restoration.

Drop Ship

Drop shipping complete server requirements for disaster recovery (including the i5, disk, HMC, tape drives, etc.) is a technique in which your organization would identify in advance the selected hardware required to meet your recovery objectives. A third-party provider would supply the hardware and would ship the agreed-upon contents based on an agreed-upon Service Level Agreement. The recovery time for a drop-ship solution ranges from 24 hours to seven days plus. The expectation is when the equipment arrives, there is provisioned supporting infrastructure (computer room) in place to plug the solution into. A drop-ship solution activates only in a disaster declaration and generally does not support regular tape recovery testing to validate the procedures or backup program in place.

Ensure the vendor can supply the equipment as advertised. Ask questions such as, "What is the committed ratio of customers to equipment?"

Cold Site

Cold sites are the least expensive option to support a disaster recovery solution. A cold site is just a physical space located in another office building. It can be owned directly by the organization or procured commercially. The latter is significantly less expensive because of the number of subscribed customers that share this common space. A cold site is an empty, vacant facility with sufficient electrical services pre-wired, HVAC, and a raised floor that can be set up with equipment and accommodate personnel in a very short time. Only the physical structure of the site is available 7/24/365.

You must remember that a cold site is just an empty room. The equipment and other resources on which the business depends will need to be procured, installed, and configured at the time of a disaster. Additional time exposure can be the length of time it takes to secure equipment for drop ship, if no contract exists with a drop-ship service provider. As a result, setting up the site will take longer (days to weeks) than setting up a site with the required equipment already installed and running (hours to days). To use a cold site, your RTO, which determines how long your organization can afford to remain down without severely impacting business, must be long enough to allow you to acquire, configure, and install all necessary systems. While a cold site keeps your initial costs very low, the cost of shipping hardware and software immediately can be quite expensive during an actual disaster. This typically supports a hardware drop-ship arrangement. An SLA should be signed with your drop-ship supplier.

Hot Site

Hot sites comprise all of the required servers, communication infrastructure, and staff resources necessary to meet business requirements in the wake of a disaster. Some hot sites are fully equipped with office suites that also include desktop recovery, telephony, fax machines, and printing capabilities, all set up and waiting for you. The servers at the hot site are already powered up, software is pre-loaded, and the network infrastructure is already installed and connected to the supporting telecommunications carriers. Hot sites can be commercially or internally owned and operated. Commercial hot-site service providers, such as Sungard, IBM, Mid-Range, and WTS, provide outsourced, managed hot sites for disaster recovery.

A commercial hot-site solution is available on a first-come, first-served basis for a tape recovery solution. If an organization owns a facility and manages the IT resources at the hot site, the facility is known as an *internal* hot site.

Such an arrangement ensures that the hot site has all the resources required to ensure business continuity. In addition, the hardware and software at the hot site will be consistent with the installed inventory in use at the primary site. This supports a typical 12- to 48-hour RTO and a 24-hour RPO.

Alternate Site

Consider a disaster in which the entire computer center or building is destroyed. In this scenario, everything that supports all critical business functions, current data, and server infrastructure is made unavailable. A duplicate site, owned and operated by the company, is an alternative. In other words, to ensure the successful recovery from a disaster, the organization chooses to self-procure the solution. You can just store all your critical information, from backup tape media all the way up to a complete duplicate of complete hardware infrastructure, running warm or even with full replication. Alternate sites are also known as *backup sites* and are used in testing and in disaster recovery.

Mirrored Site

A mirrored site is a fully redundant systems strategy. It supports organizations where traditional tape backup is not considered good enough to achieve the RTO and RPO goals for your most critical applications. Using a mirrored site involves maintaining a complete duplicate of all hardware identified as mission critical in the BIA. The hardware is fully loaded with a complete, licensed copy of the operating system and all related licensed program products. In the event of a disaster, the organization simply needs to shift operations to the alternate mirrored site and resume operations. The site would have redundant network access that would permit users to connect to it with very little down-time. Therefore, the recovery timeframe is extremely short. All of this is accomplished by implementing a high-availability third-party solution, with the assurance that the solution is fully managed 24/7. If you promise to the business a fail-over solution in 45 minutes, for example, it must work. The integrity of the data and application access must be solid.

High availability will also provide for increased RPOs. At risk is only the last transaction. Latency considerations for transaction volume must not factor in any delay in processing the data. This implies owning and operating a big enough data communications connection between both facilities to ensure minimal or no latency of data. Lastly, implementing a mirrored site also involves some strategic thinking as to the location of the site. Geographic considerations are a must. A good rule of thumb is to use a minimum of 500 miles and a different climate zone for the location of the mirror site. Having the primary data center located in Miami and a second in South Carolina does meet the distance requirements, but the climate condition is not met because a hurricane could inflict damage throughout the entire eastern coast. A better second site location would be in Nashville or Atlanta.

The drawback of the mirrored solution is the financial costs to run a second, fully licensed and managed facility. You need to consider site building costs, operating expenses, the hardware and software investment, maintenance fees, third-party replication software and training, and travel considerations. Balancing ROI with capital costs to build a mirrored site must be evaluated. Measuring financial constraints from the BIA will provide you with the financial impact of a disaster or unplanned downtime. However, this solution can also provide an ROI based on planned downtime considerations as well.

Security is often forgotten or neglected in secondary sites. Cost overruns are usually to blame. I have even heard, "We only care about security if we use the site in a disaster"! Special consideration should be given to the fact that the corporate data is live or online at the mirrored site, as is network access to the mirrored server. The mirrored site servers contain confidential and critical information as well as all your documentation. Ask yourself whether this is a security risk. Spare no effort to secure the site and actively monitor access controls. The security compliance policies should be in alignment with the audited process currently in place on the production primary facility. Additionally, all environmental-control factors that affect equipment and media should be run at the same standards of compliance.

Determine the Level of Business Resiliency You Want to Achieve

Achieving business resiliency and continuity is a step-by-step process. The BIA helps combine IT data protection practices with recovery solutions, as shown in Figure 5.3.

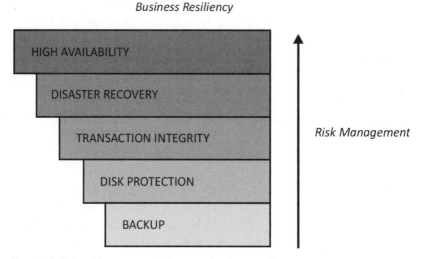

Figure 5.3: Better risk management improves business resiliency.

Business resiliency starts with a comprehensive backup recovery strategy. This is the foundation for every data protection strategy. Having this strategy in place creates the foundation for building a high-availability environment, or eventually, a business resilient solution. The first step is protecting data at the disk level, where it is most vulnerable. If your disk subsystem isn't protected in some way, you could lose all your data if you experience a single disk hardware failure. Disk protection is accomplished using either mirroring, RAID 5, or RAID 6 disk protection on the System i5.

The next level of data resiliency is transaction integrity. Transaction integrity ensures coherence of the application and data. Applications perform database updates in main store for performance reasons. Unfortunately, main storage on your system is volatile. This implies that data is stored and accessible as long as the system main storage has a continuous stream of power to the unit. On the System i5, the mechanism that allows updates in main memory while keeping track of the updates in non-volatile storage (disk) is journaling. This provides transaction-level data integrity. The point is, you need methods to ensure that you can restore data and applications to a known state after a failure has occurred. To achieve full transaction integrity, you must use applications with commitment control and provide management journal receivers.

Once you've addressed the basics of backup, disk protection, and transaction integrity, it's time to consider what type of disaster recovery strategy to deploy, so that you have the ability to recover operations at a remote location, if necessary. Finally, the ultimate step in business continuity is high availability, or the ability to keep applications available no matter what the circumstances. This provides a complete, end-to-end, mirrored integration with your System i5.

Review the selected recovery strategy checklist in Table 5.2 with the site DR coordinator and the IT recovery team to ensure that the strategies are complete and consistent with the overall recovery goals. The site DR coordinator must review and approve your strategy for several reasons:

- Ensure the overall completeness and viability of your strategy.
- Validate that the strategy is consistent with the business policies, goals, and service level objectives.
- Ensure the cost effectiveness of the strategy and identify who should incur the expenses required to implement and maintain it.
- Assist with the timely resolution of resource protection or emergency response issues.

The importance of each consideration is that it affects the very survival of your organization.

Table 5.2: Recovery Strategy Checklist	
Determination of Critical Technology & Resources Recovery Facility	**YES/NO**
Selection of data center recovery methodology complete?	YES/NO
Alternate location if production facilities unavailable exists? Where?	YES/NO
Business goals of the company understood?	YES/NO
Any special business forms (such as checks and invoices) identified? At the recovery site?	YES/NO
Vendor can replace hardware?	YES/NO
Redundant network capacity?	YES/NO
Delivery of backup data to an alternate location guarantee?	YES/NO
Transportation?	YES/NO
Recovery strategy confirmed?	YES/NO
RTO confirmed?	YES/NO
RPO confirmed?	YES/NO
Decreased capacity acceptable?	YES/NO
Increased recovery window?	YES/NO
Increased RPO or RTO objectives?	YES/NO
Mission-critical server definitions valid?	YES/NO
Date known when data last delivered to this location?	YES/NO
Tapes offsite and secure?	YES/NO
Date known when last test of recovery plan held?	YES/NO
DR plan addresses the regulatory compliance requirements of business?	YES/NO

Overall Site Restoration Strategy Sample

The flow chart in Figure 5.4 depicts the progression of events during a disaster recovery effort. This chart steps you through the overall recovery chain of events, ending with a detailed look at the site restoration progression. You must always refer to the body of your disaster recovery plan for the detailed "how to" instructions for each recovery step.

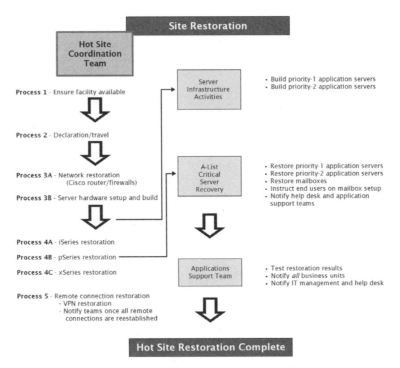

Figure 5.4: This is the basic progression of events during a disaster recovery effort.

Summary

The selection of the appropriate recovery strategies will help you in providing the direction for writing your disaster recovery procedures. Based on the RTO and RPO of individual application servers, you will probably need to use more than one type of disaster recovery solution. Both hardware-based and software-based recovery strategies might be included, in addition to traditional tape-backup resources. Once you have established how quickly you need to recover key applications (RTO) and how much data you can afford to lose (RPO), and you have obtained a budget, you can select the appropriate technology solution.

6

Backup and Recoverability

Everyone should be aware of the importance of backing up critical data. If you aren't aware, you will likely become painfully aware on the day after one of your System i5 servers or partitions crashes and there is no recoverable data. As a System i5 administrator, you need to bring all your key processes and procedures together through a backup solution that is reliable, flexible, architecturally compliant, and recoverable. Data is the backbone of today's organizations. Information is your corporation's most valuable asset. Therefore, immediate recovery and access to data after an outage is the key to every business's survival. When data is lost, damaged, or simply unavailable, it negatively affects and even completely halts your business. Adequate backups protect against permanent loss of data, but the total time it takes to rebuild and recover from a disaster can be a catastrophic business consequence if a solution is not in place.

Time is of the essence when recovering your company's lost data. While IT is busy recovering your company data, your customers might be busy contacting other suppliers. Just-in-time manufacturing, distribution, and electronic commerce all have put a premium on systems availability and access to corporate data.

Even with all this time pressure for systems availability today, the most common backup method is still to back up data onto tape once a day, and then send the tape offsite for storage. In the event of data loss, your company would recall the tapes back from their bonded offsite storage provider, and simply reload the server. A day or two later, your system is restored and you are back in business. As you know, this is a very simplified summary of activities, and it sure is not as easy as it sounds.

Tape still remains an integral part of your disaster recovery planning. The rationale behind tape is simple. Backup to tape provides the ability to produce low-cost, offsite, point-in-time copies of your vital corporate information. In a disaster, you can recover your data back from tape. The obvious drawbacks to tape backup systems are that they require a lot of oversight and that your data will only be current to the last successful tape backup. Any oversight means maintaining the tape backups manually.

System i5 and iSeries administrators have approached tape backups the same way for years. They back up the system and user data to tape, and cross their fingers that the backup process successfully completes. No thought is given to whether the backup just performed is 100% complete. Is everything necessary to recover every component of the i5 server actually backed up to tape? Is the right stuff backed up? Everyone knows about these potential problems of backing up to tape, but no one says much about it. Backup has become a dirty little secret of IT.

Plan for Data Recovery

Recovering your data is the primary element in any disaster recovery plan. Backing up data precludes a complete data restoration of all critical systems in the event of a disaster. Before you perform any system backup, you should first ask yourself what you need to save on the iSeries or System i5. In a perfect world, with no considerations for the end-user systems availability, the answer to that question would be easy: You need to save everything. Yes, everything! You might think I am crazy to even suggest that , but you should always consider the worst case. Does IT have the means to recover from a site loss, a RAID card failure, or another type of disk problem causing complete loss of data? Always consider the need for recovery in the worst scenario and having to reload the entire system for a recovery of your System i5.

The next important consideration for running backups is how often do you need to save the entire system? Once again, in an ideal world, the answer to that question is also easy: You need to save everything, every day. Seven days a week! Realistically, this is not a very common occurrence, as the system's auxiliary storage pools and user auxiliary pools have simply become too big for a daily, complete, full system backup using option 21.

In advance, you need to discuss with the business side of your organization how long you can take the server down daily to perform a backup of the system. The acceptable length of the outage will be your maximum *save window*. A save window is the amount of time that your system can be unavailable to users while you perform your save to tape. This will allow you to develop a backup strategy that fits the save window acceptable by the business. When you select a save strategy, balance what your users think is an acceptable save window with the value of the data you might lose and the amount of time it might take to recover. That is a delicate balance, and one where most system administrators tend to satisfy the business needs only, in lieu of system recovery requirements.

The key to a simplified recovery is to execute a save operation when your system is at a known consistent point and your data is not changing. This is the only process that will ensure 100% data integrity when you restore the iSeries or i5.

Things to Consider for a Backup Strategy

Today, we're more aware of the need for shortened backup windows and the need to recover data quickly. The reason for our heightened awareness might be due to increasing government regulations, corporate scrutiny, those dreaded auditors, and the obvious need for disaster recovery.

After all, what good is backing up data if you can't restore it when you need to? It's no longer a question of whether data can be restored, but how quickly it can be recovered and how much data loss your organization can tolerate. It's about making sure that your Recovery Time Objectives (RTOs) and Recovery Point Objectives (RPOs) match the true value of data at any given point during the business data lifecycle. It is all about being *recovery minded*, not over-cautious, and definitely not preaching "doom and gloom."

RPOs should be considered when restoration from tape is necessary. Keep in mind that you will be able to recover data only from the point of your last successful backup, such as 02:00 a.m. Using tape backups with other forms of disaster recovery technologies such as high availability, commitment control, continuous data protection solutions, and remote journaling will help minimize your RPO. However, some technologies might not be financially justifiable for your organization. Your choice then might be either backing up to tape more often (several times a day) or being ready to deal with the loss of up to 24 hours of data (since the last successful backup). If your organization's RPO allows the loss of 24 hours or more of data, tape backups alone are a suitable solution. A smaller RPO, however, requires using other technology in conjunction with tape. Tape also requires that you test the system to validate disaster recovery capabilities.

A traditional disaster recovery plan focuses on the technology recovery. All companies have (or should have) some form of data backup methodology in place. Unfortunately, executives assume their IT department's current data backup solution is capable of supporting every key business function, even when a disaster strikes. Nothing can be further from the truth. You need to ensure that all critical servers are being backed up reliably and consistently. This process, though it seems very obvious, is simply not exercised in many IT shops. Assigning backup responsibilities to an administrator is not enough. You need to ensure the process is followed correctly. The IT department needs to have formal, written procedures and schedules describing which systems get backed up, how backup completion is verified, when and whether the backups are executed, and whether they are full or incremental.

A backup strategy for your iSeries or i5 must address the following issues:

- How frequently should the various types of backups be performed?
- Which backup media should be used?
- How big is our backup window—daily, weekly, or monthly?
- Will backups require manual intervention or be fully automated?
- How will you verify the success of your backups?
- Where will the backup media be stored?
- How flexible is the backup design?
- How long can you afford to be down?
- How long will the restoration process take?
- How many generations of tape backups will the restoration span?
- Who is the backup and recovery owner?
- Who is the alternate?
- Is the backup solution auditable?
- Finally, is it all documented?

Backup = Recovery

Regardless of the backup software solution you use (BRMS, a third-party software solution, or native CL), certain fundamentals need to be in place to ensure better backup operations. When it comes to running a complete backup solution, it is easy to focus on the bad news: those nightly failures (media- or hardware-related), missing tapes, incomplete or unrecoverable data, or systems that failed to come up after another incomplete backup attempt. Yes, there are shops where backups are completed successfully, data is restored, and backup operations do run smoothly.

The key to a well-functioning backup infrastructure is having managed processes and controls. All computer shops have a clear understanding of the tasks to be performed and a consistent way to accomplish them.

The positive aspects of tape backups for all systems are as follows:

- Easy to run
- Easy to manage (BRMS)
- Easy to automate (BRMS)
- Today's high-speed and high-capacity reduced backup windows
- Today's reduced number of high-capacity tapes
- Virtual tape libraries (V5R4 solution)

Here are the negatives:

- Media errors
- Seldom validated
- Time to restore a hotsite in a disaster
- Loss of data because backup only runs once per day

Backup and Recovery Best Practices

As the complexity of systems increases, compliance proficiencies demand that IT become accountable to both the users and to the business. The Sarbanes-Oxley Act provides governance for many organizations today. The Act requires that the procedures used by the IT department be audited annually to ensure they have internal controls and procedures, and that they are always followed. Disaster avoidance happens long before a disaster occurs, certainly not after the fact. A commonly used framework in the IT industry is *CobiT* (*Control Objectives for Information and related Technology*). To achieve this standard, IT departments are adopting a *best practices* framework in computing services.

The System i5 backup process is a critical function to ensure business continuity for the system. The backups must be executed regularly and conform to a concise recovery program design. The system administrator of the iSeries must have the ability to restore all of its data to a consistent usable state, which minimizes the impact of your applications. That is your primary goal. You should perform a system audit of your backup and recovery program design and verify its completeness.

Ten Issues for the Administration of Backups

Many backup best practices seem basic, but accomplishing them isn't always easy. They depend on appropriate reporting and measurement capabilities, and staff competency within the organization. If you can't accomplish all of the best practices, try to address the most critical. If time and resources are the issue, develop a plan to justify them. Against these hurdles, you must, measure the acceptable risk of unrecoverable data during any major outages.

Here are two key points to remember when developing a data recovery strategy:

- Back up all critical data. Ask yourself, are you backing up the right stuff?
- Backups are the backbone to any recovery situation. In most recovery situations, the backups are not adequate, so excessive time is spent recreating parts of the operating system.

Issue 1: My backups run on the night shift, so I never hear about any issues!

The key element to recovery of your iSeries or i5 in a disaster is the completeness of the backups. If your backups are incomplete or flawed prior to the disaster, then the disaster recovery plan simply will not work, no matter how many experts you recruit. Having a process in place means a lot more than simply signing your name to it. With a sign-off, the process implies correctness. It means you have adhered to all the necessary steps in verifying the backups are fully complete. That means 100% complete. This is especially important as it pertains to your backups.

Many backup solutions are partially broken. I often observe graphs posted in IT shops stating things like, "We have a 96% backup success rate. We observe all standards to ensuring your data is backed up." A 96% on a math exam is amazing. A 96% in backups implies failure. This means that 4% of the time, the server isn't backed up completely. On a yearly calendar, you have 14 days with incomplete backups. Is this acceptable to your business? My guess is no.

Customer Backup Log Sample

- System not in restricted state, SAVSYS processing completed with errors.
- Starting SAVDLO of folder *ANY to devices TAP01.
- 2574 document library objects saved.
- Starting save of list *LINK to devices TAP01.
- 43917 objects saved. 342 not saved.
- Save of list *LINK completed with errors.
- Starting save of media information at level *OBJ to device TAP01.
- 18 objects saved from library QUSRBRM.
- Save of BRM media information at level *OBJ complete.
- DAILY *BKU 0070 *EXIT CALL PGM(BBSYSTEM/ENDDAYBU.
- Control group DAILY type *BKU completed with errors.

In this example, 342 objects were not saved on this web server. The response was, "Oh, we always get this message. It's no big deal." Backup is signed off as successful.

Was the backup really successful? Of course not. The backup could not get a lock on 342 objects, which probably means they were in use. If these 342 objects are in use, they must be critical to the function of this application. You need 100%.

The person responsible for managing the backups is under pressure to report only the good. So, if no one asks . . . hey, no one asked. Backups are typically managed by a junior staffer and on an off-shift. Many times, backup failures are not reported to management because the people performing the backups think if they tell anyone how bad the backups are, they'll be fired. They're betting that the backups will work the next night, or everything will be captured with the weekly full system option 21 save.

Examine your own house and see just how well your backups are really running.

Issue 2: Develop a backup plan.

Backups are just one component of data protection. Backup planning should be a fundamental part of every backup and recovery program's design. Your backup solution must always consider a process for rolling out new applications, adding additional partitions or guest operating systems, and being able to manage disk growth. A proper backup plan enables the system administrators to fully understand the application needs and any additional business requirements.

Issue 3: Establish a backup lifecycle program.

An effective backup strategy requires certain tasks to be completed successfully each and every day. In addition, there are weekly, monthly, and even yearly tasks that are vital to your business. An effective backup lifecycle program demands that all tasks are documented and performed on a regular, published, and agreed-upon schedule. This also lends itself to ITIL and SOX compliance.

Daily tasks are the operational fundamentals that most backup administrators are familiar with. They include items such as these:

- Backup monitoring
- Success/failure reporting
- Problem analysis and resolution
- Tape handling and library management
- Offsite tape storage
- Scheduling of special saves
- Weekly, monthly, and long-term backups
- Archiving data
- Capacity backup planning for disk and tape drives
- Review of backup policies
- Recovery testing and verification

Evaluate your daily/weekly/monthly tasks as needed. Document them, and make sure they're recorded and signed off. All this will seem very tedious at first, but as you automate these processes, you will immediately come to realize the benefits.

Issue 4: Review backup logs daily.

A review of backup job logs or BRMS reports and the QSYSOPR message queue is a key daily task, but one that's not routinely performed. It can be time-consuming, but it does pay dividends for ensuring backup completeness. DSPLOGBRM provides you with the BRMS activities per date, interactively. You can see today's history, yesterday's, last week's, or as long as you keep the history.

Backup issues tend to manifest themselves. How many times has one backup event resulted in a series of subsequent failures? A weekly backup gets run instead of a daily, thus shutting down all subsystems, including QINTER.

A very angry group of users are less than impressed. Then, you put the weekly job schedule entry on hold and forget to release it later. Now you have missed the weekend save. The system administrator responsible never informed anyone about putting the weekly backup job on hold.

It takes considerable skill to troubleshoot backup failures. It is therefore important to verify everything works. When it does not, determine the root cause rather than guess based on some symptom.

Issue 5: Protect your manual tape backup database or BRMS catalog.

BRMS backup control groups maintain a database or catalog that is absolutely critical to the recovery of your system from the backup tapes. Having no access to the BRMS catalog or worse, a corrupted catalog, means you have lost your ability to restore anything from your backup tapes.

Every backup performed through control groups automatically writes the catalog to the tape. The following objects will permit the catalog to be retrieved:

```
Saved                                                       Seq
Control           Item      Type Name    Number Date    Time Saved
Saved    Number   Group
         ----------  -----  ----------  -----  --------  --------  -------
         -------  ---------  ----------  ----------
__ QBRM            *FULL *SYSBAS  00001  xx      xx       MTHLY
__ QMSE            *FULL *SYSBAS  00001  xx      xx       MTHLY
__ Q1ABRMSF        *FULL *SYSBAS  00001  xx      xx       MTHLY
__ Q1ABRMSF01      *FULL *SYSBAS  00001  xx      xx       MTHLY
__ QUSRBRM         *FULL *SYSBAS  00001  xx      xx       MTHLY
__ QUSRBRM         *QBRM *SYSBAS  00033  xx      xx       DAILY
```

If you do not have a tape management software solution, how do you know what data is on which tapes? Many clients manually record volume information in Excel or Word and store the information on a local PC. The key to remember is to get this information offsite, so that it does not go down in flames with the rest of your infrastructure.

Issue 6: Backups run longer than your backup window.

Backup window failures are successful backups that exceed the maximum allowed time for your backup window outage. This can creep up on IT. Usually your staff only becomes painfully aware of it when users start complaining. This is often overlooked because the backup job itself completes successfully, as no errors were reported in the backup logs. This rarely happens over a short time period; generally, it creeps up as does the system disk utilization. The 2-hour window was not a problem a year ago, as the backups only took 1 hour 35 minutes to run. Now, they are taking 2 hours and 20 minutes. Record the start and end time to ensure your backup job times do not sneak up on you.

Consider when you go to the corner office, and ask for a sum of money to buy some additional disk storage. The boss says sure, because the business case supports the fact that your company needs the disk. In IT, it's easy to forget to ask for more time to back up the data during this same request. You just received approval for 500 GB of disk. How are you going to back up this extra data? System ASP is forever increasing and backup windows are shrinking. Are you backing up enough, or making concessions? Should you have asked for a faster tape drive or a second one along with the disk storage?

Issue 7: Identify and back up orphan data.

Examine the number of libraries and directories in the IFS you have, versus those actually backed up. Perform a gap analysis. BRMS provides you with some level of reporting information. By examining the BRMS recovery report, you can clearly see when libraries have been backed up. Work through the report and try to bring back the entire iSeries/400. You might be surprised that critical applications or application data are omitted and only saved monthly or quarterly. Ouch!

If you do not have BRMS, run a `PRTDSKINF *LIB` to obtain a printout of every library on your system. Examine your backup CLs, and enter the backup interval next to each library in the report. This might be a cumbersome exercise, but it sure is revealing.

Remember those hard-coded CL programs? These libraries made sense five years ago when the program was written, but has nothing been added in five years? No new applications or libraries? You tell me. Use commands built for easy recovery, like `*ALLUSR`, versus listing specific libraries one by one. Always ask yourself how you would rebuild the system after a complete loss with these backups. The orphan data problem is an excellent example of an inconsistency that can result from poor backup administration.

Issue 8: Automate your backup process.

A key to successful data protection is consistency. As the complexities of the backup infrastructure continue to grow, automation can help by providing tools to facilitate success. Manual tasks, such as checking logs on a scheduled basis, are key. Deploying automation to provide automated alerts for previously identified errors in job logs can make life easier. Scanning manually through a 100-page job log is not the way to go. Many third-party solution providers offer tremendous automated solutions for message management of the System i5. Management Central, which comes with your system, should be given careful consideration as well.

Issue 9: Backups must be integrated into the change-control process.

Your systems are, by their nature, very dynamic. System backup planning must be part of the strategic planning process, so all backup considerations must be part of the organization's formal change-control process. This demands a two-way relationship. Application changes directly and indirectly related to the backup infrastructure must be part of the notification, impact assessment, and contingency planning process that's included within change control. In every change control committee meeting, you must always consider how you will back out if the change goes bad during implementation, and how you will support it when it goes into production. The backup infrastructure is a production system, just like the most important application in an organization's environment. It requires the same respect and support.

Issue 10: Leverage your technical expertise.

Backup environments are very complex and get more so with the introduction of every new hardware or software technology. IBM continues to add additional backup and recovery functionality to the native operating systems, tape hardware, and BRMS. While much of this technology can be helpful, and it certainly all sounds good, there's a considerable challenge in understanding the functionality and how best to apply it into your own environment. All technical problems get resolved eventually, and opportunities to further enhance are always available.

Checklist for Backup and Recovery

Use this checklist as a starting point for backup and recovery activities:

- Examine the current save strategy for all mission-critical servers.
- Map out how you would rebuild one server, then multiple servers.
- Is a specific order required? Consider the big picture: enterprise recovery.
- Check the backup logs for missing objects, folders, and directories.
- Examine backup software: BRMS, third-party software solutions, or native CL.
- Examine backup software on non-AS400 platforms, such as Veritas, ArchSrv, and TSM.

- Are you saving all the required components for both application and system recovery?
- Is QUSRSYS complete? It's a users and system library.
- QSYS2, QGPL, QUSRSYS (application data restores) are required.
- Is your backup strategy flexible for a mid-week system loss as well as a weekend failure?
- Investigate levels of availability management.
- Create data exposure models. Compare static and non-static files.
- Review tape management rotations.
- Review off-site strategies.
- Model recovery to Recovery Time Objectives.
- Review special Backup & Recovery Group PTFs/Service Packs and patches.
- Optimize backups to ensure continuous availability.
- Test and validate alternate IPL functionality.
- System values setting is required for recovery.
- Consider security issues during recovery.
- Review all recovery documentation and testing activities.

Your IT department *must* provide the business with a safe and reliable iSeries or System i5 backup and recovery program. We all understand that all systems are prone to hardware problems, and possibly even disaster. Implementing a robust backup software solution eliminates extensive human interaction. By automating the routine tasks for your iSeries backup and recovery, you save both time and money and effectively guarantee systems availability by knowing the backups are executed correctly and routinely.

A special consideration when using a fault-tolerant server environment is that it does not protect against disasters, human error, or a multiple component failure. The traditional backup and recovery strategies are still required, as they must be modified to integrate with your hot standby servers, IASP, or high-availability software solution.

Backup Media Management

Managing your tapes is an important part of the backup save operation. You must be able to easily locate the tapes required for system recovery and hope they are all undamaged. Effective media management policies are essential for ensuring data protection, while controlling media and storage costs. Media management policy includes much more than just determining your tape rotations for offsite storage. Backup media management requires the following:

- Backup tape retention
- Naming and labeling tapes
- Preparing tapes
- Maintaining tape drives
- Storing tapes
- Monitoring for tape errors
- Duplicate tape volumes

Backup Tape Retention

A traditional tape retention cycle for backups is referred to as *Grandfather, Father, and Son*. This implies multiple family generations are alive and well; in other words, multiple generation of tape backups are available at any given time. An important part of a good save procedure is to have more than one available option—have more than one set of tapes available. When you perform a system or data-only recovery, you might need to go back to a previous set of save tapes if your most recent set is damaged, missing, or incomplete.

Consider the following rule of thumb for retention periods:

- Retention period for daily incremental backups: one month
- Retention period for weekly full backups: three months
- Retention period for monthly full backups: one year

These recommended minimum retention periods provide your organization with the ability to easily recover month-end, quarter-end, or even year-end data. In addition, consider tape record-retention requirements for financial data as governed by your corporate policies.

Naming and Labeling Tapes

A media naming convention can prove useful in separating tapes to correspond with your save/archive tape strategy. Tape management becomes extremely important as the tape library gets larger. Building tape volume relationships helps you in keeping track of multiple volumes and save/archive generations, as they get created. Use of LTO Tri-optic bar codes keeps things neat and tidy.

Reserving ranges of numbers to specific types of backups can prove effective for a larger tape library. Some clients name tapes 1–31, representing the day of the month. Others use color schemes with a number, to quickly distinguish between daily and weekly backups. A corresponding tape management log details each tape volume's ID, contents, owner, expiry date, and save process. This can prove invaluable in the daily operation and can be easily designed using a database application or even a spreadsheet macro. These logs should accompany the tapes to the offsite storage facility. This, of course, is all done for you if you have BRMS installed.

Preparing Tapes

Initialize each tape volume with an internal label identifier to help ensure that you load the correct tapes for the save operation. Tapes must be initialized using the initialize tape command (INZTAP). You can also specify the format or density (bytes per inch) before writing to the tape using the options on the INZTAP command prompted with an F4. It is important to ensure that the internal file identifier equals the external volume ID.

The INZTAP command prepares magnetic tape media for use on the iSeries. This command is used to write volume labels on standard-labeled cartridges. Three operations can be done by this command, depending on the values specified for the CHECK and CLEAR parameters:

- The tape can be checked for active data files (files that have not reached their expiration dates).

- The tape can be initialized. Initialization writes only on the beginning of the tape, but it makes all data on the cartridge inaccessible.

- If the tape is being initialized, any previous data on the tape can also be deleted.

If the tape is being initialized, a volume label followed by two tape markers is written at the beginning of the tape. All tapes must be initialized before use. Tapes that have been initialized do not need to be reinitialized unless the user wants to write a new volume label, or change the density of a standard labeled tape.

The INZTAP command has one required parameter, DEV. This specifies the name of the device in which the volume being initialized is placed. Specify the name of the tape or media library device, i.e. TAP01.

There are also six optional parameters:

- NEWVOL specifies the volume identifier for a tape being initialized as a standard-labeled tape. Its new-volume-identifier value specifies up to six characters to identify the new volume. The identifier must contain only alphanumeric characters and the symbols $, #, and @, and cannot have a prefix or contain blanks. Each tape should have a unique volume identifier to ensure control of the tape volumes.

- NEWOWNID specifies which tape owner's identifier to write in the volume label of the volume being written. The owner identification contains up to 14 characters (letters and/or numbers in any combination), is left-justified, and is padded on the right with blanks if fewer than 14 characters are supplied.

- CHECK specifies whether a tape volume is checked for active data files (files with an end date later than the current system date) before it is initialized. If an unlabeled volume is on the specified device for initialization, this parameter is ignored. If the volume must be checked for active files, as much of the tape is read as necessary before initialization is done. It has two values:

  » *YES: All data file labels on the tape are checked. If active files are found, the operation is ended and an error message is sent.

  » *NO: Tape initialization continues with no checking for active files. To initialize a new or empty volume, VOL(*MOUNTED) and CHECK(*NO) must be specified; otherwise, the system attempts to read labels from the volume on the specified device until the tape completely rewinds.

- DENSITY specifies the density or format in which to write the data on the tape after it has been initialized. The density used for all data files written to a standard-labeled tape is specified when the volume is initialized, and cannot be changed unless the tape is reinitialized. It has two values:

  » *DEVTYPE: The data written on the tape volume is based on the device type (the type of tape device).

  » *CTGTYPE: The data written on the tape volume is based on cartridge type (the type of tape cartridge). If the device does not support special cartridge type information, *DEVTYPE is used.

- ENDOPT specifies whether the tape is rewound only, or rewound and unloaded after the operation ends. It has two values:

  » *REWIND: The tape is automatically rewound, but not unloaded, after the operation has ended.

  » *UNLOAD: The tape is automatically rewound and unloaded after the operation ends.

- CLEAR specifies whether all previous labels and data are deleted from the tape when it is initialized. If the volume must be cleared of all data, it is spaced from the location of the initializing volume label or tape markers to the end of the tape marker. It has two values:

>> *NO: The existing data is not deleted. Even though the existing data is not deleted, the data on the volume is not accessible after the volume has been initialized.

>> *YES: After the beginning of the tape has been initialized, the remaining data on the tape is deleted. The *YES value is needed only if there are security concerns with old data. If *YES is specified, the initialize operation can take a long time.

Here is an example of using the INZTAP command:

```
INZTAP DEV(TAP01) NEWVOL(TUEBKP) CHECK(*YES)
ENDOPT(*UNLOAD)
```

This example initializes the volume on the tape device named TAP01. Its new volume identifier is TUEBKP, and the tape is checked for active files. Once the volume has been initialized, the tape is rewound and unloaded. Any previous data beyond the new volume label is not deleted, but is no longer accessible.

Expiry Dates

Accidental scratching of data can occur when there is no standard in place for file retention. When there is no tape management software installed like BRMS, you must program the prevention into the tape expiry label. An expiry date on the internal label causes the iSeries or i5 to read the information and send a message back to the system console, to QSYSOPR. If an individual mounts a tape incorrectly, a message is displayed, stating, "Data exists on this tape. Do you wish to overwrite it?" The tape-write operation will only proceed after the operator acknowledges the message.

Incorporating expiry dates in the save process on the iSeries/400 can be done in two ways:

• An expiration date EXPDATE of (*PERM) will assign a date of 999999 and make all files permanent. This would be a useful year-end option or a handy way for operators to avoid intervention for determining calendar dates. If the tape is to be re-used, the CLEAR (*ALL) and option would be used in the CL command.

- An actual expiry date on the EXPDATE parameter can be specified. This date would correspond to the rotational date in the backup cycle.

The INZBRM (Initialize BRMS) Command

To use the Initialize BRMS command, you must have the 5722-BR1 (Backup Recovery and Media Services for iSeries) licensed program installed. INZBRM performs many types of initialization:

- Initializes all major files as well as establishing default policies and control groups
- Clears and then re-initializes the device file and media library file
- Starts the subsystem for networking in a multi-system environment
- Allows you to reset BRMS and re-initialize all major files, as well as establishing default policies and control groups

Maintaining Tape Drives

All tape drives and tape units inside tape libraries must be cleaned regularly. The read and write heads collect dust and other material that can cause errors when reading or writing to tape. In addition to your regular cleaning cycle, you should also switch cleaning cartridges as per manufacturer specifications. Are you still using the original cleaning cartridge that came with the tape drive years ago?

Clean your tape drives at the following points:

- For every full system save
- At restoration of your system
- When the threshold is reached

Storing Tapes

By storing tapes with an offsite bonded data-storage provider, your data, application backups, and system saves should all be secure and readily available for recovery when needed. Do not store your backup tapes and other vital records onsite, or in an onsite vault, or at an office building across the street. Definitely do not store them in your home! Ensure your offsite storage provider is at least 30 miles away. Aligning the storage location and ability of your offsite solution provider to ship to your commercial hotsite provider will help you execute the plan successfully.

Access to your production data and system saves is vital to any successful recovery. All your current backup processes are of no value if your offsite storage provider cannot deliver the tape media back to you on a timely basis. This means 7/24/365, rain or shine. Remember, you cannot recover without data. The data component of the disaster recovery plan includes daily, weekly, and monthly backups that should be sent offsite for safekeeping the morning after they have been completed successfully. You should define the appropriate tape rotation delivered offsite to address both application and system recovery needs.

Monitoring for Tape Errors

When reading and writing to tape, it is normal for some temporary errors to occur. Tapes physically wear out after extended use. You can determine if the tape quality is degrading by printing the error log information from the iSeries/400.

There is a tendency by every system administrator to use a custom CL or repeat the same INZTAP command (F9) to initialize all tapes. This results in every tape in your entire tape media library having the same internal name, such as "Backup." Yes, the external volume IDs are unique, but the internal name is the same for all tape media. The consequence of this action shows when you examine your error log statistics. You could own hundreds of tapes, and the volume statistics will show there is a tape called "Backup" that has an excessive number of permanent write errors. Which tape of the hundred named "Backup" has the errors flagged on the media? You see you have a bad tape or tapes, but you do not know which one(s). Maybe the errors are from last night's save, or maybe they're from the year-end, full system backup.

This example report reveals numerous errors on the tape volumes:

```
Title . . . . . . . . . :           Volume Statistics Report
System type . . . . . . :  9406
System model  . . . . . :  830
System release  . . . . :  V5R3M0
System name . . . . . . :  Your System
System serial number  . . :  XXXXX
Report type . . . . . . :      Lifetime Report

Volume        ---Temporary Errors---   --------K Bytes--------
ID              Read      Write         Read      Written
PUB004          412        36          33295      1462988
PUB005            0         0              1            1
PUB029            0         0              1            1
RECK01            0         0             34     66128727
REC001            0         0              1            1
RK0001            0         0            431    898457864
RK0002            0         0            677   1465976602
RK0003            3       267           1085   2291687253
RK0004            0         0           1206   2562304148
RK0005           21       530           1299   2783519112
RK0006            0         0           1395   2652459068
RK0007            0         0           1202   2558550360
RK0008            0         0            383    805496444
RK0009            0         0            474    992852930
```

These tapes need to be identified, as they are becoming undependable and should be removed from the tape media library. The log identifies errors exceeding manufacturer recommendations on tapes PUB004, RK0003, and RK0005.

How long can you use those LTO tapes? With tape media, you just do not know which tape is bad until it fails. At that point, it is far too late. There are just no warning signs—or are there? The error log report will help you track tapes that are going bad. My own rule of thumb is permanent errors are not acceptable. One is too many. When I find a tape that has a *PERM error on the media, I execute the INZTAP command and specify the *CLEAR operand. I use the tape once more, and evaluate it again. If I get more than one permanent error on the tape media, I simply toss it. No executive of your company would be upset to hear you threw out a $30 tape to help ensure the data was indeed recoverable, especially in a disaster.

Duplicate Tape Volumes

When backing up to tape, consider tape duplication for the weekly and monthly full backups. Tape duplication is a process in which the primary backup tape is copied to a secondary tape after the backup is complete. Typically, one copy is kept onsite, and the other copy is sent to an offsite storage facility for disaster recovery purposes. BRMS has a solution that is fully capable of performing tape duplication after the initial backups have been completed.

Although tape duplication consumes more tape resources, it has two advantages: enhanced data availability in the event of a media failure on the primary copy, and faster local restore times because one copy is always onsite. There are also additional cost savings by avoiding those expensive emergency tape-recall rates charged by every offsite storage provider. This alone can justify the cost of buying more tapes for tape duplication.

Many organizations have purchased and deployed automated tape libraries (3583, 3584, 3594, 3595), among many others, to improve backup and recovery performance. Another benefit is the reduction of errors associated with manual handling of backup media. Unfortunately, management of these libraries is often overlooked. Without proper media management and retention policies, the libraries fill to capacity and require more human intervention. We tend to keep too much in the libraries themselves, thus filling up all available tape slots.

How Much to Back Up for Disaster Recovery

If a server is listed in your critical server definition of the disaster recovery plan, you have to be able to recover it. The amount of accepted data loss and recovery time expectations is also defined in this definition. An efficient DR plan supports backup and restoration of data by differentiating the criticality of your server infrastructure.

Categorize the business functions and supporting servers as *critical, essential, necessary,* or *optional.* Typically, you'll find a 30/30/20/20 breakdown. You'll find that 30% of all your servers are critical for business recovery, another 30% are essential, 20% are necessary but not required immediately, and the remaining 20% are optional or not required at all. This means you can focus on 60%, not 100% of your servers. (Detailed definitions can be found in chapter 4.)

By differentiating between critical and less critical, the DR plan helps increase operational efficiency for server backup and recovery, while reducing operating costs. Decreasing the amount of server redundancy and hotsite requirements positively impacts the business RTO while reducing IT expense and infrastructure recovery costs.

It is imperative that your DR plan specifies, in detail, when backups are executed, the complete contents of your backup, the frequency of your backups, and your offsite vaulting procedures, with all supporting documentation. In addition, an effective disaster recovery plan should detail all the steps for restoring this data within the specified timeframes of the business.

IT integrations for data protection include procedures to ensure data recoverability and integrity. The success of recovery of your DR plan is fully dependent on the individuals who ensure these procedures are being executed without flaw.

Backup Recovery and Media Services (BRMS)

Products like BRMS, shown in Figure 6.1, automate the functions of disk-to-tape backup, system restoration, and tape media management. The software provides a solution for your backup and recovery requirements, to ensure that you have a reliable, accurate backup strategy and, most importantly, can recover the saved data when needed.

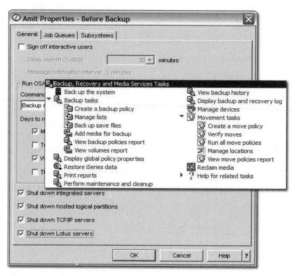

Figure 6.1: BRMS software.

BRMS is a very structured and automated backup solution. It provides the means to back up all your application libraries, systems security and configuration data, shared folders, IFS directories, and Domino databases, all regularly and automatically. Backup and recovery properties in Figure 6.2 clearly enforce the management benefits of BRMS.

BRMS has the following benefits:

- Manages your media
- Automates your backups
- Simplifies your restores and recoveries

- Provides detailed reporting
- Provides recovery reports by system
- Automates backup for i5/OS-hosted Windows, Linux, AIX 5L, and Domino servers
- Manages shutdown, save, and restart of LPARs, Domino, or Windows servers
- Performs unattended system save (SAVSYS)
- Eliminates the need to start a console monitor

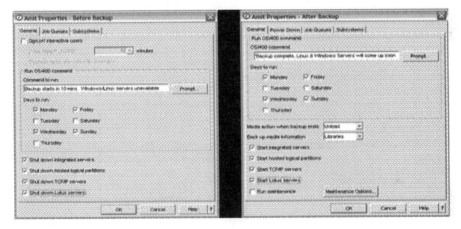

Figure 6.2: BRMS backup management.

Breaking Down Backup Needs

The backup process is a critical function to ensure business continuity for the system(s). The backups must be executed regularly, and conform to a concise recovery program design. You must be able to restore all of critical data to a consistent usable state, which minimizes the impact of your applications and meets both your Recovery Time and Recovery Point objectives. That is your primary goal.

Systems are prone to hardware problems, and possibly even disaster. Implementing a robust backup software solution eliminates extensive human interaction. Automating the routine tasks for your backup and recovery saves both time and money, and effectively guarantees systems availability by having backups executed correctly and routinely.

IBM supplies a wonderful poster called "Are you saving the right stuff?" Get this poster mounted and hang it up near the iSeries system administrators. It fully depicts the commands required to back up any component of the system, with the corresponding restoration command. This poster is very helpful in breaking down all components of the system. Figure 6.3 is an excerpt from this poster.

Consider your backup strategy and measure it against the complete system. Ask yourself whether every major block on this chart is accounted for. Examine your current backups, and cross off all the iSeries and i5 segments that are backed up. You might be in for a surprise! Also review the frequency with which each of these backup segments gets backed up. Can you afford to "mind the gap"?

Every IBM Save Option comprises numerous save CL commands specific to a unique backup requirement. You should expand the CL command structure behind every Save Option to fully understand the individual system components being saved. Understanding the differences between save menu options will help you select the backup option that best suits your backup strategy needs. Understanding the CL commands will also assist in the restoration of your libraries, objects, and other major system components. If you ask yourself, "Am I saving the right stuff?" you can answer the question with confidence, knowing what CL save commands are being executed under the menu option of a specific save command.

Save Entire System (Option 21):

```
ENDSBS SBS(*ALL) OPTION (*IMMED)
CHGMSGQ QSYSOPR DLVRY(*BREAK OR *NOTIFY)
SAVSYS
SAVLIB LIB(*NONSYS) ACCPTH)(*YES)
SAVDLO DLO(*ALL) SAVFLR(*ANY)
SAV DEV('/QSYS.LIB/tape-device-name.DEVD')
        OBJ(('/*') ('/QSYS.LIB' *OMIT)
        ('/QDLS' *OMIT)) UPDHST(*YES)
STRSBS SBSD(controlling-subsystem)
```

Save System Data Only (Option 22):

```
ENDSBS SBS(*ALL) OPTION(*IMMED)
CHGMSGQ QSYSOPR DLVRY(*BREAK OR *NOTIFY)
SAVSYS
SAVLIB LIB(*IBM) ACCPTH(*YES)
SAV DEV('/QSYS.LIB/tape-device-name.DEVD')
      OBJ(('/QIBM/ProdData')
      ('/QOpenSys/QIBM/ProdData'))
      UPDHST(*YES)
STRSBS SBSD(controlling-subsytem)
```

Save All User Data (Option 23):

```
ENDSBS SBS(*ALL) OPTION(*IMMED)
CHGMSGQ QSYSOPR DLVRY(*BREAK or *NOTIFY)
SAVSECDTA
SAVCFG
SAVLIB LIB(*ALLUSR) ACCPTH(*YES)
SAVDLO DLO(*ALL) FLOR(*ANY)
SAV DEV('/QSYS.LIB/tape-device-name.DEVD')
      OBJ(('/*') ('/QSYS.LIB' *OMIT)
      ('/QDLS'*OMIT) ('/QIBM/ProdData' *OMIT)
      ('/QOpenSys/QIBM/ProdData' *OMIT))
       UPDHST(*YES)
STRSBS SBSD(controlling-subsystem)
```

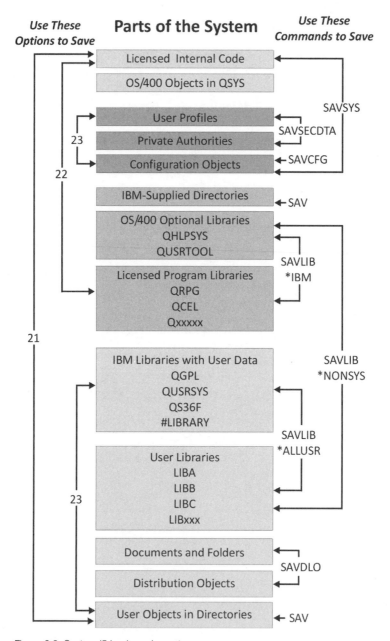

Figure 6.3: System i5 backup elements.

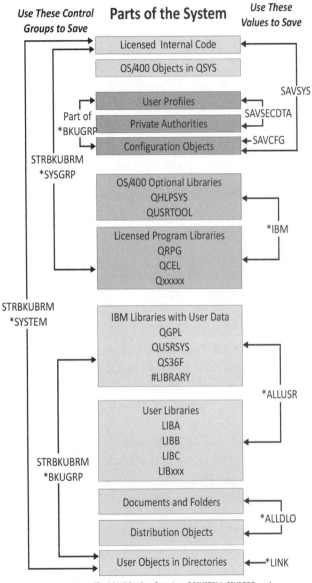

Figure 6.3: System i5 backup elements. continued

Here is some BRMS terminology to keep in mind:

- *Media*—A tape media cartridge which will contain the saved data.
- *Media Identifier*—The external name given to tape media.
- *Media Class*—A logical grouping of tape media, for example, LTO3.
- *Control Group*—A grouping of backup elements to back up and process to backup (save libraries, objects, directories, etc.).
- *Policies*—All settings or configurations that will be used for backup devices, tape media, and backup related settings.

A Simple Save Strategy

You can save your iSeries or i5 server with the GO SAVE command. It offers you plenty of flexibility based on your specific backup needs. Save your entire iSeries/i5 or portions of your iSeries/i5 server that change regularly with this simple method.

The GO SAVE command is a simple way to make sure that you have a good backup of your entire server. This command presents you with Save menus that make it easy to back up your server, no matter what backup strategy you decide to use. You can use an option 21 from the menus to do a complete full system save. In fact, option 21 is the basis for all save strategies. It allows you to perform a complete save of all the data on your server. Once you have used option 21, you can use other menu options to save parts of the server, or to use a manual save process via a CL program. Some of my clients have even customized the GO SAVE backup steps to include their ERP system shutdown sequence and tailored save commands for their environment.

The components of the option 21 Save Entire System backup are as follows:

```
ENDSBS SBS(*ALL) OPTION(*IMMED)
CHGMSGQ MSGQ(QSYSOPR) DLVRY(*BREAK or *NOTIFY)
SAVSYS
SAVLIB LIB(*NONSYS) ACCPTH(*YES)
SAVDLO DLO(*ALL) FLR(*ANY)
SAV DEV('/QSYS.LIB/tap01.DEVD') + OBJ(('/*') ('/QSYS.LIB' *OMIT) +
    ('/QDLS' *OMIT))1 UPDHST(*YES) STRSBS SBSD(qctl)
```

Weekly and Monthly Strategy

Do a full system save consisting of SAVSYS, SAVLIB *NONSYS, SAVDLO, and SAV, with the tapes sent offsite every Monday morning. This "full" backup provides the baseline for your recovery. While this method offers excellent protection, it takes a significant amount of time. Restoring data from a full backup, however, is always simpler and faster than combining many other backup methods, because all data is readily available on a single tape or on multiple tapes and in the correct sequence. Unfortunately, executing full backups daily is not a practical solution for most shops. Most full backups are done at night during non-business hours, over a weekend.

Daily Incremental Backups

Many organizations have far too much data to back up the entire system Monday to Friday. Also, having the server completely unavailable during the save window every day would be unacceptable to the business. For situations where there is just too much data and too little time, an incremental backup might be the only solution. This can be accomplished two ways:

- *Saving Changed Objects* (*SAVCHGOBJ*)—Saving changed objects or files is often used to reduce the amount of media and to complete save processing to tape sooner, thus reducing the save window. Because of their discretionary nature, incremental data backups can speed up the backup process by backing up only new or changed files and directories. This works with a file-level indicator that is updated whenever a file is changed. The system backup process reads this indicator and determines whether or not to save the file to tape. With an incremental strategy, only those files that have changed since the last backup operation will be transferred to tape.

- *Saving Critical Libraries* (*SAVLIB*)—Saving select complete libraries is also used to reduce the save processing and thus reduce the save window. This typically is used for the backup libraries deemed as ERP Production. It implies you know all your critical libraries and only want the contents of these libraries saved. Typically, this includes data only, versus application and adapt libraries in the selection criteria.

Using weekly full backups with daily incremental backups (SAVCHGOBJ or SAVLIB) is generally considered the strategic norm. Many organizations produce incremental backups on a nightly Monday–Friday schedule, and perform a full backup over the weekend. This method offers both speed and security. However, does it offer a complete backup solution? Always consider what you would do if the system were lost today. Can you get everything back to rebuild your server? What are your gaps? Are they acceptable?

Saving Security Information (SAVSECDTA)

You might do a fantastic job making sure your data is backed up regularly, while not paying enough attention to saving the system security data. Saving system security information is much more than saving the latest user-profile password changes. Security information is stored with the objects (files, libraries, directories, etc.) themselves. The object's *PUBLIC authority, ownership and owner's authority, primary group and primary group's authority, and auditing value, as well as the name of the authorization list securing the object, are all worth saving. When you save your files (with SAVLIB or SAVCHGOBJ) or save directories (with SAV), the security save information should accompany it as well. If you are only saving your objects, you are missing several critical pieces of security data.

How often you perform a SAVSECDTA depends on how often user profiles are created, changed, or removed from the system. Also consider how often private authorities are granted or removed from individual objects and authorization lists, and how often authorization lists are created or deleted. For example, if you save your security data at the beginning of the month, and you have to recover your system at the end of the month, how many user profiles and authorizations will you have to re-create?

The SAVSECDTA does not require a restricted state to run. It can run parallel with normal system job processing. I have my clients execute the SAVSECDTA at the start of every nightly backup run. The command executes prior to any special backup handling procedures you might have in place, like obtaining a dormant state for a save-while-active save. After looking through your organization's security activity, you might determine that you need to save your security data more often.

Save More with Save-While-Active

The best way to recover everything is to save everything every night. Many organizations shut down the system for end-user access nightly. The system access is restricted during an agreed-upon save window.

Suppose the nightly backup window is two hours for incremental saves, and seven hours for the weekly full system save. By implementing a save-while-active backup strategy, you can do a full system backup in the two-hour window instead of in seven hours! This means the backup window currently used to back up just changed objects or select libraries can be used instead to back up all the user libraries or *ALLUSR libraries. This will be accomplished by obtaining a snapshot of the data, and then the tape can write for hours, as it now has no impact on the users.

What Is Save-While-Active?

If systems availability is a real concern during your nightly backup window, consider implementing a save-while-active (*SWA*) solution. The best part is you already own the software. It's part of the operating system. That's one of the great things about the iSeries. SWA has been a viable solution available in OS/400 for years. However, many users are either unaware of it or choose not to implement it. Let's get all the myths out on the table now:

- SWA does not work as advertised. It never has!
- Entire objects are duplicated, using up lots of disk space.
- Exclusive locks are required.
- Opened files cannot be saved with SWA.
- ERP files cannot be opened while writing to tape.
- Applications will fail.
- Using SWA will break existing restore procedures.
- There's nowhere to go for help.

First, I can assure you that SWA does work if you use it correctly. Its name is misleading, however. To either reduce or eliminate the amount of time your system is unavailable for use during a backup (your backup outage), you can use the SWA process for particular save commands. Save-while-active lets you use the system during part or all of the backup process. In contrast, other save operations permit no access to the system while the backup runs. How you use SWA in your backup strategy depends on whether you choose to reduce or eliminate the time your system is unavailable during a backup. Simply reducing the backup window is much simpler and more common, and therefore much easier to install.

The system performs the SWA function by maintaining an image of the object being saved as it existed at a single point in time. This point in time is called the *checkpoint* for the object. The image of the object is called the *checkpoint image*. To get a consistent backup across all objects in the same state, you select the *SYNCLIB option. This allows all objects being saved to be synchronized. So, with library-level synchronization, the checkpoints for all the objects in the library occur at the same time. The term "save-while-active" might seem to imply that objects can be changed at any time during the save operation, but this is not true. The system allocates (locks) the objects as it obtains checkpoint images. Afterward, it releases them. This is why you still want to shut down user access as you have always done. The goal is to reduce the backup outage and save more.

SWA Example

Take the example of a nightly two-hour backup window. The first step is to end your system access from the users, as is the current practice. Ensure you have as much memory available as possible in the memory pool that will execute the backup command during checkpoint. Then, you execute the following:

```
SAVLIB *ALLUSR SAVACT(*SYNCLIB) SAVACTMSGQ(QSYSOPR) ACCPTH(*YES)
     OMITLIB( QPFRDATA, TESTlibs, Name of Developer libs )
```

The checkpoint will run for a while. How long depends on the number of libraries and total number of objects that need to be processed during checkpoint. Once the system has reached a synchronized state, the tape write operation is ready to start, and the locks are all released. For performance reasons, it makes sense to wait a short period of time (such as five minutes) to let the system get all memory flushed and CPU reduced back to normal. Then, you can simply start up your regular processing. So, a two-hour backup window ends up getting reduced by 30–60 minutes (depending on the size of the *ALLUSR), as shown in Figure 6.4. And you end up saving everything you need.

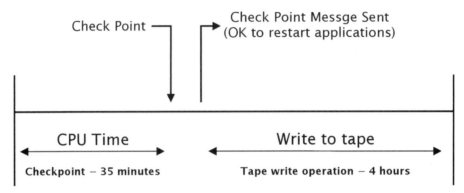

Figure 6.4: Reducing the backup window with save-while-active.

With the introduction of i5OS (V5R3), there is a solution available to further enhance SWA. It's called *Ragged*. This is the missing piece for shops that heavily use commitment control and have transactions open for long periods. This made obtaining a lock virtually impossible, thus causing SWA to time-out. Now you can run backups while users are on the system.

Richard's Backup Solution

The daily save process would be executed Monday to Friday overnight, and all tapes would be sent offsite the following morning. Use daily offsite policies, as they would support a reasonable records-retention program. This would allow for multiple daily tapes offsite at any one time.

The use of the SAVSECDTA and SAVCFG commands should also be included on a daily basis. The myth about saving security and configuration data is that you need a restricted state. I can assure you that these commands do not require a restricted state to execute. Having current security and configuration goes a long way to a full recovery:

For example, suppose the nightly backup runs at 2:00 a.m. At 1:30, issue the following:

```
SAVSECDTA
SAVCFG
```

At 1:45, send messages to users warning them to get off the system. At 2:00, restrict access (quiese your application):

```
SAVLIB *ALLUSR SAVACT(*SYNCLIB) SAVACTMSGQ(QSYSOPR) ACCPTH(*YES)
       OMITLIB ( Name of Developer libs )
```

Monitor the program for the checkpoint message. At the 3:15 a.m. checkpoint, allow access back to the system:

```
SAVDLO
SAV
```

This provides your organization with a full backup for recovery nightly (minus the restricted-state component), as the backup window is large enough to facilitate this operation. Testing must be performed on the user checkpoint to ensure the window does not exceed the acceptable maximum allowed. An option would be to save developer or test libraries as a second step, post-SAV command-level processing to reduce checkpoint times. Allow enough memory for checkpoint processing to complete. Combine this with the weekly option 21 full system save and you can recover everything on any given day of the week.

Backups for Planned Maintenance Windows

Use option 21 (the full system save) to back up your entire system before you perform an upgrade to a new release of OS/400, or apply program temporary fixes (PTFs) with a Cume package. That way, if something goes seriously wrong with your planned upgrade, you have a means to back out. A complete option 21 save should also be performed after every major system change. Getting a time window from the business large enough to perform this save is very tough. It requires plenty of negotiating, for example:

- Option 21 (save entire system): 7 hours
- Option 22 (save system data only): 40 minutes
- Operating system upgrade: 6 hours
- Cume package load: 2 hours
- Second full system save (critical): 7 hours

For installations that have a window like this one about twice a year, the second save is recommended because you will not likely get another special outage window. If a disaster occurs prior to another full option 21 save, you will not only be recovering from a disaster, but you will be forced to perform the very same operating system upgrade all over again. This would not go over well with the business! When trying to get a big enough backup window, stress the importance to the business of the second full save and the risk of waiting months to get another chance to perform an option 21. It's a game of rolling the dice and unacceptable risk. Management should see the light when it's described this way.

IBM's Virtual Tape Solution (VTL)

IBM introduced the virtual tape library (VTL) in the base operating system in V5R4. As shown in Figure 6.5, virtual tape is exactly the same thing as physical tape, except that you save your data to disk rather than physical tape media. Do not confuse this with save files. Unlike using save files (*SAVF), virtual tape mimics all aspects of physical tapes and physical tape drives. This allows you to save more than one library at a time. More importantly, you can use special save parameters, like *ALLUSR. This permits you to later duplicate these volumes to physical tapes. Now you have a copy resident on the system during the daytime for near-line restores, and a duplicate copy offsite to support disaster recovery best practices.

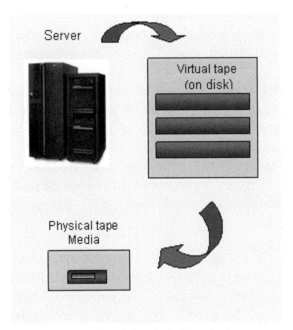

Figure 6.5: Virtual tape mimics physical tape in all ways.

Benefits of VTL

Virtual tape provides the following potential benefits:

- Increase backup performance.
- Run concurrent or parallel backups without buying more drives.
- Eliminate many save-file restrictions.
- Eliminate the impact of media errors.
- Eliminate the impact of tape hardware failures.
- Provide a backup strategy for quick restores.
- Ensure SWA processing completes by eliminating a tape drive failure.

Have you ever had a System i5 administrator forget to mount a tape before going home, only to have the system page you at 2:00 a.m. that the backup now sits in a message wait? This is not very accommodating to your beauty sleep, and you are forced to either drive in and mount a tape, or cancel the backup. (The most popular choice is usually to cancel the backup.) With virtual tape, you can specify up to 256 volumes, and never cross this bridge again.

As tape media gets older, the occasional media errors will cause the backups to fail. You are then faced with restarting the backup, which is typically difficult within the maintenance window. If you use save-while-active, you would have to start from the beginning to obtain another checkpoint. Virtual tape uses disk as the underlying media, which is typically protected by RAID5 or RAID6, or mirroring protection. Errors that occur during virtual-media duplication don't affect the production application, so they are typically less of a concern, but still need repair.

With physical tape drives, the nightly backup window would be affected if a tape drive breaks down or becomes unavailable because it's allocated to another i5 partition. With virtual tape, the backups can still be run to virtual volumes as scheduled. The duplication to physical media can be delayed until the tape drive is repaired by an IBM CSR.

Lastly, those expensive, time-consuming tape recalls from your offsite storage supplier can be eliminated, at least for data restores from the past 24 hours. By storing the virtual tape volumes on disk even after tape duplication, restores can be performed quickly, as the data reside on disk. Virtual tape volumes are unloaded and removed before the next backup is scheduled to run. The actual physical tapes are moved to offsite storage in case of a system or site loss. Remember, virtual tape is not meant to eliminate all your physical tape copies. If you lost your system due to a disk crash, you would still need tapes.

VTL Summary

If you have available disk space, virtual tape can be a simple, effective solution for saving and restoring your data. I like this solution because of the reduced impact of media errors and hardware problems during the saves. Additionally, new strategies can be devised where virtual volumes are used for onsite restores rather than recalling duplicate offsite tapes. This solution works very well with BRMS.

In addition, there are many third-party, vault-to-vault VTL software solutions using SAN device storage arrays to house tape images created by BRMS or native CL. These products work in conjunction with your backup design process. They support an externally attached SAN device to the i5, which looks like an external tape drive. In a two-tier system as in Figure 6.6, where you have a local and remote vault, this can be an effective backup and offsite data strategy, as well as a good backup solution.

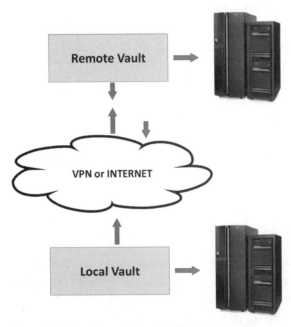

Figure 6.6: A two-tier system using VTL.

Duplicate Your Removable Media

It's never a good idea to depend on a single copy of a backup for server or data recovery. While tape media can have a long life, it is susceptible to environmental and physical damage. Most people tend to perform nightly backups and then ship those same tapes offsite the next morning without any tape verification process. The recommended best practice is to duplicate backup tapes and then send the original copy offsite. It is important that this process be executed by reading the original backup tapes and writing a copy rather than simply using an OS or third-party software feature to create two similar and potentially faulty tapes. This has the benefit of both verifying that the backup data is readable and eliminating the single point of failure of the backup tape.

The reason most often given for not having a duplication policy is lack of time. "My backups take too long to execute, and it is impossible to duplicate the data in a timely fashion." There are a number of ways to address this issue. First, the original backup runs during the designated backup window. The second copy can be made outside of the backup window, thus not affecting the system planned outage time. IBM's many high-performance tape drives, and the ability of many backup product solutions to stream to multiple devices simultaneously, makes this very achievable. Also consider the increasing popularity of disk-based devices, like VTLs. There is no acceptable excuse for not maintaining a redundant copy of backup data either on tape or disk.

Restoration Commands

With every save strategy, also consider the restoration commands required to restore a file or the complete system in a disaster. Table 6.1 displays the save commands with their corresponding restore options, while Figures 6.7 and 6.8 represent the restore commands graphically.

Table 6.1: Relationship between Save and Restore Commands	
Save Command Used	**Possible Restore Command**
SAVLIB LIB(*NONSYS)	RSTLIB SAVLIB(*NONSYS) RSTLIB SAVLIB(*IBM) RSTLIB SAVLIB(*ALLUSR) RSTLIB SAVLIB(library-name) RST
SAVLIB LIB(*ALLUSR)	RSTLIB SAVLIB(*ALLUSR) RSTLIB SAVLIB(library-name) RST
SAVLIB LIB (*IBM)	RSTLIB SAVLIB(*IBM) RSTLIB SAVLIB(library-name) RST
SAVLIB LIB(library-name)	RSTLIB SAVLIB(library-name) RST
SAVSECDTA	RSTUSRPRF RSTAUT[1]
SAVCFG	RSTCFG
SAVSYS	Restore Licensed Internal Code Restore operating system RSTUSRPRF RSTCFG RSTAUT[1]
SAVDLO	RSTDLO RST
SAVSYSINF	RSTSYSINF

[1] The RSTUSRPRF command restores authority information to temporary tables. The RSTAUT command re-grants private authorities using tables that are built as a part of the RSTUSRPRF command.

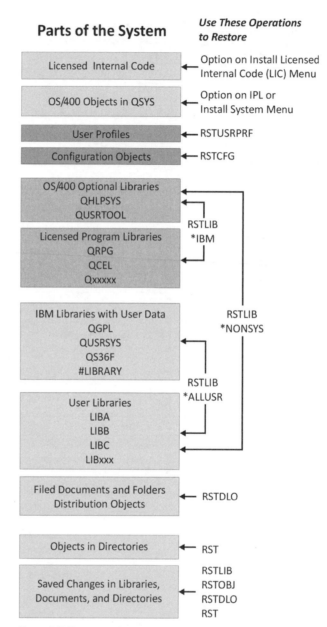

Figure 6.7: Recovery elements.

The BRMS System Recovery Report

When you back up your system using BRMS, information about each backed up item is recorded in the save history within BRMS. The information in the save history is used to create a recovery report, which steps you through a full system iSeries/400 recovery. Because of the critical nature of this BRMS recovery report, it is vital that you take a few precautions to ensure that this information is current and accessible when you need it.

You cannot use your recovery report alone to recover your system. You must also have the recovery information for your recovery to be successful. This is what I refer to as the "System Information" section of your disaster recovery plan. This report alone does not document server configuration details.

The BRMS recovery report does not tell you how to configure your disk setup, partition profiles, or recover License Internal Codes and the operating system. Your recovery is only as good as your backup, so be sure to test your backup and recovery strategy any time you change it, by doing a full system recovery. You might need to adjust your strategy to ensure that both a mid-week and weekend full recovery is possible. Test your recoveries at a disaster recovery hotsite, or by using a test system. It should be obvious, but I will advise you anyway *not* to use your production system for testing.

Send the BRMS recovery off your system. In a disaster, your iSeries will not be available, and you will not have access to the print queue containing last night's recovery report. Print your recovery report every time you do a backup, and send it to your offsite storage location. Email a copy to another server not located in the same facility as your iSeries/400.

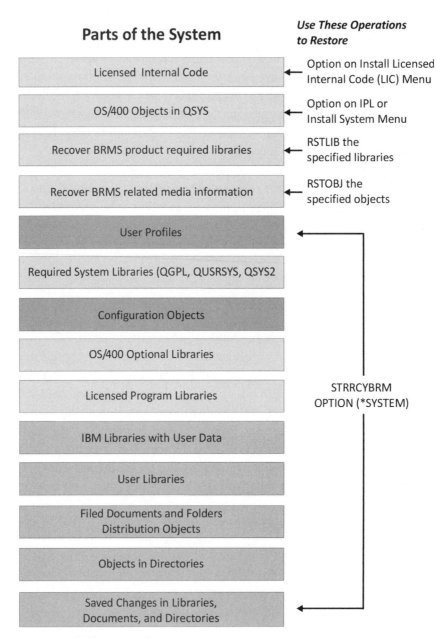

Figure 6.8: BRMS recovery elements.

How the System Restores Access Paths

When you restore a file, the system either restores the access path with the file or rebuilds the access path based on the information in the file description. The process of rebuilding the access path for a large database file can take quite a long time. The system always restores the access path for a keyed physical file of type *DATA, unless the access path was not saved. The access path for a keyed physical file should always be saved.

Access paths that are owned by logical files are restored if all of the following conditions are true:

- The system saved the access path.
- All based-on physical files are in the same library and are being restored at the same time by the same restore command.
- If the logical file exists on the system, it does not specify MAINT(*REBLD).
- The logical file owned the access path at the time it was saved.
- If the logical file is created again by the restore operation and it shares an access path that already exists, the key length for the access path must be equal to the maximum key length of the logical file.

If you meet these conditions, you minimize the rebuilding of access paths. However, during the restore operation, the system checks the integrity of each access path. If it detects any discrepancy, the access path is rebuilt . . . again!

Backing Up and Recovering a Domino Server

The Domino product resides in libraries in the QSYS.LIB file system on your iSeries server. All of your Domino databases sit in the Integrated File System (IFS), in a directory path that you specify when you configure your server. Your backup strategy for your Domino server should include saving both the libraries (infrequently) and the database directories (frequently). You must consider the need to both recover from a server-related disaster and restore a specific user mailbox.

If you are faced with a system disaster, you must restore your entire server from an option-21, full save backup. This is the most convenient and easiest scenario. If a mid-week disaster occurs, you must ensure all the Notes databases and directories in the IFS are fully saved using a save-while-active checkpoint to get the data image nightly. You must restore objects in the correct sequence to rebuild the proper links between objects; otherwise, Notes will simply not work. I recommend using BRMS in a Notes environment to ease the support of this tricky application.

When backing up Domino databases while the server is active, you *must* adhere to special considerations to avoid recovery failure. Users are always online retrieving or sending mail. With users demanding true 24/7 access to Domino e-mail and other databases, it is a technical challenge for IT.

For Domino servers, BRMS can perform online backups for Notes database files that have extensions of ns*, nt*, and .box. When Domino is installed on a system, BRMS creates the necessary control groups for online Lotus server backup. Once these Lotus server control groups are created, you start your backup by using the Start Backup Using BRMS command (STRBKUBRM) for the control group containing the Domino server (or servers) you want to save. The BRMS Domino backup then saves your database as a BRMS package, which includes the active Domino database as well as a secondary file that contains all the changes that occurred during backup, like transaction logs and journal-type information.

Run a full system save at least once a month along with your Domino BRMS online backup. I recommend performing a full Domino online (active) server backup, as it has superior restoration capabilities compared to an incremental backup. A full online backup saves the Domino server's databases and templates while the server is active. Since the Domino server is active, there might be occasions when BRMS cannot access a database to save it. This is the exception, not the norm, of course. However, since this can occur, you should monitor the logs after a save to confirm that the save completed normally with no errors. Normal compliance checks should also be in place.

The advantage to this type of backup is that users can continue working while the backup is running.

A full online backup can be run daily, as shown here:

```
                BRMS Control Group for Full Online Domino Server

        Group . . . . . . . . . : QLTSSVR
        Default activity . . . . . *BKUPCY
Text  . . . . . . . . . . Online backup of all Lotus servers

        Backup
 Seq    Items      Exit command

   10   *EXIT
   20   *EXIT    QNOTES/SAVDOMBRM SERVER('NOTEQ') TLGRP(QLTSSVR)
   30   *EXIT

                Save Domino Server using BRMS (SAVDOMBRM)

 Type choices, press Enter.

    Server name  . . . . . . . . . > 'TEST'
    Control Group  . . . . . . . . > QLTSSVR    Character value
    Files to omit:
    Files to omit  . . . . . . . .   '*NONE'

 Type of save . . . . . . . . . .   *FULL      *FULL, *INCR,
                                    *PREINCR
```

In addition, a monthly full dedicated backup is recommended to save all objects in the Domino data directory, including those not saved by the full online backup, such as ID files and configuration files.

211

Restoring a Domino Database

If you need to restore a Domino database from media to its original location, you can use the Restore Object Using BRMS (RSTBRM) command, as shown here:

```
RSTBRM DEV(TAP01) OBJ('/notes/data/database.nsf')
```

RSTBRM restores the database, along with any journaled changes or transactional logs.

Domino Control Groups

Control groups, shown in Table 6.2, are initially created within BRMS during initialization, using the INZBRM * DATA command.

Table 6.2: Domino Control Groups		
Name	**BRMS Element**	**Description**
QLTSSVR	Control Group	Back up all Domino and Quickplace servers.
QLTSDOM*nn*	Control Group	Back up databases for Domino server number, where *nn* equals the Quickplace or Domino server number instance, from 01 to 99. The description will contain the server name.
QLTSQPL*nn*	Control Group	Back up the databases for Quickplace server *nn*. The description will contain the server name.
QLTSSVR	Media Policy	The policies that represent the media class and tape retentions to be used for Notes server backups.

Domino Backup Lists

Domino backup lists are shown in Table 6.3.

Table 6.3: Domino Backup Lists		
Entry name	**User List**	**Description**
*LNKOMTONL or QLTSEXCL	QLNKOMTONL	Link list includes all the files in the IFS except Lotus server databases.
*LNKOMTLTS or QIFSXCLLTS	QLNKOMTLTS	Link list excludes all Lotus server data directories from the backup.
*LTSOMTONL or QLTSXLCONL	QLTSOMTONL	Link list includes all Lotus server data directories and excludes the online backup lotus server database.
*LINK	QLNKOMT	Any directories can be specified or excluded from a *LINK backup by adding them to the QLNKOMT user-modifiable list.

Hardware Management Console (HMC)

If you are using the Hardware Management Console for eServer (HMC), you must back up the HMC as shown in Figure 6.9. This is in addition to using the GO SAVE option 21 to obtain a complete save of your system. In disaster recovery, a systems administrator can use an appropriate recovery CD and the Critical Console Data backup to get the HMC back to the state it was in prior to the failure.

It's important to maintain a current Critical Console Data (CCD) backup to use in recovering the HMC after the loss of a disk drive or HMC. Whenever you go to a new version of HMC code, or use a Recovery CD to update the HMC, you should create a new CCD backup immediately. The same is true if you update HMC code between releases using the Corrective Service files downloadable from the web. Create a new set of CCD backups after the update.

Maintain a current Critical Console Data backup. If you use Recovery media to update your Licensed Internal Code to a new release level, make a new

CCD backup after the upgrade process. A CCD backup created at V4R3.0 will not work on a system that was upgraded to V4R4.0 using a Recovery CD. However, if you are trying to recover after losing a disk on a system that was updated using the Corrective Service files, you can use a CCD backup (created at V4R4.0) with your V4R3.0 Recovery CD. With the HMC, you must be very respectful of the rules.

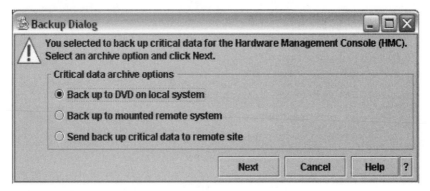

Figure 6.9: Backing up the HMC.

For additional details about the HMC backup and restoration, visit the System i5 Information Center at *http://www.ibm.com/eserver/iseries/infocenter*.

Here are good HMC practices:

- Run the initial backup (two copies) and send the DVDs offsite.
- Use the HMC scheduler to run the HMC backup daily or weekly on another DVD. It will keep overwriting the same DVD until there is a change in hardware or the code is updated or upgraded.

Summary

Backup strategies reflect the critical nature of the data. A system outage should make you reflect on the methods used in backing up the data, and how long it would take to restore that data—if you could restore it at all. When selecting a backup strategy, consider the time needed to back up versus the time needed to restore, and choose a method that fits your organization's needs.

Always build your backup strategy based on your recovery needs. By determining what data needs to be protected, what media to use for that protection, and sending the tapes offsite, you can create and maintain a reliable backup system for your organization. Such a backup system will ensure a successful recovery from a disaster. The bottom line is that even though the iSeries or System i5 seems fault tolerant and never fails, a solid backup and recovery strategy is still vital to protecting data.

7

Your Business Value of Systems Availability

When disaster recovery first emerged as a formal discipline within IT, the focus was strictly limited to the data center. Secondly, the emphasis was limited to only protecting against complete loss of the primary site. The computer room (the data center) represents the heartbeat or pulse of corporations. Today, IT has become embedded in virtually every aspect of your business. Computing is no longer something done in the background. Instead, critical business data can be found throughout the enterprise. This includes everything from large mainframe-size System i5s to local desktops, Intel servers and LANs located in the computer room. The flow of information spans many systems today.

Key business initiatives such as Enterprise Resource Planning (ERP), supply-chain management, Customer Relationship Management (CRM), and e-business have all made continuous access to information crucial to every organization. This now means your business can no longer function without information technology and its data. When information or access to it is not available, you have downtime.

Pressure to meet customer needs comes from many sources:

- Required support of both internal and external service-level agreements
- Just-in-time supply-chain requirements and penalties
- Pressure to guarantee service commitments from larger suppliers
- Strict and inflexible service-delivery-related penalties
- Tough government and industry controls
- Compliance and regulatory requirements

Until recently, the disaster recovery and system availability benefits of iSeries high-availability solutions have been reserved mostly for large enterprises. These large companies were the only ones who could afford the total cost of ownership of true high availability (*H/A*). They were the only organizations not willing to accept the risk of downtime in their business. This has changed to many other business models within corporate America. Hence, a significant paradigm shift has recently occurred in the iSeries disaster recovery world, making high availability much easier to use and dramatically less expensive. This became possible with a combination of lower hardware investment from IBM with the System i5 and Capacity Backup models, a huge market shift in the declining cost of data communications, and the significantly reduced price reduction in high-availability software with recent vendor mergers.

It is no secret that in the past few years, iSeries and i5 machines have packed significantly more CPW for the dollar. The new available configurations and pricing model of the iSeries lend themselves very well to buying a second machine for high availability. In addition, IBM periodically offers rebate and discount incentives when models are purchased with high-availability software.

The timing could not be better for the industry. Downtime has never caused more visibility when any form of disruption occurs, thus causing great expense for companies everywhere. The decreasing cost of high availability and the increasing cost of downtime to your organization is giving small and medium-sized companies (*SMBs*) the incentive to reevaluate high-availability solutions. Can you afford to make the investment in an H/A solution, or can you afford not to have the solution?

High Availability—Take the High Road

The goal for companies with no business tolerance for downtime is to achieve a state of business continuity, where critical systems and networks are continuously available, no matter what happens. For those organizations, data is something they just cannot afford to lose access to.

Data is the backbone of today's corporations and is probably your organization's most valuable asset. Therefore, immediate recovery and access to data during any type of outage is the key driver to business survival today. When data is lost or damaged, or simply unavailable, it negatively impacts your organization. It can potentially halt your business, so the success of business is directly tied to the availability of your computer systems.

In today's business world, your doors are open 24 hours a day, 7 days a week, 12 months of the year. You are always open because your customers say so! Somewhere in your enterprise, you are shipping, manufacturing goods, or getting an order from a customer either online or in person. Behind the scenes, you are probably completing all the financial elements of the sale somewhere, as well. Your organization has invested heavily in IT infrastructure because of their increasing need to rely on technology to sustain revenue and build profits.

Business continuity is directly linked to systems availability. It's all about the ability to manage the impacts of a disaster and lessen those impacts in terms of computer downtime. More precisely, it must be about the ability to meet your organization's commitments to its customers. It's about reliability, consistency, and dependability. Systems availability for your business can be a differentiating factor in today's highly competitive business world. It is also part of every organization's commitment to its shareholders, employees, customers, and suppliers.

Recovery on Your High-Availability Investment

When servers and mission-critical data are unavailable to your customers for whatever reason, you will have downtime. This usually means your business stops. When your business stops, it gets very expensive in a hurry. So, as dependence on technology grows, so does the cost of losing access to it. Downtime of any sort puts IT and business executives up against the wall.

Downtime comes in two forms: *planned* and *unplanned*. Unanticipated events—natural disasters of any kind, hardware failures, human error, fire, and power failures, to name a few—contribute to hard outages, resulting in disaster-related scenarios that cause great inconvenience to organizations.

Both planned and unplanned outages can negatively contribute to your company's bottom line. Customers everywhere, in every industry, are looking for solutions that go beyond typical high-availability practices; in other words, strictly disaster-recovery-related solutions. They need recovery time capabilities of minutes, not hours, and a recovery point objective of exactly where the application ended processing. Customers want coverage for planned and unplanned outages with minimal disruption to the end users.

The Business Impact Analysis tends to measure all unplanned downtime and its costs to the business. We focus on this because it is highly visible and considered a totally unacceptable business practice within our corporations today. However, the great majority of all downtime is planned downtime, as shown in Figure 7.1. Planned downtime accounts for 90% of all downtime, while the remaining 10% is attributed to unplanned events.

System i5 Planned vs. Unplanned Downtime

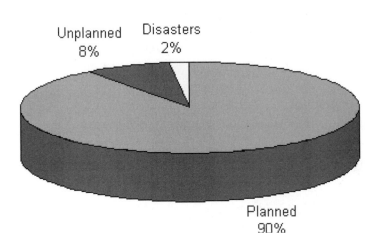

Figure 7.1: Planned and unplanned downtime.

These are the two ends of the systems availability and recovery spectrum: the old-fashioned tape-backup solution and the new age of high systems availability. The return on investment (ROI) helps your business executives decide which makes the most business sense. In the past, many felt the substantial financial investment to address just disaster recovery did not make sense. The capital expenditure to support a 10% probability did not give the organization a satisfactory return. However, another supporting argument for ROI is the serious consideration for planned outages.

As dependence on IT systems increases, so does the cost of not having access to it. Systems availability is not about the once-in-a-lifetime hardware failure. We all know and have heard about the legendary reliability stats for the iSeries/400. The iSeries/400 *never* goes down. Or does it?

iSeries/400 availability refers to all forms of downtime. We always seem to forget to include the number of hours in a year the systems are unavailable because of planned downtime. As disk farms increase in size, so does the time to back them up, implement operating system upgrades, perform PTF maintenance, and do housekeeping and database reorgs. These and similar events were always scheduled at night or on long weekends. Never forget to keep your software maintenance up to speed with IBM compliance and warranty support guidelines. You know that predictable message from the IBM support center, "Have you loaded the latest Cume level?" Of course, don't forget the time to run those dreaded batch month-ends. All these outages were only allowed to take place after serious internal negotiations— nothing short of begging for a window of opportunity.

Why eliminate planned downtime? Because:

- It's expensive.
- It's unproductive.
- It's mostly unnecessary.

By eliminating downtime, you improve profits, productivity, and performance.

Mitigating planned downtime can be fairly straightforward, but it can also quickly become very complex. A production server cannot be taken down, yet backups must be taken, various hardware and software upgrades must be performed, and housekeeping run. These activities are usually scheduled for a fixed duration of time and result in loss of system access or downtime for our users. In today's organizations, these considerations for planned outages just make your business cringe. The objective instead is to offer the organization a means to perform potentially disruptive tasks (such as backups to tape or operating system maintenance) with minimal impact on systems availability.

Planned downtime can be explained by breaking up the events into three primary groups, as Figure 7.2 shows:

- *Computer operations*—This includes activities performed regularly by your iSeries/400 administrators. These activities maintain the compliance of the System i5; ensure all the best practices that keep the box healthy and reliable; and perform backups, SQL maintenance, configuration activities, OUTQ and JOBQ management, reorgs, and other system dedicated administrative tasks.

- *Server maintenance*—This includes all IBM licensed program and third-party software activities (PTFs, Cume, or ERP application service packs, or even network changes).

- *Occasional non-routine events*—This would include deployment of new iSeries/400 System hardware, including new systems, new partitions, and disk towers. Also included are operating system upgrades, LPAR, RISC-to-RISC migrations, or major ERP upgrades. These all come with substantial planning, testing-related activities, and lots of lead time.

Planned Downtime

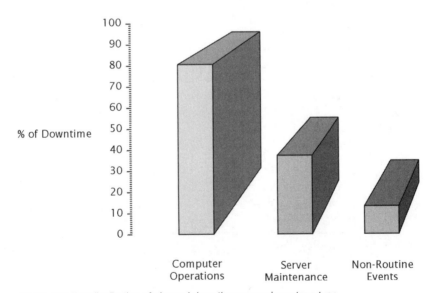

Figure 7.2: The distribution of planned downtime per major outage type.

Consider that the process of upgrading the server hardware and software is no longer a simple undertaking. With tough, rigid, and strict compliance controls in organizations, the risk-mitigation factor followed by any planned downtime is of the utmost importance. Can you afford to take the risk? Is the timing for this risk acceptable to the business?

Planned Downtime for Backups

Your system backups account for nearly 70% of the total planned downtime outage. The traditional backup window acceptable to the business continues to shrink, which can mean less data or system components backed up, while overall disk capacity continues to grow at alarming rates. Disk is becoming cheap, so you just keep buying more, and never archive. You know the result: your system auxiliary pool is growing, and there is no reason to believe it will stop anytime soon. The total time taken per year to back up the system is alarming. This can add up to many days of downtime per calendar year, as shown in Figure 7.3 for Company A.

Planned Outages per Year

Daily Backups
2 hours/day   12 hours/week or
6 times/week   624 hours/year

+ Weekly Backups
7 hours/save   7 hours/week or
4 times/month   336 hours/year
_____   _____

= Planned Backup   960 hours/year or
    Outages   40 days/year

Figure 7.3: Downtime per year for backups.

Combine the planned downtime for backups and other computer operations tasks with server maintenance and yearly events, and the numbers become even more alarming, as shown in Figure 7.4.

Additional Planned Outages

	Per Week	Per Year
Daily Backups	*12 hours*	*624 hours*
Weekly Backups	*7 hours*	*336 hours*
Server Maintenance		*30 hours*
Non-Routine Upgrades		*24 hours*
-----------------------------		-------------------
= Planned Outages		*1024 hours or 42.25 days/year*

Figure 7.4: Even more downtime for planned outages.

The 42.25 days per year in Figure 7.4 represents 11.58% of the time the iSeries/400 is unavailable to the business. Consider this total availability for your uptime stats; that represents an 88.42% uptime, which would be considered failure in most IT shops. There is a huge opportunity here.

Examine the planned impact and ROI for high availability to get most of this time back. Calculate not just the cost of downtime, but the opportunity for uptime. In this scenario, Company A can increase business productivity, reduce costs to the business, improve its IT infrastructure, and most of all remove risk from IT implementations. Use this method to determine ROI:

1. Calculate your planned downtime using the Company A example.

2. Total the complete downtime in hours or days as it relates back to your company's Business Impact Analysis.

3. Multiply this by the cost to be down per day/hour as supplied in the Business Impact Analysis. This is the *dollar value benefit* to your company due to productivity enhancements from your availability solution. The dollar value benefit can be the justification for purchasing a high availability and systems availability solution, or increasing additional technology to further enhance your systems availability.

4. Compare these savings to the costs of the solution to calculate your ROI. The numbers bring a new realization to the benefits of looking at the big picture.

What's the bottom line for Company A? The company has the opportunity to bring back 1,024 hours or 42.25 days of productivity to its business. This can be in whole or in part, but the benefits are substantial. Less downtime means more productive hours for your business. In addition, the added benefit of high availability and disaster recovery helps ensure that your company will be able to do business regardless of a planned or unplanned outage.

Server Maintenance Cost Benefits

With the length of all these backup window outages, approaching the business to ask for a long, scheduled system outage for system maintenance can be daunting. In the past, the business might have said, "IT department, you will have to wait three months or until the next long weekend for our outage." Now, however, long weekend outages are becoming unavailable. You might counter, "How about a shutdown at Thanksgiving?" "It's our busiest weekend!" the business replies.

How do you get a 20-hour outage? Is it a choice between stopping the business or falling out of IBM-support compliance? No. Just ask for two, 1-hour outages instead by using high availability, as shown in Figure 7.5.

Gracefully End System	20 Minutes
HA Software Processing	20 Minutes
Time Until System Active	20 Minutes
Total Time for Role Swap	60 Minutes

Figure 7.5: Server maintenance via H/A.

With H/A, you schedule a 60-minute outage to switch users from the source to target system and back. This keeps the business functional and is a much more reasonable amount of time to ask for. It also eliminates the risk created by IT to perform server maintenance tasks against the clock, possibly inaccurately, because of a reduced maintenance window. Instead, you switch the business to the target server and perform all the maintenance activities in a safe, controlled manner, while reducing the outage from 20 hours to 2 hours. With examples like this, the business will realize the immediate value of a high-availability implementation.

Workload Balancing Cost Benefit

When you implement the traditional two-system iSeries/400's solution to perform the roles of target and source in your high-availability architecture, you must consider the fact that the target system is basically running idle. Yes, we just discussed performing role swaps to eliminate planned outages for system maintenance—both software and hardware related. However, you have the potential to take advantage of lots of additional unused CPWs. In Figure 7.6, Company B has implemented an AS/400 Model 870 to support their disaster recovery objectives. This is a medium-sized solution supporting a production server of 10,000 CPW.

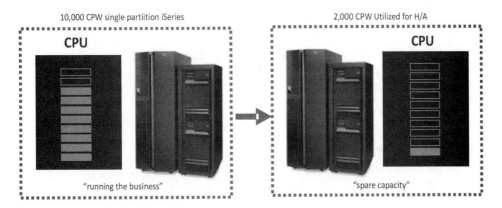

Figure 7.6: A two-system architecture.

Here are some workload-balancing options for the target or backup server that has spare capacity:

- The backup database is locked for update.
- Run query and reports on the backup server.
- Run test environments on the backup server.
- Run development environments on the backup server.
- Test OS upgrades on the target server.

Using the target server can accomplish two things for your organization. First, by moving query read-only processing to the target server, you extend the life of your production server by offloading some production CPW cycles. This means improved performance on the production server. Second, you can retire an old development server and use the target system. The result is to save you some costs. Determine how much cash you are "wasting" paying for IBM hardware maintenance and a software subscription when you could retire the old development box, and carve out a partition on the H/A target system, and use those cycles. In some cases, those dollars can be quite significant. Another consideration is to finally move those developers from your production system once and for all, to meet a key SOX compliance objective.

Any workload moved to the target server must be capable of being shut down should a production outage occur. No priority business applications can be run on this server unless the performance profile has been considered in a disaster. (A performance profile is shown in Figure 7.7.) You do not want to remove CPW cycles from the production user needs.

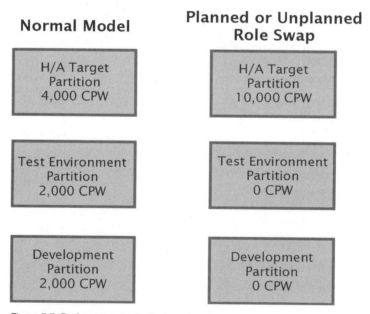

Figure 7.7: Performance profile for target and source.

Consider that fewer hardware footprints means:

- Hardware maintenance savings
- Less software
- Software subscription savings
- Software maintenance savings
- Ease of management because of a single point of control
- Technical resources

Today's high availability solutions are much more than simple IT insurance policies built strictly for disaster recovery. H/A is now an ROI-generating investment by your organization that will add value to the business each and every day. High systems availability solutions provide this value by enabling business to:

- Eliminate costs due to planned downtime.
- Save money and enhance profitability.
- Improve your business productivity.
- Sustain revenue growth and profitability.
- Minimize risks by managing planned downtime.
- Support unplanned downtime interruptions.

An information-availability solution will enable iSeries managers to better align IT with the company's business goals and objectives while enhancing the value of your existing iSeries investments. Not only does it provide benefits to the business, but it also protects the business from a potential disaster. As dependence on the iSeries/400 grows, so does the cost of losing access to it. Hardware does occasionally fail. Disasters do actually happen. Systems availability is not just a hardware, software, or design solution. It is a combination of everything.

Use H/A to get higher productivity with a totally flexible iSeries/400 infrastructure.

Real-World Example

I had a client in Mexico City, Ricardo, who for years resisted a high availability disaster-recovery solution. He insisted he did not need to worry about a disaster, as his company was situated well outside the city infrastructure, with all the amenities. His neighbor was a propane plant. Many times a month I would hear a boom as a canister ignited, followed minutes later by the sounds of fire trucks. However, Ricardo never saw this as a risk that affected him directly.

On wrapping up my consulting work in Mexico, I went to see how things were with his company. He mentioned to me that ever since I convinced IT to back up the system "properly," all the sites were down two hours every night: 20 plus downtime hours, total. He could not make, ship, nor sell product. When I explained that the system availability of an H/A solution could give him back those 20 hours a month of lost business productivity, he purchased H/A on the spot.

It is all about explaining benefits to the business. Ricardo saw the ROI instantly when it pertained to his business, rather than the relatively small chance of a disaster.

Cost Justification

Here is an ROI summary for H/A:

- Run your nightly backups from the target H/A server.
- Run reports from the target H/A server.
- Run queries on the target H/A server.
- Move development to the target server.
- Run your Web server on the target server.
- Build a data warehouse on the target server.
- Purchase a CBU edition from IBM.

Your high availability solution provides the system availability values shown in Figure 7.8.

Prevent downtime from site loss or disaster Yes / No (Depends)	YES
Prevent downtime for tape backups	YES
Prevent downtime for OS upgrades and system maintenance	YES
Prevent downtime for application upgrades	YES
Prevent downtime for housekeeping (reorgs)	YES
Prevent downtime from hardware failure	YES
Workload distribution	YES

Figure 7.8: H/A system availability to your business.

The last and most important consideration is to obtain senior management's understanding and agreement with your planned and unplanned downtime cost estimates and required Recovery Time Objective (RTO) and Recovery Point Objective (RPO) goals. Once you have established your budget, how quickly you need to recover key applications (RTO), and how much data you can afford to lose (RPO), you can select the appropriate technology solution. You will likely discover that traditional tape backup won't be good enough to achieve your RTO and RPO goals for your most critical applications. Solutions vary from shop to shop, but you must consider your acceptable loss of data and acceptable length of system outage. Those combined should drive your availability investment. I always say keeping the business up 365 days a year to support both disaster (unplanned) and non-disaster (planned) outages is a good return that even your CFO will recognize. Ask your CFO if he or she would like to get the system back 42.25 days per year. The answer, obviously, is of course!

Is Your H/A Truly High Availability?

High systems availability is not about just having invested capital expense into acquiring a second iSeries/400 server, regardless of how sweet the deal might have been from your IBM business partner. The H/A solution is also much more than simply setting up the hardware, IPL-ing the system, and loading a high availability software package. It's about designing a solution that's all encompassing. It includes networks, H/A software, and a fully monitored message-management solution. And, of course, it needs to be completely tested over and over again. Business disasters happen any time, anywhere.

You do not need a catastrophic local or regional event to have a disaster. In fact, most disasters can be as simple as a corrupted database, a bad PTF install, or a complete network failure. These scenarios can negatively affect the bottom-line profits of any organization. Consider both the serious financial impact after any disaster and the permanent damage to your reputation among your customers. Your reputation takes years and years to build, and one disaster can destroy it instantly. You can see, then, the absolute need for an implemented, H/A iSeries/400 solution.

High availability involves having redundant systems and a whole lot more, as discussed in the following pages. Having chosen a safeguarded method to manage your completely redundant solution, your iSeries is never unavailable. Yes, I am telling you it's never down, no matter what happens, planned or unplanned. It's a living process that you must care and feed to make 100% reliable all of the time. That's quite a statement to make to your business. Ensure you have not implemented or sold the executives on one of the following highly debatable myths.

Myth # 1: H/A Eliminates the Need for a DR Plan

"I have a high availability solution, so I do not need a disaster recovery plan."

Without a DR plan, how can you define what is a disaster to your organization? Forgot the obvious fire-and-rubble situation. That's easy, that's a disaster! Examine the potential for day-to-day incidents like a power failure or system loss due to a hardware failure. Are these disasters? What business functions are you supporting? Who is supporting them? Remember the classic "who, what, where, when, how" list:

- Who will execute recovery actions?
- What is needed to continue, resume, recover, or restore business functions?
- Where do we go to resume corporate, business, and operational functions?
- When must business functions and operations resume?
- How are continuity, resumption, recovery, or restoration done? What are the detailed procedures?

If you can completely and honestly answer these questions with confidence, you have the basis for a disaster recovery plan. More importantly, you will have a *complete* DR plan. Without any formal documentation and a documented supporting process, you rely strictly on human impulse and opinions and reactions. IT must rely on a proven methodology, agreed upon by both the business and IT. The choice should be obvious to everyone in your organization.

Remember, a DR plan is a set of processes developed specifically for your company. The DR plan outlines the actions to be taken by your IT staff to quickly resume operations in the event of any service interruption, as well as an outage. By establishing a firm list of detailed activities and actions to be followed, your organization will minimize potential losses incurred by downtime, planned or unplanned.

We fool ourselves by thinking disasters never happen to us. For years, I have had the opportunity to study disasters first-hand, and the one thing they have in common is that no one ever believed it would happen to them. As a disaster recovery planner, it pains me to see an organization take all the necessary steps to anticipate and invest in H/A supporting technology, develop the solution, and then be simply done with it, putting it on the back burner and assuming it will always work. Was developing the plan just a means to get an auditor off your back or deliver false hope to the business? Developing a plan and a solution does not guarantee success. You must test-drive the plan and the technology solution to ensure success. You must formally document the plan, and rehearse the documentation regularly to ensure that both the people and the technology can perform as advertised.

Having disaster recovery plan guarantees:

- Confusion
- Lack of direction
- Conflict
- Lost customers
- Potential business failure

Myth #2: Replicating = High Availability

"I replicate my database to another partition. It's another form of high availability!"

In the example in Figure 7.9, a single iSeries or System i5 is a logically partitioned server solution. This implementation is often referred to in the industry as *continuous systems availability* or *database replication*. Typically, organizations install this architecture to reduce and in most cases eliminate a backup window on their production system. Continuous availability allows you to use a high availability software solution to eliminate the downtime window on your system to perform daily and/or weekly backups. This solution is implemented using Logical Partitioning (LPAR) on the iSeries/400 to define a separate, dedicated logical partition on the same physical server.

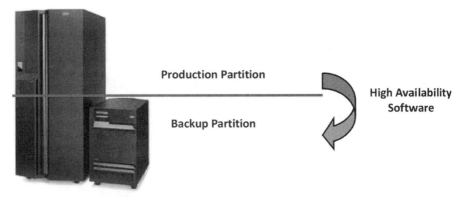

Production Partition

High Availability
Software

Backup Partition

Figure 7.9: A logically partitioned server solution.

This partition is referred to as the *backup partition*. There is typically no user access on this backup partition; its sole purpose is to house a mirrored copy of the production database and any other mission-critical libraries. This solution allows you to perform tape backups over the mirrored data, versus over the live production data.

Typically, only production databases are replicated to the backup partition. When it's time for a backup to take place, the tape activity occurs strictly on the backup partition. This allows the production partition to be available to the end users the entire time. It eliminates the need for users to sign off of the system to accommodate the backup window required to support IT operations. The business is happy because the system application is available. IT is happy because a backup is performed. The primary objective in this solution is to obtain 24-hour access to the production system Monday to Friday, and that is typically well achieved. To move this solution to the next level, you need to replicate far more than a single application database, and of course implement a second server in a second computer room, separated geographically from the first. A single point of failure is that both partitions are on the same system. If the system goes down, there is no application availability.

Myth #3: H/A Side-by-Side

"I fully replicate my H/A. Both boxes are in the same room."

Many organizations have implemented an H/A solution by placing both the production and backup iSeries/400 systems in the same computer room, in the same building. You are rolling the dice with this solution if you're trying to use it to meet any of the disaster-related objectives in your DR plan. That is why the example in Figure 7.10 refers to the organization's address as "222 Cross My Fingers Drive."

Building Address: 222 Cross My Fingers Drive

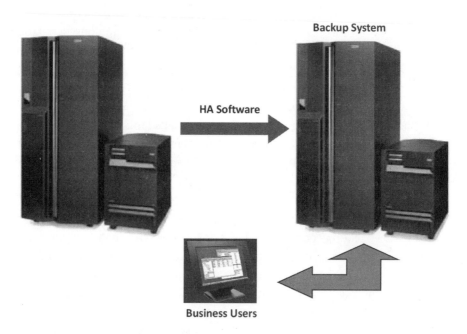

Figure 7.10: Side-by-side H/A is risky.

There are several reasons for this approach:

- The cost to build a second data center
- The cost to install environmental controls
- The lack of other available sites in the corporation
- Communication costs—latency
- Staffing

This type of implementation is a concern because the organization has implemented many components of an H/A solution, but avoided the potential primary basis for this solution: disaster recovery. Having both systems in the same location represents a single point of failure should a disaster occur. With both servers using the same power grid, sharing the same communications, and using the same physical infrastructure, you have severely decreased your chances of survival in any form of building or regional disaster.

Statistically, most disasters are power- and water-related. Having both machines in the same geographic location spells disaster and causes misconceptions in the business, which truly thought IT had a disaster recovery solution. This solution is a systems availability solution, but it does not meet any disaster recovery objectives.

There are several issues with a side-by-side implementation:

- A single point of failure
- A shared power grid
- The same central office for communications
- No alternative in a building or regional disaster

Real-World Example

A client had both the production and backup iSeries/400 H/A solution in the same office. This solution was sold to executive management as giving support to the business in a disaster. The client site supported 38 facilities, including manufacturing plants and sales offices throughout the U.S., Canada, and Mexico.

One week, this client had two close calls with a disaster. In both cases, the machines being in the same facility meant all 38 plants and sales offices were totally down. In the first situation, the telephone room was flooded under the raised floor without anyone's knowledge due to a washroom failure on the second floor. All 38 remote sites were down, but the local site stayed up. The water affected all external communications, including data and telephony. You can imagine how the corporate office looked on this one.

Later that week, the building lost power because of a traffic accident. One car lost control and knocked out a power pole. To make matters worse, the diesel generator was under repair. In this situation, both the local facility and all 38 plants and sales offices were down, even though they had a high availability implementation—so they thought.

This organization experienced a bad case of Murphy's Law, but it proved that what was purchased and implemented was by no means the H/A solution that was sold to the business. Needless to say, the target backup server was moved to a different facility the following week. However, the damage was done, and the reputation of IT was shattered.

If you are buying a second machine for the sole purpose of supporting your disaster recovery objectives, there is a statistically proven advantage to locating the server in another building across the city or state. By doing this, if a site disaster occurs in the building where the primary machine is located, the second machine will probably not be vulnerable to the same disaster.

So, the questions becomes how far is far enough. Three miles? Twenty? More? Consider generic guidelines adapted from the Army: err on the side of caution.

Companies with mission-critical System i5 servers supporting no tolerance for downtime must have appropriate DR measures in place. This must include having more than one data center. However, the answer is not to simply place the data centers as far apart as possible. Consider these important points:

- *Travel to a second data center*—When building an internally owned and managed data center or using a commercial solution, one of the first things to consider is the geographic location of the data center itself. Consider how close the staff needs to be to the second data center in an emergency. How quickly can your IT staff travel to the second location, considering alternative forms of transportation? Remember with 9/11, the entire air traffic control system was shut down for days. Traveling 3,000 miles by car is not feasible.

- *Location of second data center*—Evaluate all aspects of where the data center located, including such things as weather, natural threats, social factors, economics, and terrorism. Is your data center in a location prone to seismic disturbances or severe weather? Having the data center windows overlooking Miami Beach might look sexy, but consider the likelihood of facing a severe weather condition. It is safe to say the risk is very high and statically proven.

If your objective is purely systems availability and you want to localize the scenarios you are supporting, a nearby second data center is valid. However, you must be very clear to the senior executives in your company that this will *not* work in a site or regional disaster. You are providing a systems availability solution, not disaster recovery. Maybe a commercially available hosted and managed solution for your target system is your best alternative. Many IBM business partners provide hosting of a target server for H/A, such as Mid-Range, WTS and IBM, to name a few. You just purchase a single license of the H/A software of choice (with some restrictions from some providers), and the commercial vendor owns the target license. Now there is no need to spend the capital to buy a second system. Most importantly, the service is managed on your behalf 7/24/365.

Myth #4: Big Guy, Little Guy

"My target machine is 50% smaller. In a disaster, the users will understand. Anyway, it's only for a short time."

What is the performance profile of your production system, versus that of your target H/A solution? Some H/A implementations come about conveniently as a result of an old iSeries or worse, AS/400 hardware, as shown in Figure 7.11.

5,500 CPW
3.2 TB Disk

2,000 CPW
1.8 TB Disk

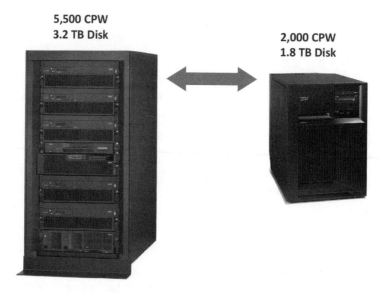

Figure 7.11: Does size matter?

The problem usually is that management decides to use the old, under-performing server as a target H/A box. It seems like a good idea until you consider the facts and repercussions. What happens, however, when you switch over to the old server? How do you think your business will react?

Does the size of the old AS/400 versus a new System i5 matter? Of course it does. If the previous machine did not meet your service-level objectives in the past, what makes you think it will in a disaster? Some IT managers will say in a disaster, the users will understand. Will the customers share the same sentiment?

The business will expect more in a disaster, not less. It's a time of crisis, and the solution you have installed will not work. You will have severe batch and system response-time issues when you switch from the production to the target server, in addition to the disaster that caused the switch in the first place.

Here are questions to ask when considering such a solution:

- Will end users accept poor response time?
- Will customers understand when it takes twice as long to turn around an order?
- What about your SLA?
- What about your contractual commitments?

Switching back to the (bigger) production system might become mandatory, not just convenient. That means a second outage, and fast.

Myth #5: H/A Takes Care of Itself

"My H/A is up and running. It does not need any special monitoring. It takes care of itself."

Once your H/A solution is in place, you need a mechanism to continuously monitor all of its related activities. As you can imagine, thousands of transactions are being replicated each and every hour, 24 hours a day. If there is any type of glitch in the system-to-system communications, like a timeout, a halt in any of the journaling components, or a halt in the journal-apply processes, one or more applications or data objects can easily lose synchronization. Now, replication is halted, and it awaits some type of manual intervention. This will immediately jeopardize the data integrity on the target system. Consider the time for the replication to catch up after a repair is finally made the next morning. It is critical, therefore, to have a monitoring process in place that ensures replication integrity 24 hours a day, every day. Replication does not take the weekend off! Otherwise, in a failure, your ability to switch to and use the backup system could be compromised. The solution might not be dependable, and you might therefore choose not to switch to it. High availability is a living, managed process, 7/24/365.

Replicating data only is not good enough. Here is what needs to be replicated and monitored:

- User data
  - » User and business data on the iSeries
  - » DB2 databases
  - » IFS
  - » Data areas
  - » Data queues

- Application objects
  - » Programs (iSeries objects used to access data)
  - » User profiles
  - » Passwords
  - » Configurations
  - » SQL stored procedures

Monitoring will ensure you always have object-level integrity. Several third-party solutions are available for systems monitoring. Another option is to use Management Central, which comes with your IBM V5R3 or V5R4 operating system. A useful monitoring process continuously monitors the status of all critical subsystem and object-level components. If a problem arises, a system alert can be generated, and an email message sent. You could even use some of the self-healing components of your H/A software to attempt to correct the problem first, and then send out an alert or simply a notification. This will support the validity of all system objects using object-level integrity. When something goes out of sync, you can use your H/A software solution to re-synchronize at the individual object, library, or link level, and mirror to the backup system the objects from the primary system.

High availability is a living process, where synchronization functions must always be checked to ensure application integrity. High availability monitoring should determine if an object on the backup system is out of synchronization with the corresponding object on the production system. If so, you should initiate a process for re-synchronizing the object, by recopying it from the production machine to the backup and applying all necessary journal entries to bring the file to a current status. Using automation and all the functional components of your H/A software, you will have a reliable go-to solution. Incorporate reporting into your system checklist for H/A integrity signoff.

Myth #6: That's IBM's Side of the Fence

"Does my target equal my source? I thought the H/A product takes care of that!"

Every vendor's H/A software solution supports the iSeries/400 differently, and every product has its own unique approach to high availability. Your job is to find out how your vendor of choice does or does not support various system user-level objects. Support for many of IBM's low-level components varies from vendor to vendor. The IBM component of the iSeries/400 infrastructure is outside of the boundaries of H/A software. You must separately maintain both the source and target systems.

On both the target and source i5, you must do the following:

- Maintain IBM system libraries.
- Maintain the same operating system level.
- Maintain the same CUME groups &PTFs.
- Ensure that any IBM applications installed on the source are installed on the target.
- Maintain the IBM job-scheduler entries.
- Ensure your H/A product supports all IBM LICPGMs.
- Mirror user profiles *only*, not "*Q" profiles.
- Ensure job queue contents are not mirrored.
- Allow special spool file considerations (not default).

Your use of IBM objects and libraries can affect your application availability in a peer-to-peer or cluster iSeries system solution. These are related directly to OS upgrade maintenance and affect H/A software. Consider the following guidelines:

- Do not place your own IT-customized objects into IBM libraries. When IBM delivers an operating system upgrade package, it might replace some objects in some libraries. Some releases will replace or combine several libraries. This is IBM's design, and they do not adhere to your specific user objects in their own library structure or upgrade process. If you don't identify and replace all of the objects you created through your change-control documentation, these objects might not exist after an operating system upgrade. This would hold true for both the target and source systems.

- Never modify IBM objects. Again, an upgrade could replace the object completely and destroy all your changes.

- Do not override QSYS or system commands. Stick with what works!

Myth #7: Communications Are a Given

"Can I get to the target system? Oh, my carrier and network folks take care of that."

Do not assume the network department in your organization will automatically configure or have in place network access to the target H/A system. You might think, "Well, the other servers in the second data center are on the network, so this should be a no-brainer." However, never assume anything. Network compatibility is crucial to the success of this solution. Secondly, you do not want the end users to have two icons on their desktops, one icon pointing to the production system and the other to the target. What are the odds that every user will know to click the second icon for system connectivity when an outage occurs? If you give the end users two roads, they will take the wrong one 9 times out of 10.

You want a seamless solution. That's why you have a network team. The network should resolve the IP address and route the end user to the system IT has deemed as production, regardless of the outage situation. Keep in mind all the network considerations for the network team:

- Configure multiple IP interfaces for switching on the same network segment.
- DNS change might be required if on a different subnet.
- Dual desktop-emulator icons for the target system might be required if DNS/interface switching cannot be done. (This is not desired.)
- Consider a dedicated DR segment, frame-relay PVCs, and firewalls.
- Is there a VPN alternative?

Also of great importance is ensuring everything related to connectivity is in place on the target iSeries/400. This is a joint solution; the network folks and the IT staff need to be on the same delivery page. Here are some additional elements to consider:

- LIN/CTL/DEV descriptions on the target
- Dial-out lines
- Fax connections to the iSeries/400
- Device-switching for attached servers
- PCs and printers
- Twin-ax (Still alive out there!)
- External feeds
- Rerouting of key phone numbers

Myth #8: No Need to Test H/A

"I have had my H/A for years. It will work when I need it. Why test? Nothing has changed."

The most talented IT support teams do not assume "we have the skills" or "practicing would be a complete waste of time." Different parts of the team need to practice working together, to improve performance, determine what works, and most importantly plan for the unexpected. In the event of a systems failure, your high availability solution requires flawless execution and teamwork. The solution and the recovery team that executes its steps need to practice, or in IT terms, test. You might have the best procedures and personnel money can buy, but the whole reason you put the solution in place was to prepare for the expected (planned outages) as well as the unexpected (unplanned outages). Why would anyone assume that in the event of a disaster everything would run smoothly? Your staff needs to know in advance what actions they need to take and how to execute them.

The process of moving users from the production systems to the target or backup system is called a *role swap*. This is because the backup system essentially takes on the role of your production system during the time your actual production system is unavailable due to a planned or unplanned system outage. The first time you attempt a role swap, it is not unusual to spend extra time working out kinks in communications, user jobs, ERP interfaces, and H/A software components and steps. This is normal, as the requirements of every system are unique, due to different types of objects being replicated. It is vital that once you have the elements of data replication and system monitoring in place, you regularly test the role-swap process to verify smooth execution of the procedures and the integrity of the data on the backup system. Test that role-swap "run book."

Running your business on the target or backup system is the ultimate test. This means staying on the system beyond the test period, to actually run your business on it. Try this for a week, a month, or a quarter, and then role-swap back to the other server. If you can conduct your business on the target solution for weeks or months at a time, your organization is ready for anything. This will show both your business and auditors that you have a fully tested fail-over system implementation. So, getting that operating system upgrade outage is no longer a threat or risk to the business.

246

Once developed, the plan should be implemented, and then tested, tested, and tested again, on a regular basis to reflect the dynamics of your computing environments. Testing has several objectives:

- Ensure the accuracy, completeness, and validity of role-swap procedures.
- Verify the capabilities of the personnel executing the recovery procedures.
- Validate data integrity.
- Identify any weakness in your solution.
- Familiarize IT personnel with the role swap and its procedures.
- Test network recovery.
- Identify any weakness in the H/A implementation.

Making a management commitment to regular testing and validating your solution will protect your company against the greatest risk of all: complacency. Today's computing environments face rapid business and technological changes. The smallest alteration to a critical application or system can cause an unanticipated failure that you might not be able to recover from if you do not test. Test because your business depends on it. Backup and recovery can be a good experience if you plan and, more importantly, test.

Disaster recovery and high systems availability are considered by many corporations today as a necessary combination. A high availability solution on its own does not automatically support both disaster recovery and systems availability. You still must employ tape backup practices, role-swap testing, and disaster recovery planning.

Take the high availability approach:

- Ensure uninterrupted access for your users and customers.
- Provide the assurance that business can function.
- Provide a measurable value to your business by virtually eliminating downtime.

Ensure your business knows what IT can deliver. Management will, of course, want a solution that is available all the time, in a 100% working state. You have invested in the infrastructure, chosen your H/A software, stand behind the IBM iSeries/400, and are willing to sign off that this will work because you test it. Eliminate all those planned and unplanned outages. Show your business the financial benefits of H/A. Show them that they are getting a return on investment because you have eliminated all those planned and unplanned outages. Remember, your iSeries/400 is always open for business because your customers say so.

IBM's Capacity Backup Offering

Disaster recovery requires capacity, but the needs are completely different from H/A. While the capacity requirement to address disaster recovery is not permanent, it might be needed for an extended period. Recovering from a situation where the data center is damaged by fire or flood will take longer than recovering from a situation where no physical damage has occurred.

Given today's financial realities, IT can no longer afford to buy double the computing assets that do not provide a return on investment to the business. IT requires a new way of addressing its unpredictable capacity requirements without spending a large amount of capital. IBM has provided a way for IT to support today's on-demand world by providing for the iSeries "capacity backup on demand." IBM's *Capacity Backup* is a new line of system offerings that will help companies have a backup system in place if their primary server fails or becomes unavailable.

The iSeries' Capacity Backup offering is intended for companies requiring an offsite disaster-recovery machine at an extremely affordable price. Capacity Backup for the iSeries includes a minimum set of startup processors that can be used for any workload and a large number of standby processors that can be used at no charge in the event of a disaster. It's a great solution because you only pay for your day-to-day needs, and you do not get penalized in a disaster.

The new "iSeries for High Availability" server described in Table 7.1 is designed to meet the needs of companies seeking to minimize both planned and unplanned downtime events. This server features H/A software packages from iSeries ISVs DataMirror, Vision Solutions, and Maximum Availability. This server is targeted at companies that require 24/7 high availability. An additional production server is actively deployed as part of a strategy to provide workload distribution and regular role swapping. This allows you to go from very low to very high power, in the event you need to activate processing power for disaster recovery.

Table 7.1: iSeries for High Availability Server	
Primary System	**Eligible CBU System**
i810 1w, 2w	i520 1w
i825 3/6w	i550 1/4w
i870 5/8w	i570 1/4w
i870 8/16w	i570 1/8w
i890 16/24w	i570 1/8w
i890 24/32w	i570 2/16w i595 2/16w
I520 1w	i520 1w
i520 1/2w	i520 1w, i520 1/2w
i520 2w	i520 1w, i520 1/2w
i550 1/4w	i550 1/4w
i570 1/2w	i570 1/4w
i570 2/4w	i570 1/4w
i570 4/8w	i570 1/4w, 1/8w
i570 9/12w, 13/16w, 8/16w	i570 1/4w, 1/8w, 2/16w
i595 8/16w	i595 2/16w
i595 16/32w	i595 2/16w, 4/32w
i595 32/64w	i595 2/16w, 4/32w

Here are some of the benefits of these solutions:

- New flexibility enables CBU editions to support the full range of business resiliency requirements, from disaster recovery to high availability.
- Organizations may now permanently activate standby processors to support additional applications or high availability operations.
- Organizations may now use processors on a CBU edition to provide failover/role-swap for processors on its "paired" production system, without purchasing additional i5/OS licenses when the respective primary system processors are inactive.
- Organizations can start with low-cost DR, then expand to a full H/A solution.
- This provides a compelling cost case for in-sourcing H/A and DR.

Summary

Making a management commitment to regular testing and validating your high availability solution will protect your company against the greatest risk of all: complacency. Today's computing environments face rapid business and technological changes. Eliminate all those planned and unplanned outages. Show your business the financial benefits of H/A by obtaining a return on investment on systems availability. Remember, your iSeries/400 is always open for business because your organization is always open for business, because your customers say so.

8

Vital Records and Critical Data Offsite Storage

When responding to a disaster or complete site loss, it must be assumed that all vital records stored within your facility will not be available. Therefore, your vital records program must focus on supporting complete disaster recovery (loss of the primary site), rather than single server failure. In the loss of a critical server, the primary facility is still available, and the data center is functional. Any required onsite recovery CDs, tape backups, and procedures are easily accessible and available (provided they can be located easily and are not locked in some system administrators desk somewhere). The opposite is true in a disaster. Everything that could possibly be required to rebuild all your servers and supporting infrastructure in its entirety must be stored and made available at the offsite storage provider.

It is always best to use a third-party vendor to rotate and store the vital records, versus a home-grown solution. Always consider housing your vital records at a location other than within the walls of your own organization.

A vital record is defined as any form of the following:

- Procedural documentation
- Infrastructure server software
- Rebuild components
- Security
- Configurations data
- Server backups
- System information
- Utilities
- Data stored elements

All these vital records are required to support the complete recovery of all the IT mission-critical servers defined by your Business Impact Analysis (BIA). Typically, all IT-related vital records are initially developed inside the data center. Procedures are written by IT, servers are backed up and managed by IT, and all supporting IT infrastructure is built and maintained by IT. Therefore, it is a natural progression to assign the responsibility for coordination and management of the vital records program to your IT staff. This responsibility should not be in the hands of the front-desk receptionist or the warehouse receiver in the back office. Coordinating, gathering, and recording the daily vital records to be shipped offsite must meet the agreed-upon requirements of the disaster recovery plan. The review of the vital records inventory and management life cycle should be handled by the Technical Recovery team as charted in the DR plan.

During the BIA phase, you identified all the vital records associated with critical servers and the supporting business-related applications. To meet the primary objective from the BIA for vital records management, all vital records must be stored offsite with a bonded, offsite storage provider. Secondly, consider geographic separation between your primary data center location and the location of the offsite storage provider. The vital records should be stored at an offsite location no closer than 30 miles from your primary computing location. Remember the obvious: no data equals no recovery. Storing records across the street in another office building, although physically offsite, does not support geographic separation from the primary data center.

Vital Record Management

Vital records are the records necessary to reconstruct a company's business in the event of some form of iSeries or i5 system failure or complete site loss. In more detail, vital records can be defined as follows:

- Items necessary to rebuild a single or all critical (predefined in the BIA) application servers and infrastructure following any form of a disaster. (Remember, we're dealing with a disaster, not an incident.)

- Records required to assure that a company can meet its responsibilities and obligations to employees, shareholders, customers, and vendors.

- Items that identify the legal identity of the company.

- Records necessary to meet retention requirements as stipulated by HIPAA, COBIT, SOX, regulatory, or other compliance-based initiatives.

In most cases, a vital record will meet more than one of these criteria. Conversely, there might be some vital records that do not meet any of the above criteria, but are determined to be vital due to special characteristics they support in disaster recovery.

Vital Records Program Retention

A vital records program should be established to assist in your disaster recovery testing and primarily to provide support for a full-scale disaster. Vital records consists of such things as a disaster recovery plan, tape media, CDs, hardcopy scripts, reference materials, all documentation, rotating backup media, installation software, application software, and license agreements. When a need arises to recall your vital records, multiple generations or sets of backup tapes, CDs, and recovery documentation can all be automatically shipped based on a pre-set rotation to a specific location. There is no requirement to keep track of which tape volumes were used for the last night's daily backup, nor which tape volumes were part of the full system save performed on the weekend. This is extremely important when considering who might need to request this offsite information.

All tape backups are taken offsite and catalogued into physical and logical sets. Tapes can then be recalled individually or by a complete set. The simplest way to set this up is to file away all tapes from a previous night's backups by the date they were sent out, for example:

- On Monday March 18, 2007, volumes 394, 222, 146, 219, and 331
- On Tuesday March 19, 2007, volumes 224, 155, and 297

The full save is always sent offsite on Mondays, so the catalog name or set could simply be *MAR182007*. When called back, all the tapes listed (394, 222, 146, 219, and 331) get recalled automatically. This removes the need to know individual tape volume serial numbers. If the disaster occurred on Wednesday, the recall would include both MAR192007 and MAR182007. This means both the full saves and incremental saves would be recalled.

Consider the role of a data center manager. There is no way you could ever expect that this individual would know which specific tapes he or she would need to recover a server. I would agree that this person's operational knowledge would include the following:

- Daily backups are scheduled nightly at 02:00.
- Weekly backups run on weekends Sunday morning at 03:30.
- All backups have run successfully as checked off by Operations.
- The backup tapes are sent offsite daily by another individual.

The tape backup process can span through many levels of system administration. By implementing a vital-records management program, the data center manager could simply identify the server name and the date he or she wishes to recover from, and the rest would be in place to successfully ship the corresponding backup media and supporting information to the desired location. Without a predefined vital-records management program, the manager would have to know the specific tape media volumes required for recovery of the server. This is just not a realistic expectation; any individual would have to depend on additional site personnel to obtain this information. Consider whether this information would even be available in a disaster such as a complete site loss, when the information containing the tape listing is sitting in a binder on the i5 system administrator's desk.

The vulnerability assessment will identify all the vital records associated with the critical servers as defined in your DR plan. The vital records are linked directly to the Recovery Time Objectives (RTOs) and the Recovery Point Objectives (RPOs) agreed upon by your organization. A vital records program must focus on disaster recovery rather than a production failure, meaning that all data for recovery must be shipped daily to the offsite storage facility. It is always best to utilize a third-party vendor to rotate and store the vital records.

Onsite Storage Will Not Cut It

Keeping all your vital records onsite is a very risky practice. It is akin to Russian roulette: there are no winners, just losers. Yes, it might be cheaper to keep the backup tapes onsite rather than at a bonded offsite service, but the risks are just too high. You might counter with, "I have a fire-proof vault located right in the secured computer room that should suffice."

It's fire-rated, but is it waterproof? If it is waterproof, is it fire-rated? A vault purchased online on eBay or at the local hardware store usually is a recipe for disaster. These products will simply not make the grade when you need them most. Ask yourself, in a disaster, what will your facility look like? Would the onsite vault containing all your vital records survive?

**Real-World Example:
Can I Go in Just to Get My Tapes Out of the Vault?**

A client called in desperation after experiencing a fire in the manufacturing plant. The data center was located in the office building attached to the plant. Everyone was safe, and the fire was extinguished. The power was cut to the building, the diesel generator was turned off by the fire department, and nobody was allowed back into the building. This was now 18 hours after the fire, and the fire marshal had still not allowed building access because he was not available. He had another fire and rescue emergency in the city, and he could not even say when someone would come by.

The DR plan, backup tapes, and other critical hotbox materials were all in the onsite locked vault. The remotes sites were getting testy, as they required the systems to continue their work. This fact meant the entire company was down—all 22 remote sites, in addition to the head office and primary manufacturing plant. The client was not in a position to declare a disaster and go to the alternate hotsite because everything was stored onsite; theysimply had nothing to go to the hotsite with.

The fire marshal declared the building accessible again in 32 hours. The tapes were all fine, and the systems came up without incident. This was a scary situation, but a valuable lesson was learned.

It is very likely that vital records and backup tapes stored onsite will not be accessible or useable after a disaster such as a fire or flood. Consider factors such as these:

- Would site access be allowed into the building by the fire chief? Typically, no.
- Would the vault be damaged in the fire? Typically, yes.
- Would the tapes inside the vault still be readable after exposure to high heat? Typically, no.
- Did water get into the vault? Typically, yes.
- Did smoke damage occur? Typically, yes.

- Would the vault be accessible after the disaster? Maybe.
- Would the vault be a complete write off? Usually!

Some organizations look to storing all vital record information in a commercial bank vault, the "ultimate safe house." It might be safe, but consider accessibility issues. The bank provides convenience and safety during regular working hours, 9:00 a.m. to 5:00 p.m., Monday to Friday. What happens after normal hours of operation?

Real-World Example: The Safe-House Customer

A client's computer room was flooded under the raised floor. Needless to say, the entire room became electrically challenged. A complete electrical short occurred, rendering all the servers useless. The water was cleaned up, and all the replacement equipment was quickly procured. Servers were set up and ready for data restoration. Then the client hit a big problem. The backup tapes and supporting vital records were all stored onsite in the same building. This is not recommended, but the client argued that the building's owner and main occupant, from whom it leased space, was a bank with an 8,000-square-foot vault with ceilings 20 feet high. It was a mini Fort Knox.

The computer room failure occurred at 01:20 Saturday morning. The bank vault did not open until 10:00 Monday morning. Instead of having the systems already restored and ready for the users Monday morning at 09:00, the systems did not come up until mid-day Tuesday. That's 1.5 days of lost business. A total of 182 office staff were set home and an additional 26 were left to answer phones and take customer inquiries (mostly complaints). This could easily have been completely averted. Even though the company that experienced the disaster was a major tenant of the bank, there was simply no way to convince anyone to open the bank vault on a Saturday. It was time-locked to open precisely on Monday morning at 10:00. (The client did consider dynamite, but thought the better of it.) Talk about being helpless!

257

Ensure your organization establishes a business relationship with a bonded offsite vendor that provides you with 24-hour, 365-day access to your data, as shown in Figure 8.1. Also ensure this access is fully automated, and that you are clear with the provider what 24/7 means. Some vendors provide service after normal operating hours by oncall staff only, versus being fully staffed around the clock. This might be important to your organization.

Without data and the server infrastructure, you have no recovery. Always consider where you are storing your data for accessibility and security. Of course, this means not storing the tapes in your house!

As recent natural disasters have shown, an onsite vault is not a preferred way to protect data, since the tapes stand a very good chance of being lost with the servers in a disaster. For recovery purposes, it is assumed that all vital records stored within the primary site will not be available following a disaster event.

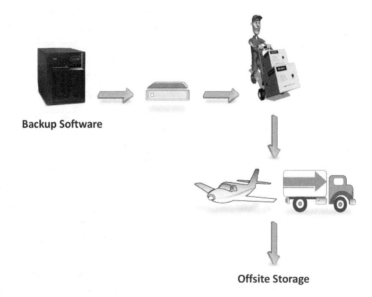

Backup Software

Offsite Storage

Figure 8.1: Store all vital records offsite, at a sufficient distance from the primary location.

All identified vital records should be stored at an offsite location no closer than 30 miles from the primary location. Proximity and access must be factors in deciding on the offsite location. Ensure your organization establishes a business relationship with a bonded off-site vendor that provides you with 24-hour, 365-day access to your data

What Is the Condition of Your Tapes?

The condition of your tape media can play a vital role in the success or failure of your backup strategy. I often find organizations that simply keep rotating the same old backup tapes, over and over again. When I ask why tapes are not being rotated out after use, the reply is, "Well, they never failed us in the past. At least, not that I am aware of . . . "

Tape media will physically wear out after extended use. Tape media will also deteriorate with tape mishandling, such as poor environmental conditions in tape storage or transport. These are facts. When reading and writing to tape, it is normal for some temporary errors to occur. You can determine if the tape quality is degrading by checking your specific backup-software tape-media usage reports or error log. Inspection of these reports typically reveals some intervention is much needed. Media errors on tapes need to be identified quickly, as they are becoming undependable and should be removed from your tape library rotations. This review process should be executed on regularly as part of the system administrator's work schedule. Consider it a compliance check.

A common tape-handling error is that tape internal labels (volume serial) are all labeled with a common default because of a custom CL program with the same name identifier. How does this happen? I find in many IT shops, the systems administrators are doing strictly what they have been trained to do: initialize tapes all the same way. Run the INZTAP command, and enter "Backup" for the internal volume name. You end up with numerous tape volumes all called "Backup" in this example. Yes, they have unique external barcode labels, but the external tape volume identifiers do not match the internal labels. When you view an error media report (PRTERRLOG * VOLSTAT) from the green screen, it is impossible to determine which tapes in the library are the damaged ones, as this reporting is based only on the tape internal labels.

The internal label must be unique and should match the external labels. Thankfully, with products like BRMS, it is not possible to have two internal labels with the same name. BRMS also manages the relationship between external and internal tape labels. If you choose not to use a tape-management solution like BRMS, you must consider the simple and obvious in manual tape-labeling procedures.

Just because you have written data to a tape, it does not ensure you can retrieve the data when you need it most. As a precaution, you can enable your backup software's "verify" option. After the files are backed up to tape, the tape is read and checked for data integrity. Although this will significantly lengthen the backup process, you'll sleep easier knowing you've made a good, retrievable backup.

The number of times a tape can be reused is determined by the type of media and by the specific manufacturer's recommendations. Never overuse a tape. It's all too common to intend to change tapes soon, but never do so. Always make sure that your tapes are in good working order. Imagine having to tell your CEO that an entire week's worth of company sales and related business activities has been lost because you tried to save the company $30 for a tape media cartridge! Validation of the tape backups' contents should be performed with an active DR test to ensure the backup completeness, that the tape media is readable, and that the contents meet the requirements for full server restoration.

Tape Drive Maintenance

All your tape drives and tape libraries must be cleaned regularly. The read and write heads collect dust and other foreign material that can cause errors when reading or writing to tape. The use of a new tape-cleaning cartridge is an important procedure to have in place, with a log sheet to record its use. As part of every vulnerability assessment, ensure that regular hardware preventative maintenance is also scheduled and that a tape drive firmware-upgrade program is in place. Ask yourself when was the last time you ordered a new cleaning cartridge? Are you still using the original unit that came with the tape drive?

Expiry Dates

Accidental scratching of data can occur when there is no standard in place for file retention. An expiry date can be placed on the internal label on a tape, thus causing the server to read and verify the date expiry information back to the system console. If an individual mounts a tape incorrectly or before the data on the tape has expired, a message is displayed stating, "Data exists on this tape. Do you wish to over write it?" The tape-write operation will proceed only after the system administrator or operator acknowledges the message and overrides it. All tape data cartridges deemed to be retained permanently should have the write-protect feature engaged on the physical cartridge itself.

Incorporating the use of expiry dates in the save process can significantly reduce errors and ensure your data is available when you need it most, in a disaster. Tape-management products like BRMS have excellent built-in tape expiry processes that move tape volumes back into a scratch pool when the data has expired automatically.

Rotating Your Offsite Tape Media

Equally strategic to a complete backup program design are your tape-rotation policies. Every organization needs to develop a tape-rotation scheme and decide where to physically store your tape media. Unfortunately, many companies store physical backup media on top of the very servers they protect, or in a so-called fire-rated safe, located in the server room.

Physical media needs to be stored offsite in a secure location from which it can be retrieved quickly if needed. To reduce costs for both media and offsite storage, a good tape-rotation scheme is essential. By reusing tapes after a predetermined period of time, tape-rotation schemes ensure that a minimum number of tapes are stored onsite.

Rotation schemes come in several flavors and complexities. The tape-retention procedure named *grandfather, father, son*, also referred to as *GFS*, is the strategy I recommend for offsite tape backup. GFS helps simplify tape handling by organizing your tapes into pre-set rotations for daily, weekly, and monthly backup tapes. In addition, you will introduce some custom backup jobs to complement the basic GFS strategy, like a yearly save or special archives backups.

GFS is by far the most widely used and effective rotation in today's IT shops. In this rotation scheme, full backups are performed monthly on Saturday, and the backup media is immediately stored offsite (grandfather). Weekly full backups are also performed on Saturday (father), and these, too, are moved offsite for a number of weekly cycles. (Five cycles are generally sufficient.) Daily incremental backups are performed Sunday to Friday (son) and stored onsite for the week of their use, and then moved offsite with the corresponding weekly backup on the same cycle schedule. At the end of a cycle for a set of tapes, they can be returned to the server and reused. Each monthly tape would be held for 12 months before being reused on the 13th month, or kept permanently (my recommendation). The weekly tapes would be held offsite for four weeks before being reused on the fifth week, and the dailies kept for 31 days and reused on the 32nd day. While this is a great system for data protection, keep in mind you will need to get those tapes back onsite for restoration purposes, which will increase courier and other costs.

Table 8.1 shows an example of the GFS tape rotation schedule. At first glance, you might think it is overkill. Maybe you are right, but it has sure helped save many of my clients looking to restore data for a specific file beyond the seven days typically stored in many IT shops. A tape rotation completes the need for disaster recovery, but it must also maintain the need for data retention for restoration purposes as well. When looking into how you are going to develop your backup strategy and rotation method, it is important to look at what data is on your system, how critical it would be if some data were lost, and how fast a system would need to be operational if the system became damaged or inoperative.

Table 8.1: GFS Tape Rotation						
Week 1						
SUN	MON	TUES	WED	THUR	FRI	SAT
Incremental	Incremental	Incremental	Incremental	Incremental	Incremental	FULL
DAILY 1	DAILY 2	DAILY 3	DAILY 4	DAILY 5	DAILY 6	WEEKLY 1
Week 2						
SUN	MON	TUES	WED	THUR	FRI	SAT
Incremental	Incremental	Incremental	Incremental	Incremental	Incremental	FULL
DAILY 7	DAILY 8	DAILY 9	DAILY 10	DAILY 11	DAILY 12	WEEKLY 2
Week 3						
SUN	MON	TUES	WED	THUR	FRI	SAT
Incremental	Incremental	Incremental	Incremental	Incremental	Incremental	FULL
DAILY 13	DAILY 14	DAILY 15	DAILY 16	DAILY 17	DAILY 18	WEEKLY 3
Week 4						
SUN	MON	TUES	WED	THUR	FRI	SAT
Incremental	Incremental	Incremental	Incremental	Incremental	Incremental	FULL
DAILY 19	DAILY 20	DAILY 21	DAILY 22	DAILY 23	DAILY 24	Monthly 1
Week 5						
SUN	MON	TUES	WED	THUR	FRI	SAT
Incremental	Incremental	Incremental	Incremental	Incremental	Incremental	FULL
DAILY 1	DAILY 2	DAILY 3	DAILY 4	DAILY 5	DAILY 6	WEEKLY 1

To implement the GFS backup and tape rotation solution, you need to allocate the following number of tapes:

- Twenty-four daily tapes ("son" tapes).
- Four weekly tapes ("father" tapes).
- Thirteen monthly tapes ("grandfather" tapes). These are not reusable; you need a new one each month. Many organizations store these tapes beyond 13 months, and even permanently.

Since some months have more than four weeks, it will take over 41 tapes for regular backups for one year.

How Long to Typically Store Tapes

It is important to observe both data protection requirements and data archival needs when deciding how long to store tapes. Always consider the need to recover an application file, such as Accounts Receivable or Sales History. Speak with the accounting and sales folks to find out how far back they would need access to any specific saved information. The answer might be to keep the daily backups available until a weekly is run, and keep the weekly backups until a monthly is run. Then, keep the monthly for 7 years, for IRS purposes. Others might say keep all daily backups until the close of the month or quarter. Now, it's 6 weeks to 14 weeks in duration. Server recovery has less lengthy retention needs, but multiple copy requirements to rebuild a server infrastructure from scratch. Figure 8.2 shows what corporate America is thinking when it comes to daily backup retention.

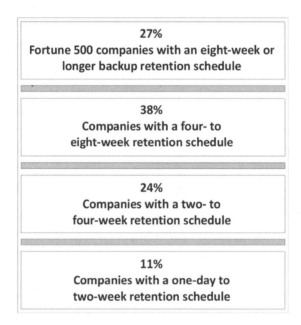

Figure 8.2: Daily backup retention policies vary by company.

Tape Media Management Policies

Media management refers to the handling, supervision, and controls of your backup tape media. The following items should be considered with regard to media management:

- Removable media should be tracked by barcodes, and reports should be generated on a daily basis detailing the current location of all backup tape media. A best practice is to report daily on tapes that are to be sent offsite and those that have expired and should be retrieved from offsite storage to be recycled or destroyed. All computer shops should document standard operating procedures to ensure that these steps are carried out.

- The offsite location and the process used to access the offsite storage should be analyzed for security concerns. Media should be placed in locked cases before leaving the computer room and subsequent tracking done at the case or container level. Cases of tape media should be signed for and should never be left unattended for someone to pick up, like in the back warehouse or front reception. Reconcile the inventory of media that is stored offsite on a monthly basis. At the end of each month, a physical scan of the offsite storage should be compared to the records of the BRMS to identify any inconsistencies. If the media is not accounted for, appropriate steps must be taken.

- Tape media cartridges contain mechanisms that are not exactly hardened against misuse. A dropped tape cartridge is probably a cartridge that won't subsequently work. How many times have you seen an operator with an armful of tape cartridges have two or three or all of them hit the floor? Accidents do happen. After a tape gets dropped, run a display tape command, or try to write to the tape to ensure it is still functional. (It would be great if media manufacturers could harden their cartridge design, or at least include a chemical indicator of impact and malfunction.)

- Once the media has reached it obsolescence or can no longer be relied upon for its integrity, it must be appropriately destroyed. There are services that will destroy the media, making it completely unreadable and environmentally disposed of.

- Dust is the number-one enemy of tape media and tape drives. To a magnetic tape drive's read/write head, a particle of dust is like a boulder on the freeway. The tape media and tape drive environment must remain clean and dust-free. A soft, static-free cloth should be used to clean the outside of cartridges, and dust should be removed from slots of a library or storage rack using compressed air. Tapes should be shipped in an electrostatic holder in a container, not piled into a cardboard box. Although appearing quite durable, tapes can be easily damaged by mishandling.

Another critical element in secure media handling is to ensure that your offsite storage vendor follows best practices. Here is a quick list of some of the things to consider:

- *Onsite vulnerability*—Pickup of tapes should be a standard operating procedure, where a responsible IT person hands over and receives a signature from a known (ID-carrying) vendor representative.

- *Barcode support*—The vendor should be able to understand barcodes on either your tapes or cases. This will allow the vendor to scan in the cases or tapes before they leave your facility, and scan them into the vault once they arrive at their facility. This will help to keep your tape inventory accurate.

- *Secure transport*—Talk to your vendor about the entire process of how your media is handled, from start to finish. Look for an emphasis on physical security, and audit and control mechanisms to ensure that the process is being followed. It is inadvisable to move sensitive data from point A to point B in a truck or vehicle with the vendor's name, easily identifying it as carrying sensitive data.

- *Container vaulting*—Container vaulting is when you send the vendor a box of tapes, and they track only the case or box. They should support this type of vaulting.

- *Individual media vaulting*—Individual media vaulting is when you send them a case of tapes, and they track each piece of media in the case. They should support this type of vaulting.
- *Environmental controls*—Tapes and other media should not be stored in a vehicle's trunk, or any other non-environmentally controlled location. If a vendor is going to be storing your tapes, the environment must be strictly managed, including temperature, humidity, and static controls.

Offsite Tape Pickup Schedule

Backup tapes must be sent offsite daily to ensure minimal exposure to loss of data. A regular delivery and pickup schedule should be established with your bonded offsite supplier. This schedule governs when your delivery and/or pickup occurs. The delivery schedule should include a combination of daily, weekly, and special monthly service pickups, as shown in Figure 8.3. Consider the security and sensitivity of the tape media contents. Leaving the tapes out front, in the corporate lobby, for pickup makes no sense. Assigning the front receptionist to ensure the tapes go offsite and are collected regularly is not a reasonable expectation. Have your bonded offsite storage provider come to reception, and then the receptionist can contact your IT staff. Leave the tape-media coordination in the hands of the people responsible for it in the first place.

You must incorporate and formally document the following key information:

- The type of schedule, which can be daily, weekly, monthly, or on request. Multiple schedules may be incorporated.
- Any special requirements, such as the first Sunday of every month. There can be more than one of these specified.
- The service windows available. Pick a specified time delivery of a one-hour interval, such as every day 10–11 a.m., so that the tapes will be picked up on a strict schedule. Consider that waiting until late in the business day to arrange for tape pickup causes two issues. First,

it means that tapes will be onsite, and therefore vulnerable, for an additional six hours every day. Second, an end-of-day pickup could be missed by the offsite company because of traffic, weather, or other factors.

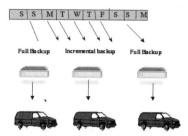

Figure 8.3: Schedule a combination of daily, weekly, and monthly service pickups.

Offsite Storage Considerations

Consider creating a *hotbox*, or recovery box, for your disaster recovery. This box would contain specific items that your technical staff would need if your building were not accessible to rebuild your servers. The box would contain an up-to-date copy of the disaster recovery plan, all server software infrastructure components, and the recovery CDs that have been identified and designated for use when a disaster occurs. Seal the box to ensure security best practices.

Set up a two-hotbox rotation. The contents of both boxes are identical. One box resides at the offsite storage; the other resides in the computer room for localized support issues and maintenance. For additional redundancy, a third box can be stored at your hotsite or alternate processing facility.

When changes to the contents of the hotboxes are necessary, the box at the home site is first updated. The new content is then shipped to your offsite storage provider and swapped with the current box stored. The box and an inventory listing of its contents are both critical vital records and should be documented as such in the DR plan.

Here are some items that could be included in the hotbox:

- A complete, printed copy of the disaster recovery plan.
- A complete copy of the DR plan, suitable for viewing through a file browser like Netscape. This copy will also be on a CD-ROM

- A sealed envelope containing the root, QSECOFR or administrator passwords for every computer system. Whenever the seal is broken on an envelope containing these passwords, all of the passwords within that envelope must be changed to avoid security problems.
- Software for the rebuild of iSeries/400 servers:
  » LIC (License Internal Code) CD IBM V5R3/V5R4
  » BRMS restoration report
  » LPAR LVT
  » Full system save
- Software for the rebuild of Intel servers:
  » Windows 2003 and service packs
  » MS Office
  » Office service packs
  » WinZip
  » Adobe
  » Client Access 5.3
  » PC Anywhere
  » MDAC
  » Printers and video drivers
  » Visual C++
  » Exchange
  » Oracle
  » SQL
- Backup software:
  » Veritas backup exec and patches
  » TSM
  » Legato
  » ARCHSERV

- » Installation guides
- » Recovery CDs (Bare Metal or Christie, etc.)
- Software licenses for servers:
  - » Software installation keys
  - » Proof of entitlement documents
  - » Software key installation procedures
- Stand-alone utility tapes
  - » Stand-alone IPL tape ICKDSF (Device Support Facilities)
  - » Stand-alone IPL tape FDR for MVS/ESA
  - » Stand-alone IPL tape VM/Syback
  - » MKSYSB
- VM Starter System tapes
  - » IPL-able stand-alone ICKDSF and DDR
  - » I/O configuration program (IOCP) tape
- Sun Microsystems Solaris server media kit; copy of the Solaris language products installation CD
- Documentation CDs:
  - » Networking documentation set
  - » Red Books documentation set
  - » CISCO router and firewall documentation
  - » Device support facilities documentation Set
  - » ERP software manuals (Peoplesoft, SAP, BPCS, etc.)

The hotbox itself should be a lockable case, labeled as shown in Table 8.2. The elements of the label are as follows:

- The case ID refers to the identifying number on the outside of the physical box.
- The storage location refers to the name of the off-site storage facility.

- The contact name refers to the person who coordinates inventory control and retrieval of recovery boxes.
- The item identifier and contents description identify the items stored in the box.

Table 8.2: Hotbox Label	
Case ID Number:	
Storage Location:	
Storage Location Contact Information:	
Contact name:	
Item Identifier	**Content Description**

Choosing an Offsite Storage Provider

Ensure the offsite storage provider supplies proper tape storage carrying cases. These cases better protect your data. A hard cover and locking case protects your data cartridges from any exposure during pickup and delivery of your media. Physical movement of your data is safeguarded. Locking cases should also be available for transportation and storage of tape media.

Does your offsite supplier provide full support to your commercial hotsite service provider? In the event of a disaster, will your vital-records management system allow you the flexibility to automatically ship all your tapes there? Does the commercial hotsite accept or recognize your offsite storage provider as creditable?

Here are some other things to look for:

- A vendor dedicated to protecting and managing the tape media
- A facility that is structurally sound, protected from natural and manmade hazards, and with an internal disaster preparedness plan
- Adequate security, fire protection, and backup power systems that are inspected and tested regularly
- Temperature humidity and static electricity controls
- An online Web-based records-tracking system
- A flexible routing schedule, and delivery vehicles equipped with climate control, two-way communication, fire extinguishers, and security systems
- A bonded courier staff

Here are questions to ask potential vendors:

- How do you differentiate yourself from competitors?
- Are documentation procedures in place for pickup and delivery, retrieval, and removal?
- Do you use barcode tape media handling?
- Is your record-tracking system manual or automated?
- Is there a segregation of customer media?
- How do you separate clients' tapes and ensure no mix-ups occur?
- Do you have additional services available for disaster recovery?
- Have all employees signed a confidentiality agreement as a condition of employment?
- What insurance coverage is provided? What is the liability limit?
- What references are available?

Here are questions to ask vendor references:

- How similar to my own are your company's offsite records protection, storage, and management needs?

- How long have you been with this provider?
- Is service consistent? Is weekend and holiday service adequate?
- Do you have any experiences with lost or misplaced shipments of tapes?
- Is the invoice clear, accurate, and easy to understand?
- Have costs exceeded original quoted estimates?
- Is there a support contract?

As always, you get what you pay for. Here are some additional factors to consider:

- Moving companies sometimes offer storage services as a sideline.
- Twenty-four-hour service to one provider might mean the facility is staffed around the clock. Another might deliver 24-hour service through employee on-call arrangements.
- Are you paying for space reserved just for you, or are your tapes shelved wherever space is available?
- Transportation services: some providers maintain their own vehicles; others subcontract the service. Are you comfortable with subcontractors?
- Pay special attention to records storage providers who share buildings with other companies.
- Be aware of the location of your site relative to your facility, as well as regional natural hazards such as flooding or earthquakes.

Summary

Implementing a robust vital-records management solution in your IT shop will provide you with the means to meet all of your stated recovery objectives as derived from your Business Impact Analysis. Having the means in place to successfully recover the IT infrastructure is only facilitated when an effective vital records practice is documented and maintained within the scope of the disaster recovery plan. Only then can you ensure business continuity in the event of a disaster.

9

Building Your Teams

The success of your disaster recovery team is directly related to the quality of its people. The behavior they exhibit during an emergency is the critical factor in determining the ultimate success or failure of your server recovery. People, not machines, recover the System i5 and supporting infrastructure that your business demands. Do not lose sight of the obvious, that your staff members have needs in a disaster, too!

A common mistake is for companies to build their DR teams with the wrong people. Far too often, junior staff members populate these teams, holding positions of great importance to the survival of the organization in a disaster. One of the qualifiers for DR team members should be years of experience within the IT field specific to your operating platform (System i5) and years of experience within your company. For example, Larry is a new hire. He has lots of experience in large IT shops, is very motivated, and is a great hire. However, he has only been with the company for eight weeks. Larry might eventually be the perfect team leader for the system recovery of the iSeries and supporting business functions, but today he must first understand the company's IT infrastructure, business practices, backup and recovery process, and most of all, the corporate culture. Typically, your company will have numerous custom applications that require special recovery procedures unique to your organization. There is no way Larry would have this company-specific application knowledge to lead the effort in rebuilding your iSeries. He has industry experience, but not company experience. Picking the low man on the seniority pole is a dangerous proposition. What can the new hire say, "no"?

Another staffer to avoid is the unmotivated person seeking an easy assignment, the kind who joins the disaster recovery team thinking to get out of "all those other crazy IT projects." Maybe you have a team member who has been with your organization for 30 years, looking for an easy assignment on which to do the absolute minimum until retirement. This person does not have the long-term interests of your company at heart in a disaster.

In a disaster, things will become extreme in terms of stress, conflict, and natural adrenaline. Consider the situation and conditions your recovery teams will face. These individuals must perform under the most intense pressure during a stressful recovery. The right people are folks who understand your enterprise's computer systems and can usually identify and rectify most problems quickly. They truly understand all the ramifications of their actions because they have "been there"— they have seen it all before and are not afraid to face it. Not only are these people thought of as leaders in your organization, they are the most knowledgeable, trusted, and capable team members. They are great both technically and in leadership.

Always consider that the team you select will be charged with the responsibility of recovering your entire multi-million or even billion dollar enterprise. The very survival of the business depends on these folks. That is a huge responsibility. Ask yourself, "Have I selected the best people possible to do this job? Am I sure they can deliver?"

Unfortunately, the effects of short-sightedness in selecting your recovery teams is only discovered during a disaster, as minutes turn to hours, and then days go by in a totally messed-up server recovery. Even worse, sometimes *no* recovery is possible at all. I have seen this scary event all too many times. Imagine not being able to recover your iSeries, and the impact that would have on your organization! Remember the level of service delivery you promised to the business in all the walkthrough meetings. You have formally documented this in your Recover Time Objective (RTO). The difference between a great recovery team and one that falls down on the job is the caliber of its members.

Selecting Candidates: Pick Me! No, Don't Pick Me!

What should you look for when selecting the best people to be on your recovery teams? Table 9.1 lists desirable and undesirable traits.

Table 9.1: Evaluating Candidates for the DR Team	
Ideal Candidates	**People to Avoid**
Considered an expert by his/her peers	Hands-off; does not understand the total picture
A go-to person for anything and everything	A new hire or part-time employee
An active contributor to many IT integrations	Totally unfamiliar with the systems
Works well under pressure	Folds under pressure
Cool, calm, collected	Hot under the collar; loses his/her cool
Confident in his/her work	Always needs reassurance
Trusted by peers	Tends to blame others (excuses, excuses, excuses)
Always online; dedicated to the company	Pure 9-to-5'er; unreachable after hours
Willing to fix problems	"Not my problem; sorry, I cannot help you"

Consider the type of individuals you are placing on your team. Screen your members to ensure you're getting the ideal candidate. Ask a series of questions to see how potential candidates would handle themselves, but remember, you work with these people, so you should be familiar with what they can deliver. If an individual displays several of the negative traits in Table 9.1 under normal working conditions, think carefully before including him or her on a DR team, when things are anything but normal. It is pretty likely that the negative traits will come up.

Real-World Example: The Hot-Headed Executive

I was called in by a company that had moved its late-model AS/400 literally five feet to make room for a new iSeries and disk tower. Things looked good until the unit was powered on. Five disk drives went bad at once, causing total data loss.

An executive named Barb (name changed to protect the guilty) came storming into the data center, tossing verbal obscenities at everyone in sight and looking for the system administrator. She yelled at the admin, "How could you have messed this up? You are totally incompetent!"

I stepped in to tell Barb we were doing everything in our power to get the company back in business ASAP. I instructed the admin to run a full Save Option 21, and IBM arrived to replace the drives. Barb again confronted the admin, telling her to either shape up or ship out (with much more vulgarity). This unnerved the admin so much that I took her outside to get some air. Our dialogue went like this:

Me: "Don't worry, we are not leaving you alone on this one."

Admin: "Easy for you to say! I'll be lucky if I have a job Monday."

Me: "You ran the Save Option 21 like I asked you, right? So, all will be fine."

Admin: "Well, I'm no longer sure."

Me: "I'm sure you did. . . . It ran just fine, right?"

Admin: "I'm not sure. Maybe the 21 save ran a little quicker this time. Maybe I made a typo and ran an option 22 or 20, or something else."

Me: "An option 22 is just the IBM operating system layer save, but I am sure you would have seen it in the log."

Admin: "I never had a chance to check the log. Barb was all over me to turn the system over to you guys so she didn't pay you to stand around. Oh my gosh, I did screw up! I better fess up to Barb. At least I might still have a chance to keep my job."

Me: "Look, I am sure you ran what we asked you. We'll know in less than an hour. Let's not throw in the towel just yet."

The executive was so overpowering and so abusive, she was able to raise doubts in the iSeries administrator's ability to do her own job. The story ends happily, as the admin did indeed run the correct backup and we got the system back that very night, before it caused any impact to the business.

The moral of the story is keep executives out of the computer room, stand up for what you believe in (yourself), and most importantly, do not include hot-heads on your disaster recovery team.

Preparing Your Staff for Success

The success of your IT organization is measured by the investment in capital, the education and training, and the results it brings. In order for your organization to be resilient, management must invest time, money, and more time to ensure your staff are well prepared. The recovery teams must find time to practice and then practice again. Employee the Boy Scout motto, "be prepared." Your team must practice disaster recovery regularly, not just when an auditor deems it time, or when there's a break in the project schedule (which, of course, never seems to happen). The objective in testing a disaster recovery plan is to learn what doesn't work and make your team members comfortable with its activities so they can perform them under duress.

Experienced team members are the most likely to recognize gaps or assumptions made in the plan when conducting tests regularly. They will read between the lines and not make assumptions. Nor will they simply follow the documents blindly, knowing that there might be some gaps.

Your DR team members will be more comfortable in familiar situations, particularly during stressful times. If a team has practiced its recovery plan several times before an actual disaster, its members can more easily perform technically and visualize the recovery goal. More importantly, they will not be overwhelmed by recovery-scenario tasks. The confidence that comes from frequent testing can actually result in excitement and satisfaction in a job well done. Although no one wishes for a disaster to happen, it can be exciting for a recovery team to see a well-tested plan actually work in a real exercise for the benefit of the company. Team members will know they can deliver if the situation calls for it. Your teams will always remain prepared.

How Disasters Affect People

The most critical part of any recovery team's responsibility is dealing effectively with the issues of being human. In actual disasters, the situation will cause changes in people's behavior. A disaster can affect people in unpredictable ways:

- A disaster can devastate people.
- A disaster can affect others around those on the DR team.
- A disaster can make an individual unable to function.
- A disaster can cause an emotional breakdown.

The rapid, traumatic change in people that results from a disaster will be unpredictable. Disasters might bring out the best in some people, who will rise above everyone's expectations. Disasters might devastate other people, making them unable to function effectively. An individual's reaction to a disaster can affect those around them, and thus dramatically alter the reactions and delivery capabilities of the entire recovery team. The team's recovery focus can become unfocused. This can become counterproductive and damaging. Respect these possibilities, and be prepared to deal with them. We all deal with stress in different ways.

The backbone of any disaster recovery plan is preparedness, as disasters will impact employees' personal lives, as well as their work lives. You must be able to provide a solution for both your business and the family needs of your team members. Freedom from personal concerns among recovery team members tends to mitigate stress. It makes sense to develop a family disaster-recovery plan (discussed in chapter 19) to help alleviate staff concerns about their personal situations in a regional event.

When There Is Loss of Life or Missing People

There are many uncontrollable factors in a disaster, including death, personal injury, or staff who are missing. These factors will prevent recovery team members from delivering some or all of their recovery objectives. They will not stay focused on the task at hand. Even the most complete recovery plan can fail if key team members are not present to execute their roles, physically or even mentally.

If a key member unexpectedly fails to appear during a disaster, two things must be done as soon as possible:

- Efforts must be made to locate the missing DR team member, preferably by non-team members. This should be the responsibility of the disaster recovery coordinator. Other team members will naturally be concerned for the missing colleague, and will be distracted. Knowing that efforts are being made to locate him or her can alleviative some concern.

- An alternate for the missing team member must be assigned, so recovery can proceed on schedule as per the plan. These substitutes or alternates will have already been identified within the teams.

Real-World Example: September 11 Story

During 9/11, many organizations were faced with not knowing the status of their staff. The telephone infrastructure could not support the demands placed on it by sheer volume, and this damaged the phone system's ability to function. A recovery that I participated in was completely stalled because of this issue. The phone system was overloaded in New York, and the crisis at hand made it unreasonable to communicate with anyone. We decided to go with the recovery plan we had practiced several times. I talked to the DR team leader, who was some thousand miles away from New York, in the Tampa office. He was in a panic, "What if all my people are dead?! I cannot locate anyone, I cannot get through. What am I going to do? Everyone is dead!"

There was a fully redundant solution, tested, documented, and in place. I told him, "Turn off CNN. Turn off all these outside distractions." The TV was simply repeating the same bleak details. It was time to stop watching TV, open the disaster recovery plan, and execute the script. We had far exceeded all of our Recovery Time Objectives already, so the decision was simple. It was time to switch systems.

This system ran banking machines for Latin America and involved satellite communications to be switched as well. I got him refocused, and he simply executed the steps to switch data centers from New York to Tampa with the installed Clustered High Availability solution. The systems were now back on-line. The disaster recovery plan worked as written.

The staff did surface over the next few days. There was no loss of life, but lots of permanent bad memories. The company's New York site was not damaged; its power was simply cut. They ran in Tampa for the next two months, as many of the staff simply refused to go back to work initially. Who could blame them?

The moral of this story is to stick to your disaster recovery plan, regardless of the events!

Death or Serious Injury

When a staff member is seriously injured or killed, it brings great pause to everyone concerned. People will naturally grieve the situation. First and foremost, the company should express its condolences, and offer the victim's family immediate support and assistance. Helping a victim's family is one important way for an organization to show that it cares for its own people. Secondly, the affected staff member's coworkers should be apprised of the situation. With injuries, regular reports on the injured colleague's condition can help keep the rest of the teams' spirits up. No news is always perceived as bad news! Ensure your company shows it does care about its people.

Command-Center Stress

When a disaster affects an organization, stress will affect the employees who work there, particularly the senior executive and IT management teams. This stress should be confined to the "Command Center," where all the important efforts to achieve recovery will be concentrated. This is where the decision to declare a disaster, damage assessment, recovery operations, and business restoration decisions will be made.

During a disaster-recovery operation, the assumption is that all stress levels are considered negative and counterproductive. When a disaster strikes, an organization that has a tested meeting-room stress-management disaster recovery plan has already begun to reduce the effects of stress because it is far better prepared than a company that does not have such a plan.

Reduce the level of stress:

- *Practice your Command Center manners and procedures*: The better prepared you are, the more effective the outcome. The better you treat everyone, the better the outcome. Do not point fingers. Getting along goes a long way.
- *Clarify your roles*: Team members must know what is expected of them so they can fulfill their roles. Be very clear in advance of a disaster event, and there will be no surprised faces in the room.
- *Establish communication*: Communicate well with all team members and key business leaders for effective recovery. It is also important to manage the media effectively. Employ regular debriefings of recovery personnel. Open all outgoing and incoming lines of communication to include all recovery team staff, and tell all staff when they can expect the next update.
- *Get to the point:* Use short, clear statements to convey information. Do not make everything into a long-winded story. In a stressful time, the patience level is a little short. Keep people on track by sticking to what you know and what you plan to do next.

Best practices for your recovery teams:

1. Does your team have the right stuff?

   » You want the best leaders from your company.

   » The success of the recovery team is directly related to the quality of the people. (There are *no* exceptions to this rule.)

2. Practice doesn't make perfect; only perfect practice makes perfect.

   » Allow all team members ample opportunity to practice recovery scenarios.

   » Do it all over again.

   » Make sure primary and alternative team members are equally trained.

   » Develop skill sets and develop confidence.

3. Shift work—this is now a 24-hour shop.

   » Plan for rotating shifts (12-hour shifts are the maximum).

   » Encourage people to take breaks.

   » This is no time for heroes.

   » Emphasize some good nutritional habits to fuel the effort.

4. Ensure team members' families are cared for.

   » Family comes first. Have a DR family preparedness program.

   » Pre-arrange care for team members' families.

   » Ensure team leaders are sensitive to team members' personal needs.

   » Provide crisis-counseling services.

   » Provide support services to the families of injured staff.

Building Your Recovery Teams

Teams should provide leadership in a disaster. When a disaster strikes your organization, everyone will look immediately to the IT management team for leadership and direction. How quickly and effectively the IT management and technical team leaders respond during the first few critical hours after a disaster will determine your company's success, both short term and long term. The recovery team leaders must be prepared to demonstrate that rare combination of technical awareness, business urgency, and compassion for staff. That is a pretty a tall order! Their leadership must provide for the ability to meet the delivery expectations from your disaster recovery plan as agreed upon by the business.

The recovery can only be facilitated when a team leader can assess the physical impact or loss of the computing facility at hand. Recovery team leaders must manage the individual team members and successfully transition them to the next recovery steps. A team leader must lead everyone from the complete chaos of the situation and the impact caused by the disaster. Leadership is only achieved by doing the following:

- Communicate pre-planned and tested directions effectively.
- Gain control of the emergency situation as quickly as possible.
- Provide structure as soon as possible.
- Start the recovery process quickly.
- Ensure everyone follows the recovery plan to the end, to accomplish its goals.

The individual selected for the position of team member must be very competent and confident. This individual does not minimize the effect of the disaster, but rather communicates the expectation of recovery. Decisions will be impulsive, and sometimes be viewed as extreme, but they will all be based totally on the proven, tested roadmap of your DR plan.

Selecting Team Leaders

Each recovery and management team should have a designated team leader and alternate. These people play an active role in the guidance of team members during a disaster, and participate in all DR planning exercises. A team leader must have an overall awareness and appreciation for all tasks assigned to the recovery team members and the dependencies with every task performed. The number of activities required to successfully execute a disaster recovery can be huge. Knowing everyone's precise roles, the timing of tasks, when they are completed, when tasks are pending, and dependencies to other teams are key for a successful leader. He or she must always know what the next step requires.

The designation of team leaders, alternates, and members should never be arbitrary. Giving the responsibility to the highest ranking official in the company's organization chart is not the way to do things. Leadership requires the individual to have an intimate knowledge of the technologies and procedures currently used by the business. You are not looking for someone to execute all the keystrokes in your server recovery, but rather someone who has a holistic view of all installed computer technology—not just restricted knowledge of the i5. This individual will fully understand how each server application interfaces into the business and the specific business needs it meets.

Team members, on the other hand, are generally selected on the basis of whether they have prerequisite skills and knowledge of specific system areas. Just look around your organizations and you will find many people who possess these skills, I am sure.

In an emergency, the team leader or designated alternate will be responsible for contacting other team members to initiate recovery activities as soon as the IT management team declares a disaster. As part of recovery plan maintenance, the team leaders ensure that procedures are current with the changing business objectives. When things get out of date, assign team members to align IT with the business to ensure ongoing completeness.

Consider where your team leaders live. A candidate who lives within a certain proximity to the corporate office might be more preferable, or possibly less preferable, than one who lives further away. If a prospective team leader is always out of town on company business, he or she might not be a logical choice. How is the individual under stress? Visionary, a logical thinker, and a true leader?

Above all, you must not lose sight of your team member's real-life situations. Can your technical staff relocate to a hotsite location for the duration of a declared disaster? A candidate for team leader who is afraid of flying is probably not a good choice. Some of your recovery team members might be single parents, with no ability to even work emergency overtime, much less relocate out of state for a period of time. Other employees might rely exclusively on public transportation to get to and from work, and might not be able to get to a site requiring a car.

You can help uncover such situations by having all employees sign a form on a yearly basis, indicating that they have read and understood the disaster plan as it pertains to them personally. Have every team member identify any limitations they might have in the required commitment in a disaster. By knowing in advance, you can plan around some of the obstacles.

Many considerations enter into the selection of the team leader. The ultimate consideration, however, is whether the candidate possesses the knowledge and skills to accomplish the responsibility at hand.

Communication Between Team Leader and Members

The most important contribution a team leader can make is to ensure a recovery environment that enables team members to speak up and address the real issues preventing the goal from being achieved. A leader with good communication skills must be able to speak openly and deal with problems as they arise. A team leader's goal should be to listen, understand different viewpoints, and work toward a problem resolution. A team leader must make recovery team members feel comfortable enough to express their needs and wants during this stressful exercise.

Recovery team members will need to know what is going on at all times, and they need to be informed about things such as outstanding tasks, plans, priorities, and progress. The most important part of communication is not so much the tools you choose, but the dedication by each member of the team to use the chosen tools regularly.

Your DR plan will require a set of team leader tasks that speak to the following:

- Activate the team in the event of a disaster.
- Meet with the IT recovery team to understand the impact of the disaster. You will need to understand the impacts to your clients.
- Notify the business and meet with other recovery teams.
- Perform other specific tasks to direct the recovery.

Team-member tasks must also be created in advance. Answers to the following questions should help with the development of these tasks:

- Who will receive the call from the team leader?
- What will the team members need to know about the disaster and its impact on the team's processes?
- Were any personnel injured? Do any team members require assistance? If yes, work with Human Resources accordingly.
- Who needs to be notified about the disruption?
  - » IT staff?
  - » Business units? All, or specific ones?
  - » Vendors? Which ones?
  - » Business partners? Which ones?
- Where is your alternate recovery location?
- How will team members get to the recovery location?
- What do they need to take with them to the recovery location?
- When should team members report to the recovery site?
- How will you obtain the required recovery resources?
- If the team has to purchase extra equipment or supplies to assist with the recovery, what procedures do they follow?

Goal Setting

Establishing goals within the team is essential. It is important for the team leader to establish goals early, so the recovery team members understand their purpose for participation. If the recovery objectives are clear, the recovery team members are motivated to excel in the activities and develop trust for their leader. Goals give the team direction and provide a feeling of value and importance.

It is very important for a team leader to make sure the team knows how the work will be done, how important the work is to the success of the project, and how they will accomplish their tasks. Without any formal DR planning or recovery goals, the team has nothing to strive for, and members may lose motivation. Remember that disaster recovery is not the most exciting project in the technology sector because of all the documentation required. Keeping the goal simple and achievable will be very beneficial to the team.

Assigning Roles

Assigning roles to team members helps them know their places on the team. Each member should be assigned a specific, clearly defined role that relates to his or her technical role within the IT department. Defining roles to team members makes assignments more straightforward, helps them understand the decision-making process, and assures that tasks will be completed. It is important to clarify each role at the very first meeting so members know exactly what they have to do. Making a list of everyone's skill sets, preferences, and work experiences helps in assigning achievable roles.

How to Work Together

To be productive and successful, a recovery team must know how to work together. A team that can work together will be able to raise and resolve issues that are standing in the way of accomplishing system-restoration goals. Working together under the stress of a disaster might not come easily at first, but with proper training, the team will be able to adapt quickly. The training may include instructions on how to communicate better, manage stress and conflict, or understand the skills and talents that everyone brings to the table. If people are working together effectively rather than working by themselves, more work will be accomplished. Effective use of resources is essential to the success of the recovery team. In the business world, companies are very serious about how they use their resources. The same should hold true in disaster recovery. Many companies use team techniques in systems development to effectively use their resources.

Disaster Recovery Team Overview

The disaster recovery plan is invoked in stages, or *recovery phases*, by specifically assigned staff organized into recovery teams. It is important that these teams function efficiently, so independent tasks can proceed simultaneously. The plan can be executed by any number of teams, depending on the size of your organization. Additional teams might need to be added to your plan to support regulatory or legislative requirements specific to your industry.

The types of teams required are based on the number of system(s) within the scope of the disaster recovery plan. The size of each team and specific team titles will depend on the organization. Here is a typical outline of teams to support a DR plan:

- Executive sponsor
- Recovery management team
- IT management team
- Executive management team
- Damage assessment team
- Media relations team
- Technical recovery team
- Platform recovery team, made up of the following sub-teams:

- » iSeries recovery

- » pSeries recovery

- » Intel server recovery

- » Unix/Linux recovery

- » Network recovery

- Applications team

- Security team

- Insurance recovery team

- Site restoration

- Facilities build team

- Procurement team (for equipment and supplies)

Personnel should be chosen to staff these teams based on their skills and knowledge. Ideally, teams are staffed with the personnel responsible for the same or similar operations under normal conditions. Team members must understand not only their roles and responsibilities associated with the DR plan, but also the procedures necessary for executing the recovery strategy. Teams should be sufficiently large to remain viable if some members are unavailable. Team members should also be familiar with the goals and procedures of other teams to facilitate coordination of the recovery. This team concept will allow for the effective and timely management of all disaster recovery activities, regardless of the size of your company, the type of disaster, or the magnitude of the disaster's effects.

Team Tasks, Roles, and Responsibilities

Create team member tasks for every team. You will need a set of team leader tasks that speak to the following:

- Notification from the team leader that the recovery team has been activated as a result of a disaster

- Meeting with the team leader to understand the impact of the disaster and initiate the recovery efforts
- Specific tasks to help the various team members restart the critical processes

The specific team-member tasks should be developed to provide answers to the following questions:

- Who will receive a call from the team leader? Who is the alternate choice?
- What will the team members need to know about the disaster and its impact on the team's processes?
- Were any of the recovery team members injured?
- What do we need to take with us to the recovery location?
- When should team members report to the recovery site?
- How do we obtain the required recovery resources?
- Who will help us install and enable the resources?
- If we have to purchase extra equipment or supplies to assist with the recovery, what procedures do we follow?
- Will we need any special assistance from any of the functional support organizations to accomplish the recovery? (If so, provide timely notification to the team leader, who will ensure that the team obtains the required support.)
- When did the incident occur, and at what time were our processes interrupted?
- What do we do to restart the critical processes and servers?
- What server should be recovered first, second, third, etc.?
- What processes may be suspended, and for how long?
- Should we keep a detailed log of the actions we are taking to recover our servers, as well as issues that arise?
- How do we do a damage assessment of our normal work area?

- What kind of reports should we prepare to document the impact of the disaster on our computer room?

- What kinds of records are required for insurance purposes?

- Do we have to help prepare insurance records or reports?

- Do we have to take any special measures to protect our records and other assets while operating at the recovery location?

- What regular status reports do we need to provide to the site recovery team and our senior management?

- Who will help us resolve problems or issues that may arise during the recovery operations?

- How long do we operate at the recovery location?

- How do we add (restart) additional processes and personnel to the recovery location?

- What do we have to do to plan for the return to our normal work area?

- What lessons did we learn during the recovery effort, and how should we document these lessons?

You need to designate roles and responsibilities for each team member and assign an alternate team member whenever feasible. This is done by developing a checklist of critical functions for each team member, which will keep even the most stressed-out individual on track in the midst of a disaster. Having a "what's next" list goes a long way to success in a disaster. Checklists also provide a foundation for a coordinated response, eliminating the question of who is doing what. Each recovery team has a specific role and set of responsibilities that work together to ensure a successful disaster recovery operation.

The IT Recovery Management Team

The IT recovery management team's required activities include preparedness prior to any disastrous event, administrative requirements during the recovery effort, rebuilding activities, and overall recovery responsibilities. Your first step is to identify the decision makers in your company and establish a chain of command. This will help to eliminate potential problems of authority and conflicts when a disaster occurs. Usually, there are multiple decision makers who need to coordinate closely with each other on a regular, timely basis (hourly, twice daily, etc.) in order to appropriately manage the crisis. Identifying the most skilled members is challenging, to say the least. Often, the best team members are not necessarily the people with the highest-ranking titles, but those who possess the required skill and talent to handle the situation at hand. Including the top-ranking senior executives of your organization strictly based on job title is a recipe for failure. In general, this level of business executives is too busy to participate in planning or testing, or to attend meetings, let along contribute required documentation on time. While you need senior management's input to the disaster recovery process, you should choose to invite them for periodic planning sessions as business contributors only.

Members of the IT recovery management team will be actively involved in the recovery operation of the partially or totally destroyed server room. This team will be responsible for the declaration of a disaster, commercial alternate site processing, and any computer hardware required to support the production processing environment if a re-build is required. This may involve purchases, leases, and restoration of the server room and communication hardware, as the situation warrants. Based upon the damage-assessment estimates and the lead times required to obtain and install the hardware components, management will dedicate the appropriate resources to the task.

The members of the IT recovery management team must be very well-versed in the technical integrations and IT infrastructure within your organization. These folks are unique, as they either directly or indirectly support IT's day-to-day activities and service delivery. Their roles in the organization might include CIO, VP of Technology, Director of Infrastructure Services, or Manager of Technical Services.

The primary function of this team is to prepare a preliminary assessment of the condition of the building, the data processing facilities, and the computer systems affected by the disaster. The IT recovery management team oversees the whole recovery process, coordinating the activities of both the recovery solution (hotsite or high systems resiliency) and the restoration of the primary site. The leader of this team has the final authority on decisions that must be made during the recovery process. This includes damage assessment, alert, and declaration. This is done by monitoring all the activities of the respective teams responsible for the recovery of the data center and the restoration of the primary site.

The IT recovery management team is activated immediately upon discovery of any potential disaster. This team will make the decision to activate the disaster recovery plan or consider the event just an incident that can be resolved quickly. This team provides the unique business knowledge necessary to develop an initial response and supporting actions.

The IT Recovery Management Team's Leader

The IT recovery management team is led by the *Recovery Coordinator*, which is a formal title for the team leader. This individual has the final authority regarding decisions during every phase of the recovery process. Each of the remaining individuals acts as a coordinator and uses specialized skills to address portions of the recovery roadmap. As the recovery process gets underway, there will likely be areas of overlap between teams, and detailed communications will be required. The IT recovery management team will have regular meetings to provide support and communications between various team coordinators.

The Recovery Coordinator should always remain accessible for strategic decisions, recovery strategy resolution, resource conflicts, the sourcing of hardware, and major expenditure approvals. This individual needs to be a skilled leader who is accustomed to dealing with pressure. This individual will have a broad knowledge of the hardware and software used in your organization. The Recovery Coordinator should also be a problem solver, as there will be many tasks that arise that have not been anticipated in advance. The individual must also be able to delegate responsibility to others, and have signing authority to source funds as part of the disaster recovery process. The Recovery Coordinator must be identified to the rest of the recovery teams, to publicize the chain of command.

The Recovery Coordinator's duties include the following:

- Open the communication interface to senior management.
- Notify the controller or C-level execs and request assistance to brief all involved personnel regarding statements outside the organization, and act as an interface with news media during the recovery period.
- Manage and maintain the disaster recovery effort—ensure control, integrity, and compliance with your organizational policies.
- Coordinate the disaster recovery activities, including damage assessment, recovery strategy, and site restoration (primary or alternate site).
- Keep management of each of the departments serviced by your organization informed about the status of the recovery.
- Provide resolution of conflicts and problems that cannot be resolved at lower levels.
- Monitor the progress of the recovery team in rebuilding and restoring critical server operations.
- Ensure that recovery team members are aware of any changes in the course of action.

Table 9.2 lists more specific duties of this key person.

The selection of the members of the IT recovery management team is very important. It is performed by the Recovery Coordinator. It is almost impossible to document exactly what each of the individual recovery team members will be required to do, as each disaster will have its own special set of circumstances, many of which will be completely unanticipated. Most importantly, each member of the team must be capable of stepping in with the leadership, technical, and management skills to make the on-the-spot decisions necessary to complete the task at hand.

Table 9.2: IT Recovery Management, Team Leader Checklist	
Action	**Status/Remarks**
1	Coordinate damage assessment activities with the team leader of the Technical Recovery team.
2	Place hotsite on alert.
3	Notify members of the IT recovery management team to convene in the Control Room
4	Notify other senior management, as appropriate.
5	Decide to cancel the alert or invoke a disaster.
6	Notify the hotsite that your organization is declaring a disaster and that your hotsite provider is to be ready at its facility.
7	Ensure that all transition team functions (recovery, network, application support, and technical support) are staffed.
8	Ensure that all recovery materials needed to restore applications data at the hotsite or locally are available.
9	Determine the restoration capability.
10	Ensure that IT technical recovery team is deployed to the appropriate recovery location (onsite/hotsite).
11	Verify that the production restoration is underway.
12	Ensure that the application support team has been notified and is in place to support primary applications.
13	Coordinate with HR representative to ensure that all members of the disaster recovery teams have been briefed regarding communications with the news media.
14	Coordinate with technical recovery team leader to develop a project schedule for reconstructing the server room.
15	Review the restoration project schedule and monitor progress during the restoration period.

Chain of Command

Clearly identify the chain of command in effect when a disaster is declared. Be very clear. *Be very clear.* (This repetition is intentional.) The most important element to consider is to separate the recovery management team from the senior management of your corporation. Non-IT executives are typically not involved in the technical workings of the organization, and in most cases, they should not be involved in the technical details of disaster recovery, either. Direct presence from senior executives can hinder progress and might develop into intimidating situations for your technical recovery staff.

You must determine what is the norm in your organization. If a senior executive rarely steps foot in the computer room, then ensure that the same is true during a disaster. Having a former IT guy who is now a senior executive looking over a technician's shoulder at every keystroke is inappropriate. However, this is not meant to imply that you should leave your senior executives in the dark. You must provide them with regular status reports so they can continue to run the business and support your customers. Keep them in the know, but keep them away.

Whatever the chain of command you adopt for disaster recovery, it is important that the DR plan's organization chart and your company's day-to-day organization chart remain *totally independent*. You must reinforce the principle that once a disaster has been declared, the DR chain of command takes precedence. All significant decisions must be made through this command structure, not the traditional organization chart. Sometimes, this is a bitter pill for senior executives to swallow. They simply do not wish to let go. This is the primary reason why it is so important for an organization to have a formal process for declaring a disaster, both internally and with your hotsite. If leadership during disaster recovery differs from normal organizational lines, a recovery organization chart should be formally published as part of the recovery plan. It should be clear to the entire organization that it will be in effect from the time of a declaration until the recovery management team completes its job and the disaster recovery is no longer considered active.

The IT Technical Recovery Team

Members of the IT technical recovery team will be actively involved in the recovery operations of the partially or totally destroyed computer room.

This team provides onsite technical staff and supports all related recovery scenarios. Levels of support include: server setup, system initialization, system startup, application restoration, database load, application verification, and establishing proper network communications with the LAN/WAN. All servers would be made available at a commercial hotsite or alternate computing facility as identified in the mission-critical equipment list.

The IT technical recovery team coordinates the technical recovery to ensure that all activities are completed in a timely manner to achieve the Recovery Time Objective (RTO) of the critical business functions, as stated to the user community.

Larger IT shops with several unique hardware platforms in addition to the iSeries, or large quantities of mission-critical Wintel servers, will have more complex recoveries. They typically require additional specialized team members to perform several different functions, all reporting to the team leader.

The IT Technical Recovery Team's Leader

The team leader is often referred to as the *Technical Recovery Manager*. This individual needs to be highly skilled in a number of areas. He or she must have a strong background in all the server hardware and software installed, as well as knowledge of the complete IT infrastructure, including network communications. A working knowledge of the installed platforms in use is mandatory. The Technical Recovery Manager needs to be able to communicate easily with vendor technical representatives and hardware engineers concerning installation options, performance issues, hardware problem resolution, and interfacing with the management team. He or she must also be able to schedule and manage people.

The Technical Recovery Manager will be responsible for initiating damage assessment activities of the damaged or failed infrastructure, recovery actions, and notification procedures until such time as the recovery management team's leader is available.

Technical Recovery Manager Checklist

If it is determined that your organization cannot continue processing in the primary computer room on a timely basis, the Technical Recovery Manager has the following responsibilities:

1. Notify the hotsite that your organization is exercising its option to declare a disaster and take over the hotsite.

2. Notify appropriate members of your organization's management, as identified in the contact list.

3. Notify the regional management of the business locations served by your organization. Keep them informed of the recovery status.

4. Brief all recovery-team personnel as they arrive at the command center; initially, this will be the transition teams and later, user representatives.

5. Determine if recovery will be local or whether travel to a hotsite (maybe out of state) will be necessary.

6. Arrange for a list of team members who require air transportation to the hotsite and supply this list to the Recovery Coordinator from the IT management recovery team.

7. Recover the operating system and user data environment by restoring the latest copy of the backup delivered to the hotsite by the offsite storage facility or the technical team members.

The Network Recovery Team

The network recovery team will be led by the Technical Recovery Manager. The network engineer should also be a part of this team if it is necessary to use an alternative site. Individuals on this team need to be skilled in network design and maintenance. They should be trained in diagnosing and correcting network outages and in connecting and debugging new additions to an existing network. Members of this team will be responsible for selecting any other team members they require.

This team will be responsible for overseeing the restoration of the organization's network and all network connections necessary at the primary or alternate site. It is entirely possible that the network recovery team might be the only team convened as a result of a particular disaster. For instance, if a fire in the communications cabinets destroys fiber-optic connections and network equipment, this team will be charged with the recovery. The network team should have detailed recovery procedures to support the basis of the disaster recovery plan.

Typically, there is a high degree of dependency on the network, so a very high emphasis must be placed on restoring it as quickly as possible. Switching or rerouting networks is typically required.

The Hardware Recovery Team

The hardware recovery team will be led by the Technical Recovery Manager. Individuals on this team will be the leaders in restoring one or more of the computer platforms described in the DR plan. Some technical recovery team personnel will be responsible for restoration of several unique hardware platforms. The hardware recovery team is responsible for communicating needs and status information to other recovery teams and coordinating restoration operations between parties working on different computer platforms.

Each hardware platform recovery team/member will follow this plan of action:

- Assess damage.
- Determine which hardware, software, and backups will be required to start the restoration of a specific server.
- Communicate a list of components to be purchased and their specifications to the Technical Recovery Manager.
- Review the recovery steps documented in the DR plan, and make any changes necessary to fit the current situation.

- When hardware begins to arrive, work with vendor representatives to install the equipment.
- When all components have been assembled, begin the steps to restore the operating system(s) and other data from the off-site backup tapes.

Application Recovery Team

The application recovery team will be led by the Technical Recovery Manager. This team will be responsible for conducting activities leading up to the approval and acceptance of application systems for production use after they have been rebuilt. In general, this team's activities will begin after the hardware recovery team has completed work on the target platform. Some of the team members might, in fact, be from the hardware recovery teams.

Some of the anticipated tasks for this team include the following:

- Perform analysis for additional recovery activities, such as database restores or individual file restores.
- Perform application-restart activities.
- Perform SQL database maintenance after a recovery.
- Develop programs/procedures to address specific problems.
- Interface with application users to test applications.

The application team members will need to use available diagnostic tools to ascertain the status of files, application servers, and database objects. Secondly, they will need to determine if additional restoration versions from backups are required. This team will also need to interface with users to verify that applications are functioning as expected and develop solutions to problems that arise.

Facility Recovery Team

The facility recovery team is typically led by the Recovery Coordinator and includes the Technical Recovery Manager. It probably also includes select members from all the other teams. This team will be responsible for the details of preparing the recovery site to accommodate the hardware and personnel necessary for recovery. Detailed layouts and instructions for the site preparation would have to be determined at the time of the incident.

This team is also responsible for the activities to repair and/or rebuild the primary site (or the primary data center). It is anticipated that the major responsibility for this will fall to building engineers and contractors. However, the facility recovery team must oversee these operations, to ensure that the facility is repaired to properly support the operation of mainframe and networking equipment per the original design of the primary site.

The primary function of this team is to manage and coordinate the restoration of the primary site's server room. This team must evaluate the extent of damage to buildings, equipment, power, and communications. The scope of this team's responsibilities includes the following:

- **Facilities and environmental control equipment**—The computer room's infrastructure and supporting environmental systems are the responsibility of facilities management.
- **Computing and peripheral equipment**—The data processing systems and supporting peripherals are the responsibility of the Technical Recovery Manager.
- **Communications equipment**—The telephone-switching system and other equipment required to support the communications network is the responsibility of the Technical Recovery Manager.
- **Supplies and forms**—Special forms and standard supply stocks are the responsibility of the Recovery Coordinator.

Replacement Equipment

If there is a need for replacement equipment as directed from the facility recovery team, the DR plan contains a complete inventory of the server components currently housed in the computer room. Where possible, agreements should be made in advance with IBM and your local Business Partners to supply replacements for drop-ship hardware on an emergency basis.

To avoid problems and delays in the recovery, every attempt should be made to replicate the current system configuration. However, there will probably be cases where components are not available or the delivery timeframe is unacceptably long. The recovery management team will have the expertise and resources to work through these problems as they arise. Some changes will be required to the procedures documented in the plan. Different models of equipment or equipment from a different vendor might be needed to expedite the recovery process.

Disaster Recovery Preparedness

To ensure that the activities are fully supported by the team's recovery capabilities on an ongoing basis, each member of the recovery management team and the technical recovery team is responsible for preparing and training the employees within his or her area of responsibility. Preparedness includes the following:

1. Maintain a current copy of your computer contingency plan at home and at the office.
2. Ensure that all team members and alternates maintain a current copy of this computer contingency plan at their homes and offices.
3. Ensure all recovery team personnel consider recovery preparedness as a part of their normal duties.
4. Maintain your recovery plan, including all procedures, checklists, and team rosters. Provide any updates to the Recovery Coordinator for any of the following reasons:

    A.   Changes to personnel identified within the teams

    B.   Significant changes to IT recovery requirements that reflect changes to the recovery plan's steps or timeline

    C.   Significant changes to the business recovery procedures, such as the addition of new business functions, support systems, new business practices, or organizational changes

5. Participate in overall recovery plan exercises as required.

6. Participate in hotsite testing as required.

Administrative Responsibilities

These Administrative responsibilities outline the tasks that the recovery management team and the technical recovery team must perform to maintain proper recordkeeping and control throughout the recovery effort:

1. Maintain proper written documentation of any changes or modifications to standard operating procedures.

2. Ensure all temporary changes or modifications do not carry over to normal operations following the recovery effort.

3. Review recovery activities against the documented recovery plan and initiate updates or complete changes as required.

All the recovery teams must be well acquainted with the day-to-day server activities and be able to interface with all the business-continuity processes currently in place.

Care for Your Recovery Teams During a Disaster

Care for your recovery teams involves meeting the psychological and emotional needs of your personnel, as well as making sure basic needs are met for things like food and rest.

Shift Work

Schedule teams to work in shifts of no more than 12 hours to reduce the potential for overstress from burnout. Ensure the complete team does not engage in your recovery immediately. Although it might seem logical to invoke the complete recovery team with "Just call everyone in. I'm declaring a disaster," quite the opposite is true.

For example, suppose a disaster were to happen during regular working hours. After the decision-making process and damage assessments are complete, I recommend sending some staff home. This might come as a surprise to senior executives, who question, "What is he thinking, sending his key technical resources home? It's a disaster, for crying out loud! We should have everyone working on it."

The truth is that you do not want every team member to experience burnout at the same time, and have nobody who can continue the recovery effort. Having fresh staff coming in after an initial eight hours is a welcome relief. At this point, 12-hours shifts can commence. The reasoning for a shorter start is that the current team onsite has had to face many of the initial stresses of the disaster. Who knows? They might have already been at work for many hours.

If people show signs of overstress during the recovery, one remedy is simply to take a break from the work at hand. Step outside. Take a walk outside your building; a breath of fresh air can do wonders. It will give your body a well-deserved break. Have a (non-alcoholic) beverage, and listen to some music. All of this can restore a team member's perspective and send him or her back to the task at hand better able to deal with the unexpected. Twenty to thirty minute breaks can go a long way to clearing your head.

Food

Everyone has to eat. Everyone's food habits are unique, and people can be picky in many different ways. Efforts must be made to supply good, nutritious, favorite types of food to your recovery teams. They must be cared for during a crisis by putting someone (the Recovery Coordinator) in charge of ensuring there is a constant, varied food supply. There can never be too much food, caffeine, or water at a recovery site. If your team likes eating pizza and subs, then get them what they prefer, versus cottage cheese and salads. This is not the time to count calories or change bad eating habits.

Here are some tips about providing food:

- Have snacks handy.
- Stay away from high-energy drinks (a major issue these days).
- NO alcohol.
- Make sure to supply plenty of fresh fruits and comforts foods.

Provide the food that the team needs on your company's behalf. Yes, pay for the staff's meals upfront. Figure out the expense reports later! I once saw a manager look for money from each person, "Ok, guys, ante up. That's $10 from each of you." Imagine what he would have said if someone had no cash. "Sorry, no food"?!

This team had been on the job for over 48 hours at that point. Of course, you would show more sense and respect in that situation.

Recovery Coordinator Duties

The Recovery Coordinator provides administrative support to all the recovery teams, as well as support to employees and their families. One of the most important functions of this individual is to take on the burden of administrative details, so that the recovery-management and technical-recovery teams can concentrate on their recovery work.

The efforts of your teams are critical to the successful recovery of mission-critical servers. Recovery teams must be able to focus on their work. The

Recovery Coordinator supplies a single focal point for posting statuses, keeping track of the all-important timeline, recording requirements and events that occur, and reminding team members of upcoming events. This helps streamline recovery. Timeline reporting is made available to the team leaders of the recovery management team.

The Recovery Coordinator also interfaces with Human Resources, as the designated family contact for team members. This person will be made available throughout the recovery process to provide assistance to employees' family members or update them on progress.

Some of the other anticipated tasks for the Recovery Coordinator and the recovery management team include the following:

1. Provide DR plan maintenance activities.
2. Arrange air travel and hotel accommodations at the hotsite.
3. Arrange for tape media to be shipped via air cargo or ground transport.
4. Determine the status of staff working at the time of the disaster.
5. Coordinate with HR to provide counseling services for staff or family members having emotional problems resulting from the disaster.
6. Assist the individual team coordinators in locating potential team members.
7. Coordinate food and sleeping arrangements of the recovery staff, as necessary.
8. Provide support to track time and expenses related to the disaster.
9. Coordinate testing activities (both desktop and active testing).
10. Ensure that plan changes are made.
11. Distribute updated versions of the disaster recovery plan.

Guidelines for Travel

The Technical Recovery Manager will provide the Recovery Coordinator with the names of individuals who will be required to travel to the hotsite, along with information on all their hotel requirements, an estimate of any travel money needed, and any special instructions relating to travel. All the travel arrangements and itineraries, tickets, and advance travel money will then be supplied.

To prepare for travel, the Technical Recovery Manager should complete the form in Figure 9.1 in advance, for each team member who might be required to travel in a disaster. Also in advance, the Technical Recovery Manger should create a profile of each of these team members, including the following information:

- Name
- Title
- Address (street address)
- Home telephone number
- Pager number, if available
- Cellular telephone number, if available
- Personal e-mail address, if available
- Alternate telephone number

Having the correct spelling of names is extremely important. Also ensure the travel documents correspond to the travelers' photo identification. Many people go by different names in the workplace, like their middle name, for example. With the state of airport security, there are no exceptions.

Do all of this upfront, not under duress. With this process completed upfront, the Technical Recovery Manger can simply say, "John, Joe, and Sue will need to get to the Philadelphia hotsite on the first available flight."

Name:	Destination:	Departure Date:	Departure Time:
Hotel Reservation?	Yes ( ) No ( )		
Rental Car?	Yes ( ) No ( )		
Cash Advance:	$		

Figure 9.1: Fill out this form in advance for each recovery-team member who might need to travel in a disaster.

The Team's Meeting Place

Most disasters are isolated. During those situations, the board room at the main office can be used for the recovery operation's command center. However, some disaster situations eliminate the option of using the local facility. In those instances, a local hotel or restaurant might have to suffice. Make sure to choose a backup location in advance, and make sure this location is fully documented and directions to it are supplied in the disaster recovery plan. Make sure all the team members in your disaster recovery plan know the primary and alternate locations. Have maps available, if necessary.

In choosing the primary and alternate meeting places, think about any key resources you would need there during the initial steps. Here are some specific considerations to keep in mind:

- *Location*—When selecting your alternate meeting place, consider its location relative to your normal work place and to the key staff members you would call together there. The location should not be so far away that staff members would have difficulty getting there. Conversely, it should not be so close to your normal work location that it could be affected by the same incident. If your meeting place is across the street from your office, you might not be able to get to it. I have used everything from a Starbucks to a hotel meeting room for a meeting place.

- *Alternate to the alternate*—Consider selecting at least two alternate meeting locations. The first alternate could be close to your facility, while the second should be further away, ensuring availability if your primary location is not accessible.

- *Communications capability*—Since the ability to communicate with others is essential to effectively respond to any incident, make sure that the location you choose has enough telephones for your needs. If you have a cellular phone, plan to take it with you to the meeting place as another means of communication, and in case regular phones are not working.

If you have a laptop computer with Internet or e-mail capabilities, your meeting place should have the capability to connect that computer as well. Assuming your laptop computer was not in the affected building, you should plan to take it to the meeting place. Also make sure that stationary supplies, such as notepads, pens, and pencils, are available.

Conducting the Meeting

Recovery team leaders should meet to determine actions to be taken and establish the priority of restoring business functions based on the situation and resources available. Review tasks to be performed and assign personnel. Personnel should be assigned to contact vendors and advise them about the situation and when they can expect service to be restored. Here are additional tasks during this meeting:

- Determine if some personnel will have to travel to the alternate recovery site.
- Distribute copies of any forms that will be needed during the recovery operation.
- Distribute copies of the news media statement that has been prepared. Instruct everyone not to make statements to the news media.
- Assign recovery team members to provide support to other teams, as needed.
- Identify personnel who should stay home and remain on standby.

- Implement procedures to resume time dependent functions based on the priorities established.

As progress continues during the recovery operation, the team should be prepared to move back to the affected facility and resume normal business operations.

DR Testing and Plan Maintenance

The Recovery Coordinator will coordinate planning, set test objectives, and implement the overall recovery of the organization. He or she will coordinate disaster recovery activities and track their progress.

Publishing updated documentation is also the responsibility of the Recovery Coordinator. Maintenance and creation of technical documentation is the responsibility of the Technical Recovery Manager. In order for all the diverse technical responsibilities to continue to be fulfilled on an ongoing basis, the approach employed here is one where each technical and management function coordinates activities through the Recovery Coordinator, who has overall maintenance-coordination responsibility.

The Recovery Coordinator's duties include the following:

- Coordination and administration of testing activities
- Testing objectives and summary reporting
- Documentation and updates
- Distribution of disaster recovery plans
- Review and approval of changes to the DR plan
- Interface with management objectives
- Liaison with the hotsite facility

The Recovery Coordinator is the key individual in the maintenance and testing of your DR plan. He or she acts as the focal point and coordinator for all maintenance and testing activities. The following must be accomplished yearly:

- Annually budget for disaster recovery capability.
- Review changes required to the hotsite configuration.
- Update the disaster recovery plan semi-annually.
- Update the critical server listing.
- Schedule two tests per year.

The Recovery Coordinator is also responsible for maintaining a continuing awareness of the disaster recovery capability. This is done through periodic communications regarding events relevant to the capability and process involved in its maintenance. Communications typically are through chaired meetings.

The Recovery Coordinator should publish a report semi-annually that highlights the events of the past six months related to capabilities, gaps, testing results, documentation updates, and projects pending. This report should be circulated to all individuals who are in the distribution list for the DR plan, as well as other appropriate individuals.

All changes to the documentation will be coordinated through the Recovery Coordinator, who will approve or disapprove each change request. Disapproved change requests will be returned to the originator for revisions, and resubmitted. Approved changes will be accumulated and maintained in the secure offsite storage facility and updated on the company's common DR drive. On a semi-annual basis, the Recovery Coordinator will retrieve all changes and circulate them with new CDs and obtain the old CDs distributed previously. This occurrence can be scheduled more frequently when major changes occur.

Testing will be coordinated by the Recovery Coordinator, but will actually be performed by the technical recovery team. All testing objectives will be coordinated through the Coordinator well in advance of any testing. Booking and coordinating access to the hotsite, scheduling travel and accommodations for staff, and auditing the testing will all be coordinated.

The role of the Recovery Coordinator during a technical test is to do the following:

- Manage the conduct of the test.
- Ensure that each objective is fully realized.
- Ensure that each test participant follows the procedures from the computer contingency plan as precisely as possible.
- Document any changes necessary to the procedures of the disaster recovery plan.
- Record changes to the information database as they are noted during the test.
- Record problems and their resolutions as they arise.
- Record the duration of each of the procedures.
- Liaison with the hotsite staff.

The Recovery Coordinator is also responsible for writing the summary report for the test. The summary report should include the following:

- The objectives of the technical test
- The participants
- The changes needed for the DR plan
- Any recommendations resulting from the test
- The schedule for the next test

Summary

The success of the disaster recovery plan depends totally on your teams' abilities to fully understand what is expected of them. You must ensure that each team member fully comprehends his or her roles in recovery of the IT infrastructure. Specific definition of roles will vary from organization to organization, but we can agree that the foundation must be laid out and clearly defined. A true testament of clearly understanding your roles is to have your team members stand up and verbalize what they are responsible for.

During a walkthrough, make sure the recovery team members can answer the following:

- Where does the electronic version of the DR plan reside?
- What actions will they take, and where will they go to exercise those activities?
- What is the recovery scope in their area of responsibility?
- What is the agreed-upon timeframe to restore the systems?
- What is the chain of command?

When everyone clearly understands their roles in rebuilding the corporate computing facility, the recovery is just a question of following the plan, step by step.

10

Effective Communications

The cost of setting up a robust disaster-notification system is relatively low, especially when compared to the potential cost of being unable to get in touch with critical staff during a disaster. Having a well-developed and tested disaster-notification plan is vital to the success of every disaster recovery plan, yet it simply does not get enough attention. Are you confident that the right people in your organization can be contacted in a reasonable amount of time, and that these team members are able to respond to any possible disaster-related scenario? Do you have a predefined location to convene, evaluate, react, and manage the complete recovery process? Can you do it quickly, reliably, and consistently? The call-notification procedures and command center location cannot be rigid. The foundation must be flexible and task-driven, thus allowing DR plan administrators to pre-plan the notification process for any number of scenarios.

Now, how do you effectively communicate with everyone during a disaster? That is the million-dollar question. When things are calm and normal, you can simply walk over to "Maria's" office, or call a key supplier on her cell phone. Things are normal, so people are available. However, will the same be true during a crisis, or in the midst of a regional disaster? Consider that contact then might be required after regular business hours, on a long weekend, or in the middle of the night. Can you reach everyone on your notification list effectively and in a timely basis to invoke the disaster recovery plan?

To respond to a disaster, or even a potential disaster (or alert), you need to ensure you can get in contact with all your essential staff as outlined in the DR plan. Organizations go to great lengths to develop and test their disaster recovery plans. The IT recovery team must gain confidence through testing that they can restore the systems and supporting infrastructure in a timely manner. Build the confidence that you can recover the systems with a minimal loss of data, as agreed to and stated in your Recovery Point Objective (RPO). Secondly, meet the Recovery Time Objective (RTO) as agreed to in your mission statement. These are the only components of the disaster recovery plan that organizations tend to test over and over again. While it's reasonable to emphasize these components, is enough consideration and testing given in your organization to ensuring how effective the notification process is?

As you can see in Figure 10.1, a considerable percentage of organizations (13%) never test their call-notification procedures, and 32% only test yearly. These are sobering statistics. A large number of corporations are taking significant risk by assuming call notification will work every time. You can only recover your IT infrastructure if your team members are contacted and made available. Do not let this be the missing link to the success of your DR plan.

Call Notification Testing Fequency

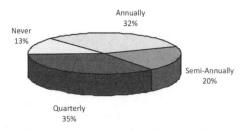

Figure 10.1: Far too many organizations do not test their notification process thoroughly. (Source: Gartner)

Develop an Employee Call Sheet

In today's mobile world, there are many ways to reach your team members, and the effectiveness or preference of being reachable varies from person to person. Every team member identified in your disaster recovery plan should have a corresponding contact sheet, as shown in Figure 10.2. The information on that sheet provides multiple means of achieving the initial response. The following information should always be detailed for each member of the teams:

- Team member name
- Job title on the disaster recovery teams
- Official job title in your organization
- Home address (street address, not a post-office box number)
- Office telephone number
- Home telephone number
- Pager number, if available
- Cellular telephone number, if available
- Preferred number to be reached at (i.e. cell versus home)
- Personal email (not the corporate email address)
- Alternate telephone number (i.e. vacation home, other family member)
- Blackberry or PDA address
- Fax number

The employee's home address is required in case telephones are out of order or constantly busy. This is often the case in regional disasters. Another employee (not directly from the technical recovery team) might need to be dispatched to physically locate a critical team member. A valid home address (not a PO box) provides a means of contact during a critical time. I have found this to be especially effective on long weekends, where you might find the team member performing yard work or enjoying the family pool. In a computer-room disaster, finding a key individual is always preferred, regardless of how you locate the individual. Many times, the team member was oblivious to the urgent situation at hand at the office, so a colleague coming by is highly welcomed.

Employee Call Information Sheet

Name: _____

DR Job Title: _____

Corporate Job Title: _____

Home Address: _____

City/State/Zip: _____

Office Phone: _____ Home Phone: _____

Pager: _____ Cellular: _____

Alternate Number: _____ Fax Number: _____

Personal Email Address: _____

Blackberry/PDA Email Address: _____

Please return the completed sheet to the Recovery Coordinator by:
_____ *(Specify an acceptable completion date.)*

Figure 10.2: Fill out this sheet for each member of the recovery team.

An alternate telephone number is any number by which the team member can be contacted. Examples include the individual's weekend cottage number, a neighbor's number, or even the phone number of a relative (maybe a parent) who will usually know the whereabouts of the team member. You might wonder how you'll convince a team member to give away his or her cottage phone number, a personal refuge away from the office. You might hear, "That's where I go to turn the office off!" Your answer is, "That's exactly why we need it!"

Everyone has a preferred method of being reached. Some rely exclusively on a cell phone, as the device is always handy. Others will suggest the cottage they go to every weekend. Knowing this can save time in dialing the primary reachable number first.

Personal email can be through a local Internet Service Provider, or through a Hotmail, MSN, or Yahoo account. Never include corporate email accounts here. You must always assume that your primary data center has been affected by the disaster, making any corporate email systems unavailable.

Unlike the cell-phone networks, Blackberry or PDA service is typically available for service during a regional disaster. So, the email addresses of these devices are important. Text messaging or IM'ing is an excellent alternative to calling in a regional disaster. Determine in advance whether an employee's device service package supports messaging.

If any of the team members do not have pagers, cellular phones, or personal email addresses, do not leave those entries blank on the information sheet. A blank information field leaves too much to question. Instead, specify a comment like "not applicable" ("N/A").

When distributing the contact information sheet, set a completion and return date. Otherwise, this quickly becomes a very low priority for everyone in their busy daily work schedules. Accuracy of the information is most easily assured in this way. Have a checklist that confirms the receipt of the sheet, as auditors might wish to see this process signoff. It's always easier to confirm if any call sheets remain outstanding with a checklist. Send the sheet electronically to ensure that the responses are easily read and transcribed. Deciphering a team member's handwriting can be challenging in the best of times.

The primary assumption of most disaster recovery plans is that your facilities and everything in them will be completely inaccessible or destroyed. Under no circumstance will you be able to go back to your office to get something, nor will you have access to the systems online from anywhere in your network. Consider that everything is lost. This is why you need accurate contact information handy and available to execute the call notification procedures as your first step to a successful disaster recovery.

Privacy of Contact Lists

The assumption is that the recovery team leaders will be able use all the information on the contact lists to communicate with their teams when required in an emergency. Is this realistic? Some team members might be concerned about having their personal information published in a company document. They might, for example, have an unlisted home telephone number, and might simply refuse to provide it. In today's era of personal privacy laws like the PIPEDA legislation (Personal Information Protection and Electronic Documents Act, also known as The Privacy Act), both personal and legislative considerations must be followed. In addition, there are several white papers describing privacy legislation specific to industry sectors, as well as unique pieces of legislation specific to individual states.

Can you count on your teams not to disclose the contact information you've gathered? The answer has to be yes! You must reinforce to your management and recovery teams the need to protect the privacy of all individuals. No team member is permitted to disclose contact information to anyone, regardless of the circumstance. The most important consideration in every organization is that the DR plan is strictly a private and confidential document, owned and operated only by your organization.

The team members must be assured that their personal information will in no way become available for public consumption. As the disaster recovery plans are distributed, everyone must sign on the dotted line and agree that this is a corporate confidential document. This level of signoff will uphold the level of privacy you are trying to achieve. You must also stress that failure to comply with the confidentiality will be considered grounds for dismissal of employment. This level of assurance should give all your team members the comfort that their personal information will be treated securely at all times by everyone identified in your plan.

Official Privacy Notice

Here is a sample of the legal disclaimer to be read by each team member and then checked off as accepted:

> *The information you provide will be used within boundaries of the Corporate Disaster Recovery Plan and is strictly intended for this use only. In the event of any potential disaster recovery response, you are giving permission to Recovery Team Leaders to contact you away from your place of employment. Your contact information will only be made available within the Disaster Recovery Plan and will have limited distribution. This contact sheet will be considered Private and Confidential property of this corporation. After reading this, please check off the box below, agreeing that you fully understand and accept this policy as written.*

This privacy statement is a place to start. However, you should always consult your organization's legal counsel, as they might have a standard statement or a publication of notice that they would prefer. Legal folks always prefer to use their own wording in any corporate legal notice. You must also educate your counsel of the intent and use of this document, so they can give the best legal advice.

Who Do You Contact?

Consider that many times, you will not know initially if the reason for the call notification is for a disaster response or simply an incident response. In Table 10.1, the names identified are members of the Technical Recovery Team.

Table 10.1: IT Technical Recovery Team	
Member N16ame	**Role**
Richard lastname	Team Lead–Technical Coordinator
Maria lastname	i5–Primary
Alexander lastname	i5–Alternate
Nicholas lastname	i5–Alternate
Franca lastname	Intel–Primary
Matthew lastname	Intel–Alternate
Cassandra lastname	Communications–Primary
Jonathon lastname	Communications–Alternate
Trent lastname	ERP Application Support–Primary
Chris lastname	ERP Application Support - Alternate
Barb lastname	Linux Support–Primary

Each member listed in Table 10.1 would have a specific page dedicated in the disaster recovery plan as shown in Figure 10.3. This page details all the information captured by using the contact sheet.

Contact Information

Richard Dolewski

Team Member Title:	Team Lead, Technical Coordinator
Home Phone Number:	933-111-2222
Cell Phone Number:	644-333-4444
Pager Number:	644-555-6666
Home Email Address:	Rich@yahoo.com
Home Address:	22 Skyview Lane Boulder, Colorado
Alternate Phone Numbers:	Parents' Place (Louie & Bernice) 933-123-4567 Family Cottage 933-321-7654
Blackberry Email Address:	msd339@yourcarrier.com
Home Fax Number:	933-765-4321

Figure 10.3: This is a sample page in the disaster recovery plan.

When you have a disaster, your goals are essentially the same. You want to know what happened, how it happened, where you stand, and what it will take to get things back on track. The worst thing you can have at this point is a bottleneck. Information must travel upward and downward in the company effectively for all recovery team members and managers to know what's going on. You must allow for several different lines of communication to make sure that the correct message gets out quickly.

There will be an obvious need to reach your team leaders or designated alternates, so they can start executing the disaster recovery plan. The management teams will need to be in contact with each other to coordinate activities and exchange information with the business. Some team members might need to be notified to stay home, while others will need to know to go to a command center or commercial hotsite facility. Still others might need to be contacted for their business knowledge and feedback. No matter what the reason for establishing contact, it is important to be able to reach everyone quickly.

You will need to record who has been contacted successfully at what time, and who remains to be contacted. This tracking of contact notification is necessary for effective communications. Keep in mind that things will be moving very fast in a disaster, and you will forget details regardless of how organized you think you are. Having a contact reference sheet will go a long way toward staying organized.

Communicating with Your Teams

For communications to be effective, the message needs to be very clear and direct. Do not indulge in extensive storytelling, rehashing every detail. Also, do not try to predict or presume the outcome of the situation at hand. With plenty of stress and adrenaline, assumptions can lead to possible blaming and misconceptions. Instead, everyone needs to get together to assess the situation, decide on recovery actions, and execute the next steps as a team.

Establishing and maintaining communications throughout the course of the recovery effort is crucial. Continuous contact is especially important during the early hours of a large regional disaster, when rumors are flying around and the situation is probably very unstable. Regular phone calls to update team members at agreed-upon update intervals are the key to your success.

Disasters require notification and response procedures to include:

- Notifying key team members quickly and accurately
- Knowing and supplying the right information
- Executing notification in an effective and timely manner
- Obtaining information from the respondents
- Escalating to additional team members or alternates as required
- Managing, monitoring, and tracking the entire notification process

Your Phone Dialogue

Having a dialogue prepared in advance is a very important process. Communicating your message person-to-person is always preferred over all other forms of communication. You will want to receive a reply from the recovery team members, including their statuses. Can they participate in the recovery? How long will it take for them to get to a specified location? The ability to interact is an important element, but it is sometimes a forgotten dimension in a disaster. Ensuring that everyone in your plan understands before a disaster occurs whom they should contact during a crisis is one of the most prudent steps you can take. Keeping the conversation to a minimum is very important as well. Keep the information clear, brief, concise, and above all, accurate. This is not a social call that lasts 30 minutes or more. You will simply run out of time! Often, we spend far too much time getting into unnecessary details that are simply not required as part of the initial call notification. That type of detail is reserved for the onsite command center discussions.

The team leader or designated alternate will start the notifications of a potential disaster alert or declared disaster. Upon activation of the disaster recovery plan, all team-member notifications will be completed, in their entirety. It is always important to read and understand the complete procedure prior to making any calls.

Notification of Personnel

Before you engage in any calls to team members on your notification list, you need to review the items in Table 10.2, as you will be the "traffic cop" for instructing the team members on their next move.

Table 10.2: Information to Obtain Before Making Any Phone Calls
Command Center Location
Address
Access Requirements
Command Center Phone Number
Team Leader Phone Number
Brief Description of Disaster Situation
Brief Description of Potential Next Steps
Where Team Members Will Assemble
Contact Name at Commercial Hotsite

The team leaders should notify all team members that a potential disaster event has occurred. Keep a record of each team member you reach, with a simple checkmark and time called. Now you are ready to start the notification process:

1. Place the phone call, and with a composed voice, say, "May I speak with (individual's name)?"

2. If the team member answers, provide all necessary information about the potential disaster situation. Instruct the individual that this is a disaster alert and a full damage assessment needs to be performed onsite immediately. Tell him or her the time and location at which

327

the team is convening. Remind the team member to make no public statements about the situation. Reiterate with the team member not to call other coworkers (unless instructed to) and to advise family members not to call other employees' families to discuss the situation. All of this is very important. Tell the individual to provide enough details to family members so that they are not forced to make assumptions or draw conclusions, but to stay away from technical analysis. Remember, this is not a CIA operation! Just remind the team member to keep the information private.

3. If the individual is not available, try to find out where he or she can be reached. Obtain a phone number if the ones on your call sheet aren't working. *Do not* discuss the disaster situation with the person answering the phone. Simply leave a message that it is imperative that the team member calls you back urgently at the number you provide. Make the phone call to the next team member and provide the information stated in the previous step.

4. If an answering machine picks up, make no detailed statement regarding the situation. Provide the phone number to return your call and ask that the team member call you back at that number provided as soon as possible as a work related emergency has transpired.

5. If there is no answer at all, you should still record the status of the call, noting the time of the call. Make a reasonable number of attempts, and then move on to the next team member. Do not get stuck searching for one team member. Move on and get things rolling. The DR coordinator can continue trying to reach the team member.

6. If there is no response after you have exhausted all telephone and email alternatives on the employee contact sheet for a team member, it must be assumed that something has happened to make that person unavailable. How do you determine if he or she has received the message? Set a return call-back time criteria, so that the process moves forward. Typically, you contact the backup or alternate on the

list. If the situation escalates to a full disaster, it might make sense to have your DR coordinator attempt to have someone look for them at the home address provided.

Selecting a Meeting Place for the Command Center

In the event of a declared or potential disaster, getting the command center up and running is the first activity on the list. The command center is the place for all communications among the recovery teams members involved in the disaster recovery activities. Its purpose is to eliminate confusion, by establishing a single meeting place for all recovery team members. Select a place to meet with your recovery teams in advance if your primary office facility is unavailable. In choosing this meeting place, consider its location, transportation access, and facilities. Typically, a primary location and an alternate is chosen to ensure that there is an agreed-upon location in advance of a disaster.

The command center will always be staffed by the disaster recovery coordinator and the recovery team leader who is knowledgeable with the written elements of the disaster recovery plan. The team leader will understand the command structure and be familiar with the plan's objectives, as well as all the recovery and management teams involved in disaster recovery. This is now a 24-hour operation, so additional personnel might be required to support multiple shifts.

Location

If the disaster is limited to a portion of the primary site, the location will always be on the premises. If the disaster prevents the entire site from being used, then the command center must be located at the pre-established backup site specified in the disaster recovery plan.

When selecting your meeting place, consider its location relative to your normal work place and to all the recovery team members. The natural thought is to choose a location far away from the primary computing facility. However, the location should not be so far that staff members have difficulty getting there. Conversely, it should not be so close to your normal premises that it could be effected by the same incident. Choosing the donut shop across the street in a hurricane disaster, for example, would just not work.

Some location suggestions include the main board room (for a disaster limited to the server room), a local hotel, or a corporate satellite office. The key is to have 24/7 access to this location. This is another reason why a retail location like a coffee shop will not suffice.

Alternate Meeting Place

Select at least two possible meeting locations. Some of the specifics for choosing a second location are mentioned below. Your primary location could be close to your facility, and be used if access is feasible. Your alternate location should be further away, thus ensuring availability if your primary location is not accessible. Ensure all your options are always fully documented. Also make sure the recovery teams know which location is chosen as the place to convene. Having recovery team members dispersed across multiple meeting locations is a poor start to your recovery process.

Staffing

The command center should be staffed by at least one senior person from the IT recovery management team at all times and the disaster recovery coordinator or another administrative person knowledgeable with the disaster recovery plan. Above all, this person must know the command structure and be familiar to all the management teams involved in disaster recovery.

Rules

The most basic rule is this: The command center is responsible for establishing and maintaining control over the disaster recovery process. Ensure effective communications are established between recovery teams and the senior management of your organization.

The following documentation must be present:

- The disaster recovery plan for the organization
- Contact lists for the recovery management team and the other teams
- Guidelines for communications policy, establishing and controlling internal and external communications

When a catastrophic event affects an organization, stress permeates all the employees who work there. Stress should be concentrated in the command center—that's why many call it the "war room." This is where the important efforts to achieve the recovery activities will be concentrated. During a DR operation, the assumption is that all stress is negative or counterproductive. However, that is not necessarily always the case. When the DR plan also accounts for the human elements, it increases the likelihood that the "war room" will be staffed by people who are selected and trained to cope with stress more effectively than those on the outside.

Command Center Equipment

The minimum equipment required includes a phone number and an e-mail address that will be available for the duration of the disaster. In many cases, some of the specialized equipment required will not be immediately available. Procurement folks must be engaged to try and resolve any potential problems.

The command center will need to include the following equipment:

- Several landline phone sets. Verify the following:
  - » A dial tone
  - » Active voicemail
  - » Procedures for using the phone set
  - » Conference-call capabilities
- A PC running the required imaged applications needed by management as detailed in the disaster recovery plan. Verify that the PC is functional and any required passwords are available.
- E-mail capabilities with the company standard applications (such as Lotus Notes or Microsoft Exchange) and with a known IP verifiable address, preferably within the company's domain and firewall. Verify the following:
  - » Active e-mail to server
  - » Necessary password
  - » Security
- Web access. Verify the following:
  - » Any special browser
  - » Firewall considerations
  - » Web passwords or keys
- A fax machine and copier
- Food for the staff

Here are other important factors to consider:

- *Vulnerability*—When selecting a location for your meeting place, particularly for your alternate location, ensure you consider the types of vulnerabilities that may face your organization in a disaster. For example, if your primary location is prone to floods, your alternate location should be on high ground or somewhere considered safe and away from the event. If your primary location is in the path of a hurricane, your meeting location should be at a reasonable distance from the hurricane path and out of the evacuation zone.

- *Communications access*—Since the ability to communicate with others in your organization is essential to effectively responding to a disaster, you must ensure that the location you choose has enough telephones lines and Internet bandwidth. That is why a hotel is typically a better choice than, say, a coffee shop. Yes, the sign might say "Internet café," but it would not work for a long period of time as a command center. Short term . . . maybe. You will, of course, bring with you any laptops that will be used with the Internet for e-mail capabilities. This, of course, assumes your laptops were not damaged in the disaster. (Another provision that must be accounted for!)

- *Size of the location*—The location you choose must be big enough for the number of recovery personnel expected to meet in this location. Keep in mind this is strictly a place for you and your key recovery staff to discuss your plan of action and disaster response. It's not a space for all of your staff to work.

When documenting your meeting place, include its street address, who to contact when you get there, where to park, any special check-in procedures, or any special security requirements. See Figure 10.4 for an example. Also provide a complete map to the location, with driving directions, suggested route, specific entrance, and floor plan of the facility if it's a large place like a convention center.

Primary Location	
Facility Name: : The James Hotel and Convention Center	
Street Address: 612 King Street	Floor: 2nd Floor Meeting Rooms
City/State/Zip: Boulder, Colorado	
Contact Person: Front Desk Manager	
Alternate Contact: Assistant Manager	Phone No: 933–555-1212
24 Hour No: Same	
Alternate Location	
Facility Name: The Drake Convention Center	
Street Address: 16 Front Street	Floor: 1st Floor
City/State/Zip: Boulder, Colorado	
Contact Person: Front Desk Manager	Phone No: 933–555-1234
Alternate Contact: Assistant Manager	24 Hour No: Same
Check-in Instructions: A meeting room is booked under the name "Richard Smith." Room name and location will be supplied by hotel and/or convention-center staff. Wireless Internet Web keys supplied.	
Food Arrangements: Arranged.	
Meeting Room: 15 chairs classroom style. Projection device and screen.	
Drive Time: 25 minutes from office facility. Map and driving instructions below.	

Figure 10.4: This is a sample meeting place description.

Facing and Dealing with the Media

In every disaster recovery plan, there should be a principal company spokesperson designated in advance to face the media. Believe me when I say that this is not a job for nervous types. Great care and caution must be taken in selecting and training the right person for this role. Are you prepared to face the media when a disaster strikes? Who from your organization will face the press, and what will that person say? More importantly, how will he or she say it?

The media will be aggressive and very demanding in getting everything they possibly can get their hands on. Remember they put into print or run the video with the message they and only they wish to express. This might not be your view.

Real-World Example

Several years ago, a customer had a terrible situation occur: a liquid chlorine explosion caused great damage to the manufacturing plant, and there was, unfortunately, loss of life. The media was everywhere. The huge fire was contained in the far back of the manufacturing property. One of the computer administrators came outside and was rushed by media crews. Immediately, the lights were on and the cameras were rolling. They asked him, "What's it like in there? How many people are hurt?" He replied, "Hell, don't ask me! I don't even know what's going on! I was simply doing my job when I saw all this commotion outside the window, so I came out to see what's going on out here."

The reporters immediately snapped back, "You mean nobody warned you? Didn't you hear a fire alarm? Was there no evacuation of the building? Is this a common occurrence in your company? Didn't you smell the chlorine?"

"Well," he replied, "I didn't hear any alarm. In fact, I'm not sure that it even works. When I came out the stairway it sure reeked of chlorine, but it's a smell I've gotten use to. It's like that most evenings."

Talk about all the wrong things to say! The very last thing you want is to see one of your computer operators on CNN, giving his opinions of the disaster.

Here were some of the misrepresented facts about the administrator's statements:

- The chlorine smell he referred to was that of the janitor bleaching the stairway floors nightly.

- The fire alarm wasn't heard because the administrator routinely listened to music on headphones.

> - There was an evacuation. The administrator did not use his entry key to get into the computer room. Instead, he left the room's door propped open, so security was unaware of any entry that might have been made into the computer room.
>
> To paraphrase the legendary newscaster Paul Harvey, "You heard the news and now you've heard the rest of the story."

If a disaster strikes your company, the last thing you want to worry about is the opinion of the public. Unfortunately, the news media will beat the fire trucks to the scene of a disaster every time. Count on this to happen. While you are trying to recover your computer systems, the media will be stationed around the corner, waiting with microphone in hand. However, you can help make sure it's not a picture of total gloom and doom to the public. Traditionally, this is part of your organization's business continuity plan. However, you might not have a business continuity plan, so insert this vital role into your DR plan under damage assessment and notification tasks.

Is Your Company Prepared for the Microphone?

There are several steps you can take to prepare pre-selected members of your management recovery team to work with the media. Keep in mind, typically we have ourselves to blame for miscommunication, not the media. We are all thirsty for up-to-the-minute, live news. That is our expectation from the media today. We all watch 24-hour news channels, or even flip between competing networks to hear the exact same breaking news story all over again.

The media prefers to report bad news rather than good news. That's what keeps the viewers glued. So here are some very important things to consider:

1. Decide in advance exactly who will speak to the media. Always assign one primary spokesperson and an alternate. When more than one person communicates with the media, it can create inconsistencies in your story. That is the last thing you want to do.

2. Journalists tend to seek out the worst possible prognosis for your company, as bad news is what they prefer to report on. The savvy spokesperson should learn how to quickly redirect any negative, baited question from a newsperson and restate the question in a more positive way. Also inform the media what your company has done to improve the situation. Be aggressive in stating your company's position.

3. Practice this role just as you would practice your technical recovery. There are professional agencies available that will give you the "lights, camera, action" experience, even including a thousand microphones pressed up against you. This will help you train for handling this type of pressure. This should be part of every desktop disaster recovery test.

4. Answer all questions as directly and briefly as you can, in a positive manner. Say something like, "Yes, we had a disaster and we are in the process of recovering all our mission-critical systems. We will be serving our customers tomorrow." Keep it brief and to the point. Don't elaborate; too much gets read into every word you speak.

5. Never lie . . . end of story. Do not "ASSume" the reporter knows little about your situation, and that you can lie your way out of a sticky situation. The media will catch you. And then you will have some serious explaining to do.

It is inevitable that the public will hear your story. This is beyond your control. What you can control is how they hear it. By being careful, credible, and above all brief, you can turn a bad situation into a positive public relations opportunity. Show the media how organized and responsible your organization can be in the face of a disaster. When the news truck arrives, you will simply say to the disaster recovery team, "Excuse me, I have an interview with the press. They will hear our story."

Notification Solution Design

Provide instructions in advance to let your team members know how to best use the notification process. While there are many ways to address the disaster notification process, the best solution is one that does not depend on your own internal computing systems or any component of your local IT infrastructure. If there is a disaster in your facility, any homegrown systems will probably be affected. The ideal communications system is independent of your operations and is fault tolerant.

Web Site Notification in a Regional Disaster

The problem, unfortunately, in many regional disasters is that many companies, specifically smaller enterprises, do not have a Web site offering emergency response information. Not having a clear channel of communications for customers, suppliers, or employees other than those listed in the disaster recovery plan only adds unnecessary turmoil.

A Web site can serve as an extremely valuable method of communication during a crisis. No front-desk receptionist or human resources department can be expected to handle the potential volume of requests for information, even if they were in their offices during an emergency. You must have a way to instruct employees on where to pick up their paychecks, confirm they will be paid promptly, stay in touch with the workers' union, and inform employees when to next report into work. What about telling your customers that everything will be normal again in 48 hours? This will go a long way to keeping their loyalty.

Use an external provider for the Web site. Relying on your internal server might not be possible in a site loss. I recommend housing the Web server with a service provider a thousand miles away. This will ensure the site is up and running. Administration and updates to the Web site can be made by a technical recovery team member.

Using a 1-800 Service

If a disaster strikes after normal working hours, or if you need to send people home initially, you will need a means to communicate with your recovery teams. I have found that you can use the phone network more effectively by setting up an 800 number with voicemail capability, in advance. Remember that 800 numbers are virtual, and long-distance toll charges are not a factor. Employees should be given a wallet-sized card to carry with them at all times that contains this 800 number and a copy of the notification call tree information. Should a regional event occur, they are instructed to call the 800 number to listen to the updated information. This technique is a great solution in a regional disaster and should be in place in addition to setting up local calling trees.

If using an 800 service, regular updates must take place. The notification system should also authenticate the person requesting access, to ensure that a false notification is not given. To eliminate any hesitation for activation of the 800 service in a perceived emergency, there should be a clearly defined policy of what constitutes an emergency and a procedure to execute the plan. Your disaster recovery plan will dictate your declaration timelines and all parameters. Your designated recovery team personnel should be trained in advance on any specific procedures or specialized equipment for administering the 800 service. Training always reinforces the procedures to ensure continued success.

Phone List Maintenance

It's virtually guaranteed that the members of the IT recovery and management team will change. Even if the team members stay the same, their contact information will change. People move, change cell phones, change e-mail addresses . . . and often, it seems! Your disaster recovery coordinator is responsible for keeping the contact information for recovery team personnel up-to-date. All changes to contact information, including contracted personnel, should be maintained on an agreed-upon, regular interval.

I suggest distributing employee contact information forms quarterly, to confirm their accuracy and completeness. For predictably volatile periods, like an upcoming hurricane season, distribute the forms in advance to maintain a state of readiness.

Summary

Disaster notification is an important DR plan element, yet it is often severely neglected. It is the missing or weak link because disasters are often viewed as unlikely events. With recent events like Hurricanes Katrina, Rita, and Francis, we have learned that this is not the case. Just turn on CNN on any given day, and you will quickly realize disasters do happen—and a lot more frequently than most people like to believe.

Disasters come in many forms, but they are indeed real and do need to be adequately planned for. Ensure you can reach your recovery teams in times of need. Effective communications is key to properly executing plans and restoring your IT infrastructure in a timely fashion.

11

How to Develop and Document a Disaster Recovery Plan

T he purpose of writing a disaster recovery plan is to provide a detailed roadmap for developing all actions and responsibilities to be executed in the event of a disaster. While planning for disaster recovery, it is essential to account for recovery from all the disaster-related scenarios that apply to your organization. The disaster recovery plan must be written so that it is flexible and scalable to the types of failure that your organization is faced with.

The DR planning project is approached in phases. As you start writing the plan, you must conceptualize as a team, not individually, what it should accomplish. What are your business and IT organizational recovery goals? As a group, walk through what the ideal DR plan would need to support your IT delivery objectives. What would the DR plan scope look like, and who would be involved? This is determined by working with the team members throughout the documentation process. As a team, you must reach a consensus on the assumptions for the planning project. You need to analyze the findings of the vulnerability study, risk assessment, and finally the business impact analysis. The team can then use the scope of this project to identify disaster recovery strategies and solutions to meet the organizational recovery requirements.

The disaster recovery plan must document all procedures necessary for effective and timely recovery. That implies you need to get documentation in place before an event occurs. When a disaster strikes, you don't want to be forced to sift through loose notes to resolve the issue. A proper disaster recovery plan should include all aspects of systems recovery. This will go beyond the bits and bytes of server restoration to include procedures for dealing with executive management and other departments in your organization, and for working with local police and fire officials. This document becomes all-encompassing for the IT recovery team. Include as much detail as required to ensure that the IT response in an actual disaster does not lead your teams into chaos, but rather to a successful recovery.

Disaster Recovery Plan Development Overview

There are seven major steps to developing a disaster recovery plan:

1. Understand the objectives of the disaster recovery plan.
2. Understand the DR plan's structural attributes.
3. Understand the phased disaster recovery approach.
4. Understand the established disaster recovery organization.
5. Finalize the basis of your disaster recovery plan.
6. Define and document server restoration procedures.
7. Define testing and a recovery validation program.

The chart in Figure 11.1 provides an overview of these steps, including input and output requirements.

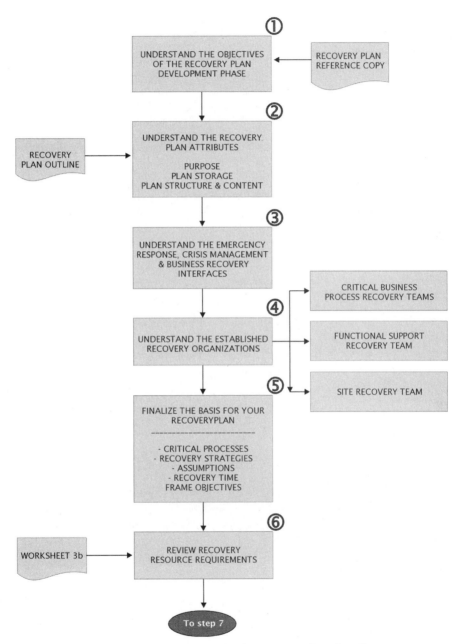

Figure 11.1: An overview of disaster recovery development procedures (part 1).

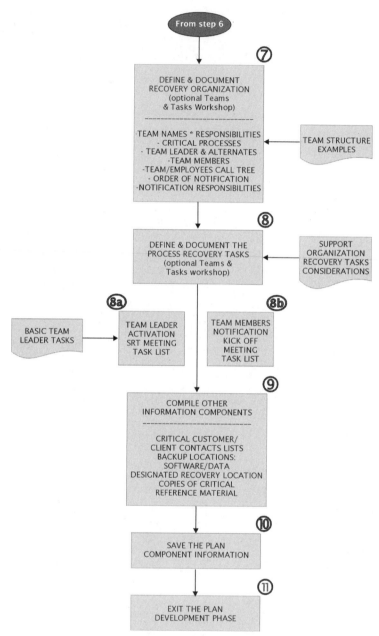

Figure 11.1: An overview of disaster recovery development procedures (part 2).

Step 1: Understand the Objectives of the DR Plan

The objectives of the disaster recovery plan are as follows:

- The DR plan will provide for the resumption of a business unit's critical processes within the established Recovery Time Objectives (RTOs).
- The development of IT recovery team plans will enable designated staff to activate and execute their recovery plans following any major disruption.

These activities include the preparation of the necessary information for all of the required sections of the recovery plan. Word documents, Excel spreadsheets, Visio diagrams, tables, links, and any other electronic materials may be used to supply the necessary contents of the DR plan. All of the information compiled during this phase will be used to construct the final electronic copy of the disaster recovery plan for distribution.

Step 2: Understand the DR Plan's Structural Attributes

The disaster recovery plan organizes and documents the agreed-upon arrangements by the business. Detailed procedures describe how IT will recover all previously defined mission-critical application servers within agreed-upon recovery and time objectives. The DR plan specifies the following:

- Who will be responsible to recover the servers
- What critical applications processes must be recovered
- Where they will be recovered
- When they must be recovered
- How they will be recovered

These plans should ensure that, in the event of a disaster, your IT recovery team will do the following:

- Recover servers according to the documented process.
- Ensure systems availability to the business within agreed-upon timelines.
- Ensure systems are restored to a consistent, useable state.
- Ensure minimal data loss.

The opening chapter of the DR plan will include executive-level statements that set the baseline and expectations of delivery for the plan. These include such areas as the following:

- Documentation overview
- Plan objectives
- Assumptions
- Mission statements
- Disaster-related definitions

Step 3: Understand the Phased Disaster Recovery Approach

Figure 11.2 identifies the disaster recovery phases for a site disaster.

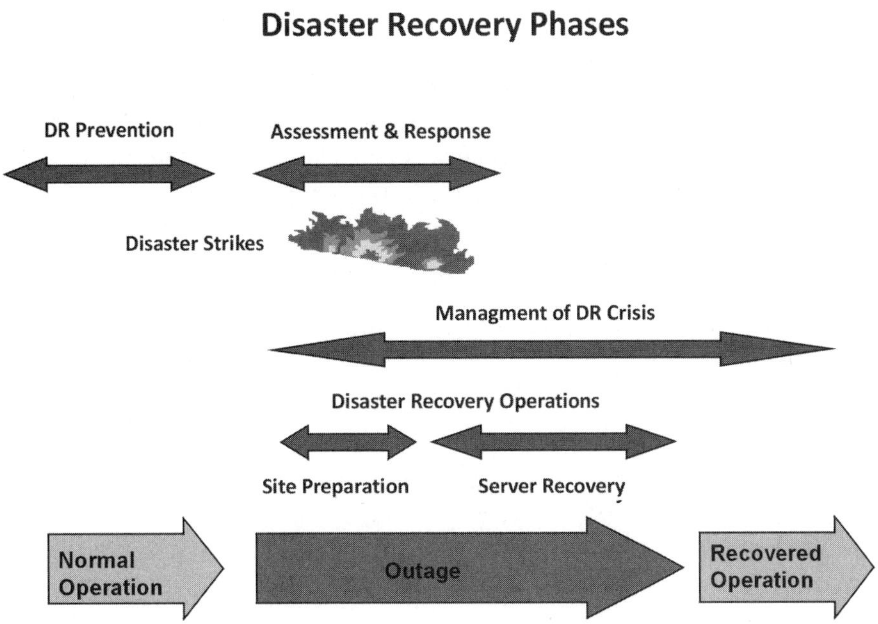

Disaster Recovery Phases

Figure 11.2: Here are the major phases for disaster recovery.

DR Prevention Phase

Disaster prevention does not have a true start or finish line. This phase (or this ongoing, living process) identifies and mitigates the risks within your organization and minimizes the potential for disaster loss. This means always maintaining disaster preparedness by evaluating your IT support infrastructure and levels of acceptable risk. You must constantly update the procedures for handling any unplanned interruption of critical business functions within the data center. Times will change, as will the levels of acceptable risk and the prevention approaches. The vulnerability assessment will bring forward any data-center vulnerabilities as part of the DR planning project.

Whether risks are natural or manmade, the goal of this phase is to implement effective systems and procedures to protect the company's assets and manage these risks. The IBM System i5 server and computer room facility must be properly managed, fully functional, and tested regularly.

Adequate backups protect against permanent loss of data. The iSeries and i5 backup process is a critical function to ensure recovery capabilities and business resumption for the system(s). The backups must be executed on a regular basis and conform to a concise recovery program design. You must maintain the ability to restore all data to a consistent useable state, which minimizes the impact to your applications. That is complete prevention!

Assessment and Initial Response Phase

The assessment and initial response phase includes the actions that must be taken to protect personnel, assess the extent of damage to the computing infrastructure, evaluate means for delivering computing services, and develop an initial response to the disaster scenario or incident. The scenario or incident may range from a power loss causing a temporary business interruption to a regional natural event involving employee evacuation and considerable damage to the computer facilities. The damage assessment and evaluation of the incident will determine the level of response from your disaster recovery plan.

Your response procedures might require the support of external organizations, such as IBM, Business Partners, IT consultants, and of course the local fire and police departments. If the event has the potential to cause significant computer downtime, the disaster declaration phase may be implemented immediately to enable the IT management team to provide guidance and assistance to the rest of the business.

Management of the DR Crisis

The complete management effort for the disaster includes the directions given to the IT recovery team from the IT management team and their actions required to address the outage, restart or restore server operations, and reestablish computing services. During this phase, there will be periods of significant instability that will threaten the company's ability to do normal business. Things will get stressful.

During this phase, the IT management team will provide for overall management guidance and direction to both senior executives and the IT recovery team. This includes activation of the recovery teams and DR plan, disaster declaration, command center activation, and updates to the business executives on a regular basis.

Disaster Recovery Operations Phase

This phase supports the recovery efforts to provide for the timely resumption of mission-critical business operations within the pre-established recovery timeframe. This phase includes two major steps: site preparation and server recovery.

Site preparation includes all initial disaster preparation activities to bring the computing services back online for the business. This starts with retrieving vital records from offsite storage, and continues to travel (either local or out-of-state) and setup of an internal alternate site or commercial hotsite.

Once the site-related activities are in place, the IT recovery team performs server configuration, data restoration, and server startup. The data and server recovery will be fully documented and include a managed set of procedures detailing all recovery actions that must be executed. This step-by-step set of procedures explains all required actions to ensure complete and timely restoration of the data and server infrastructure. This would include activities related to preparing server hardware and the operating system, restoring the data, switching systems in a high-availability recovery strategy, and rerouting networks. All of these activities must be completed within the timeframes agreed upon by the business.

Facilities Restoration Phase

After a disaster, you need to have a strategy to get back to normal business operations at your primary office facility. Disaster recovery supports interim services. In other words, get the business back to normal in the agreed-upon timelines. Once you are running computing operations at a commercial hotsite, for example, you need to consider how to return the services back to your company. You cannot live at the hotsite forever, even if you could afford it. The facilities restoration phase includes all of the facility, computer room, server repair and/or replacement, and rebuild activities required to enable the company to return to a normal operating mode.

Note that the individual business recovery teams are activated upon notification from the site recovery team.

Step 4: Understand the Established Disaster Recovery Organization

Three types of recovery teams may be activated at a site to accomplish a recovery effort. Their roles, responsibilities, contact information, and authority must be clearly defined:

- *The IT management team*—Following a disaster that involves significant impact to the site facilities and the ability to provide computing services, this team is responsible for the following:
  - » Damage assessment
  - » The determination of whether a disaster should be invoked
  - » The commencement of all related recovery and communication activities

  The site recovery team leader will be responsible for the overall management and coordination of the efforts required to recover the mission-critical systems.

- *The IT recovery team*—This team is responsible for ensuring that the systems are recovered within the established recovery timeframe and recovery point objectives. The team members will follow the DR tasks as documented in the plan based on the agreed-upon recovery strategies, scope, and assumptions.
- *The site restoration team*—This team is comprised of representatives from the IT management team that will interface with other members of the organization to help facilitate the recovery of the primary data center.

Team members may come from many organizations, including these:

- Facilities
- Human resources
- Security
- Engineering
- Administration
- Purchasing
- Safety
- Finance
- Procurement
- Corporate communications
- Business partners

Step 5: Establish the Basis for Your DR Plan

The components of the approved recovery strategy resulting from the business impact analysis will be used as the basis for the development and implementation of your recovery plan. You need to clearly define the established recovery roadmap. Make sure the following information from the BIA is clearly stated:

- Define all the critical server applications that must be restored.
- Document the recovery strategies for each critical server. They might all have the same recovery approach, or several different solutions might be needed.
- Ensure that the recovery strategies reflect the assumed disaster scenario.
- List the assumptions on which the recovery strategies are based.
- Document the recovery time objectives for all servers.
- Document the recovery time objectives for all critical servers.
- Define what is in scope and what is *not* supported in the disaster recovery plan.

Step 6: Define and Document the Server Restoration Process

The IT recovery team must develop all required server procedures (step-by-step restoration and system information) that would be executed in a disaster. These procedures must clearly illustrate every required step to support a successful recovery. That means no details are assumed or excluded. However, the premise is that the information supplied will be executed by an IT professional, so a basic IT skillset can be assumed.

All documentation will be compiled to support the system information, in the form of Word documents, Excel spreadsheets, Visio diagrams, and links to other files. The procedures will be used in all aspects of recovery training and testing, and in the event of a real disaster.

Step 7: Define Testing and Recovery Validation

For a DR plan to provide the expected capabilities in a disaster, it must be tested. The document will contain testing strategies that will provide a foundation to validate the contents of the plan for effectiveness as well as for completeness. Training and formalized testing will support the plan objectives. Forms of testing should be documented that best suit your organization. Include active testing, passive testing, and desktop exercises. Document the results of all tests. All of this will drive a change-management process that will ensure the plan is kept up-to-date at all times.

Ready, Set, Write the Plan

Once the recovery strategies have been agreed on, the disaster recovery plan must be defined and documented. Considerable time and effort will be necessary to develop the initial plan. Effective documentation and procedures are extremely important to the ongoing success of any DR plan. Poorly written procedures can be extremely frustrating and difficult to use for your IT recovery team and IT management team. If the procedures are difficult to use or locate, team members will simply not reference them. They will deviate and start to execute procedures as they remember them. DANGER!!

Ensure the plan is easy to use. An unusable document becomes extremely difficult to maintain, and spirals quickly into an outdated DR plan. Well-written plans reduce the time required to read and comprehend the procedures, therefore resulting in a better chance of success. Keep in mind that all DR plans are used under very stressful situations. The plan *must* be well-written, or it will fail you when you need it most.

Even though you are just starting the DR planning process, consider the maintenance of the plan. I know it might sound like you are getting ahead of yourself, but you should consider maintenance right from the beginning of plan development. When writing every section of this document, consider whether its contents will seem precise and logical when it comes time to update it. Is the procedure clear and where you would expect to find it? Or is the information scattered across various pages, maybe even spanning chapters?

You might remember the legendary IBM CISC to RISC AS/400 migration book. That manual won the award hands-down for forcing users to flip back and forth endlessly in trying to determine what step to execute next. There was no flow or structure. If information is scattered about, when it's time to write any updates, you will have to "un-scatter" all those pages and not miss any pertinent changes. By planning a structured approach in advance, the maintenance of the plan will be straightforward and simple, versus a fearful project in itself.

Assign each member of the planning group a section to write. Stick to the strengths of the technical resource or author. Establish a timeline with specific goals. Provide enough time to complete the work, but not so much as to allow assignments to linger. Establish a schedule for the following:

- First draft
- Review
- Second draft
- Tabletop review as a group
- Final draft
- Printing
- Distribution

How to Write the DR Plan

The DR plan must be well organized, action oriented, and comprehensive, as shown in Figure 11.3. Remember, the plan will be written by IT professionals to be used by IT professionals. Suppose your finance director makes the following statements at the DR planning kick-off meeting:

Finance Guy: I want this plan to contain everything! *Agreed.*
Finance Guy: The plan must not make any assumptions. *Agreed.*
Finance Guy: I want nothing left for reading between the lines. *Agreed.*
Finance Guy: I want this plan to contain every single detail, so that even I can recover the system. *Whoa!! Hold the phones.*

The last statement is where I disagree; it's very old thinking. Documenting to a level such as "Right-click, drag down, left-click Properties, right-click Select and then click OK" is way to much. You will need a forklift to carry such a document about. Remember the recovery of any server will be executed by a System i5 or iSeries professional. Some level of skill is required and rightfully assumed. After all, would the finance director let a computer operator manage the company money? I rest my case.

Disaster Recovery Planning
cannot be approached casually

The plan must be ...

- Well organized
- Action oriented
- Comprehensive

Objective: Total restoration of services in a timely manner

Figure 11.3: The three success factors of a DR plan.

Here are some tips to help in writing the plan:

- Assume that the users of the plan are IT personnel unfamiliar with your actual i5 implementation, but possessed of the required technical skillset.

- Use short and direct sentences, and above all keep it simple. Long sentences will overwhelm or confuse the reader. Technical people tend to skim over words and not read stories. Don't force the reader to read a sentence over and over again.

- Use subject headings to start major sections of the plan, and use short paragraphs within a section. Long paragraphs can be detrimental to the average reader's comprehension.

- Read a procedure to yourself after you write it. Ensure you are clearly expressing the points you wish to get across, and then read it again.

- Use bullets for technical steps. If the user needs to press the Enter key or right-click the mouse, state it! Use your organization's standard symbols for keystrokes, such as *<Enter>*.

- Compliment technical steps with screen images. Be careful, however, not to make the file size too big by importing high-resolution graphics.

- Use the same standard format throughout the plan.

- Avoid excessive computer jargon. Sometimes we get caught up in all those three-letter abbreviations. Spell out an acronym or abbreviation on first use, for example, "Now turn to the Hardware Management Console (HMC). The HMC is used to manage. . . ."

- Use position titles as they relate to the DR plan rather than names of individuals. This will significantly reduce the maintenance needed later. Staff will change, but the recovery-related positions will typically remain the same.

- Use both sides of the paper (front and back).

- Identify events that can be done in parallel, and those that must occur sequentially.

- Avoid "This page has been left intentionally blank."

Tools and Style for the Plan

Is your trustworthy word processing software good enough for creating the plan? YES! Microsoft Word is probably the most convenient tool anyone could use and, more importantly, little or no training is required to use it. Also, you can easily incorporate other Microsoft attachments, like Excel spreadsheets, right into the document. We all have a licensed copy of Word, so there's no need to purchase specialized software.

A standard format for the procedures should be developed to ensure consistency and conformity in the plan, and assist in its future maintenance. Documentation should not be new to your organization. Examine current formats and styles in use. They might be easily adapted, and your staff is already familiar with them. Maintaining standard practice is especially important because many people will be writing, reviewing, and updating procedures during the plan's inception. The creation of the plan's structure is vital to the success of the disaster recovery project. This structure must be multi-level to ensure coordination between different recovery teams and departments within your organization.

The procedures in the plan should contain the following:

- The name of the procedure
- Headings
- A footer that contains the procedure's name and page number
- A section for the purpose of the procedure
- Revision control
- A section for the scope of the procedure (what it covers)
- How and where other related pieces of information exist
- References like a URL and author's name
- An area for authorizations or signoffs, if required

Keep the following in mind when designing the plan:

- Minimize dependency on specific individuals.
- Distribute the recovery effort equally.
- Ensure the completeness of every procedure.
- Include timelines for major steps in the plan.
- Ensure the establishment of criteria for critical decisions.
- Minimize dependency on specific outside entities.
- Ensure the plan is current, and a living document.
- Get any necessary signoffs.

The Content of Your Procedures

When you are writing a page, a section, or even a chapter of your plan, ask yourself the basic questions *who*, *what*, *when*, *where*, and *how*. A procedure should always answer two or more of these questions. Here are some examples of how to apply them:

- Who will execute recovery actions?
- What is needed to continue, resume, recover, or restore business functions?
- When must business functions and operations resume?
- Where do we go to resume corporate, business, and operational functions?
- How detailed do the procedures need to be for continuity, resumption, recovery, or restoration?

Here are some additional questions to keep in mind about content:

- Does the DR plan contain clear and concise statements and describe the critical server functions covered within the scope of the plan?
- Does the DR plan provide sufficient information for each section of the document to allow the reader to understand how to execute the plan?
- Does the plan contain a brief description of critical systems used, including the criticality of the area?

- Does the plan describe the roles and responsibilities of the teams?
- Are all notification call trees properly documented and updated at least quarterly?
- Does the plan describe the necessary actions to ensure that the proper coordination of activities is carried out?
- Does the plan describe how it will be maintained, tested, reviewed, and updated to ensure that it accurately reflects the most current information?
- Does the documentation follow a standard format and guidelines?
- Is the plan distributed to all disaster recovery personnel?
- Is there adequate provision for emergency communication among key personnel?
- Has a command center been designated at which all relevant personnel are to convene in the event of a disaster?

The Disaster Recovery Plan's Structure

The DR plan must follow a common outline to provide a consistent, simple, and readable structure. The structure must be easy to use, so any specific piece of information can be quickly located. Poorly written procedures are extremely frustrating to use and difficult to maintain. A well-written DR plan reduces the time required to read and understand the procedures, and therefore, results in a better chance of success.

A disaster recovery plan would imply that there is only one way to write a plan. In fact, every plan should be unique and reflect the specific business requirements of your organization. The following outline is a sample of suggested sections for a disaster recovery plan, but additional items relevant to your site and organization should always be considered. This list is by no means all-encompassing:

- Chapter 1, Documentation Overview
  - » Plan Objective
  - » Mission Statement

» Definitions

» Scope of Plan

» Assumptions

» Disaster Recovery Plan Support Services

» Software Overview

» Network Configuration

» Critical Systems Definition, A List

» Critical Systems Definition, B List

» Disaster Recovery Team Overview

» Disaster Recovery Team Roles, High-Level Overview

» Distribution List

- Chapter 2, IT Management Team Overview

  » Team Roles and Responsibilities

  » Disaster Recovery Preparedness

  » Overall Site-Restoration Timeline

  » Strategy Overview

  » Management Team Leader Responsibilities

  » Management Team Leader Checklist

- Chapter 3, IT Technical Recovery Team

  » Team Roles and Responsibilities

  » Disaster Recovery Preparedness

  » Administrative Responsibilities

  » Team Recovery Responsibilities

  » Technical Recovery Manager Checklist

- Chapter 4, Plan Activation Procedures

  » Determining Personnel Status

  » Plan Activation Process

- » Disaster Alert Notification Procedure
- » First-Alert Response
- » Disaster Verification
- » Placing Hotsite and IT Recovery Team on Alert
- » Assembling Team Leaders at Command Center
- » Damage Assessment Evaluation
- » Notification of Personnel
- » Response and Recovery Recommendations
- » Activating Staff Department Support
- » Responsibilities during Actual Disaster

- Chapter 5, Hotsite Activation
  - » Declaring a Disaster with the Hotsite
  - » Disaster Declaration Authorized Personnel
  - » Directions and Map to Primary Hotsite
  - » Directions and Map to Secondary Hotsite
  - » Travel Procedures
  - » Recalling Tapes from Offsite Storage
  - » Offsite Storage Authorized Personnel
  - » Opening the Hotsite

- Chapter 6, IBM System i5 Environment Restoration
  - » Licensed Internal Code Restore
  - » Licensed Internal Code Restore at Hotsite
  - » Building Your Disk Configuration at the Hotsite
  - » Licensed Internal Code Restore at Raymond
  - » Recovering Your Disk Configuration at Raymond
  - » Restoring the Operating System
  - » User Profiles Restore

» Configuration Data Restore

» Restoring IBM Product Libraries

» Recovering User Libraries

» DLO Recovery

» Recovering Objects in Directories

» Spooled Files Restore

» Restore Authority

» Finishing Steps

» Verifying System Information

» The Print Job Log

» Resource Integrity Recovery

» Varying Online Device Recovery

• Chapter 7, IBM System i5 System Information

» System Overview

» Working with System Status

» Display PTF and Group Status

» LPAR LVT

» Hardware Management Console Configuration

» Licensed Program Products, Product Option

» Licensed Program Products, Installed Release

» TCP/IP Interface Information

» TCP/IP Route Information

» TCP/IP Host Table Entries Information

» Network Attributes

» System Values

» Ethernet Line Description

» ECS Line Description

» System Startup Program

» Software Keys Procedures

» iSeries/400 Tape Management Policies

» Backup Program details

» Backup and Tape Management Policies

» Hot Box Contents

- Chapter 8, Intel Restoration

  » Windows 2003 Setup

  » Windows Post-2003 Setup Configuration

  » Installing Service Packs

  » Installing IBM Director

  » Installing Intel Network Drivers

  » Installing Configuration Drivers

  » IBM Update Express

  » Installing Backup Software

  » Rebuilding Backup Software Database

- Chapter 9, Intel System Information

  » Server IP Summary

  » Hardware Rack Configurations

  » Servers Software Inventory

  » Disk Logical Partitioning

  » Disk Partition Information

  » SAN Wiring Information

  » Tape Switch Details

  » Fiber Switch Layout, Fabric

  » Configuration of Zones

  » VMWare Server Configuration

  » Citrix Server Configuration

- » Exchange Server Installation
- » Active Directory

- Chapter 10, Site Restoration Procedures
  - » Restoration Activities
  - » Roles and Responsibilities
  - » Site Construction Specifications
  - » Environmental Issues
  - » Safety and Security
  - » Insurance Inspection
  - » Team Leader Responsibilities
  - » Management Checklist
  - » Transition Planning Checklist
  - » Site Restoration Checklist
  - » Funding Approval

- Chapter 11, Testing Overview
  - » Document Standards on the Home DRP Directory
  - » Testing Overview
  - » Disaster Recovery Coordinator Duties for Testing and Plan Maintenance
  - » Testing Objectives
  - » Passive Testing
  - » Active testing
  - » Plan Maintenance
  - » Testing Results

- Appendices
  - » Appendix A, IT Management Team Call Tree
  - » Appendix B, IT Technical Recovery Team Call Tree
  - » Appendix C, Staff Department Contact List

» Appendix D, Preferred Vendor Information

» Appendix E, License Key Retrieval Information

» Appendix F, Revisions Schedule

Developing and Writing the Procedures

The procedures should start with a section that includes the following:

» Title page

» Table of contents

» Introduction

» Plan objective

» Mission statement

» Definitions

» Assumptions

You then continue to other sections, which provide details about hardware, software, teams, responsibilities, etc.

The Title Page

The title page is an important part of the disaster recovery plan, but it typically gets little or no attention. The title page should include the name and location of the organization for which the plan was developed. If your organization uses unique facility names or building names, or is a service bureau to the supporting company, then the title page should include these references.

The title page should include the date the initial disaster recovery plan was developed, along with the most recent revision date. This revision date is used for change control by all plan owners. The title page should also state that the document is "Confidential, for internal use only." In some organizations, the page immediately following the title page has a legal disclaimer outlining the confidentiality and strict use of this document. You should discuss this with your legal counsel to ensure the disaster recovery plan meets the privacy disclaimer requirements of your specific organization. The title page can also list the name of the DR plan coordinator, as he or she is the owner of the document itself.

Include the company logo to add legitimacy to the plan, as well as visually giving it a little color. Additional artwork on the title page can go a long way to giving this very important document some reader appeal. Also include a title page for each chapter in the disaster recovery plan. These become logical separators.

Table of Contents

The table of contents for your plan should be detailed enough to show all the section headings, chapter titles, and major subheadings. The table must be organized in the order in which the parts in the plan occur. Secondly, include references to any tables, diagrams, or charts that are included within a chapter. This very important element is typically omitted.

The contents of any appendices should also be displayed in detail, including testing reports, risk assessment documents, business impact analysis reports, and revision schedules. Some organizations also include a table of contents within each chapter, as an easy reference tool for that chapter. All pages referenced in the table of contents should be bookmarked for direct access.

Introduction

The introduction in the DR plan should provide an overview of the plan's contents and delivery expectations. It should summarize any specific compliance or regulatory guidelines, like Sarbanes-Oxley or HIPAA, as well as any organizational policies that relate to the disaster response. It might make sense in some industries to dedicate an appendix to further detail specific adherence to stated compliance or other policies, levels of compliance audited, and compliance reporting documents. Make your auditors happy at the onset, and your DR plan will not face initial scrutiny.

Plan Objective

The disaster recovery plan's objective states that the plan is designed to provide immediate response and subsequent recovery from any unplanned computing service interruption, such as the complete loss of utility service, critical server failure, or catastrophic loss of the facility. The plan's objective provides an overview of the requirements, strategies, and proposed actions necessary to rapidly and effectively recover computing services in such events. State all plan objectives and outline specific details for incident response, subsequent disaster recovery actions, and activities that are included within the respective recovery team plans.

Here is an example of a plan objective:

The Disaster Recovery Plan has been developed to meet the following objectives:

1. *Provide an organized and consolidated approach to managing response and recovery activities following any unplanned incident or business interruption, avoiding confusion and reducing exposure to error.*

2. *Provide prompt and appropriate response to any unplanned incident, thereby reducing the impact resulting from short-term business interruptions.*

3. *Recover essential operations in a timely manner, increasing the ability of the company to recover from damaging loss to the facility.*

The purpose of this document is to describe the specific contingency procedures, recovery strategy, and resources required to safeguard the processing capabilities and financial integrity of OurCo's computer facilities. This is required in order to be in compliance with OurCo's accepted standards for computer operations, risk assessment, and contingency planning.

Mission Statement

A mission statement is a brief description of the disaster recovery plan's fundamental purpose. The mission statement articulates the company's disaster recovery solution and summarizes the approach to the organization. Have the IT management team leader provide a mission statement to demonstrate the company's commitment to disaster recovery. The statement should define the purpose of the disaster recovery plan and indicate that it will involve the entire organization.

Here is an example of a mission statement:

The disaster recovery plan has been developed to provide immediate response and subsequent recovery from any unplanned computing service interruption such as a critical server failure, or a catastrophic event such as a loss of the corporate computing facility. The plan supports all critical computer-based applications as defined in this document to be fully recovered within two days (48 hours) of a full-scale disaster.

The plan is for recovery of the corporate data center, located at 1234 Smith Avenue in YourTown, Ohio, from a site disaster or lesser incident causing a disruption in service delivery exceeding 48 hours. The plan includes all tasks, resources, and time estimates developed and maintained by the DR plan coordinator. The plan also consists of procedures to be executed at the time of a disaster.

Figure 11.4 illustrates the server-room recovery and relocation of operations.

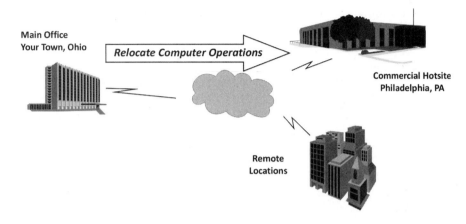

Main Office
Your Town, Ohio

Relocate Computer Operations

Commercial Hotsite
Philadelphia, PA

Remote
Locations

Figure 11.4: An illustration like this might be included in the plan's mission statement.

Definitions for Disaster Recovery Planning

The following are samples of some terms you might include in the "Definitions" section of your plan.

Alert Declaration of Potential Disaster

An alert declaration of potential disaster is the notification to a commercial hotsite that a potential disaster situation exists or has occurred. It tells the hotsite to stand by for possible escalation or activation of the computer contingency plan. The alert triggers internal escalation and potential set up of hardware in advance of the actual disaster declaration.

Declaration of Disaster

A declaration of disaster is a formal announcement by preauthorized personnel that a disaster or severe outage is predicted or has occurred at your primary computing facility. Declaration of a disaster triggers the activation of the disaster recovery plan, procedures, activities, and response to the emergency or disaster event. All prearranged mitigating actions (e.g. moving to an alternate site) will be implemented.

Disaster

A disaster is any sudden, calamitous event that results in great damage or loss to your organization. A disaster causes a prolonged disruption or creates an inability for your organization to provide critical business functions for a predetermined period of time, as stated in the mission statement. The time factor determines whether an interruption in service is an inconvenience or a disaster.

Disaster Recovery

Disaster recovery is the reaction to a sudden, unplanned event that enables an organization to continue critical business functions until normal business operations resume. Disaster recovery includes all the activities and responses to an interruption necessary to reestablish the processing capabilities of essential computing services after a disaster has occurred.

Disaster Recovery Plan

A disaster recovery plan is a document listing your recovery objectives and priorities in the event your company experiences a disaster. This document will address the business case and recovery sequence for business processes that are critical, and how much time a recovery should take before it financially affects your company.

The document will identify leadership responsibilities, alternate computer locations, technology solutions, and staffing requirements. The plan will contain the following:

- Advanced planning and arrangements for recovery of an organization's critical server functions and processes
- Sufficient preparations, and a set of agreed-upon procedures to respond to a disaster
- Coverage of all events resulting from a partial to total loss of primary computing facilities
- Arrangements to ensure the availability of equipment and personnel
- What mission-critical computing services will be resumed
- When they will be resumed
- Where they will be resumed
- How they will be resumed
- Who will perform the actions required for resumption of services

Hotsite

The disaster recovery hotsite is an alternate location to be used to recover business critical services when the primary facilities are inaccessible because of a disaster. The alternate commercially operated facility includes supporting technical support staff, hardware, workstations, and communications to be used in the event of a disaster. Location and size of the hotsite will be proportional to the equipment and resources required to support the needs stated.

IT Management Team

The IT management team is a group of senior managers, directors, and business/IT line managers who will assume overall management responsibility for the response to and resolution of any disastrous incidents that could affect the company's personnel, profitability, image, or survival resulting from a loss of computing services. This team is responsible for directing and controlling all of the actions required to address and resolve the event.

Prevention

Prevention refers to policies, procedures, and measures that speak to the identification and mitigation of the different types of risks within the IT-provided computing services. Risks may be natural or manmade. Prevention activities include the implementation of effective systems and procedures that will lessen the possibility or the impact of adverse incidents occurring at your site. The primary goals of prevention are to protect the organization's assets and manage risk.

Recovery

Recovery activities speak to the activation of previously developed tasks and teams to provide for the timely resumption of the critical business processes within the established recovery timeframes.

Recovery Point Objective (RPO)

The RPO is the point in time to which server data must be restored to resume normal processing of transactions involving the data. This is the amount of data that can be lost without adversely affecting the organization. The RPO indicates the data that is stored offsite. All critical business functions and interfaces will be synchronized to the same point in time when systems become available again.

Recovery Team

The recovery team is a group of individuals charged with the responsibility for recovering a business unit or process following disaster, also known as the *IT recovery team*. Members of the team will be actively involved in the recovery operation of the partially or totally destroyed computer room. Following the containment of the disaster, this team will be responsible for damage assessment and the determination of which recovery actions should be invoked, and in what order. They will be responsible for the overall management and coordination of the effort required to recover from the disruption. The team will provide onsite technical staff and will support all related issues. All servers will be made available as identified in the mission-critical equipment list.

Recovery Time Objective (RTO)

The recovery time objective (RTO) is the length of time required to recover from an unplanned outage as a result of a disaster. It is the acceptable time to recover all applications used in the business process, including recovery of applications, data, and end-user access to those applications. The RTO is directly related to the business impact analysis and is normally stated as a specific time value in minutes, hours, or days.

Restoration

Restoration refers to the plans and procedures that provide for the configuration, recovery of system and user data, set up of mission-critical server applications, and related activities to enable the company to return to a normal mode of operation.

Test

A test is an exercise of the disaster recovery plan under simulated conditions. A test enables the recovery team members to rehearse and enhance the recovery plan procedures that will be executed during an actual disaster recovery effort. Testing can be done in the form of active tests at a commercial hotsite or desktop exercises performed in a board room. Both activities support the validation and completeness of the DR plan.

Disaster Recovery Plan Assumptions

The disaster recovery plan is based on the assumption that a full disaster situation (complete loss of computing services) or loss of building facilities has occurred. The goal is to ensure that mission-critical servers and communication services are restored to the business user community. The resources and logistics necessary to make this happen are described in this document. The plan is also adaptable to lesser disasters, such as the loss of a single piece of equipment or a Raid5 failure in a System i5 partition.

For a DR plan to be effective, it must be current. Regularly scheduled maintenance of the plan will ensure the information necessary for a successful recovery. Testing will check the procedures and information stored in the plan for accuracy and suitability to the tasks of recovery.

Here is an example of a plan's assumptions:

This plan is written based on the following assumptions:

- *Only the primary facility has been disabled by the disruption; all other organizational facilities are unaffected.*

- *The offsite storage location for critical backup files (currently located at Your Offsite Storage Vendor on 3295 5th Avenue) is intact and accessible.*

- *Qualified personnel as identified in this document are available to perform disaster recovery responsibilities.*

- *Disaster recovery is performed in accordance with the procedures set forth within this plan.*

- *Data backup and tape rotation practices are performed on a regular schedule and validated by IT support staff.*

- *The hotsite is accessible and available for use by the company.*

- *Plan review, maintenance, and updates are performed on a regular basis to ensure a viable state of readiness.*

- *Disaster recovery awareness and training programs have been implemented.*

- *Plan exercise strategies have been tested on a regular basis.*

DR Plan Supported Services

It is important to outline what IT-related services are being supported by the contents of the disaster recovery plan. This is a high-level, executive summary that will formally state the intentions and deliverables of the plan. This section should outline the following:

- The RPO
- The RTO
- Formal contractual commitments in place with providers
- A high-level overview of what has been committed contractually

Here is an example of a summary of services:

OurCo has developed a disaster recovery plan that will return the company's computer-based systems to near normal operation within 3 days of a disaster that disrupts normal computer processing capabilities.

A contractual commitment is in place for computer hotsite access with ABC Company, a commercial provider. The primary disaster-support center of ABC Company is located in Phoenix, Arizona, with a second alternate site located in Denver, Colorado. ABC Company's disaster-recovery services subscription includes access to three iSeries/400s, Blade Center, SAN, and multiple Intel servers. A work area at the recovery center will provide office facilities for 15 people, including standard desktop configurations.

The hotsite facility would be used as a command center for system support and recovery of computing services.

All recovery will be performed using the media stored from the offsite storage facility located at StorageNow in Phoenix, Arizona. The operating system and all business applications will be recovered to the most recent time available from tape backup media. Some loss of data will be inevitable. The Recovery Point Objective is 24 to 48 hours, depending on the support application.

Everyday normal operations will not be available in an emergency situation; only the critical business needs will be supported at the hotsite. All functions not supported at the hotsite will require a manual system to be established by the business units, or they will not be performed until return from the hotsite is facilitated. All manual system functions performed during the contingency period will be maintained by the business units. Upon restoration of the primary site, the data from these functions will be keyed into the system and updated.

The disaster recovery plan is independent of the business continuity plan.

Software Overview

Summarize all software used in your organization and supported in the disaster recovery plan. A brief paragraph describing the name of the software and the business function it supports will help illustrate the contents covered within the plan. The corresponding supporting server infrastructure for these core applications should also be included. The core applications govern the ongoing operation of the enterprise.

A typical statement of software would include the following:

The core systems supporting OurCo's client base include PeopleSoft, JDEdwards Enterprise One, IBM's Lotus Notes/Lotus Domino, and SeaGull's GUI400. These systems use an IBM iSeries and IBM Intel compatible computer equipment. The Intel servers provide Web and Citrix CNC infrastructure. The Intel servers operate Windows 2003. The corporate standard on the iSeries/400 is version V5R3 and the ERP software is JDEdwards E1, Microsoft

Office, and Lotus Notes for e-mail. The file servers are SQL databases using a SAN solution, which is Windows 2003 based.

Oracle JD Edwards ERP Software Overview

The organization is currently running Oracle JDEdwards OneWorld E1 8.10 Base with Tools Release 9.86.

Environments

Currently, our organization uses the following environments: JD810 (Pristine), DV810, PY810, and PD810. In addition, other environment "skeletons" are fully configured. This allows the organization to quickly drop data into an environment without overwriting data in one of our existing environments. For example, CP810 uses PY objects, with its own set of data.

Application Servers

Currently, one Windows 2003 application server is in use. JDEAPP2 is a batch server that runs UBEs that are time-consuming and CPU-intensive. This server also runs UBEs that populate the OCR database files, since these files need to be on a Windows-based server.

Each application module depends on the other for information. Therefore, no module could be restored and be expected to perform its function without the other modules and the entire database in place. With few exceptions, all of the production environment will be restored in the event of a disaster. Access to the recovered systems will be in a phased process, to provide the maximum processing power available to areas of the business regarded as critical.

In the example, the system is hosted on an IBM System i5 partition. A pristine environment and other environments are configured to meet specific business requirements. JDEdwards is a modular, integrated suite of business applications that includes the following:

- Financials

  » Financial Reporting provides the controller's office with financial reports on a regular basis.

  » Job Cost manages projects and jobs and monitors the associated costs and revenues.

  » Fixed Assets tracks fixed-asset information and computes period depreciation.

  » Accounts Receivable provides accounts-receivable information.

  » Accounts Payable provides accounts-payable information.

- Human Resources

  » Health and Safety tracks accident information.

  » Payroll processes the company's payroll.

  » Benefits Administration administers the company's benefits packages.

  » Human Resources maintains the employee's profile information.

- Plant Maintenance optimizes maintenance, repair, and operations inventories and automates the fulfillment of spare parts and supplies.

- Address Book is a central database that contains the names and addresses of all employees, vendors, customers, suppliers, retirees, etc.

A complete ERP software solution diagram (Figure 11.5) and hardware topology (Figure 11.6) should represent the critical applications running the business. This helps illustrate the flow of data across the ERP application model.

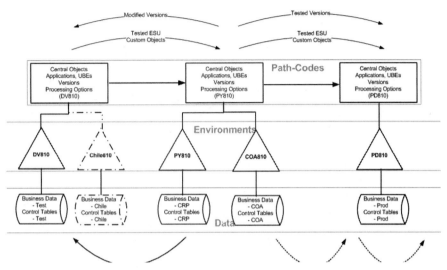

Figure 11.5: Software architecture.

Rack 01	Rack 02
Flat Screen	**Fat09**
	Fat10
	PC Console
Blade Centre **TS01, TS02, TS03, TS04 TS05, Deployment, CreateForm**	
	Switch
KVM/Keybroad	
Active Domain Controller	
LTO (Tape Drive)	**iSeries (810)**
SPACE	
Fat05	
Fat06	
Fat07	
Fat08	
Fat01	
Fat02	
Fat03	
Fat04	
SAN	

Figure 11.6: Business software/hardware topology.

379

Critical Systems Definition, A-List

As a result of the business impact analysis and critical server definitions, your organization will have an agreed-upon list of mission-critical servers that are within the scope of the disaster recovery plan. The purpose of this section is to identify to the business which computing services have been identified as critical and will be recovered within the RTO of the mission statement. These servers are identified as "A-list" recovery servers, as shown in Table 11.1. Appropriate backup and recovery program modifications would have been implemented and tested to support this list. The servers in the A-list will be recovered at the commercial hotsite. The noncritical business systems will have a lower priority. These are referred to as the "B-list" servers. Efforts should be first directed at critical applications.

Table 11.1: Sample A-List Servers List	
Server Name	**Function**
iSeries/400 – JDESYS	JDE
ISeries/400 – NOTES	Lotus Domino Cluster
System i5 – JDEwal	Linux Fire Wall
DC1	Primary Domain Controller
WEB01	External Web Server
CITSEC	Citrix Secure Gateway Server
JJGM	Node 1 of SQL Cluster
DBM7	Database Server
JJPRINT	Node 1 of Print Cluster
VMCLust	VMWARE Node 1—Scanning Server
	VMWARE Node 2—RSA Secure ID
	VMWARE Node 3—JJ-30
	VMWARE Node 4—Backup Server
Blade Center	TS01—Citrix Presentation Server
	TS02—Citrix Presentation Server
	TS03—Citrx Presentation Server
	TS04—Citrix Presentation Server
	TS05—Citrix Presentation Server
	TS06—Citrx Presentation Server
BKSRV	Veritas Server

Critical Systems Definition, B-List

The business must identify which computing services are non-mission-critical. These will be recovered some time after the initial RTO has been satisfied from the mission statement. These non-critical business systems are referred to as the "B-list" of servers, as shown in Table 11.2. Efforts should be first directed at critical applications on the A-list. There may or may not be hardware initially available at a hotsite or other facility. The procurement of this hardware may be required.

Table 11.2: Sample B-List Servers List	
Server Name	**Function**
L02	JDE—Development
FAX	Faxing Server
FORMS	Special Forms Overlay
EVAUL	Electronic Data Vault
DEV01	Development
DEV02	Development
DEV03	Development
TS13	Citrix Presentation Server
TS14	Citrix Presentation Server
TS15	Citrix Presentation Server
SQL05	Staff Benefit Server
SQL06	Human Resources
SQL07	Human Resources
DB2	Data Warehouse 2
DB3	Data Warehouse 3

Disaster Recovery Teams Overview

The disaster recovery plan is executed in recovery phases by specifically assigned staff organized into recovery teams. A high-level overview and diagram of the recovery efforts, as shown in Figure 11.7, should outline the recovery progression. It is important that the teams function efficiently and independently, so tasks can proceed simultaneously. The disaster recovery plan is developed using a recovery management organization consisting of the following:

- IT Management Team
- Technical Recovery Teams
  - » iSeries Recovery
  - » pSeries Recovery
  - » Intel Server Recovery
  - » Network Recovery
  - » Applications Team
- Site Restoration (IT Management Team)

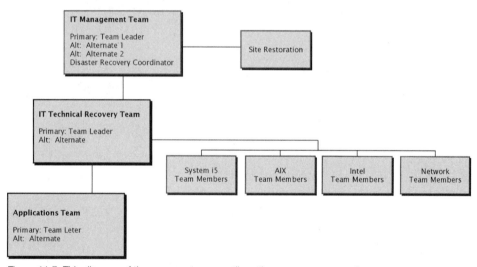

Figure 11.7: This diagram of the recovery teams outlines the recovery progression.

IT Management Team Overview

The primary function of the IT management team is to manage and coordinate the activities of the recovery hotsite and the restoration of the primary site. This will be done by monitoring the activities of the respective teams responsible for the recovery at the hotsite and the restoration of the primary site. The initial function of this team is to prepare a preliminary assessment of the condition of the building, the data processing facilities, and the computer systems affected by the disaster. The management team oversees the whole recovery process. This team has the final authority on decisions that must be made during the recovery process, including damage assessment, alert, and declaration.

This team will convene at the predetermined command center. It is composed of other team leaders and led by the senior executive. The contact information for the members of this team is provide in an appendix to the plan.

Table 11.3 is an example of a table that might be included in the plan, in the section that describes the management team.

Table 11.3: Sample IT Management Team List	
Member Name	**Role**
Maria Alvarez	Team Lead, Recovery Manager
Paul Evans	Alternate
John Chung	Alternate
Josie Novak	Team Lead, Technical Recovery Team
Art Weisman	Disaster Recovery Coordinator

IT Technical Recovery Team Overview

The primary function of this team is to ensure that the user community has full data processing and communication capabilities. The critical business applications are to be re-constructed at either the company computer room or at the contingency site as directed by the IT management team. Recovery includes IBM System i5 or iSeries, and all mission critical Intel servers, applications, and communications. The Technical Recovery Team Leader will be responsible for initiating damage assessment, recovery actions, and notification procedures until such time as senior executives are available. All reporting will flow to the recovery management team. The contact information for this team should be located in an appendix to your DRP.

Table 11.4 is an example of a table that might be included in the plan, in the section that describes the technical recovery team.

Table 11.4: Sample Technical Recovery Team List	
Member Name	**Role**
Josie Novak	Team Lead - Technical Coordinator
Kevin Doyle	iSeries - Primary
Ed Powers	iSeries - Alternate
Ron DiGiovanna	Intel - Primary
Rani Patel	Intel - Alternate
Mike Rozansky	Intel - Alternate
Martha Howard	Intel - Alternate
Lisa Young	Communications - Primary
Paul Mandel	Communications - Alternate
Harry Cho	Application Support - Primary
Ann Carter	Application Support - Alternate

Primary Site Restoration Team (IT Management Team)

The primary function of the primary site restoration team is to manage and coordinate the restoration of the primary site's server room. This team must evaluate the extent of damage to the primary site's building, equipment, power, and communications.

This team must also estimate the time it will take to restore and staff normal operations. The team can be located at the recovery hotsite, but must be available to migrate to the primary site as soon as the emergency is over.

Recovery Progression

The flowchart in Figure 11.8 depicts the high-level progression of the recovery effort from the event to the activation of each recovery team, hotsite activation, and vital records retrieval. This chart lists the progression of major milestones and walks you through the steps used to determine whether to activate the plan. Refer readers to the body of the plan for detailed "how to" instructions.

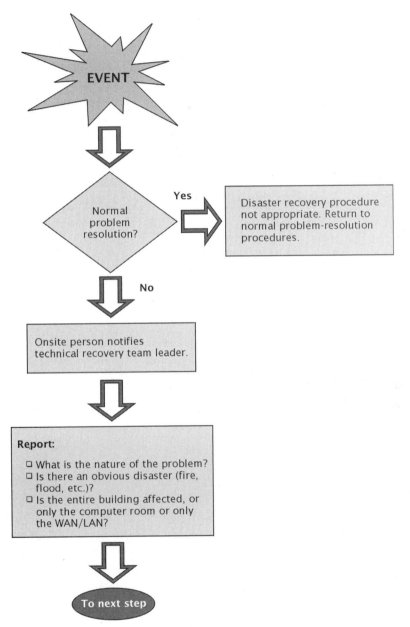

Figure 11.8: This flowchart depicts the high-level progression of the recovery effort (part 1).

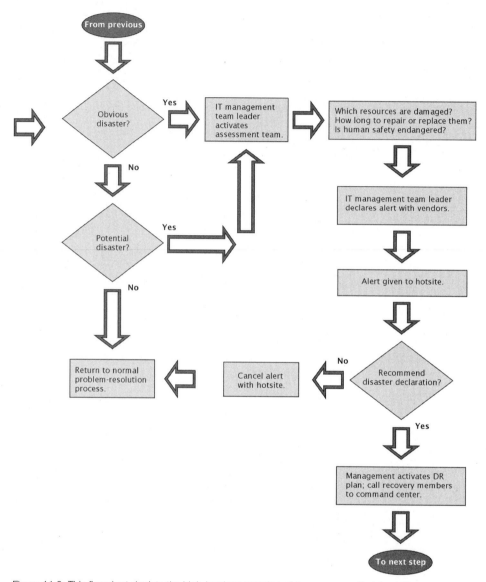

Figure 11.8: This flowchart depicts the high-level progression of the recovery effort (part 2).

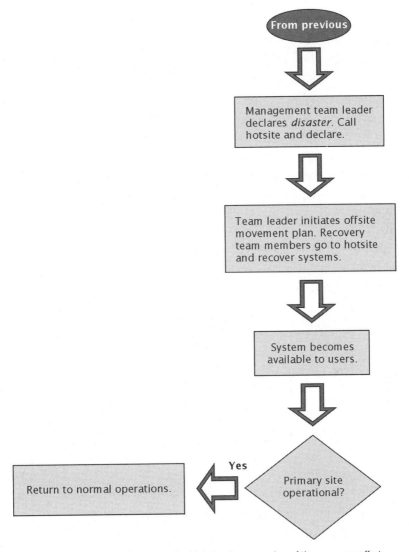

Figure 11.8: This flowchart depicts the high-level progression of the recovery effort (part 3).

Disaster Recovery Plan Distribution List

The disaster recovery plan is distributed to authorized personnel to assist in the definition and understanding of responsibilities and procedures related to a business disruption that has been caused by a disastrous event. Make sure to include a statement that the plan is intended for an individual's use only while an employee of the organization, and that the document is considered strictly confidential. Upon any departmental change of employment status, it is the individual's responsibility to return his or her assigned copy and all duplicates to the appropriate manager. Nobody outside of your organization should be permitted to read, review, copy, or audit the plan without prior written approval.

The purpose of this section is to identify the individuals receiving copies of the plan and to provide the documentation for distributing updates to the plan. Table 11.5 shows a sample distribution list.

Table 11.5: Sample Distribution List		
COPY #	NAME	TITLE
1	Server—Primary	Network Drive Copy
2	Offsite Storage	Offsite Storage Vendor, in Hot Box
3	Server—Backup	Second Network Drive Copy
4	Hotsite	Commercial Hotsite Copy
5	Maria Alvarez	IT Management Team Leader
6	Paul Evans	IT Management Alternate Team Leader
7	John Chung	IT Management Team Member
8	Josie Novak	IT Recovery Team Leader
9	Art Weisman	Disaster Recovery Coordinator
10	Kevin Doyle	I5/iSeries—Primary
11	Ed Powers	I5 /Intel—Alternate
12	Ron DiGiovanna	Intel—Primary

Summary

Developing a DR plan requires a detailed set of procedures that will provide the roadmap for the recovery teams through all aspects of disaster recovery. By fully understanding the complete disaster recovery objectives, recovery planning phases, and the recovery goals, you are ready to start your planning efforts. Writing a comprehensive plan that is action oriented and complete will leave nothing for chance in the event a disaster strikes your organization. You must ensure that the DR plan's structure is logically designed, which will permit information to be easily located. A logical, flowing plan will help ensure your IT recovery teams follow the roadmap as designed . . . page by page.

12

Effective Plan-Activation Procedures

You need a roadmap to clearly illustrate the steps required to formally activate a disaster recovery plan. The "Plan Activation" section of the plan must document how an incident is identified, who is notified, what the damage assessment criteria are, how and who can make the decision to declare a disaster, and finally the specific steps for declaring the disaster. The plan activation procedures document the initial evaluation, decision, and response for each individual recovery team. These specific activation activities are all initiated and performed by the IT recovery management team. This team provides the unique business and disaster-recovery preparedness knowledge necessary to follow all the initial alert activities and develop a formal initial response. Once the plan is activated, the activation procedures must also document the alternate-site alert process and setup, offsite storage retrieval, emergency notification to the teams, and procedures for activating the emergency command center and its selected location.

The IT recovery management team is activated immediately upon the discovery of any potential disaster identified within your business. The purpose is to determine if any disruption in IT-related services is deemed to be an "incident" or declared a "disaster." This level-sets the expectations and requirements for a formal declaration of disaster recovery activities. The delegation of team assignments can be modified based on particular recovery circumstances. Sometimes, things will change on the fly. An incident can become a disaster in hours, days, or minutes. Conversely, an alert can be called off when it's determined that the situation is just an IT incident. The IT recovery management team provides the centralized coordination point for the following recovery activities:

- Initial assessment
- Plan activation
- Subsequent support and recovery resource acquisition
- Hotsite coordination—alert and disaster authorization
- iSeries/System i5 infrastructure restoration
- pSeries infrastructure restoration
- xSeries infrastructure restoration
- zSeries infrastructure restoration
- Network activation
- Licensing of software

A combination of one or more of the following teams is generally activated, depending on the size of the business and the number of critical functions to be recovered:

- The IT recovery management team operates in the emergency command center and is responsible for managing and controlling the disaster recovery efforts. This team is the primary owner in a disaster. It is in charge!
- The executive business team is made up of senior executives representing the business units who have overall responsibility to your company for the day-to-day management of critical business functions. These folks are *not* in charge in a disaster!

- The IT technical recovery teams can be assigned to the various critical hardware functions. In smaller shops, there tends to be just one technical recovery team designated to recovery across hardware platforms. These are the people who go to the alternate site and execute the recovery procedures for server restoration and make the applications available after a disaster.

There should be an activation system in place that incorporates the IT recovery management team as the primary stakeholder, the executive business team, and the IT technical recovery teams necessary to support recovery.

The Disaster-Alert Notification Procedure

When your organization is faced with a potential disaster, many personal anxieties will surface. With your recovery team members' adrenaline flowing at an all-time high, there is a natural response to do things quickly. This sense of urgency makes you impatient. You just want to get things moving along, and now!

Well, I ask for you to be patient during the initial phase. You might recall an instructor or professor telling you to read the entire test before you answer any questions. The same is true for the plan-activation procedures. I always have a bullet in all my plans that reads like this and is in red:

» Please read the entire procedure FIRST, before executing any steps.

The details of the disaster recovery plan should be familiar to everyone on the IT recovery management team. That is a given. After all the testing exercises, these procedures should be very clear. However, the need to re-read the plan is fueled by the fact that it might not have been tested in recent months, or the stress of the situation at hand might mean people are not thinking clearly. By reading through all the steps first, you familiarize everyone's thinking before you start actually performing the tasks.

Normally, awareness of any potentially disastrous event will be initiated first from the computer room, facilities management, site security, or computer operations personnel who are actually onsite during the disaster. The sequence of events to be followed during a potentially disastrous occurrence are as follows in the plan activation procedures:

- Perform first-alert response.
- Make initial assessment.
- Verify disaster.
- Determine personnel status.
- Activate command center.
- Place hotsite on alert.
- Assign team responsibilities during the disaster.

The high-level overview illustrated in Figure 12.1 is designed to activate the disaster-recovery process.

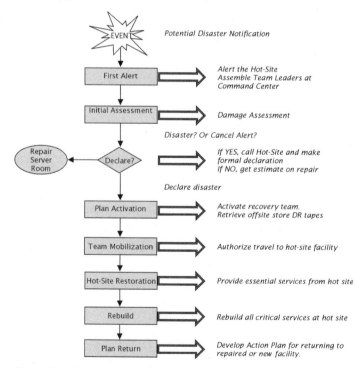

Figure 12.1: The plan-activation process flowchart.

- The technical services manager or operation manager learns of an event in the computer room that he/she deems requires a response. He/she will execute the call-notification phone list documented in the disaster recovery plan. The call sequence proceeds as follows:
    » The technical services manager calls the IT recovery-management team's manager or alternate.
    » The manager of the IT recovery management team contacts the disaster recovery coordinator and all members of the team.
    » The manager of the IT management team notifies senior executive business members as per internal notification procedures.
- The leader of the IT technical recovery team begins notifying the appropriate vendors and requests their assistance in assessing the damage to the computer room.
- The leader of the IT technical services team notifies representatives from the appropriate hardware and communications vendors, requesting their assistance in assessing the damage to the server room or communications facilities.
- The manager of the IT recovery management team informs the building or facilities manager of the potential disaster and requests his/her assistance in the initial damage assessment and subsequent insurance inspections. A corporate insurance representative prepares to notify the appropriate agencies and initiate claims as necessary.
- The manager of the IT recovery management team and the manager of building facilities make initial contact with the appropriate civil authorities (fire, police, etc.) not already notified, to alert them to the possibility of a disastrous event at the server room's facility.
- The manager of the IT recovery management team notifies the management of each of the critical user departments within the business. The manager also keeps senior management informed throughout this process.
- All of the individuals notified above meet with the manager of the IT recovery management team or the technical services team

in the command center to conduct an initial damage assessment. They determine whether to continue data processing operations at the primary office location or to transition to the hotsite.

- If the decision is made to transition to the hotsite, the disaster recovery coordinator assists the members of the technical recovery team in securing necessary support items such as cash advances, lodging, and travel to the hotsite.

First-Alert Response

The following sections provide a problem-review and escalation process to ensure that management and support personnel are appropriately notified following any potentially disastrous event in the server room. This first-alert procedure is followed by a multi-tiered problem review and escalation plan for the following:

- Verifying the disaster
- Determining personnel status
- Assembling team leaders and recovery team members at the command center
- Assessing and evaluating damage
- Activating the plan

Identification of a problem or disaster might come from a number of sources. In the event of a fire, explosion, or bomb threat, normal building emergency-evacuation procedures should always be followed first. Personal safety considerations are paramount.

Initial Assessment: Verify the Disaster

During the disaster verification process, a preliminary damage evaluation is performed to determine whether or not all the recovery teams are to be activated. This procedure is also used if a non-emergency problem is escalated to a disaster alert. The first contact person notified of a potential disaster assumes the responsibilities of performing the tasks listed below:

1. While on the telephone with the individual performing the first alert, obtain the following information:
   » Name of the person making the alert
   » Nature of the problem
   » Best estimate of recovery effort
   » Preliminary assessment of the incident, including personnel injuries and physical damage
   » Building accessibility
   » Immediate dangers or restrictions
   » Status of other contact attempts
   » Phone number where the person performing the first alert can be reached

2. Provide information as to when you will arrive and where you will meet the person performing the first alert.

3. Arrange for damage assessment with recovery team members.

4. Attempt to verify the magnitude of the disaster situation by calling the company's main switchboard, or by contacting the building manager or the security monitoring company. Check out network connectivity as well.

5. Obtain a copy of the disaster recovery plan and report to the command center.

6. Upon arrival, meet with the individual who made the first alert to start all the related damage-assessment activities. Use the building security staff, fire, or police to obtain the following information:
   » When the building can be accessed
   » Extent of damage to building
   » Extent of damage to contents
   » Extent of damage to computer equipment
   » Extent of damage to communications equipment

7. If the facility can be entered, quickly evaluate the extent of the damage. Contact the manager of the recovery management team and the leader of the IT technical recovery team, and instruct them to meet at the command center.

8. If the facilities, equipment, and data are not affected, and the issue can be resolved by regular IT staff procedures, then notify the recovery management team and senior management that disaster activities have been terminated.

Determine Personnel Status

One of the recovery manager's important early duties is to determine the status of the recovery personnel working at the time of the disaster. Safety of personnel onsite after the disaster will effect any rescues or first aid necessary for staff caught up in the disaster itself. The recovery manager should produce a list of the able-bodied team members who will be available to aid in the system salvage and recovery process. It is imperative in any disaster to locate all personnel first, and determine status and availability.

Traditionally, the duty of determining all recovery staff situations and availability lies with the disaster recovery coordinator. This individual's responsibility will be to identify any individuals who might have been physically or emotionally injured, missing, or killed in the disaster. The disaster recovery coordinator will work closely with the human resources department, who in turn will work with families and employees, administering to their situational needs. This may include obtaining counseling services or other personal needs outside of the normal day-to-day needs.

Taking special care of your people is a very important task and should receive the highest priority from your company immediately following the disaster. Of course, there is a huge technical task of restoring the complete server infrastructure and network operations ahead, but you simply cannot lose sight of the human interests at stake.

Assemble the Team at the Command Center

Select an alternate place to meet in advance of any potential disaster event when your primary facility becomes inaccessible. Make sure that the members of your IT recovery management and technical recovery teams know the precise location. Location maps should be supplied, and location details included in the DR plan. This predefined meeting place will serve as a location for you and your key staff to plan your technical response to the potentially disastrous event.

When selecting your meeting place, consider its location relative to your normal work place. It should not be so far away that recovery team members have difficulty getting there. Conversely, it should not be so close to your normal work location that it could be affected by the same disaster scenario. It is recommended that you select at least two possible meeting locations. Your primary location could be close to your facility or inside the facility's boardroom, if access is possible. Your alternate location should be further away, ensuring availability if your primary location is not accessible.

Since the ability to communicate with others is essential to effectively respond to any incident, make sure that the location you choose as a command center has enough telephones (land lines) and Internet bandwidth for your needs. If you have a cellular phone, plan to take it with you to this meeting place as another means of communication, in case regular phones are not working. However, do not strictly count on cell phone technology. Often, the cellar networks cannot support voice traffic in a regional disaster. If your laptop computer was not in the affected disaster, plan to take it to the meeting place with you. Laptop wireless capabilities can be very helpful. Connectivity to the Internet will be mandatory for email, access to documentation servers, and other special communications requirements.

After the manager of the IT recovery management team has assessed the situation, that individual will contact all remaining members of the IT recovery management team (as identified in team rosters) and request that the team meet at the designated command center. All IT recovery management team members or their alternates (as identified in advance) will attend the meeting at the command center.

Place the Hotsite on Alert

Whenever an event takes place within your organization that warrants the need to perform a disaster assessment, it make sense to put the commercial hotsite vendor on alert. By calling in the members of the recovery management team, the situation suggests the event is greater than can be solved with a simple IPL of the System i5. I would encourage you to put your hotsite vendor on alert when a situation poses an unacceptable degree of risk. Placing the commercial hotsite vendor on alert is a "heads up" process to allow the provider time to make the necessary preparations for a smooth transition in case of an actual disaster declaration by your company.

Consider the following when determining whether to alert the hotsite:

- Alert startup gives no additional priority towards hotsite access or equipment rights.
- Some vendors have an associated fee with an alert.
- Some vendors do not accept any form of alerts—strictly disaster declarations.
- Any customer testing will continue at the hotsite vendor.
- Disaster declarations will continue to be serviced on the normal "first come, first served" basis.

It makes sense for the recovery team manager to inform the hotsite vendor on the status of the potentially disastrous situation at prearranged intervals. Situation updates must be maintained until the event is resolved by an alert termination or declaration of disaster. There are two types of alerts: pre-planned and emergency.

400

A pre-planned alert would include a server room move, major construction, or a power upgrade or transfer. These activities involve some form of high risk to your data center. When the risk is too high, risk-mitigation activities might involve parallel hotsite-related services. For example, if you are moving the System i5 from one computer room to another across town, running a parallel DR recovery is a good plan in case the truck goes off the road during the move or the server is damaged in some way from the move.

An emergency alert includes a customer outage where you are unsure if you might declare a disaster. Possible causes include an extended power outage, a severe equipment failure, or adverse weather conditions. Ensure you enforce control with the hotsite provider, that *you* determine whether the incident is considered an emergency or disaster, not the vendor. Too often, the vendor will not allow you to declare because of the stated pending emergency. In other words, you have to wait for the hurricane to rip your building to shreds instead of going into prevention mode before the event!

Assess the Damage

The IT recovery management team will participate in all the damage assessment activities in coordination with the leader of the IT technical recovery team. This team will also be responsible for all detailed damage-assessment reports for purposes of insurance claims.

Here are the steps to assessing damage:

1. Evaluate the situation presented and provide a sound technical decision to select the choice of the recovery activation.
2. Provide an assessment of the major hardware components that can be salvaged.
3. Provide an assessment of the onsite vital records that can be salvaged.

This damage assessment is intended to establish the extent of damage to critical server hardware infrastructure and the facility. The assessment scope is all about the mission-critical servers and the ability to get the critical business functions back up and running. The primary goal is to determine whether the recovery of the server infrastructure should take place at the hotsite or locally. Secondly, determine what hardware must be ordered immediately. Based on the assessment report, the IT recovery management team can begin the process of either a disaster declaration and acquiring replacement equipment or canceling the alert.

Team members should be liberal in their estimate of the time required to repair or replace a damaged server. Take into consideration situations where one repair cannot begin until another step is completed. Hardware dependencies can be paramount. Estimates of repair time should include equipment ordering, shipping, installation, restoration, and testing before the systems are made available.

When considering hardware, evaluate first the equipment lists provided in the recovery and system information sections for each platform. These lists were constructed primarily for recovery at the hotsite, so they consist of the critical servers necessary for your recovery. You will need to separate servers into two groups. One group will be composed of those missing or destroyed. The second will be those considered salvageable. These salvageable servers will have to be evaluated by IBM hardware engineers and repaired as necessary. There will be warrantee considerations as well.

With respect to the building facility, evaluation of damage to the physical structure, electrical systems, air conditioning, fire suppression, and building networks should all be conducted. If estimates from this process indicate that recovery at the original site will require more than the stated RTO in the mission statement of the DR plan, migration to the hot site is recommended immediately.

During disaster assessment and evaluation, the manager of the IT recovery management team must determine whether or not a disaster should be declared and the entire recovery organization activated. When the IT recovery management team members assemble at the emergency command center, they will perform the following activities:

1. Place the commercial hotsite vendor on alert. This will enable preparatory activities to begin for possible recovery operations.

2. Dispatch selected team members to reassess the extent of the damage to the facility and its contents.

3. Obtain complete facility and content damage reports from onsite damage assessment, as provided by the leader of the IT technical recovery team.

4. Obtain injury reports and staff whereabouts from the disaster recovery coordinator and/or local authorities.

5. If access to the primary office facility or computer room is restricted, obtain an estimate of when access will be allowed by the local emergency authorities.

6. Formulate a disaster recovery plan "activation" or "termination" recommendation. Some organizations decide by committee, while other companies simply take the direction of the IT recovery management team's manager. Recognize what works best within the walls of your organization, and respect the authority that has been agreed upon in advance.

7. Reassemble the team at the command center.

8. Perform a final review of the findings from the assessment activities.

9. Determine the level of recovery plan activation:

    9.1 Temporary interruption—Facilities, equipment, and data are not seriously affected; the problem can or will be handled by the technical recovery team, building engineers, or vendor personnel with a minimum of processing and service outage.

    9.2 Limited recovery plan activation—Certain team members, but not all, will be activated based on the effected areas and services.

    9.3 Full recovery plan activation—All team members will be activated.

10. If after evaluation from the damage assessment reports, no further recovery activities are required, terminate all recovery activities and notify the hotsite vendor to cancel the alert.

11. If recovery operations are required, activate the DR plan and initiate recovery operations:

    11.1 Data processing recovery activities will be initiated in the recovery operation activation meeting, conducted by the leader of the IT recovery management team.

    11.2 Activate disaster declaration with the hotsite vendor and follow vendor-specific activation steps.

    11.3 Contact all IT technical recovery team members or alternates. Request that they report immediately to the command center.

12. Contact all remaining technical recovery team members and/or alternates using the call list. Request that they report immediately to the command center.

Notify Personnel

The IT recovery management team has determined that the DR plan must be implemented to support the critical needs of the business. The current findings from the damage assessment suggest a recovery time greater than what has been agreed upon by the business and IT in the mission statement.

All team-member notifications will be completed by the team leaders, who are notified by the disaster recovery coordinator. Obtain the following information before making any phone calls:

- Command center location
- Address
- Access requirements
- Phone number
- Brief description of disaster situation
- Location where member(s) will assemble
- Contact name at hotsite

Notify all technical recovery team leaders and their alternates. Request them to meet at the command center, and identify the location. The team leaders should notify all team members that a disaster has occurred and a formal declaration is currently being evaluated. A record of each team member reached should be kept.

Use the following procedure for contacting team members:

1. Place the phone call, and with a composed voice, say, "May I speak with (individual's name)?"
2. If the individual is available, explain the potential disaster situation and supply all necessary information. Tell him or her when and where the team is meeting. Remind the team member to make no public statements about the situation. Provide enough details to family members (staying away from technical jargon) so that they are not forced to make assumptions or draw their own conclusions.
3. If the individual is not available, determine where you may reach him or her. Try to find out where the individual might be. *Do not* discuss the disaster situation with the person answering the phone. Simply leave a message that it's imperative that the team member calls you back urgently, at the number you provide.
4. If contact is made with an answering machine, make no statement regarding the situation.
5. If there is no response after you leave a message, contact the backup or alternate on the list. There will be situations when you have tried to reach an individual, and you have simply exhausted all telephone and email alternatives on the employee contact sheet. It might make sense to have the disaster recovery coordinator attempt to continue to locate the individual.

The status of all calls made should be recorded. Note the person you called, the time the call was placed, and whether the person was contacted. Make a reasonable number of attempts, but if the phone continues to be busy or there is no answer, continue to the next person on the list. Forward the completed call-notification list to the disaster recovery coordinator.

Hotsite Call-up Procedures

A formal call procedure must be detailed that will provide the steps for notifying your hotsite vendor. Always assume that the IT technical recovery team's leader or alternate will need explicit details as he or she does not interface directly with the vendor on a regular basis. List the following vendor information:

- Vendor name
- Contract number
- The organization name on the contract (the parent company)
- The vendor's call number (both the 800 number and a local number)
- Special vendor call procedures
- Information that the vendor will require for disaster declaration

In addition to the vendor call procedure as part of the DR plan, you will need to document the list of recovery team personnel who are authorized to formally declare a disaster with the hotsite vendor, as shown in Figure 12.2. The vendor contract that was signed by your organization will be accompanied by a hotsite subscriber guide. This guide will list the authorized staff from your organization who may communicate with the hotsite. It is vital to your organization to ensure that this be maintained and in line with the hotsite vendor's records. A hotsite vendor will not accept the fact that "Brendon Tucker" left your company and you are his replacement, regardless of how convincing your argument might sound. Simply put, they will not accept your call, regardless of your situation or level of urgency. This declaration list is a living document that you must maintain with the supplier, not the other way around.

Disaster Declaration Authorized Personnel

Contact Details

Subscriber Name:	Your legal company name
Address:	123 New IT Drive
	Mytown, New York
	12345
Contract Number:	32-K4567-NY
Primary Product:	iSeries/400, Intel, pSeries, Desktop Recovery

Recovery Team Members Authorized to Declare a Disaster

Primary Contact to Declare Disaster

Name:	
Title:	
Work:	
Cell:	
Home:	
Personal Disaster Code:	

Primary Contact to Declare Disaster

Name:	
Title:	
Work:	
Cell:	
Home:	
Personal Disaster Code:	

Primary Contact to Declare Disaster

Name:	
Title:	
Work:	
Cell:	
Home:	
Personal Disaster Code:	

Figure 12.2: This information is needed to declare a disaster with the hotsite.

At the acceptance of a commercial hotsite vendor contract, your organization must provide the vendor's customer service coordinator with a list of at least three people who have authority to declare a disaster on behalf of your company. This list should contain primary and alternate names, and telephone and pager numbers for each individual. This disaster authorization list should reflect the sequence in which individuals are to be contacted. To declare a disaster, authorized recovery team members should call the hotsite as soon as possible. As you might recall, hotsite access is available on a first come, first served basis. Hesitation to declare a disaster is not in your company's best business-survival interest.

The customer services coordinator at the hotsite, upon receipt of the disaster declaration from your organization, will validate the disaster declaration authority list with those kept on file with the vendor. The company authorized representative will be directed to provide a password by the hotsite vendor to verify authority upon declaration of a disaster. If confirmation of a valid disaster declaration is received, the customer services coordinator will inform the company-authorized designee that the hotsite will be turned over to you in the agreed-upon time interval, as stated in the contract. This can be anywhere from three to 12 hours, depending on the vendor. Now the disaster will be officially declared, and the disaster recovery contractual services will begin.

When all authorizations are confirmed, the hotsite vendor will activate its own internal procedures to provide your company with a restore-ready iSeries or System i5 and all supporting equipment listed in the equipment schedule of the hotsite contract. This typically includes adding disk drives to the System ASP and loading the License Internal Code.

Hotsite personnel will return your call to secure the final authorization and to confirm that a disaster situation actually exists typically within 30 minutes. To confirm final authorization, your hotsite coordinator will request your company's authorization code once again. When all authorizations are confirmed, the hotsite recovery coordinator will activate your recovery checklist. This checklist will identify the tasks that the hotsite will perform to assist in the disaster recovery effort.

Immediately upon notification of your disaster, the hotsite recovery coordinator will begin preparation for your arrival at the facility. Upon your arrival at the facility, hotsite personnel will acquaint the technical recovery team with the customer areas and appropriate local procedures or policies.

Directions and Map to Primary Hotsite

The disaster recovery plan should provide directions to the personnel who will be traveling to the alternate site or hotsite. If travel by automobile is not feasible because of time considerations, arrangements must be detailed for air travel. Your recovery team members will need plane tickets, hotel accommodations, and expense money in advance. You cannot assume that an IT staffer has a credit card ready to charge full-fare airline tickets.

The disaster recovery coordinator's role is to prearrange the logistics and ensure that during a disaster-related event, all requirements are facilitated. The technical team leader should supply the disaster recovery coordinator with the names of all the individuals required to travel, their destination, hotel requirements, and any special needs they might have. Figure 12.3 shows a sample of the type of direction details to document.

In chapter 8, you learned how a hot box stores essential software elements for server recovery at your offsite storage provider. Some organizations will set up an additional small box for disaster recovery staff needs at the offsite storage facility. This box could contain the following:

- Travelers' checks
- Cash
- Airline tickets—open, full-fare, and valid for one year
- Car rental corporate account number
- Hotel directions from primary office and/or airport
- Hotel corporate account number
- Hotsite driving directions from primary office and/or airport

- Hotsite-to-hotel driving directions
- Cell phone chargers, both car adapter and desktop
- Blackberry chargers
- Additional spare phones

Some organizations also have a corporate policy restricting staff from traveling on the same airplane. They will send staff on two different carriers not because of safety concerns, but rather to avoid being delayed by one airline. In a disaster, you must make the call as to what makes the most sense for your organization.

Directions to Primary Hotsite
ADDRESS: 34 Waycroft Drive
                  Pittsburgh, Pennsylvania
                  33216

From Pittsburgh Airport
› Follow airport exit signs to 76 North.
› Take 76 North 15 miles to exit 33, Dover Avenue.
› Exit right on off-ramp heading east on Dover Avenue.
› Proceed straight through to first intersection.
› Turn left on Steeles Road and head north.
› Turn right onto Waycroft Drive.
› Hotsite is on the left side (north), address 34. The parking lot is located in front of the main entrance of the building.

Directions and Map to Alternate Hotsite
ADDRESS: 80 West Beaver Creek
                  Richmond Hill, Ontario
                  L4B 1H3

From Toronto Pearson Airport
› Follow 401 East to the 404.
› Follow 404 North to Hwy 7 exit.
› Turn left onto Hwy 7 and proceed to West Beaver Creek.
› Turn right onto West Beaver Creek.
› Hotsite is on the left side (west), address 80 and unit 6. The parking lot is located in front of the main entrance of the building.

Alternate route from Toronto Pearson Airport
› Follow 409 East out of the airport.
› Take the 427 North exit.
› Follow 407 east to the Leslie exit.
› Turn north (left) onto Leslie Street and proceed north to West Wilmot.
› Turn left onto West Wilmot and proceed to West Beaver Creek.
› Turn right (north) onto West Beaver Creek.
› Hotsite is on the left side (west), address 80 and unit 6. The parking lot is located in front of the main entrance of the building.

Figure 12.3: Sample direction details, including a map to the hotsite. (part 1 of 2))

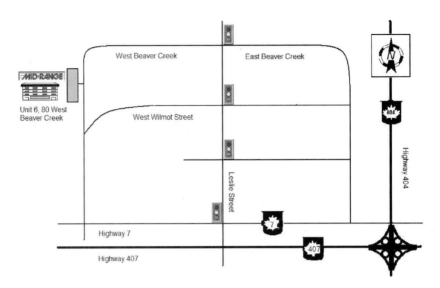

Figure 12.3: Sample direction details, including a map to the hotsite. (part 2 of 2))

Hotsite Opening

Here is a sample of the required policies a recovery staff must adhere to when working out of a commercial hotsite:

1. All employees must park their cars in the prescribed areas of the parking lot, clear of any emergency/fire routes or the loading docks. All staff requiring access to the hotsite should proceed to the reception desk in the main lobby.

2. Every individual who enters the hotsite will be required to sign in. The receptionist will maintain a sign-in book in the lobby. All members of recovery teams will receive an identification badge that must be worn at all times while at the hotsite. Photo identification is always required during sign in. No photo ID means you *do not* gain access to your hotsite.

3. A hotsite staff member will acquaint the recovery team members with the facility and appropriate procedures upon their arrival.

4. Any additional staff arriving from your organization, who are not part of the restoration team, must be approved in advance. Hotsite personnel will escort them into the recovery area.

5. After all staff have signed in and received badges, they may proceed to unload material required during the disaster. The loading docks are usually available for large items and should be used whenever extended in/out trips are required.

6. Any office supplies, special forms, manuals, tapes, or other required materials can be ordered for arrival at a later time.

7. Review the restoration process with the hotsite coordinator and ensure all the correct tapes have arrived before proceeding with the recovery.

Recalling Tapes from Your Offsite Storage Provider

In the event of a disaster where server recovery is local or at a hotsite, you will need to recall all your backup tape media and vital records in order to rebuild the server infrastructure. Just like it is important to keep your hotsite vendor involved in the potential disaster as it unfolds, or when a declaration is called, your offsite storage vendor should also be notified. Advance thinking can save your organization hours of wait time while tapes are recalled.

A formal call procedure must be detailed that provides the steps necessary for notifying your offsite storage vendor. Always assume that the recovery team leader requires explicit details, as he or she does not interface directly with the vendor on a regular basis. List the following vendor information:

- Vendor name
- Contract number
- The organization name on the contract (the parent company)
- The vendor's call number (both the 800 number and a local number)
- The Web site, account number, and password for tape retrieval
- The vendor's vital-records recall procedures (by Web and by phone)
- Destination where you wish to have the tapes and vital records delivered (address, contact name, contact phone number, and ZIP code)

Offsite storage providers will only permit access to your backup tapes by pre-authorized staff. Every vendor limits the access of customer records to requests made by authorized agents. List the authorized agents from your organization and the level of authority they may have for tape handling, as shown in Table 12.1.

Table 12.1: Authorized Agents for Handling Tape		
Last Name	**First Name**	**Authority Level***
Travino	Lee	1
Jones	Bobby	1
Sneed	Sam	2
Crenshaw	Benjamin	2
*1=full authority, 2=send and receive tapes to and from primary office		

Site Restoration Activities

A final consideration in any disaster recovery scenario is the preparation to return home to a fully functional data processing facility in as short a time as possible. You cannot run your business indefinitely from a hotsite, even if you could afford the daily charges. Many hotsite vendors limit onsite access from six to eight weeks.

The restoration activities are defined as a recovery management team objective. These activities will be managed under the leadership of the manager of the IT recovery management team. The responsibilities include the completion of the tasks necessary to rebuild the servers and/or the complete server infrastructure. The computer room rebuild must be equal to or better than it was prior to the disaster. These tasks involve a variety of activities, ranging from the initial assessment of damage to the final transition of operations back to the fully restored server room.

The team definition includes the following areas:

- *Facilities and environmental control equipment*—The server room infrastructure and supporting environmental systems are the responsibility of facilities management.

- *Computing and peripheral equipment*—The data processing systems and supporting peripherals are the responsibility of the technical recovery team leader.

- *Communications equipment*—The telephone switching and other equipment required to support the communications network is the responsibility of the technical recovery team leader.

- *Supplies and forms*—Special forms and standard supply stocks are the responsibility of the disaster recovery coordinator.

This team will also be responsible for overseeing the activities for the repair and/or rebuilding of the primary site (the administrative services building). It is anticipated that the major responsibility for this will lie with building engineers and contractors. However, this team must oversee these operations to ensure that the facility is repaired to properly support the operation of mainframe and networking equipment according to the original design of the primary site.

Replacement Equipment

A disaster recovery plan contains a complete inventory of the server components currently housed in the computer room that have been deemed mission-critical as identified on the A-list. The scope of the DR plan defines the network and all the servers containing the most recent data and software applications that must be restored after a disaster. Where possible, agreements should be made with vendors to supply replacement equipment on an emergency basis. To avoid problems and delays in the recovery, every attempt should be made to replicate the current system configuration. However, there will likely be cases where components are not available or the delivery timeframes are unacceptably long. The recovery management team will have the expertise and resources to work through these problems as they arise. Some changes will be required to the procedures documented in the plan; using different models of equipment or equipment from a different vendor may be suitable to expediting the recovery process.

Safety and Security

It will also be the responsibility of the IT recovery management team or facilities management, in conjunction with the local fire department, to conduct a safety inspection of the disaster site prior to the admittance of any cleanup or damage assessment crews.

When the damaged area is considered safe for access, facilities management will advise the leaders of the IT recovery management and IT technical recovery teams that the safety and security phase has been completed and that the facilities are free from hazards.

The leader of the IT recovery management team will then

- Advise the insurance department that the insurance inspection procedure for the damaged area can commence
- Coordinate all requests for entry into the damaged area with the corporate legal department, as well as the corporate insurance department.

The Insurance Inspection

It is important for the leader of the IT recovery management team to fully understand the insurance coverage details in place within the organization. The details should be known in advance for the following insurance items:

- Insurance provider's name
- Contact information for the insurance provider
- Type of insurance

- Policy numbers covering the business
- Type of deductible
- Policy limits

Frequently review the type of coverage you have. Does it cover floods or earthquakes? Are there measures or additional insurance you need to operate your business in the event of an emergency?

Under no circumstances will any cleanup at the facility or server equipment maintenance activities begin prior to the insurance inspection. Upon receipt of the approval to commence with the inspection, the IT recovery management team leader will coordinate contacting the underwriters with the corporate insurance representative, begin notifying appropriate hardware vendors, schedule the inspection, and make all necessary arrangements for obtaining site access passes from facilities management.

During the equipment insurance inspection by the underwriters and hardware vendors, the leader of the IT technical recovery team will be onsite to record all damage-related details and to provide technical advice, as required. This individual will use the hardware inventory in the "System Information" section of the DR plan as the master list for all insurance claims. The hardware inventory serves a dual purpose by providing detailed feature information for the reordering of new computer hardware and for server restoration.

Upon completion of the inspection, the leader of the IT technical recovery team should immediately notify the leader of the IT recovery management team that the inspection has been completed and the restoration and building phases may begin.

Restoration Phase

The restoration of the data center back to the primary facility is another form of disaster recovery. The only difference is that this one is planned, so the event can be scheduled with the business. The restoration is executed as documented in the disaster recover plan:

1. Assist in notifying corporate insurance to request assistance in initial safety and insurance inspection activities.

2. Coordinate requests for entry into the damaged area with corporate insurance and corporate legal representatives.

3. Establish schedules for salvage, new facilities preparation, and new equipment installation with the responsible individuals.

4. Specifically coordinate the restoration of the computing and peripheral equipment, auxiliary equipment, and supplies and forms.

5. Assist team members in obtaining the cooperation and participation of outside vendors during the restoration process.

6. Provide funding for the rebuild.

7. Coordinate the transition of operations through the various stages of recovery with server room operations and technical personnel and with the applications support team.

8. Brief team members regarding restoration activities.

9. Secure equipment and provide a timeline for operations to resume at the primary site.

10. Schedule an outage with the business to perform special save activities.

11. Schedule an outage with the business to shut down and move operations from the hotsite to the data center.

12. Move the operations.

Recovery Script

A recovery script is a timeline to help your organization execute major steps based on your Recovery Time Objective (RTO). To build a timeline script, you must first understand what your committed RTO is to the business. Second, you must determine how long it will take you to restore your mission-critical servers. The timeline forces you to stick to a schedule, thus guaranteeing the stated delivery objectives. This procedure will pre-determine your company's course of action. The recovery script must answer to the following questions:

- What is my recovery timeline?
- When do I inform management?
- When do I put the hotsite on alert?
- How long does it take to get the recovery started?
- How long do my recovery activities take to execute?
- When do I declare?
- What actions are taken at what time?
- Who will execute them?

The following is a hypothetical timeline for the initial actions taken during a possible disaster situation, shown in Figure 12.4.

Sequence of Events

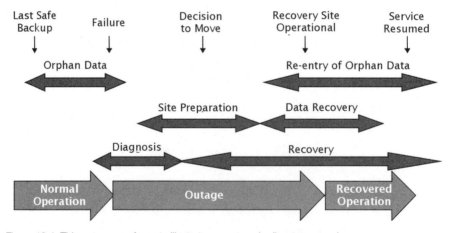

Figure 12.4: This sequence of events illustrates an example disaster scenario.

Timeline Sequence

The scenario is that an iSeries hardware failure occured after a sprinkler head had dumped water in the computer room. Here are the recovery parameters:

- The RTO is 24 hours.
- The commercial hotsite is located in the same city.
- Travel time to the hotsite is one hour.
- The system rebuild takes 12 hours.

Tape recalls are available in 90 minutes in an emergency.

Time: 0 hour

At the first indication of any total service outage, the organization will initiate standard troubleshooting and problem-escalation procedures. Every attempt to resolve the problem at the operations level is made at this time. Second-level technical staff are engaged.

Time: 1.0 hour

- Can the issue be resolved? Yes, but you cannot activate power to the computer room until the water-spill issue is resolved.
- Office services are engaged to start the water cleanup. (Estimate 2 hours.)
- The sprinkler water system has been bypassed.

Time: 3.0 hour

- Water issues are resolved and computer power can be restored again.
- Technical support staff determine the problem requires external help from an IBM hardware engineer. The SRC light on the front panel indicates a hardware failure. A severity-one call is placed to IBM field services.

- Onsite staff will escalate the problem to the appropriate management levels.

Time: 4.0 hour

IBM hardware engineers arrive and start problem diagnostics.

Time: 5.5 hour

- IBM has diagnosed the hardware problem and replacement parts are required. No time estimate is available until replacement hardware is located.
- Notification of incident is now escalated.
- Upon notification of an incident, the IT management recovery team leader notifies the technical recovery team leader that a major problem has occurred at the computer center and advises the team leaders to come onsite.
- All team leaders assemble at the designated control center.

Time: 6.0 hour

- IBM states parts are in another city and will arrive in three hours.
- The impact assessment activities continue, with the preparation of recovery team activities.
- The hotsite is placed on alert.
- Tapes are now recalled from offsite storage.

Time: 7.5 hour

- Offsite storage tapes arrive onsite.
- The technical recovery team is placed on standby.

Time: 10.0 hour

IBM parts arrive. Three possible scenarios exist:

- The parts replaced by IBM resolve the server outage and the alert is cancelled.
- The parts replaced by IBM resolve the server outage, but the server requires a full system and data reload. The alert remains open until the system is restored and fully functional again. All offsite materials remain onsite as delivered from the offsite storage vendor.
- The hardware failure is not resolved. Declare a disaster and start restoration activities at the hotsite to run parallel with server hardware repairs.

The recovery script must detail what time you will do which activity. The most common mistake organizations make is that the hotsite is not placed on alert until hour 10.0 or even after all the repair activities have been concluded. Now it's hour 14.0. With a restoration time of 12 hours, it is imperative that restoration activities have already started. The advantage in this example is that the hotsite vendor is local and no air travel is required. This could have easily been a few hours in the planning activation. It is beneficial as well to build a hardware recovery timeline, as shown in Figure 12.5, to clearly display the efforts required to rebuild the server infrastructure.

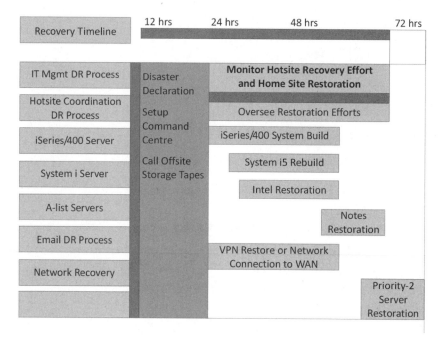

Figure 12.5: A server recovery timeline.

Summary

Here is an abbreviated disaster action checklist:

1. Plan Initiation:
    a. Notify senior management.
    b. Contact recovery teams.
    c. Determine the degree of disaster.
    d. Implement the proper application-recovery plan, depending on the extent of the disaster.
    e. Contact the backup site and establish schedules.
    f. Contact all other necessary personnel—both user and data processing.
    g. Contact vendors—both hardware and software.
    h. Notify users of the disruption of service.

2. Follow-Up Checklist:

   a. List teams and tasks of each.

   b. Obtain emergency cash and set up transportation to and from the backup site, if necessary.

   c. Set up living quarters, if necessary.

   d. Set up eating establishments, as required.

   e. List all personnel and their telephone numbers.

   f. Establish the user participation plan.

   g. Set up the delivery and receipt of mail. Establish emergency office supplies.

   h. Rent or purchase equipment, as needed.

   i. Determine the applications to be run and in what sequence.

   j. Identify the number of workstations needed.

   k. Check out any off-line equipment needs for each application.

   l. Check on forms needed for each application.

   m. Check all data being taken to the backup site before leaving, and leave an inventory profile at the home location.

   n. Set up primary vendors for assistance with problems incurred during the emergency.

   o. Plan for transportation of any additional items needed at the backup site.

   p. Take directions (map) to the backup site.

   q. Check for additional magnetic tapes or optical media, if required.

   r. Take copies of system and operational documentation and procedural manuals.

   s. Ensure that all personnel involved know their tasks.

   t. Notify insurance broker.

13

The Need for System-Related Documentation

Writing a disaster recovery plan is a documentation exercise that requires much thought, determination, and collaboration. As you have realized by now, it can be a very time-consuming project. There is considerable effort in writing a cohesive, comprehensive, and fully functional disaster recovery plan. One result of the DR planning project is that there will typically be a positive impact on your IT department. Yes, I am serious! Many IT staff members will realize the upfront importance and criticality of systems documentation. Before the project, you would typically find documentation lacking inside IT shops. DR plans force you to document, and for some, it is for the first time.

Prior to a writing a disaster recovery plan, try to find an i5 administrator who feels motivated to produce documentation for a process that is "never to be used by anyone." There lies the problem, and that's the wrong perception within IT. The individuals charged with the documentation task might view it in the beginning as a complete waste of time and effort. Many i5 system administrators would argue, "What's the point?"

Let's consider this. How many times have you been asked to install a new iSeries or i5 system? How about building a new partition? Maybe even a test system to validate a business solution that you put into production some years ago? Can you remember exactly how to do it right? Do you know all the prerequisites, dependencies and gotchas?

If only you had made some notes, you could simply reuse them, and not make this into a major project. Possibly another individual in your IT department has performed the procedure. Wouldn't it be nice to borrow that person's knowledge and experience to make your own IT life easier?

Now consider rebuilding servers without documentation in the most stressful situation: in a disaster, a real disaster. I can tell you from experience that recovering the complete data center in 24 to 48 hours will change your entire IT life. You will remember it for the good and for the bad. Will you rise to the occasion or go down with the IT ship? Can you rebuild the server infrastructure in the acceptable timeframe? Will you struggle to rebuild it at all? The only road to success is to follow documented, tested steps to rebuilding the servers exactly as they were running prior to the disaster. That's the primary consideration for spending the initial time and effort to write documentation. It's a roadmap for rebuilding your facility. This will give you your only chance to succeed.

There is no doubt that some feel that the documentation process slows the pace of progress within IT. The technology field is so fast-paced that it's hard to keep up with all the changes going on. That's exactly the reason for documentation! Consider how much time can be saved in training and preventing the duplication of effort. Now the justification of documentation becomes totally unavoidable and very logical.

A Change in the i5 Philosophy Silos

Writing a disaster recovery plan changes the server management philosophy of most IT staffs. i5 system administrators typically work in their own little silos. This is not a dig against iSeries/400 or i5 people. It is common across all computer professionals, regardless of hardware platform. They are handed the responsibility of maintaining a server or several logically partitioned servers to support a variety of business requirements. Specifically what are those business requirements? You will find that most administrators do not truly know or care. The i5 system administrator has never had a need to know prior to the DR planning initiative.

Techies are always near to their support discipline, and that is technology itself. Therefore, they are not linked directly to the business operation. They do know the uptime and technology requirements for every server, and that is a very important discipline to maintain. Upgrades to both hardware and software are again all managed within the administrator's little silo, or maybe even a department-wide silo. No one outside this department knows the scope nor what the specific changes involve, or how many changes have been performed to date. They just know that changes or upgrades are done on a regular basis and the servers remained operational. Expand that to other server platforms within your IT infrastructure, and the number of silos increases. What about network administration, or remote office technical support? Sometimes, cubicle walls separate one department silo from another. Maybe the only walls are the ones created within the silo's. This obviously presents the need for documentation and change management so that everyone knows the drill. Every time, all the time!

Let me introduce you to an iSeries colleague named David. He typically goes out of his way to avoid the whole responsibility of systems documentation. The process of creating documentation is very limiting to his technical creativity, not to mention just plain tedious. So what does he do? He always wants to move on to the next exciting thing. Find the next technical challenge! In his thinking, typical documentation simply gets in the way of that goal. Installing the latest operating system upgrade or working with the Hardware Management Console to create additional logical partitions is far more intriguing. However, as he would readily admit, documentation implies the process is sufficiently well documented to become somebody else's problem, and hence David never has to deal with it again. He can get rid of the problem and pass it along. Interested? Then there are the disaster recovery considerations. Now, David needs to sing a far different tune. He must realize the need to make something work long after he has done his initial tedious documentation efforts and wiped his hands clean. The disaster recovery project brings on a whole different layer of ownership.

When a DR planning project sweeps through an IT department, the silos topple as support of this project internally rises to the top. Formal documents need to be written and constantly maintained. It's no longer acceptable to have notes scattered on the i5 system administrator's desk, or worse, stored in his or her personal storage device (the brain). The success of the DR planning project will require this very same IT system administrator to produce professional working documents that will be needed to formally document the servers. All this, in turn, is critical to the success of your recovery of the IT infrastructure.

Successful management and completion of a DR planning project, like any other complex, large-scale project, is not an easy undertaking. Project delivery complications are inevitable, and the recovery planning team must react quickly and decisively. The success factor of this team will be its ability to be proactive, anticipate obstacles, and deliver timely corrective actions. Systems documentation within this project and future projects must be incorporated into the IT planning process. Therefore, it is never completely closed.

Write It All Down

With the ever-increasing need for uptime of computing systems, system documentation assumes a greater importance. In DR, server documentation is one of the most visible components of the project and ongoing recovery success. When there is no available documentation, we all have problems.

Unfortunately, server documentation is often late in development or completely overlooked. Every critical server identified during the business impact analysis must have detailed system documentation. Your disaster recovery plan must provide immediate, logical access to current, detailed configuration settings. Only this level of documentation will permit faster and complete recovery of the server infrastructure. Neglecting this part of DR planning will add hours or days to the recovery process. In the worst situation, lack of documentation prohibits a successful recovery from taking place at all. Do not underestimate the importance of this section in your disaster recovery plans.

All DR plans must include complete configuration information to a level that will enable you to rebuild your mission-critical servers. Without this critical supporting documentation, your restoration efforts will be severely impeded. This holds true for recovery of a single iSeries server and for the complete loss of a site. When access is available to your data center in a disaster, your backup data tapes alone will not entirely enable IT staff to rebuild a server. Detailed configuration documentation of every mission-critical server is essential to reestablishing a working IT framework.

I Thought Those Backup Tapes Had Everything!

One of the most common reasons detailed configuration system information is not documented is the simple belief that last night's backup tapes contain everything needed to restore servers to the state they were in prior to a server failure or disaster. Nothing can be further from the truth. The effectiveness and completeness of backup tapes depends on the nature of the disaster.

A mid-week failure with only daily data backup tapes preserves business data, but typically contains absolutely no server configuration data or settings. This backup availability will cause severe issues in restoration timelines. The backup tapes would only permit restoring the applications during the functional restoration phase of disaster recovery. In reality, this phase can only be done once the infrastructure has been properly restored, or rebuilt and reconfigured.

A second critical element to server recovery is whether the most recent system security is available. This is referred to as the daily running of the SAVSECDTA command. Many companies choose not to document their security policies and choose to omit saving critical security data daily. You need to ensure that the restored applications do not have any security issues when they are returned to production. A locked-down application might be completely open after a system restore. With proper supporting documentation, you can verify the level of system policies needed to support the iSeries or i5 application as it was in production.

Throughout the recovery process, a disaster recovery plan that contains detailed configuration documentation will permit the restoration team to easily navigate a recovery, troubleshoot issues, and verify and make modifications to any configuration settings required. Primarily, this level of information enables other personnel unfamiliar with that infrastructure to get the servers rebuilt and business running again.

Real-World Example: Customer Recovers iSeries/400 Because of Documentation Availability

I had a client that lost its data center due to a prolonged power failure. It ran a centralized operation that supported 28 manufacturing, shipping warehouses, and sales offices throughout Canada and the U.S. On Thursday, August 14, 2003, at precisely 4:12 p.m. EST, the lights went out. The blackout affected electric systems in northern Ohio, eastern Michigan, northern Pennsylvania, New Jersey, much of New York state, and Ontario. This was a notable regional disaster event, far more serious than a local power grid going down. The northeast went completely dark!

The remote sites all started calling in. Yes, there were concerns about how things looked at the primary facility, but the real question quickly became "when will the systems be up?" The sites had product to manufacture, sell, and move.

The client's representative declared a disaster and came to the hotsite. He arrived with a box of 12 tapes and said, "Here you go." He had no IT staff available; they were all working through issues or on vacation. After all, it was August. So, he left the hotsite staff with the task of recovering the iSeries system. In addition to the backup tapes, he produced the disaster recovery plan that he had tested successfully in previously visits to the hotsite. The difference in this disaster declaration was the system information documentation provided in the DR plan. It clearly spelled out the backup process, recovery procedures, and all the system-related information. This included system values, network attributes, working with third-party vendors for license keys, system startup procedures, etc. The network piece was also well defined, so the hotsite was able to work in conjunction with the isSeries/400 build, connecting the remotes into the hotsite's facility, which became the new production target location.

The disaster recovery was successful for three reasons:

- A solid backup program design
- Clear documentation for system recovery
- Supporting documents for server configuration.

Remember, with proper supporting documentation and skilled iSeries/400 professional, you can rebuild your server every time.

Collecting and Maintaining System Information

Normally, collecting and maintaining detailed configuration documentation is accomplished in one of the following ways:

- Manually check all the required server settings on each system.
- Develop a program or a tool specially designed to provide required server configuration settings through an automated process.
- Use the IBM-supplied command PRTSYSINF.

- Don't store the information resident on the iSeries. The information must be stored offsite, either at a storage provider, another server, or an office facility.

Whether the collection process is done manually or with tools that provide the required system information, automation makes the collection task easier by eliminating the work hours required and guaranteeing this critical operation gets performed regularly. With automation, the selection process for documentation is performed according to a predetermined schedule. It is therefore assured to be done. Manual collection always becomes a second or third priority in any given business day, which means it gets missed altogether.

The PRTSYSINF Command

The PRTSYSINF command is available in OS/400 versions V4R5 onward. Printing the system information provides valuable information about your iSeries/400 or i5 server that will be useful during a system recovery. The Print System Information (PRTSYSINF) command prints system information that should be maintained for disaster recovery and system verification purposes. You can schedule this command to run on a regular basis, say every weekend or monthly prior to the full system save. It will execute in under five minutes and does not need a restricted state to execute. It is especially useful if you cannot use your SAVSYS media to recover your system, and you are basically back to square one.

Consider what you would have to do if you were forced to use the V5R3 distribution media. There are literally hundreds to thousands of configuration settings currently running on your system. How could you possibly remember them all?

You might need your security administrator to provide the special authorities to execute this command. The PRTSYSINF command requires *ALLOBJ, *IOSYSCFG, and *JOBCTL authority and produces many, many, *many* spooled file listings.

You will have to find a means to electronically send the specific reports of concern (via PDF) to another location or burn a CD with the listings. Printing, of course, is another option, but do not be surprised if this command produces 300 to 500 pages of spooled reports. This output should be used as a reference.

The following reports are produced with the PRTSYSINF command:

- Library backup list (from the GO BACKUP menu)
- Folder backup list (from the GO BACKUP menu)
- Current settings for all system values (DSPSYSVAL)
- Current settings for all network attributes (DSPNETA)
- Edit descriptions (one report per description)
- PTF details (DSPPTF); details of all fixes installed on your server
- Network storage (DSPNWSSTG); information about network server storage spaces
- Reply list entries (WRKRYPLE); all reply list entries
- Recovery for access paths (DSPRCYAP); settings for access path recovery times
- Service attributes (DSPSRVA); settings for service attributes
- Power on/off schedule (DSPPWRSCD)
- Communications hardware resources
- Local workstations hardware resources
- Processor hardware resources
- Storage hardware resources
- LAN adapters hardware resources
- Coupled hardware resources
- Distribution services (DSPDSTSRV); SNADS configuration
- Subsystem descriptions (DSPSBSD); a separate spool file per subsystem description
- Software resources (DSPSFWRSC); installed licensed programs (the software resources list)

433

- Journal objects (DSPOBJD TYPE(*JRN)); all the journals on your server
- Journal attributes (one report per journal)
- Cleanup information (CHGCLNUP); settings for automatic cleanup
- QSECOFR user profile attributes (DSPUSRPRF)
- Current values for the QSECOFR user profile
- QDFTJOBD job description attributes

Complete Site Loss versus Server Loss

The important aspect of total infrastructure disaster recovery is to have detailed documentation for your environment. Approach documentation from the assumption that you will eventually have to completely rebuild the entire server and network infrastructure from scratch. With this in mind, consider every critical element to document in its entirety, from the PTFs installed, to IP addressing. Besides documenting the server configuration specifics, ensure the server hardware and operating system features are also documented. If you ever need to rebuild your iSeries or i5 server, it would be nice to be able to rebuild the logical partition performance profiles, disk configurations, OS levels, etc., exactly as they were running in production.

While a system will generally be able to be recovered eventually even without good documentation, additional downtime equates to lost revenue. Saving significant time in a rebuilding process by making use of documentation and well thought-out diagrams greatly assists in the successful restore.

iSeries/400 System Information

The following information is required to be included in the iSeries/400 or i5 system information section of your disaster recovery plan. This information must be detailed in a logical manner for every iSeries and i5 server and partition identified as a critical application:

1. Document iSeries/400 topology
   » System name
   » Partition name
   » Partition role and description of business function
   » VSIO of the LPAR configuration
2. Hardware configurations
   » Partition-level rack hardware details
   » System rack level details
   » LVT for LPAR-ed system
3. Hardware management console (HMC)
   » Configuration profile
   » Firmware
   » Backup
   » System planning tool report
4. Partition and hardware profile information for each partition
   » Performance profile
   » Disk allocation
   » Switchable features (IASP, tape drives, etc.)
5. Operating system information
   » Version
   » Installed product options
   » Special licensed products
   » Cume level
   » Group levels
   » Special Hypers
6. Third-party software inventory
   » Software name
   » Version number

» Service packs

» Vendor name

7. Third-party software contact information

» Vendor name

» Customer number

» Product name

» Support line phone number

» Vendor Web site URL

» Client representative name

» Contract number

8. BRMS and native backup software

» Daily backup policies

» Weekly backup policies

» Monthly backup policies

» Offsite tape-rotation policies

» Exit programs

» Backup schedule

» Backup shutdown and startup process

9. System values per system

10. Network attributes per system

11. Network configuration

» TCP/IP interface information

» TCP/IP routes

» Host tables

» TCP/IP servers active

» APIs

» Security management of FTP, ODBC, DDM, and HTTP

12. Ethernet line description per system

13. Additional line descriptions
    - » Any unique line descriptions
    - » Secondary Ethernet configuration descriptions
    - » Fax configurations
14. System startup program CL source per system
15. Any network storage spaces
16. IXS or IXA
    - » Configuration
    - » Setup
    - » Backup policies
    - » Operating system environment
17. Software license repository information
18. Work management
    - » Wrksyssts F11 screen shot displaying share pools per system
    - » Private pools
    - » Unique subsystem descriptions
    - » Specific system values
19. Considerations for hot-box
    - » Operating system software CD
    - » LIC CDs
    - » LPAR LVT
    - » Proof of Entitlement documents
    - » License keys
    - » DR plan

Intel System Information

The following information is required to be included in the Intel system information section of your disaster recovery plan. This information must be detailed in a logical manner for every Intel server identified as a critical application.

1. Hardware configurations of all servers
   » Brand
   » Model number
   » Hardware configuration – RAM, disk, processor
   » Special card features
   » Disk partitions
   » Disk SAN or NAS
   » Drivers used with each hardware components
   » IRQ, DMA, and base memory address for each component
   » Operating system level
   » Service packs Installed

2. Software inventory running on all servers
   » Which applications are running on each server
   » Detail version and release level
   » Current applied service patch levels
   » Critical application level settings
   » Path to specific databases and transaction logs

3. Backup software
   » Daily backup policies
   » Weekly backup policies
   » Monthly backup policies
   » Offsite tape-rotation policies
   » Tape naming convention
   » Backup topology exit programs
   » Software installed
   » Backup software patch levels

» Bare-metal or DR agents

» Tape drives

» Virtual tape libraries

» Electronic data vaults

4. Security management

» Security network topology

» Firewalls overview

» Spam filtering

» DMZ

5. Network configuration

» TCP/IP interface information per NIC

» TCP/IP routes

» Host tables

» Network segments per NIC

» WAN/LAN overview

» Network diagram

6. Third-party software contact information

» Vendor name

» Customer number

» Product name

» Support line phone number

» Vendor Web site URL

» Client representative name

» Contract number

7. Standard desktop configuration

8. Server install procedures

9. Server recovery procedures

10. Considerations for hot-box

» Operating system software CD

» Application CDs (such as SQL)

» Backup software CDs

» Backup software agent CDs (such as Exchange)

» License key CD

Network System Information

The following information is required to be included in the network-administration system information section of your disaster recovery plan. This information must be detailed in a logical manner for every Intel server identified as a critical application.

1. The physical network

   » Routers

   » Switches and hubs

   » Access points

   » Network cable segments

   » Hub or switch ports wired to each network jack.

   » Internal settings for switches, routers, access points, and fire walls

   » Server used as a DNS server

   » All DNS settings

   » The locations and settings of WINS and DHCP servers

2. Network diagram

3. Active Directory

   » All domains

   » Domain controllers and Active Directory roles

   » Trust relationships

   » All OUs, servers, computers, and groups

   » The rights assigned to each group

» Group policies

» Group settings

4. Third-party hardware and software contact information

» Vendor name

» Customer number

» Product name

» Support line phone number

» Vendor Web site URL

» Client representative name

5. Network data elements

» Carrier details

» Customer number

» Circuit numbers

» Application use of circuit

» Circuit configuration details

6. Procedures for uploading router configuration

7. Procedure for VPN client connectivity

8. All VPN tunnels and site locations

9. Backup policies

Summary

Managing configuration settings will reduce IT recovery time and errors significantly. Collecting system information is a painful task that few companies accomplish. Simply put, you must be disciplined. Collecting this information not only helps reduce downtime following a disaster, but it will assist you in successfully recovering your server infrastructure. Automate all server-information data collection for every hardware platform, so that it is gathered on a consistent, regular interval, without compromise.

14

System i5/iSeries Restoration Procedures

Restoring the IT infrastructure is the most crucial phase in keeping the business running in the event of a disaster. The high cost of downtime goes well beyond lost sales revenue. Imagine that a disaster has occurred. You have the data backed onto tape; now, what should you do with it? If you do not have fully documented recovery procedures, your data won't be available to you. With the data sitting in your hands, you need to be able to re-create your entire business from brand-new systems or alternate systems at your hotsite. Simply stated, you are going to need procedures for rebuilding systems and network infrastructure. System recovery and restoration procedures are typically best written by the people who currently administer and maintain the system i5. Your restoration procedures will be backed by your system information section for each critical server.

Without recovery procedures written in advance and tested at a hotsite, your chance of recovery is not very good. Yes, you can open up the "IBM Backup and Recovery Guide" for the first time and navigate through it. However, consider that this manual is 600+ pages of quality reading. Second, I am sure it's safe to say you will have many customized components that this manual will not be able to anticipate. Restoration or recovery procedures supporting your servers is a step in the right direction.

Recovery Procedures

To facilitate the recovery of the mission-critical servers, the disaster recovery plan should provide detailed procedures to restore the IT systems by your IT recovery team members. Considering the extensive variety of system types, configurations, and applications housed in computer rooms today, this chapter is even more important. Recovery procedures should be written in a straightforward, step-by-step style. To prevent difficulty or confusion in an emergency, no procedural steps should be assumed or omitted. Every step should be numbered with supporting start and end times to help the reader understand how long the tested steps will take to execute. Do not make assumptions, nor presume the reader will read between the lines to get from one step to another. Screen captures will also help demonstrate technical points.

Case Study Sample

Here is the backup strategy of a sample client:

- Monthly, a full system save Option 21 is performed: SAVSYS, SAVLIB *NONSYS, SAVDLO, and SAV.
- Daily, SAVLIB is performed for all production libraries using Save While Active.
- IFS save is performed daily.
- Configuration and security information is saved daily.
- Tapes are sent offsite daily.

After your System i5 has been repaired/replaced and the IBM CSR has given you the green light to proceed, what steps will you execute? Your decisions will determine the success or failure of your System i5 recovery. Use the procedure in the following pages as a guideline to help you develop your own customized procedures based on your backup strategy. The procedure is based on the above backups, and presumes all tapes are available for this system recovery. This recovery is a native CL-based system save, rather than a BRMS system backup.

Licensed Internal Code Restore

Run Schedule: Used to replace a damaged LIC from a complete system loss or replacing the load source disk.

Licensed Internal Code: This is the layer of the i5 architecture just above the hardware. The Licensed Internal Code is an important part of the i5 architecture. You must have a working LIC loaded on your machine before you can restore the operating system.

Load Source Unit: This is the first disk unit in the system ASP (1). It contains the LIC and disk configuration. You must use the control panel to initiate this process.

Step 1: Obtain the most recent copy of the SAVSYS backup. If you do not have a SAVSYS available, use the IBM supplied CD-ROMs that came with your current i5 operating system and all the program temporary fixes that you have applied.

Start time: _____   Stop time: _____

Use media from *SAVSYS and the procedure for recovering the Licensed Internal Code.

Step 2: You must use the control panel on the system unit to select the IPL device for an IPL from the alternate device. Insert the black key to unlock the control panel. On an HMC-based system, an alternate IPL device is selected by right-clicking the profile and making the selection of the alternate IPL device. On an 800 series, selection is done from the primary or management partition.

Step 3: Press the Mode select button to position the panel to Manual mode. The green indicator light will illuminate beside the selected mode. On an HMC-based system, Mode is selected by right-clicking Partition and From the Properties. On an 8xx series, partitions mode is selected from the primary system.

Step 4: Press the Function Select button to display 02 (IPL) in the Function display and press Enter. On an HMC-based system, set this from Partition by right-clicking and selecting Properties. On an 8xx series, this is done from the primary partition by taking option 10 beside the logical partitions.

Step 5: Press the Function Select button to display D (IPL from tape or CD- ROM) your alternate IPL device in the function display, and press Enter. On an HMC-based system, this is done by right-clicking Partitions and choosing Restart or Activate Partition and Open 5250 Emulation Session. On an 8xx series, this is done from the primary partition by either choosing Power on Partition or Restart Partition.

Step 6: Place the tape in the tape drive or place the CD-ROM in the optical disk unit. When the IPL is started, the system searches the alternate IPL devices for the Boot program. Ensure the HMC device is online and the console is powered up.

Step 7: Turn on power to the i5 or iSeries/400.

Step 8: After approximately 15 minutes, the Install Licensed Internal Code menu will appear. Select one of the following:

1. Install Licensed Internal Code
2. Work with Dedicated Service Tools (DST)
3. Define alternate installation device

If the system attention light illuminates and one of the SRC codes in Table 14.1 appears, perform the appropriate recovery instructions.

Table 14.1: SRC Codes	
SRC Code	**Description**
A1xx 1933 A12x 1933	The tape unit for the alternate IPL is not ready.
B1xx 1803 B1xx 1806 B1xx 1938	The tape unit for the alternate IPL was not found or was not ready.
B1xx 1934	The wrong tape is loaded.
2507 0001 2642 0001 2643 0001	A tape is not loaded in the tape unit for alternate IPL.
Any other SRC	The system has encountered a problem loading the LIC.

Step 9: Select option **1** in the Install Licensed Internal Code menu and press Enter. The Licensed Internal Code menu shown in Figure 14.1 provides several methods for loading your iSeries or System i5.

```
              Install Licensed Internal Code (LIC)

        1.  Restore Licensed Internal Code
        2.  Install Licensed Internal Code & Initialize system
        3.  Install Licensed Internal Code & Recover configuration
        4.  Install Licensed Internal Code & Restore Disk Unit
        5.  Install Licensed Internal Code & upgrade load source
```

Figure 14.1: The LIC menu.

447

Option 1 restores the Licensed Internal Code without removing other information that is on the system. This option is normally used in the following situations:

» Damaged objects in the operating system
» After replacing a failed disk subsystem other than unit 1 in the system ASP
» Upgrading to a new release of OS/400
» SLIP install

Option 2 installs the Licensed Internal Code and removes all data from all disks. This option is normally used when you are restoring to another hardware configuration to recover from a complete system loss. This would be used at the hotsite location or if you have experienced a failure on a RAID5 disk array.

Option 3 installs the Licensed Internal Code and requires you to provide information on how the disks were configured on your system (including ASP disk assignments and protection level). This option is normally used in the following situations:

» Replacing the load source unit
» Complete system restore to your existing iSeries or System i5
» Recovering back to your iSeries or i5 and not at the hotsite

Option 4 installs the Licensed Internal Code and restores data to a replacement disk unit. This option is used only by a service representative after data was successfully pumped from a failed disk unit.

Option 5 is used as part of the hardware migration path.

Step 10: Select option **2** (at the hotsite) and proceed to step 11.
Select option **3** (at your site on your equipment) and proceed to step 25.

If you selected option 2, the screen in Figure 14.2 will appear.

```
Install LIC and Initialize System    -    Confirmation


Warning:
        All data on the selected disk will be destroyed and
the Licensed Internal
        Code will be written to this disk if you choose to
continue the initialize and
        Install.



        Press F10 to continue the install.
        Press F12 ( Cancel ) to return to the previous screen
        Press F3  ( Exit ) to return to the install selection screen
```

Figure 14.2: Installing the LIC and initializing the system.

Step 11: Press **F10** on the Confirmation screen to proceed.

Step 12: The initialize disk status screen is displayed, as shown in Figure 14.3. The actual time to initialize the disk will be considerably less than the estimated time displayed.

```
Initialize the Disk - Status


The load source disk is being initialized.


Estimated time to initialize in minutes :        36

Elapsed time in minutes . . . . . . . . :        0.0


Please wait.

Wait for next display or press F16 for DST main menu
```

Figure 14.3: Initializing the disk status.

449

Step 13:   You are shown the Install License Internal Code status display, as in Figure 14.4. You do not need to respond. You have finished loading the Licensed Internal Code.

```
              Install Licensed Internal Code - Status

Install of the Licensed Internal Code in progress



               +----------------------------------------------+
Percent        | XXXXXXXXXXXXXXXXXXXXX 75% XXXXXXXXXXXXXXX |
Complete       +----------------------------------------------+



Elapsed time in minutes . . . . . . . . : 4.0

Please wait.



Wait for next display or press F16 for DST main menu
```

Figure 14.4: Finishing loading the LIC.

> **Note:**   During this process, the terminal session will disconnect. No intervention is required. The session will reestablish prior to proceeding to the Disk Configuration Attention Report screen.

Building Your Disk Configuration at the Hotsite Using Option 2

Step 14: When you install the Licensed Internal Code by using option 2 from the Install Licensed Internal Code menu, the system does the following:

» Clears disk unit 1 that contains information about how all the other disk units on your system are configured.

» Prepares to delete all data in the system ASP. The system ASP is not actually cleared until you perform the IPL after installing the LIC.

The resulting screen is shown in Figure 14.5.

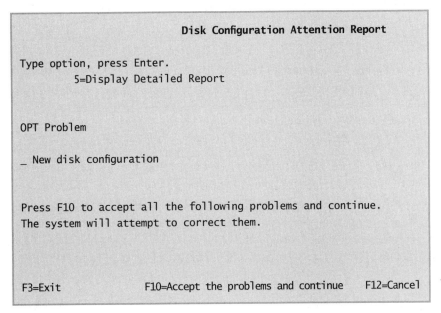

```
                      Disk Configuration Attention Report

Type option, press Enter.
        5=Display Detailed Report


OPT Problem

_ New disk configuration


Press F10 to accept all the following problems and continue.
The system will attempt to correct them.




F3=Exit              F10=Accept the problems and continue    F12=Cancel
```

Figure 14.5: After the LIC is installed.

Step 15: Press **F3** (Exit). You will be shown the Use Dedicated Service Tools menu. Select option **3** to use Dedicated Service Tools.

Figure 14.6 shows the Service Tools profile QSECOFR password expired after first use. At the Change Service Tools User Password screen, enter *in all uppercase* the current password (QSECOFR) and a new password, with verification of the password.

```
                    Dedicated Service Tools (DST) Sign On
                                                      System: Mid-Range


   Type choices, press Enter.



   DST user . . . . . . . . . . . . . . . .    QSECOFR
   DST password . . . . . . . . . . . . .     _____




   F3=Exit                                              F12=Cancel
```

Figure 14.6: Changing the password.

Step 16: In the DST User field, type QSECOFR and in the DST password field, type QSECOFR. Sign on *in all uppercase* as DST user QSECOFR with password QSECOFR. (The DST QSECOFR password is not the same as the previous QSECOFR password on your iSeries/400.)

The Use Dedicated Service Tools menu is shown:

1. Select an IPL
2. Install the Operating system
3. Work with licensed internal code
4. Work with disk units
5. Work with DST environment
6. Select DST Console mode

    7. Start a service tool

    8. Review Disk and determine if Parity is set

Step 17: Select option **4** (Work with disk units).
Select option **1** (Work with disk configuration).
Select option **5** (Work with device parity).

Step 18: Select option **2** (Start device parity protection). The display will list all the disk subsystems for which you can start the device parity protection. Type **1** in the Options column for the disks on which you wish to start device parity protection, and press Enter.

Step 19: To proceed, the system must perform directory recovery, which will take a significant amount of time. The system might appear inactive during this time. Press Enter to continue.

At this point, pressing Enter initiates the procedure for starting device parity protection. Once begun, this procedure must continue to run to completion.

Step 20: Select option **4** (Work with disk units).
Select option **1** (Work with disk configuration).
Select option **3** (ASP Configuration).
Select option **3** (Add units to ASPs).

Step 21: The next display identifies the possible disk configuration. The display shows the disk units assigned to the system ASP. The warning on this display means that it will clear all data on the disk units in the system ASP:

*Unit possibly configured for Power PC

This message is OK and can be ignored.

Step 22: If the configuration is correct, press **F10** to confirm the configuration. The system builds the configuration information and returns to the DST menu.

Step 23: Press **F12** to cancel the DST menu. This will display the IPL or Install the System menu.

Step 24: Proceed to step 39 to restore the operating system.

Building Your Disk Configuration on Your Home System Using Option 3

If you selected option 3, the screen in Figure 14.7 will appear.

```
Install LIC and Recover Configuration    -    Confirmation


Warning:
            All data on the selected disk will be destroyed and the
            Licensed Internal
         Code will be written to this disk if you choose to
            continue the install



         Press F10 to continue the install.
         Press F12 ( Cancel ) to return to the previous screen
         Press F3   ( Exit ) to return to the install selection screen
```

Figure 14.7: Continuing the installation.

Step 25: Press **F10** on the Confirmation screen to proceed.

Step 26: The Initialize Disk Status screen is displayed in Figure 14.8. The actual time to initialize the disk will be considerably less than the estimated time displayed.

```
   Initialize the Disk - Status


   The load source disk is being initialized.


   Estimated time to initialize in minutes :       36

   Elapsed time in minutes . . . . . . . . :          0.0


   Please wait.

   Wait for next display or press F16 for DST main menu
```

Figure 14.8: The Initialize Disk Status screen.

Step 27: You are shown the Install License Internal Code status display, as in Figure 14.9. You do not need to respond.

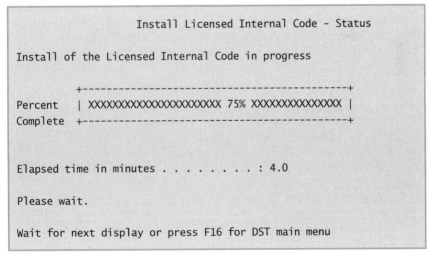

```
                     Install Licensed Internal Code - Status

   Install of the Licensed Internal Code in progress

           +-----------------------------------------+
   Percent | XXXXXXXXXXXXXXXXXXXXXX 75% XXXXXXXXXXXXXX |
   Complete +-----------------------------------------+


   Elapsed time in minutes . . . . . . . . : 4.0

   Please wait.

   Wait for next display or press F16 for DST main menu
```

Figure 14.9: The progress of initialization.

> **Note:** During this process, the terminal session will disconnect. No intervention is required. The session will reestablish prior to proceeding to the Disk Configuration Attention Report screen.

Step 28: When you install the Licensed Internal Code by using option 3 from the Install Licensed Internal Code (LIC) menu, the system does the following:

> » Clears disk unit 1 that contains information about how all the other disk units on your system are configured.
>
> » Prepares to delete all data in the system ASP. The system ASP is not actually cleared until you perform the IPL after installing the LIC.

Every disk unit on your system contains information on how it's configured. DST provides an option to recover the disk configuration on your system. The system will read every disk, assign it to the System ASP, and rebuild the disk unit information on unit 1.

Step 29: At the Disk Configuration Attention Report screen in Figure 14.10, press **F10** to accept the problems and continue.

```
                     Disk Configuration Attention Report

Type option, press Enter.
        5=Display Detailed Report


OPT Problem
_ New disk configuration




Press F10 to accept all the following problems and continue.
```

Figure 14.10: Starting the disk configuration. (part 1 of 2)

```
The system will attempt to correct them.

F3=Exit              F10=Accept the problems and continue
                     F12=Cancel
```

Figure 14.10: Starting the disk configuration. (part 2 of 2)

Step 30: Press **F3** (Exit to use Dedicated Service Tools). You will be shown the Use Dedicated Service Tools menu. Select option **3** to use Dedicated Service Tools.

The Service tools profile QSECOFR password is expired after first use. At the Change Service Tools User Password screen, enter *in all uppercase* the current password QSECOFR and a new password, with the verification password.

Step 31: In the DST User field, type QSECOFR. In the DST password field, type QSECOFR. Sign on *in all uppercase* as DST user QSECOFR with password QSECOFR. (The DST QSECOFR password is not the same as the previous QSECOFR password on your iSeries or System i5.)

The Use Dedicated Service Tools menu is shown:

1. Select an IPL
2. Install the Operating system
3. Work with licensed internal code
4. Work with disk units
5. Work with DST environment
6. Select DST Console mode
7. Start a service tool

Step 32: Select option **4** (Work with disk units).
Select option **2** (Work with disk unit recovery).
Select option **5** (Recover disk configuration).

Step 33: When you see Figure 14.11, press **F10** to ignore problems and continue.

```
Problem Report

OPT      Problem

_____    Load Source has been re-built

_____    ASP's will be cleared

Press F10 to ignore problems and continue
```

Figure 14.11: A standard problem-report screen.

Step 34: The Confirm Recover Configuration display identifies the possible disk configuration. The display shows the disk units that are assigned to the system ASP. The warning on this display means that it will clear all data on the disk units in the system ASP.

If the configuration is correct, press **F10** to confirm the configuration. The system builds the configuration information and returns to the DST menu.

The Use Dedicated Service Tools menu is shown:

1. Select an IPL
2. Install the Operating system
3. Work with licensed internal code
4. Work with disk units
5. Work with DST environment
6. Select DST Console mode
7. Start a service tool

Step 35:   Select option **4** (Work with disk units).
Select option **1** (Work with disk configuration).
Select option **5** (Work with device parity).

Step 36:   Select option **2** (Start device parity protection). The display will list all the disk subsystems for which you can start the device parity protection. Type a **1** in the Options column for the disks on which you wish to start device parity protection, and press Enter.

Step 37:   To proceed, the system must perform directory recovery, which will take a significant amount of time. The system might appear inactive during this time. Press Enter to continue.

At this point, pressing the Enter key initiates the procedure for starting device parity protection. Once begun, this procedure must continue to run to completion.

Step 38:   Proceed to step 39 to restore the operating system.

Restoring the Operating System

Run Schedule: Used to restore the operating system. This procedure can be performed either after restoring the Licensed Internal Code or after a manual IPL from the alternate IPL device. You must have a working LIC loaded on your machine before you can restore the operating system. You will be required to use the control panel to initiate this process.

Step 39:   Is the IPL or Install the System screen displayed?

   » *No*: Execute steps 1 through 7 and return to step 23.

   » *Yes*: Continue onto step 40.

Step 40:   Ensure that the tape loaded is the most recent SAVSYS.

Start time _____   Stop time _____

Use media from *SAVSYS and the procedure for restoring the operating system.

Warning! Use the IBM distribution tapes or the installation CD-ROMs only if no SAVSYS tape exists. If you use the IBM distribution CD-ROMs or tapes, all cumulative PTF and individual PTFs applied after the initial installation of the system must be installed again.

Step 41: At the IPL or Install the System screen, select **2** to install the operating system, as shown in Figure 14.12.

```
                    IPL or Install the System

                                              System: PLAKE
Select one of the following:

1. Perform an IPL
2. Install the Operating System
3. Use Dedicated Service Tools (DST)
4. Perform automatic installation of the Operating System
5. Save Licensed Internal Code

Selection
2

Licensed Internal Code - Property of IBM 5722-999 Licensed
Internal Code (c) Copyright IBM Corp. 1980, 2001.
```

Figure 14.12: Starting the operating system installation.

Note: Option 4 (Perform automatic installation) can only be used for installing a new version of the operating system, not for system recovery.

Step 42: Select **1** for a tape device if you are using tape SAVSYS, as shown in Figure 14.13. Press Enter at the Confirm Install of Operating System display.

```
                    Install Device Type

                                              System: PLAKE
Select one of the following:

1. Tape
2. Optical
3. Virtual Optical - Image catalog

Selection
1
```

Figure 14.13: Installing from tape.

Step 43: The Select a Language Group display in Figure 14.14 shows the primary language on the SAVSYS or CD-ROM that you are restoring. Type **2924** and press Enter to set the primary language as English.

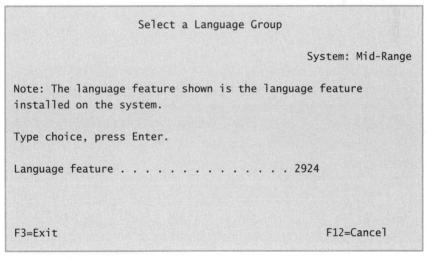

```
                  Select a Language Group

                                           System: Mid-Range

Note: The language feature shown is the language feature
installed on the system.

Type choice, press Enter.

Language feature . . . . . . . . . . . . . 2924




F3=Exit                                    F12=Cancel
```

Figure 14.14: Setting the primary language.

Step 44: At the Confirm Language Feature Selection screen, press Enter to confirm the language code.

Step 45: You will be presented with the Add All Disk Units to the System display if there are any disks attached that are in non-configured status. Is the Add All Disk Units to the System screen displayed?

 » *No*: Continue to step 46.

 » *Yes*: Select option **1** to add all disk units to the system auxiliary storage pool (ASP).

Step 46: The IPL in Progress display will show several steps. The steps take varied lengths of time, and some could exceed 20 minutes. The LIC IPL in Progress screen is presented as shown in Figure 14.5, indicating the IPL progress.

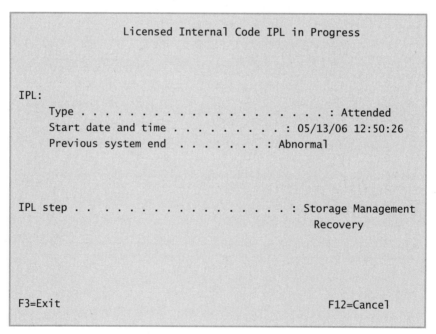

```
                    Licensed Internal Code IPL in Progress



IPL:
     Type . . . . . . . . . . . . . . . . . . . . : Attended
     Start date and time . . . . . . . . . : 05/13/06 12:50:26
     Previous system end  . . . . . . . : Abnormal




IPL step . . . . . . . . . . . . . . . . . : Storage Management
                                             Recovery




F3=Exit                                          F12=Cancel
```

Figure 14.15: The IPL in progress.

These subsequent status screens continue to present the IPL progress:

» Authority Recovery

» Journal Recovery

» Database Recovery

» Journal Synchronization

» Start the Operating System

Step 47: From the Install the Operating System display in Figure 14.16, select the default installation option.

```
                    Install the Operating System

Type options, press Enter.

     Install
        option . . . . . 2              1=Take defaults (No other
                                          options are displayed)
                                        2=Change install options

Date:
        Year . . . . . 01               00-99
        Month. . . . . 05               01-12
        Day  . . . . . 13               01-31
Time:
        Hour . . . . . 14               00-23
        Minute . . . . 15               00-59
        Second . . . . 00               00-59
```

Figure 14.16: The IPL in progress.

The following steps should be used when restoring to a system with a different serial number. Network attributes and system information will be recovered from save media, so the manual entry will not be required:

» At the Install the Operating System screen, select **2** for "Change install options." Confirm that the date and time values are correct, and press Enter to continue. The required OS/400 Installation Profiles and Libraries are installed as shown in Figure 14.17, and the Specify Install Options screen is displayed.

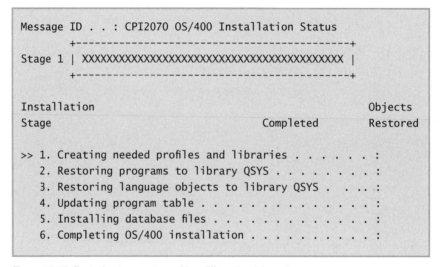

```
Message ID . . : CPI2070 OS/400 Installation Status
       +--------------------------------------------+
Stage 1 | XXXXXXXXXXXXXXXXXXXXXXXXXXXXXXXXXXXXXXXXXX |
       +--------------------------------------------+


Installation                                      Objects
Stage                             Completed        Restored

>> 1. Creating needed profiles and libraries . . . . . . :
   2. Restoring programs to library QSYS . . . . . . . . :
   3. Restoring language objects to library QSYS . . . . :
   4. Updating program table . . . . . . . . . . . . . . :
   5. Installing database files . . . . . . . . . . . . :
   6. Completing OS/400 installation . . . . . . . . . . :
```

Figure 14.17: Restoring to a system with a different serial number.

» Messages show the number of program and language objects being restored into library QSYS. This is strictly for information purposes. No response is required. This set can take up to 30 minutes to 1 hour to restore.

» At the Specify Install Options screen shown in Figure 14.18, select **1** for "Restore option," and then **2** for "Job and output queues option."

```
                        Specify Install Options
Type options, press Enter.


Restore option  . . . . . 1   1 =  Restore programs and language
                                     objects
                                     from the current media set
                               2 =  Do not restore programs or
                                     language objects
                               3 =  Restore only language objects
                                     from current media set
                               4 =  Restore only language objects
                                     from a different media set
                                     using
                                     current install device
Job and output
    queues option  .  . . 2     1=Clear, 2=Keep


Distribute OS/400 on
    available disk units  1     1=Yes, 2=No
```

Figure 14.18: The Specify Install Options screen.

> » At the Specify Restore Options screen in Figure 14.19, select
> **1** for System information. The default value is set as 2. Select
> **1** for all other items listed.

```
                      Specify Restore Options


Type options, press Enter.


    Restore from the installation media:


        System information . . 1     1=Restore, 2=Do not restore
        Edit descriptions  .   1     1=Restore, 2=Do not restore
        Message reply list. .  1     1=Restore, 2=Do not restore
        Job descriptions . .   1     1=Restore, 3=Keep customization
        Subsystem descriptions 1     1=Restore, 3=Keep customization
```

Figure 14.19: The Specify Restore Options screen.

Step 48: The next message to appear will be "Operating system has been installed. IPL in progress". Normal IPL SRCs will be displayed, as shown in Figure 14.20.

```
Message ID . . :  CPI2070                      OS/400 Installation
                                                     Status
+----------------------------------------------------+
| XXXXXXXXXXXXXXXXXXXXXXXXXXXXXXXXXXXXXXXXXXXXXXXXXXX |
+----------------------------------------------------+
Installation                                         Objects
Stage                          Completed              Restored

      1 Creating needed profiles and libraries . . . . : X

      2 Restoring programs to library QSYS. . . . . : X      09222

      3 Restoring language objects to library QSYS  . : X    04863

      4 Updating program table . . . . . . . . . . : X

      5 Installing database files . . . . . . . . . : X

   >> 6 Completing OS/400 installation  . . . . . . :
```

Figure 14.20: The operating system being installed.

Step 49: When the Sign-On screen appears, sign on as QSECOFR without specifying a user password. SRC C900 2965 will be displayed.

Step 50: On the Select Product to Work with PTFs screen, press **F3** (Exit).

Step 51: On the IPL Options screen shown in Figure 14.21, enter the correct date and time, select **Y** for the following options, and press Enter:

> » Start system to restricted state
> » Set major system options
> » Define or change the system at IPL

```
                          IPL Options

Type choices, press Enter.


System date. . . . . . . . . . . . 05 / 13 / 06 MM / DD / YY
System time  . . . . . . . . . . . 14 : 32 : 00 HH : MM : SS
Clear job queues . . . . . . . . . N        Y=Yes,  N=No
Clear output queues . . . . . . . . N        Y=Yes,  N=No
Clear incomplete job logs . . . . . N        Y=Yes,  N=No
Start print writers . . . . . . . . N        Y=Yes,  N=No
Start system to restricted state . . Y       Y=Yes,  N=No


Set major system options . . . . . . Y       Y=Yes,  N=No
Define or change system at IPL . . . Y       Y=Yes,  N=No



Last power-down operation was ABNORMAL
```

Figure 14.21: The IPL Options screen.

Step 52:   You are now shown the Set Major System Options screen. Set the options as follows, and press Enter:

>> Enable automatic configuration . . . . **Y**

>> Device configuration naming . . . . . . ***NORMAL**

>> Default special environment . . . . . . ***NONE**

Enabling automatic configuration is an important option to avoiding an A900 2000 SRC code later in the recovery process. By enabling the option, a console device description and tape device descriptions will be automatically configured. The downside is that all powered-on devices will also be auto-configured. These devices might have to be deleted.

Step 53:   When you restore your machine, the system resets some system information, such as system values and network attributes, to the IBM-supplied defaults. On the Define or Change System at

IPL screen, select option **3** (System value commands), and press Enter. Locate and change the following system values:

QALWOBJRST to ***ALL**

QJOBMSGQFL to ***PRTWRAP**

QJOBMSGQMX to **30**

QMAXSIGN to ***nomax**

QPFRADJ to **3**

QALWOBJRST to ***ALL**

QVFYOBJRST to **1**

QSCANFSCTL to ***NOPOSTRST**

QJOBMSGQ2 to **24**

Step 54: Press **F3** to return to the System Value Commands screen.

Step 55: Press **F3** to return to the Define or Change the System screen. Press **F3** to exit and continue the IPL. Press **F3** to exit the Display Messages screen.

Step 56: When restoring a complete system, the following network attributes maybe be reset to the IBM defaults:

» System Name

» Local network ID

» Local control point name

» Default local location name

» Default node

» Default type

» Maximum number of sessions

» Network node servers

Select option **4** (Work with Network attributes).
Select option **2** (Change Network Attributes) if your system name does not appear correctly.

Step 57: Upon completion of all required changes to network attributes, press **F12** to return to the Define or Change the System screen.

Step 58: Press **F3** to exit and continue the IPL.

Step 59: On the Edit Rebuild of Access Paths screen, press Enter.

Step 60: Press **F3** to exit the Display Access Paths Status screen.

Step 61: Press **F3** to exit the Display Messages screen.

The installation of the LIC and the operating system is complete when the iSeries/400 main menu appears. (GO MAIN or the command line in your sign-on session.)

Step 62: Delete all devices except the DSP01 console and tape drive, which have been auto-configured.

User Profile Restore

Run Schedule: Used to restore user profiles. You can restore a single user profile, a list, or all user profiles. All user profiles must be restored prior to a complete system reload. If you have a damaged user profile, it can be deleted unless it's an IBM-supplied user profile. The only way to recover an IBM profile is to slip install/restore the operating system again.

When you restore user profiles, the system will build an authority reference table for each profile that is restored. User private authorities are stored in this table.

Step 63: Mount the most recent tape containing the security data. The backup of security data is performed daily. If no daily tape is available, then use the latest SAVSYS.

Step 64: CHGMSGQ MSGQ(QSYSOPR) DLVRY(*BREAK) SEV(60)

Step 65: ENDSBS *ALL *IMMED

Step 66: Is the security data input tape a daily?

> » *Yes*: RSTUSRPRF DEV(TAP01) USRPRF(*ALL) ENDOPT(*LEAVE) ALWOBJDIF(*ALL)

> » *No*: RSTUSRPRF DEV(TAP01) USRPRF(*ALL) ENDOPT(*LEAVE) ALWOBJDIF(*ALL)

Note: CHGUSRPRF QSECOFR PASSWORD(RECOVERY) is very important!

Device Configuration Restore

Run Schedule: Used to restore configuration objects. You can restore a single configuration, a group of configurations, or the system resource management information. If you have a damaged object, it can be deleted and restored from tape. The file on the tape is named QFILEIOC. All device descriptions will need to be deleted to correct any devices auto-configured. First set QAUTOCFG to 0 (zero) prior to deleting devices. Omit TAP01 and DSP01.

Step 67: Mount the most recent tape containing the configuration data. The backup of configuration data is performed daily on a tape labeled SAVCFG. If no daily tape is available, then use the latest SAVSYS.

Step 68: Is the configuration data input tape a daily?

» *Yes:* RSTCFG DEV(TAP01) OBJTYPE(*ALL) ENDOPT(*UNLOAD) ALWOBJDIF(*ALL) SRM(*NONE):

» *No:* RSTCFG DEV(TAP01) OBJTYPE(*ALL) ENDOPT(*LEAVE) ALWOBJDIF(*ALL) SRM(*NONE)

IBM and User Library Restore (*NONSYS)

Run Schedule: Used to restore all IBM LICPGM, user programs, and user data libraries. The restore can be done on an individual library level or as a global complete restore.

Step 69: Mount the most recent tape containing last SAVLIB *NONSYS. This backup is performed every month-end.

Step 70: Load the first tape from the SAVLIB *NONSYS backup and issue the following command:

RSTLIB(*NONSYS) DEV(TAPXX) ENDOPT(*UNLOAD) MBROPT(*ALL) ALWOBJDIF(*ALL) OMITLIB(QMPGDATA)

Specify the OMITLIB parameter only if a more recent version of the daily tapes is available, in addition to the full system save.

Ensure all logical files have been rebuilt correctly by checking the job log, if required:

RSTLIB LIB(XXX) ENDOPT(*LEAVE) OPTIONS(*NEW) ALWOBJDIF(*ALL)

where *XXX* is the name of the library that has missed logical files from the above restore.

Step 71: Restore the most recent libraries from daily tapes, if available:

RSTLIB LIB(XXX) ENDOPT(*LEAVE) MBROPT(*ALL) ALWOBJDIF(*ALL)

where *XXX* are the daily save libraries, i.e., LIB1, LIB2, and LIB3.

Proceed to step 75.

User Library Restore

Run Schedule: Used to restore all user program and data libraries. The restore can be done on a library level or as a global complete restore.

Step 72: Locate the most recent tape containing the latest SAVLIB *ALLUSR.

Step 73: Load the first tape from the SAVLIB *ALLUSR backup and issue the following command:

RSTLIB *ALLUSR DEV(TAP01) ENDOPT(*LEAVE) ALWOBJDIF(*ALL) MBROPT(*ALL) OMITLIB(QMPGDATA)

Specify the OMITLIB parameter only if a more recent version of the daily tapes is available, in addition to the full user library save.

Ensure all logical files have been rebuilt correctly by checking the job log, if required:

RSTLIB(XXX) ENDOPT(*LEAVE) OPTION(*NEW) ALWOBJDIF(*ALL)

where *XXX* is the name of the library that has missed logical files from the above restore.

Step 74: Restore the most recent libraries from daily tapes, if available:

RSTLIB(XXX) ENDOPT(*LEAVE) MBROPT(*ALL) ALWOBJDIF(*ALL)

where *XXX* are the daily save libraries, i.e., LIB1 and LIB2.

Document Library Restore

Run Schedule: Used to restore all user documents, mail, and shared folders.

Step 75: Mount the most recent tape containing the document save set. The backup of the DLO is performed daily. If no DLO save set is available, the IBM distribution media will be required. This will include *only* IBM-supplied programs. All user data will be lost.

Step 76: RSTDLO(*ALL) SAVFLR(*ANY) DEV(TAP01) ENDOPT(*UNLOAD)

Step 77: The directories need to be restored:

RST DEV('QSYS.LIB/TAP01.DEVD') OBJ (('/*') ('/QSYS.LIB' *OMIT) ('/QDLS' *OMIT)) ENDOPT(*UNLOAD)

Step 78: Save the job log with SIGNOFF *LIST and press Enter.

Restore Verification

Run Schedule: Used upon completion of the restore steps, to ensure the entire system has been restored successfully.

Step 79: Display the job log to verify that all libraries and objects were restored. Scan the log for CPC3700, CPF3700 and CPC9000 messages. Restore commands used provide the following system messages:

» CPC3703—Sent for each library restored.

» CPF3773—Refers to the number of objects successfully restored or not restored.

» CPF3839—The completion message for the RST command from a tape input operation.

» CPF383E—The completion message from the RST command for a Save File input operation.

» CPF9003—The completion message for the RSTDLO command.

A restore operation can be unsuccessful. When the system cannot restore an object successfully, it is usually because of the following:

- The object exists on the system already.

- The object is currently in use by the system. Restoring an object requires an exclusive lock on the file.

- The object on the media is damaged.

- The user does not have the necessary authority to restore the object.

- Object difference exist. For example, information about a database file does not match.

- Security-sensitive objects are not restored because the system value QALWOBJRST was set to *NONE.

System Security Rebuild

Run Schedule: After all user profiles and user libraries have been restored.

Restoring a user's private authorities to objects is a separate process from restoring user profiles. Security-related messages will be produced under some conditions when the system cannot resolve security conflicts. It is essential that security information is restored in the correct order.

Step 80:   RSTAUT and press Enter.

Step 81:   CHGSYSVAL SYSVAL(QSTRUPPGM) VALUE(*NONE)

Step 82:   Place scheduled jobs on hold:

HLDJOBSCDE JOB(*ALL) ENTRYNBR(*ALL)

REVIEW SUBMITTED JOBS

Step 83: PWRDWNSYS OPTION(*IMMED) RESTART(*YES *FULL) IPLSRC(B)

Step 84: Sign on to the system. Verify the device names for local devices. Verify all application environments work. Reset the startup program.

Step 85: ENDSBS *ALL *IMMED

Step 86: STRSBS QCTL

Summary

Following a complete, documented, and tested process helps ensure systems recovery. This chapter provides a recovery foundation for supporting a native CL backup program design. It is important to become very familiar with your backup strategy and document a complete recovery set of procedures to reflect you backup strategy. Opening up the 600-page "Backup and Recovery" manual for the first time in a disaster is not forward-thinking. Detailing every recovery step helps ensure that your recovery team members can successfully recover every level of the iSeries or System i5 system.

15

System i5/iSeries BRMS Restoration Procedures

To facilitate the recovery of the mission-critical servers, the disaster recovery plan should provide detailed procedures to restore the IT systems by your IT recovery team members. Considering the extensive variety of system types, configurations, and applications housed in computer rooms today, this chapter is even more important.

Utilizing IBM BRMS software to manage your backup and recovery solution can greatly assist in your success. The BRMS solution provides a recovery report that will help your recovery team roadmap the System i5 recovery steps. This can be very useful as this report will constantly be updated automatically as backups are executed daily. The key is to ensure this system recovery report is printed or emailed from your system after the backups have been executed successfully. Having the report reside in an output queue on the failed server will be of no value during a disaster.

In the event that your recovery procedures are not available from BRMS or you wish to have more elaborative procedures outline your recovery efforts, a case study help illustrate the basic BRMS recovery up to a successful catalog recreation.

Recovery procedures should be written in a straightforward, step-by-step style. To prevent difficulty or confusion in an emergency, no procedural steps should be assumed or omitted. Every step should be numbered with supporting start and end times to help the reader understand how long the tested steps will take to execute. Do not make assumptions, nor presume the reader will read between the lines to get from one step to another. Screen captures will also help demonstrate technical points.

The following resources are required for iSeries recovery using BRMS:

1. All system components backed up using BRMS, including a SAVSYS

2. The most current set of BRMS recovery reports, including the following:

    a. "Recovering your Entire System" report

    b. "Recovery Volume Summary" report

    c. "Display ASP Information" report

3. All media listed on the "Recovery Volume Summary" report

This recovery is based on a BRMS backup strategy where utilizing this process will assist your organization in a successful recovery of the BRMS base system in order to proceed with full BRMS restoration procedures.

Licensed Internal Code Restore

Run Schedule: Used to replace a damaged LIC from a complete system loss or replacing the load source disk.

Licensed Internal Code: This is the layer of the i5 architecture just above the hardware. The Licensed Internal Code is an important part of the i5 architecture. You must have a working LIC loaded on your machine before you can restore the operating system.

Load Source Unit: This is the first disk unit in the system ASP (1). It contains the LIC and disk configuration. You must use the control panel to initiate this process.

You must have a working LIC loaded on your machine before you can restore the operating system. You will be required to use the HMC or physical control panel to initiate this process.

Step 1: Using the BRMS "Recovering Your Entire System" report, obtain the media volume required to recover the Licensed Internal Code from the SAVSYS.

If you do not have a SAVSYS available, use the IBM supplied CD-ROMs that came with your current i5 operating system and all the program temporary fixes that you have applied.

Start time: _____   Stop time: _____

Use media from *SAVSYS and the procedure for recovering the Licensed Internal Code.

Step 2: You must use the control panel on the system unit to select the IPL device for an IPL from the alternate device. Insert the black key to unlock the control panel. On an HMC-based system, an alternate IPL device is selected by right-clicking the profile and making the selection of the alternate IPL device. On an 800 series, selection is done from the primary or management partition.

Step 3: Press the Mode select button to position the panel to Manual mode. The green indicator light will illuminate beside the selected mode. On an HMC-based system, Mode is selected by right-clicking Partition and From the Properties. On an 8xx series, partitions mode is selected from the primary system.

Step 4: Press the Function Select button to display 02 (IPL) in the Function display and press Enter. On an HMC-based system, set this from Partition by right-clicking and selecting Properties. On an 8xx series, this is done from the primary partition by selecting option 10 beside the logical partitions.

Step 5: Press the Function Select button to display D (IPL from tape or CD- ROM) your alternate IPL device in the function display, and press Enter. On an HMC-based system, this is done by right-clicking Partitions and choosing Restart or Activate Partition and Open 5250 Emulation Session. On an 8xx series, this is done from the primary partition by either choosing Power on Partition or Restart Partition.

Step 6: Place the tape in the tape drive or place the CD-ROM in the optical disk unit. When the IPL is started, the system searches the alternate IPL devices for the Boot program. Ensure the HMC device is online and the console is powered up.

Step 7: Turn on power to the i5 or iSeries/400.

Step 8: After approximately 15 minutes, the Install Licensed Internal Code menu will appear. Select one of the following:

1. Install Licensed Internal Code
2. Work with Dedicated Service Tools (DST)
3. Define alternate installation device

If the system attention light illuminates and one of the SRC codes in Table 15.1 appears, perform the appropriate recovery instructions.

Table 15.1: SRC Codes	
SRC Code	**Description**
A1xx 1933 A12x 1933	The tape unit for the alternate IPL is not ready.
B1xx 1803 B1xx 1806 B1xx 1938	The tape unit for the alternate IPL was not found or was not ready.
2507 0001 2642 0001 2643 0001	A tape is not loaded in the tape unit for alternate IPL.
Any other SRC	The system has encountered a problem loading the LIC.

```
   Install Licensed Internal Code (LIC)

Restore Licensed Internal Code
Install Licensed Internal Code & Initialize system
Install Licensed Internal Code & Recover configuration
Install Licensed Internal Code & Restore Disk Unit
Install Licensed Internal Code & upgrade load source
```

Figure 15.1: The LIC menu.

Step 9:   Select option **1** in the Install Licensed Internal Code menu and press Enter. The Licensed Internal Code menu shown in Figure 15.1 provides several methods for loading.

Option 1 restores the Licensed Internal Code without removing other information that is on the system. This option is normally used in the following situations:

» Damaged objects in the operating system

» After replacing a failed disk subsystem other than unit 1 in the system ASP

» Upgrading to a new release of OS/400

» SLIP install

Option 2 installs the Licensed Internal Code and removes all data from all disks. This option is normally used when you are restoring to another hardware configuration to recover from a complete system loss. This would be used at the hotsite location or if you have experienced a failure on a RAID5 disk array.

Option 3 installs the Licensed Internal Code and requires you to provide information on how the disks were configured on your system (including ASP disk assignments and protection level). This option is normally used in the following situations:

481

» Replacing the load source unit

» Complete system restore to your existing iSeries or System i5

» Recovering back to your iSeries or i5 and not at the hotsite

Option 4 installs the Licensed Internal Code and restores data to a replacement disk unit. This option is used only by a service representative after data was successfully pumped from a failed disk unit.

Option 5 is used as part of the hardware migration path.

Step 10: Select option **2** (at the hotsite) and proceed to step 11.
Select option **3** (at your site on your equipment) and proceed to step 25.

If you selected option 2, the screen in Figure 15.2 will appear.

```
Install LIC and Initialize System   -   Confirmation


Warning:
     All data on the selected disk will be destroyed and the
     Licensed Internal
   Code will be written to this disk if you choose to continue
     the initialize
   and Install.



     Press F10 to continue the install.
     Press F12 ( Cancel ) to return to the previous screen
     Press F3  ( Exit ) to return to the install selection
     screen
```

Figure 15.2: Installing the LIC and initializing the system.

Step 11: Press **F10** on the Confirmation screen to proceed.

Step 12: The initialize disk status screen is displayed, as shown in Figure 15.3. The actual time to initialize the disk will be considerably less than the estimated time displayed.

```
Initialize the Disk - Status


The load source disk is being initialized.


Estimated time to initialize in minutes :      36

Elapsed time in minutes . . . . . . . . :     0.0


Please wait.

Wait for next display or press F16 for DST main menu
```

Figure 15.3: Initializing the disk status.

Step 13:   You are shown the Install License Internal Code status display, as in Figure 15.4. You do not need to respond. You have finished loading the Licensed Internal Code.

```
              Install Licensed Internal Code - Status

Install of the Licensed Internal Code in progress



              +----------------------------------------------+
Percent       | XXXXXXXXXXXXXXXXXXXXX 75% XXXXXXXXXXXXXXX     |
Complete      +----------------------------------------------+


Elapsed time in minutes . . . . . . . . : 4.0

Please wait.


Wait for next display or press F16 for DST main menu
```

Figure 15.4: Finishing loading the LIC.

> **Note:** During this process, the terminal session will disconnect. No intervention is required. The session will reestablish prior to proceeding to the Disk Configuration Attention Report screen.

Building Your Disk Configuration at the Hotsite Using Option 2

Step 14: When you install the Licensed Internal Code by using option 2 from the Install Licensed Internal Code menu, the system does the following:

» Clears disk unit 1 that contains information about how all the other disk units on your system are configured.

» Prepares to delete all data in the system ASP. The system ASP is not actually cleared until you perform the IPL after installing the LIC.

The resulting screen is shown in Figure 15.5. You will have to change the DST password here.

```
                        Disk Configuration Attention Report

Type option, press Enter.
        5=Display Detailed Report


OPT Problem
_ New disk configuration


Press F10 to accept all the following problems and continue.
The system will attempt to correct them.



F3=Exit     F10=Accept the problems and continue        F12=Cancel
```

Figure 15.5: After the LIC is installed.

Step 15: Press **F3** (Exit). You will be shown the Use Dedicated Service Tools menu. Select option **3** to use Dedicated Service Tools.

Figure 15.6 shows the Service Tools profile QSECOFR password expired after first use. At the Change Service Tools User Password screen, enter *in all uppercase* the current password (QSECOFR) and a new password, with verification of the password.

```
                    Dedicated Service Tools (DST) Sign On
                                                     System: Mid-Range


Type choices, press Enter.


DST user . . . . . . . . . . . . . . . . .    QSECOFR
DST password. . . . . . . . . . . . . . .    _____




F3=Exit                                                         F12=Cancel
```

Figure 15.6: Changing the password.

Step 16: In the DST User field, type QSECOFR and in the DST password field, type QSECOFR. Sign on *in all uppercase* as DST user QSECOFR with password QSECOFR. (The DST QSECOFR password is not the same as the previous QSECOFR password on your iSeries/400.)

The Use Dedicated Service Tools menu is shown:
1. Select an IPL
2. Install the Operating system
3. Work with licensed internal code
4. Work with disk units
5. Work with DST environment
6. Select DST Console mode

7. Start a service tool
8. Review Disk and determine if Parity is set

Step 17: Select option **4** (Work with disk units).
Select option **1** (Work with disk configuration).
Select option **5** (Work with device parity).

Step 18: Select option **2** (Start device parity protection). The display will list all the disk subsystems for which you can start the device parity protection. Type **1** in the Options column for the disks on which you wish to start device parity protection, and press Enter.

Step 19: To proceed, the system must perform directory recovery, which will take a significant amount of time. The system might appear inactive during this time. Press Enter to continue.

At this point, pressing Enter initiates the procedure for starting device parity protection. Once begun, this procedure must continue to run to completion.

Step 20: Select option **4** (Work with disk units).
Select option **1** (Work with disk configuration).
Select option **3** (ASP Configuration).
Select option **3** (Add units to ASPs).

Step 21: The next display identifies the possible disk configuration. The display shows the disk units assigned to the system ASP. The warning on this display means that it will clear all data on the disk units in the system ASP.

Step 22: If the configuration is correct, press **F10** to confirm the configuration. The system builds the configuration information and returns to the DST menu. You will get a message stating that the "selected units have been added successfully." This step can take several hours to complete, depending on the number and size of disk drives and the total quantity of disk to be added.

Step 23: Press **F12** to cancel the DST menu. This will display the IPL or Install the System menu.

Step 24: Proceed to step 39 to restore the operating system.

Building Your Disk Configuration on Your Home System Using Option 3

If you selected option 3, the screen in Figure 15.7 will appear.

```
Install LIC and Recover Configuration    -   Confirmation


Warning:
          All data on the selected disk will be destroyed and
            the Licensed Internal
          Code will be written to this disk if you choose to con
            tinue the install



          Press F10 to continue the install.
          Press F12 ( Cancel ) to return to the previous screen
          Press F3   ( Exit ) to return to the install selection
            screen
```

Figure 15.7: Continuing the installation.

Step 25: Press **F10** on the Confirmation screen to proceed.

Step 26:   The Initialize Disk Status screen in Figure 15.8 is displayed. The actual time to initialize the disk will be considerably less than the estimated time displayed.

```
Initialize the Disk - Status


The load source disk is being initialized.


Estimated time to initialize in minutes :        36

Elapsed time in minutes . . . . . . . . :        0.0


Please wait.

Wait for next display or press F16 for DST main menu
```

Figure 15.8: The Initialize Disk Status screen.

Step 27:   You are shown the Install License Internal Code status display, as in Figure 15.9. You do not need to respond.

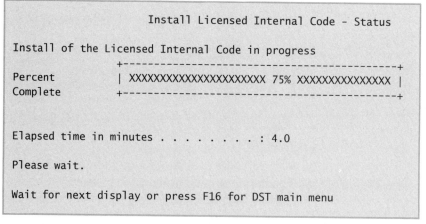

```
                      Install Licensed Internal Code - Status

Install of the Licensed Internal Code in progress
                    +-----------------------------------------------+
Percent             | XXXXXXXXXXXXXXXXXXXXXX 75% XXXXXXXXXXXXXXX |
Complete            +-----------------------------------------------+


Elapsed time in minutes . . . . . . . . : 4.0

Please wait.

Wait for next display or press F16 for DST main menu
```

Figure 15.9: The progress of initialization.

> **Note:** During this process, the terminal session will disconnect. No intervention is required. The session will reestablish prior to proceeding to the Disk Configuration Attention Report screen.

Step 28: When you install the Licensed Internal Code by using option 3 from the Install Licensed Internal Code (LIC) menu, the system does the following:

» Clears disk unit 1 that contains information about how all the other disk units on your system are configured.

» Prepares to delete all data in the system ASP. The system ASP is not actually cleared until you perform the IPL after installing the LIC.

Every disk unit on your system contains information on how it's configured. DST provides an option to recover the disk configuration on your system. The system will read every disk, assign it to the System ASP, and rebuild the disk unit information on unit 1.

Step 29: At the Disk Configuration Attention Report screen in Figure 15.10, press **F10** to accept the problems and continue.

```
                    Disk Configuration Attention Report

Type option, press Enter.
        5=Display Detailed Report


OPT Problem
_ New disk configuration




Press F10 to accept all the following problems and continue.
```

Figure 15.10: Starting the disk configuration. (part 1 of 2)

```
The system will attempt to correct them.




F3=Exit      F10=Accept the problems and continue      F12=Cancel
```

Figure 15.10: Starting the disk configuration. (part 2 of 2)

Step 30: Press **F3** (Exit to use Dedicated Service Tools). You will be shown the Use Dedicated Service Tools menu. Select option **3** to use Dedicated Service Tools.

The Service tools profile QSECOFR password is expired after first use. At the Change Service Tools User Password screen, enter *in all uppercase* the current password QSECOFR and a new password, with the verification password.

Step 31: In the DST User field, type QSECOFR. In the DST password field, type QSECOFR. Sign on *in all uppercase* as DST user QSECOFR with password QSECOFR. (The DST QSECOFR password is not the same as the previous QSECOFR password on your iSeries or System i5.)

The Use Dedicated Service Tools menu is as follows:

1. Select an IPL
2. Install the Operating system
3. Work with licensed internal code
4. Work with disk units
5. Work with DST environment
6. Select DST Console mode
7. Start a service tool

Step 32: Select option **4** (Work with disk units).
Select option **2** (Work with disk unit recovery).
Select option **5** (Recover disk configuration).

Step 33: When you see Figure 15.11, press **F10** to ignore problems and continue.

```
Problem Report

OPT        Problem

_____      Load Source has been re-built

_____      ASP's will be cleared

Press F10 to ignore problems and continue
```

Figure 15.11: A standard problem-report screen.

Step 34: The Confirm Recover Configuration display identifies the possible disk configuration. The display shows the disk units that are assigned to the system ASP. The warning on this display means that it will clear all data on the disk units in the system ASP.

If the configuration is correct, press **F10** to confirm the configuration. The system builds the configuration information and returns to the DST menu.

The Use Dedicated Service Tools menu is as follows:

1. Select an IPL
2. Install the Operating system
3. Work with licensed internal code
4. Work with disk units
5. Work with DST environment

6. Select DST Console mode

7. Start a service tool

Step 35: Select option **4** (Work with disk units).
Select option **1** (Work with disk configuration).
Select option **5** (Work with device parity).

Step 36: Select option **2** (Start device parity protection). The display will list all the disk subsystems for which you can start the device parity protection. Type a **1** in the Options column for the disks on which you wish to start device parity protection, and press Enter.

Step 37: To proceed, the system must perform directory recovery, which will take a significant amount of time. The system might appear inactive during this time. Press Enter to continue.

At this point, pressing the Enter key initiates the procedure for starting device parity protection. Once begun, this procedure must continue to run to completion.

Step 38: Proceed to step 39 to restore the operating system.

Restoring the Operating System

Run Schedule: Used to restore the operating system. This procedure can be performed either after restoring the Licensed Internal Code or after a manual IPL from the alternate IPL device. You must have a working LIC loaded on your machine before you can restore the operating system.

Step 39: Using the BRMS "Recovering Your Entire System" report, obtain the media volume required to recover the operating system from the BRMS SAVSYS.

Is the IPL or Install the System screen displayed?

» *No*: Execute steps 1 through 7 and return to step 23.

» *Yes*: Continue onto step 40.

Step 40: Ensure that the tape loaded is the most recent SAVSYS.

Start time _____   Stop time _____

Use media from *SAVSYS and the procedure for restoring the operating system.

Warning! Use the IBM distribution tapes or the installation CD-ROMs only if no SAVSYS tape exists. If you use the IBM distribution CD-ROMs or tapes, all cumulative PTF and individual PTFs applied after the initial installation of the system must be installed again.

Step 41: At the IPL or Install the System screen, select **2** to install the operating system, as shown in Figure 15.12.

```
                    IPL or Install the System

                                            System: PLAKE
Select one of the following:

1. Perform an IPL
2. Install the Operating System
3. Use Dedicated Service Tools (DST)
4. Perform automatic installation of the Operating System
5. Save Licensed Internal Code

Selection
2

Licensed Internal Code - Property of IBM 5722-999 Licensed
Internal Code (c) Copyright IBM Corp. 1980, 2001.
```

Figure 15.12: Starting the operating system installation.

> **Note:** Option 4 (Perform automatic installation) can only be used for installing a new version of the operating system, not for system recovery.

Step 42: Select **1** for a tape device if you are using tape SAVSYS, as shown in Figure 15.13. Press Enter at the Confirm Install of Operating System display.

```
                         Install Device Type

                                                    System: PLAKE
Select one of the following:

1. Tape
2. Optical
3. Virtual Optical – Image catalog

Selection
1
```

Figure 15.13: Installing from tape.

Step 43: The Select a Language Group display in Figure 15.14 shows the primary language on the SAVSYS or CD-ROM that you are restoring. Type **2924** and press Enter to set the primary language as English.

```
                      Select a Language Group

                                              System: Mid-Range


Note: The language feature shown is the language feature
installed on the system.

Type choice, press Enter.
```

Figure 15.14: Setting the primary language. (part 1 of 2)

```
Language feature . . . . . . . . . . . . 2924



F3=Exit                                          F12=Cancel
```

Figure 15.14: Setting the primary language. (part 2 of 2)

Step 44: At the "Confirm Language Feature Selection," press Enter to confirm the language code.

Step 45: You will be presented with the "Add All Disk Units to the System" display if there are any disks attached that are in non-configured status. Is the Add All Disk Units to the System screen displayed?

» *No*: Continue to step 46.

» *Yes*: Select option **1** to add all disk units to the system auxiliary storage pool (ASP).

Step 46: The IPL in Progress display will show several steps. The steps take varied lengths of time, and some could exceed 20 minutes. The LIC IPL in Progress screen is presented as shown in Figure 15.5, indicating the IPL progress.

```
             Licensed Internal Code IPL in Progress


IPL:
    Type . . . . . . . . . . . . . . . . . . : Attended
    Start date and time . . . . . . . . : 05/13/06 12:50:26
    Previous system end  . . . . . . . . . . . : Abnormal



IPL step . . . . . . . . . . . . . . . . . : Storage Management
  Recovery
F3=Exit                                          F12=Cancel
```

Figure 15.15: The IPL in progress.

These subsequent status screens continue to present the IPL progress:

» Authority Recovery

» Journal Recovery

» Database Recovery

» Journal Synchronization

» Start the Operating System

The following steps should be used when restoring to a system with a different serial number. Network attributes and system information will be recovered from save media; therefore, the manual entry will not be required.

Step 47: From the "Install the Operating System" display in Figure 15.16, select the default installation option.

```
                    Install the Operating System

Type options, press Enter.

     Install
          option . . . . . 2        1=Take defaults (No other
                                          options are displayed)
                                     2=Change install options

Date:
          Year . . . . . . 05                   00-99
          Month.  . . . . 05                    01-12
          Day . . . . . . .13                   01-31
Time:
          Hour . . . . .  14                     00-23
          Minute . . . . . 15                    00-59
          Second . . . . . 00                    00-59
```

Figure 15.16: The IPL in progress.

» At the Install the Operating System screen, select **2** for "Change install options." Confirm that the date and time values are correct, and press Enter to continue. The required OS/400 Installation Profiles and Libraries are installed as shown in Figure 15.17, and the Specify Install Options screen is displayed.

Messages show the number of program and language objects being restored into library QSYS. This is strictly for information purposes. No response is required. This set can take up to one hour to restore.

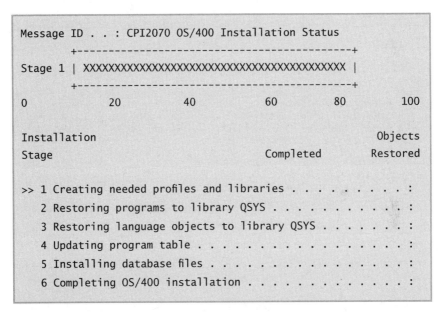

```
Message ID . . : CPI2070 OS/400 Installation Status
        +--------------------------------------------+
Stage 1 | XXXXXXXXXXXXXXXXXXXXXXXXXXXXXXXXXXXXXXXXXXX |
        +--------------------------------------------+
0           20          40          60          80          100


Installation                                                Objects
Stage                                        Completed      Restored


>> 1 Creating needed profiles and libraries . . . . . . . . . :
   2 Restoring programs to library QSYS . . . . . . . . . . :
   3 Restoring language objects to library QSYS . . . . . . . :
   4 Updating program table . . . . . . . . . . . . . . . . :
   5 Installing database files . . . . . . . . . . . . . . . :
   6 Completing OS/400 installation . . . . . . . . . . . . :
```

Figure 15.17: Restoring to a system with a different serial number.

Messages show the number of program and language objects being restored into library QSYS. This is strictly for information purposes. No response is required. This set can take up to 30 minutes to 1 hour to restore.

» At the Specify Install Options screen shown in Figure 15.18, select **1** for "Restore option," and then **2** for "Job and output queues option."

```
                        Specify Install Options
Type options, press Enter.

Restore option . . . . 1  1 =  Restore programs and language objects
                                  from the current media set
                          2 =  Do not restore programs or
                                  language objects
                          3 =  Restore only language objects
                                  from current media set
                          4 =  Restore only language objects
                                  from a different media set using
                                  current install device
Job and output
   queues option . . . . . . 2      1=Clear, 2=Keep

Distribute OS/400 on
   available disk units . . . 1      1=Yes, 2=No
```

Figure 15.18: The Specify Install Options screen.

» At the Specify Restore Options screen in Figure 15.19, select **1** for System information. The default value is set as 2. Select **1** for all other items listed.

```
                        Specify Restore Options

Type options, press Enter.

     Restore from the installation media:

        System information . . . . . 1   1=Restore, 2=Do not restore
        Edit descriptions . . . . . 1   1=Restore, 2=Do not restore
        Message reply list . . . . . 1   1=Restore, 2=Do not restore
        Job descriptions . . . . . . 1   1=Restore, 3=Keep customization
        Subsystem descriptions . . . 1   1=Restore, 3=Keep customization
```

Figure 15.19: The Specify Restore Options screen.

Step 48: The next message to appear will be "Operating system has been installed. IPL in progress". Normal IPL SRCs will be displayed, as shown in Figure 15.20.

```
Message ID . . :  CPI2070              OS/400 Installation Status
+----------------------------------------------------+
| XXXXXXXXXXXXXXXXXXXXXXXXXXXXXXXXXXXXXXXXXXXXXXX |
+----------------------------------------------------+
0        20          40          60          80          100

Installation                                        Objects
Stage                        Completed              Restored

    1 Creating needed profiles and libraries . . . : X

    2 Restoring programs to library QSYS . . . . . : X      09222

    3 Restoring language objects to library QSYS . : X      04863

    4 Updating program table . . . . . . . . . . : X
    5 Installing database files . . . . . . . . . : X
 >> 6 Completing OS/400 installation . . . . . . . :
```

Figure 15.20: The operating system being installed.

Step 49: When the Sign-On screen appears, sign on as QSECOFR without specifying a user password. SRC C900 2965 will be displayed.

Step 50: On the Select Product to Work with PTFs screen, press **F3** (Exit).

Step 51: On the IPL Options screen shown in Figure 15.21, enter the correct date and time, select **Y** for the following options, and press Enter:

- Start system to restricted state
- Set major system options
- Define or change the system at IPL

```
                          IPL Options

Type choices, press Enter.

System date . . . . . . . . . . . . . 05 / 13 / 06 MM / DD / YY
System time . . . . . . . . . . . . . 14 : 32 : 00 HH : MM : SS
Clear job queues  . . . . . . . . . . N          Y=Yes, N=No
Clear output queues . . . . . . . . . N          Y=Yes, N=No
Clear incomplete job logs . . . . . . N          Y=Yes, N=No
Start print writers . . . . . . . . . N          Y=Yes, N=No
Start system to restricted state  . . Y          Y=Yes, N=No

Set major system options  . . . . . . Y          Y=Yes, N=No
Define or change system at IPL . . . . Y          Y=Yes, N=No


Last power-down operation was ABNORMAL
```

Figure 15.21: The IPL Options screen.

Step 52: You are now shown the Set Major System Options screen. Set the options as follows, and press Enter:

- Enable automatic configuration . . . . **Y**
- Device configuration naming. . . . . . ***NORMAL**
- Default special environment. . . . . . ***NONE**

Enabling automatic configuration is an important option to avoiding an A900 2000 SRC code later in the recovery process. By enabling the option, a console device description and tape device descriptions will be automatically configured. The downside is that all powered-on devices will also be auto-configured. These will have to be deleted.

Step 53: When you restore your machine, the system resets some system information, such as system values and network attributes, to the IBM-supplied defaults. On the Define or Change System at IPL screen, select option **3**, (System value commands), and press Enter. Locate and change the following system values:

QALWOBJRST to ***ALL**

QJOBMSGQFL to ***PRTWRAP**

QJOBMSGQMX to **30**

QMAXSIGN to ***nomax**

QPFRADJ to **3**

QALWOBJRST to ***ALL**

QVFYOBJRST to **1**

QSCANFSCTL to ***NOPOSTRST**

QJOBMSGQ2 to **24**

Step 54:   Press **F3** to return to the System Value Commands screen.

Step 55:   Press **F3** to return to the Define or Change the System screen.
Press **F3** to exit and continue the IPL.
Press **F3** to exit the Display Messages screen.

Step 56:   When restoring a complete system, the following network attributes
maybe be reset to the IBM defaults. Ensure all configuration settings
for your system information by verifying the following settings:

- » System name
- » Local network ID
- » Local control point name
- » Default local location name
- » Default node
- » Default type
- » Maximum number of sessions
- » Network node servers

Select option **4** (Work with Network attributes).
Select option **2** (Change Network Attributes) if your system name
does not appear correctly.

Step 57: Upon completion of all required changes to network attributes, press **F12** to return to the Define or Change the System screen.

Step 58: Press **F3** to exit and continue the IPL.

Step 59: On the Edit Rebuild of Access Paths screen, press Enter.

Step 60: Press **F3** to exit the Display Access Paths Status screen.

Step 61: Press **F3** to exit the Display Messages screen.

The installation of the LIC and the operating system is complete when the iSeries/400 main menu appears. (GO MAIN or the command line in your sign-on session.)

Step 62: At the Sign-on Information screen, press Enter to change the default QSECOFR password. Enter the current password, QSECOFR, and a new password with verification of the new password.

Step 63: At the Main Menu screen, type WRKMLBSTS to determine the status of any Media Library devices.

> **Note:** To run the BRMS/400 recovery "automated," using a Media Library Device in Random mode, the BRMS/400 Save needs to have been performed with the client's Media Library Device set to Random mode.

Step 64: Unload the *SAVSYS tape and reload the Media Library with all tapes required for the BRMS/400 recovery. At the transport, set the Media Library to the appropriate state for Library (*Random) mode operations. Use the steps 66-68 to rename the Media Library Device back to the client's Media Library device name at the time the BRMS/400 save was performed.

Step 65: At the Work with Media Library Status screen, select **2**. Vary off the Media Library Device. Select **8** (Work with description).

Step 66: Select **7** (Rename the Media Library Device). Use device name indicated above. Select **1** (Vary on the Media Library Device). Ensure the Media Library device you are using is varied on, then select option **4** to allocate the tape resource you are using.

Device type and name used (Media Library/Tape unit): _____

Step 67: To prevent messages that are not related to the recovery from interrupting, type the following:

CHGMSGQ MSGQ(QSYSOPR) DLVRY(*NOTIFY) SEV(99)

Recovering the BRMS Product

Use the media shown in Table 15.2. The BRMS/400 product and associated libraries must be recovered before you can use the product to perform other recovery operations.

Table 15.2: Media to Recover BRMS									
Saved *S*System	Type	ASP	Save Date	Save Time	Objects	Omit	Sequence Number	Control Group	Volume Identifier
*System	*FULL	01			0		1	*System	xxxxx

Step 68: To prevent messages that are not related to the recovery from interrupting the recovery process, run the following command:

CHGMSGQ MSGQ(QSYSOPR) DLVRY(*NOTIFY) SEV(99)

Use the following command to see which tape devices are configured:

WRKCFGSTS CFGTYPE(*DEV) CFGD(*TAP)

503

Or use the following command to see which media library devices are configured:

WRKCFGSTS CFGTYPE(*DEV) CFGD(*TAPMLB)

> **Note:** Please read this entire section before proceeding to the BRMS System Recovery report.

Step 69: You will now leave this document and continue the recovery using the BRMS "Recovering Your Entire System" report.

> **Note:** Do not recover all user libraries. Exclude libraries deemed to be nonessential as stated in the DR plan. Examples of such libraries might be the QMPGDATA, QPFRDATA, and DEVELOPER libraries.

Step 70: Complete all the steps in the BRMS Recovery Report, beginning with the step entitled "Recover the BRMS Product" and ending with the step entitled "Recover Authorization Information."

> **Note:** For each step, review the job log to confirm that the step was successful. Compare the number of objects restored with the number of objects backed up, as indicated on the BRMS Recovery report.

Step 71: Return to this step after executing the BRMS recovery process.

Step 72: To copy the Restore Job Log to a spool file, enter the following command:

DSPJOBLOG OUTPUT(*PRINT)

Step 73: To create a library-level summary of the restore process, perform the following:

» DSPLOG and prompt using **PF4**.

» Press **F10** for additional parameters.

» Change output to *PRINT. Page forward and enter the message identifiers of CPC3700, CPF3700, and CPC9000.

Step 74: To ensure the spooled files are maintained on the system for the duration of your recovery exercise, change the save attribute for the associated files to *YES.

WRKSPLF to display the spool files created during this session.

Locate files QPJOBLOG and QPDSPLOG.

Place a value of **2** next to each file, type the text string SAVE(*YES) on the command line, and then press Enter.

Step 75: Place selected job queues on hold. This will prevent scheduled batch jobs from executing before the second IPL, and before they have been reviewed:

» Type WRKJOBQ.

» Type a **3** next to selected job queues and press Enter.

Step 76: Perform an Initial Program Load (IPL) of the system. At the CPU control panel, press the **Mode Select** button until the green indicator is in the NORMAL setting.

PWRDWNSYS OPTION(*IMMED) RESTART(*YES *FULL) IPLSRC(B)

Summary

Following a complete, documented process helps ensure systems recovery. This chapter provides a recovery foundation for supporting the IBM BRMS recovery system report. Detailing every recovery step helps ensure that your recovery team members successfully recover every level of the iSeries or System i5 system.

16

Testing Your Disaster Recovery Plan

Your organization's disaster recovery plan has been completely assembled, signed off by the IT and business functions, and finally distributed. The mission-critical applications and server infrastructure supporting your business have been identified and agreed upon. The scope of your plan is in complete alignment with the business. Contracts have been established with your commercial hotsite provider, including additional services unique to your organization. Now, if some natural or manmade event interrupts your ability to provide essential computing services, the IT recovery team is ready! The business fully expects IT to be ready regardless of the type of disaster or the magnitude of the event.

Ask yourself, are you really prepared? Many surveys would suggest not. On average, only 55% of the CIOs surveyed by *CIO Journal* were confident they could recover their mission-critical systems in a disaster. The rest were only somewhat confident or not confident at all that their disaster recovery plan would work.

- How does your organization ensure all the work of recovery planning is truly complete?
- How do you ensure the recovery plan will be used correctly in the event of a disaster?
- How do you ensure the recovery plan will work as written?

The answer is your DR plan must be completely tested to see if your disaster preparedness and recovery procedures really work. Testing is an integral part of every comprehensive DR planning methodology. Auditors insist on it. The business insists on it. IT must insist on it. Simply stated, testing just makes sense. It is the scope, frequency, and amount and type of testing required that varies, however. Testing is difficult because it is a complicated process that does not always bring desired results.

How close to realism should your testing go? In my experience, the first rule of testing is that it should *never* interrupt production IT processing or any other profit-making business processes. The costs and ramifications are substantial if anything goes wrong with the test. Testing in a production environment can actually cause a disaster. That is unacceptable risk. Therefore, true realism is not an option. Gone are the days when the CIO could walk into the computer room, and hit the main power switch, and declare an instant disaster. (Actually, I think that must be an old wives' tale.)

As a disaster recovery planner, I regrettably see organizations take all the time and effort to document the necessary steps for disaster preparedness, but then place the disaster recovery plan on the shelf in the CIO's office. It sure looks impressive! Ask yourself, though, what good is a leather-bound document doing if it's just collecting dust?

Only 70% of today's businesses have fully documented disaster recovery plans.

Of those companies with plans:

- Pre-9/11, 64% NEVER test their plan.
- Post-9/11, 35% NEVER test their plan.

Developing a plan does not guarantee success because planning itself is not the total solution—you must exercise your plan to validate the stated readiness and technical integrity. Most importantly, you must train your IT technical recovery teams.

Disaster recovery testing is an essential part of developing an effective disaster recovery strategy. Testing will identify where a company's DR plan falls short. Therefore, it can assist you in finding ways to better prepare for possible future events. The worst way to test a disaster recovery plan is to wait for an actual incident to occur. You are simply rolling the dice with your career and your company's future. An actual disaster is not conducive to gathering results without stress or emotion. Above all, it's not a very productive learning environment. Consider the financial impact on the bottom line for your business, and the fact that using an untested plan during a real disaster is a career-limiting exercise. Other corporations down the supply chain that depend on your organization's ability to provide services or goods will not be happy to learn this is your debut. Ultimately, do not underestimate the legal liabilities associated with this unproven approach.

To be truly ready for a disaster, you need to experience simulated disasters and evaluate the effectiveness of your current procedures in meeting the disaster recovery challenge. Disaster testing is more than just going through the motions; it requires a post-mortem analysis of every test to identify where the plan failed. The failure might not be due to a bad plan; it could be the result of changing business conditions or the performance of an outside organization, such as a hotsite or communications provider. Testing is an exercise involving stated objectives, scenarios, evaluation, and remediation. Learn what's important in a disaster recovery test and how to make such tests effective, and you'll be well-positioned to ensure your organization's survival.

Practice Just Like the Pros

How many professional sports teams do you see taking the field without any preparation? Even the most talented teams do not assume they have the skills, so practicing would be a waste of time. Different parts of the team need to practice working together to improve performance, determine what works, and most importantly, plan for the unexpected by making appropriate adjustments.

In the event of a systems failure, your disaster recovery plan requires flawless execution and teamwork for success. Your disaster recovery teams need to practice on a regular basis. Put into IT terms, test. You may have the best-written DR plan money can buy, and the best technical personnel, but the entire reason you put the plan in place is to prepare for the unexpected. You cannot assume that everything will run smoothly or automatically in a disaster. Your staff must know in advance what actions to take and how to execute them. The fact is, implementing a disaster recovery plan without testing is almost as bad as not having a plan at all.

"But I have tested my plan," you might be saying. "Our records show we tested in the first quarter . . . last year." Testing your disaster recovery plan once would be great, if your critical servers and staff never changed. When has your company ever completed a year without any infrastructure changes, however? No new technology, no growth, no changes to ERP software or applications, no new personnel? Never, right? That is why I recommend companies test their plan at least twice a year. A yearly DR test cycle has a way of getting stretched, and before you realize it, 18 months or even two years have gone by. Other projects or events always seem to get in the way.

In many instances, testing will reveal that changes made in your company's IT systems infrastructure should have necessitated a change in your disaster recovery plan. It is worth the inconvenience to find that out ahead of time, rather than when the lights go out and your computer room is in the dark. With technology becoming more advanced and pervasive, it has become both more complex and necessary than ever to test plans. Make sure that your team and equipment are ready ahead of time.

Satisfy the Need for Testing

Testing is a continuous process. Disaster recovery testing ranges from a simple review of the test plan to detailed exercises of your company's ability to restore your computing environments as stated, either internally or at a commercial hotsite. You should incorporate a variety of tests designed to exercise all components of the plan, staggered throughout the year.

Furthermore, you should incorporate the element of surprise into some of these tests. This brings on some sense of realism, as true disasters vary in the amount of warning they give you before they actually occur. Disasters such as those that might occur during a data center move offer a substantial amount of warning. Others, such as power outages or employee sabotage, can occur with no warning at all. Blizzards and hurricanes offer some advance warning, but their magnitude and impacts are completely unpredictable. Weather tracking is far from an exact science. All disasters offer some element of surprise; so your recovery testing should do the same.

When I ran an IT division, I found it ironic that each testing activity related to disaster recovery was scheduled. We spent much time and effort scheduling to ensure it fit well with everyone's business calendar. The majority of DR events, however, are completely unexpected. A good compromise that makes perfect recovery sense is to execute small parts of your DR plan as unplanned activities for your team members. I can guarantee that you will find a major kink or two in every plan's execution. A great place to start is with backups. Without solid backups, you have no recovery. I've done this by asking my staff to immediately (not this afternoon or after lunch) get me a detailed list of every offsite DR tape, and the vital records we would need to recover our computer room today. My recovery team came back with the precise list of the offsite storage tapes required and the associated tape-recall procedures. We did not stop there, however. My next question was, "How did you get this listing?" The bad news was that the list was stored online on the iSeries. As a result, we changed the procedures to ship the BRMS recovery reports offsite daily.

Testing will accomplish the following:

- Ensure the accuracy, completeness, and validity of recovery procedures.
- Ensure the capabilities of the personnel executing the recovery procedures.
- Validate the information recorded in the disaster recovery plan.
- Verify that the timeline estimates for recovery are realistic.
- Validate that all changes in the computing environment are reflected in the DR plan.
- Familiarize IT personnel with the plan and its procedures.
- Verify that outside agencies, such as backup data centers, perform as expected.
- Discover business conditions that require changes to the plan.
- Document required changes.
- Enlighten staff that this is not like all the other tests.

The Embarrassment of Testing: What If We Fail?

You are probably familiar with the concept of testing a disaster recovery plan. You might know all about tabletop exercises, walkthroughs, and multiple simulations, and even the dreaded full-blown "just like the real thing" tests.

To pull off a good test, you have to develop a test plan, create a realistic test scenario, and identify participants. That's a lot of work, and you're probably fully booked as it is! So, you might find yourself treating a scheduled test as a hassle versus an opportunity. You first need to find a convenient time when all the key players will be available. You can't take the chance of having one of your key recovery team members unavailable because of a family vacation, right? After all, you want everything to go smoothly. That way, you can let those "beloved" auditors know they can check off testing for another year. Then, you can put the plan back on the shelf and forget about it, until you're forced to do another bothersome round of testing next year.

This philosophy seems to have passed the test of time. All the participants know what to do . . . after all, they have done it over and over again. The observers also know what to expect . . . after all, they have seen it over and over again. You're very busy with your regular job, and a disaster isn't really going to happen to you anyway, so why bother? You're good at your job. You always step up to a challenge (and you have your résumé stored offsite).

Instead of thinking of testing as an annoyance to you, think of it in terms of teamwork. It is a stress test to see what will break. After all, don't you really want to find the flaws in your plan (and you are pretty much guaranteed to have some)? Of course—you want to discover all of them, if possible! But if you take these risks and try to find flaws in your perfectly developed plan, won't you look bad? Won't management be angry?

Not if you do your homework and educate senior management properly, in advance. Granted, this might be an unfamiliar perspective for managers who always expect a glowing "success" to support promotions and profits. This is an obstacle that can be overcome. It just requires properly educating management on the benefits gained from a different perspective. It means preparing, training, and validating every step so you are prepared for a disaster. What better benefit is there than having the level of assurance that a viable disaster recovery plan will be in place when needed? An added benefit that is often realized by using the "exercise" approach is that it takes the pressure off the participants to "pass the test" in the traditional sense. They now can be allowed the freedom to be honest, putting forth their efforts where they should be focused, which is towards improving the plan.

In my experience, participants often take a much more enthusiastic role with this approach. They start to enjoy and look forward to the test, rather than dread the process. They are better able to understand why it is so important. Recovery team members become active participants, who can truly see the merits of their efforts. After all, the time to find out which items are out of date and/or missing is when you have the time and resources to make a correction. This is the only way to not suffer any serious consequences resulting from wrong or incomplete information.

The measure of success when exercising a recovery plan should *not* be that everything went as planned. If you're not finding something in your plan that can be improved, you're not exercising strenuously enough. Just keep testing!

Know your responsibilities when testing:

- Define key responsibilities.

- Determine ownership.

- Measure and report on roles performed by your staff and/or your partners.

Open-Book Testing

Think back, way back, to your days in school. Suddenly, your teacher announces that there is to be a major exam. If you're like me, the terror of these words has left a permanent scar. The only relief in such an announcement is the news of an "open-book" exam. While the relative merits of this form of academic testing can be argued, it has been a source of comfort to students for generations.

Open-book testing only teaches you how to find answers that are already clearly documented. If it's missing in the first place, you simply will not find what you're looking for. The open-book approach is a search-and-retrieve technique that is highly dependent on a person's information-gathering techniques and ability to locate information quickly.

How does this relate to disaster recovery testing? Obviously, a plan must be well-organized and have a logical flow. It provides the "open book" you will need to access quickly and in an organized manner if a disaster occurs. During such an occurrence, a well-organized DR plan will be of great importance. However, there is a greater need to ensure your team members become familiar with the plan's layout and structure, and the electronic shortcuts built into it for data retrieval. Knowing the plan's roadmap ensures your team will find the information on a timely basis. It provides an assessment of the documentation itself.

Review your plan for the following:

- *Organization*—Is it easy to locate specific items?
- *Consistency*—What is the structure or layout?
- *Clarity*—Is there enough information, or is too much left for interpretation?
- *Action orientation*—Look for step-by-step details, with a natural progression to the next logical step.
- *Comprehensiveness*—Are things missing or overlooked? On the other hand, are things over-documented?

The objective of the documentation review is to have a plan that is readable and will serve as a complete reference for all your recovery actions.

Define a Complete Testing Project

The disaster recovery owner (that's you) should outline the testing objectives and develop the test project plan for computer systems recovery. This test should include a combination of active and passive tests (desktop exercises). The test project plan shows the planned tests with their timing, duration, staff requirements, objectives, and stated scenarios.

Here are the basic steps for conducting a testing project:

1. Create a detailed project plan.
2. Assign owners and completion dates for all the tasks.
3. Recruit an executive sponsor.
4. Create your test plan timelines.
5. Review custom application needs.
6. Don't forget third-party products.
7. Complete a desktop exercise.
8. Document changes and gaps from the desktop exercise.
9. Develop active testing objectives.
10. Develop active testing scenarios.
11. Document changes and gaps from the active test.
12. Determine whether to include the users or auditors.
13. Make required changes.
14. Decide on the next testing date.

Types of Testing

There are a wide variety of tests that can be performed. Examples include the following:

1. Call communication carriers to verify their internal network switch procedures.
2. Call staff members in the personnel file after hours to validate their home and alternate contact information.
3. Call vendors after normal business hours to ensure that their hotline and service numbers are correct and staffed.
4. Execute the notification, escalation, and assembly tasks on a non-business day.
5. Put the hotsite on alert and meet staff at the command center location.
6. Recall backup tape media and have them shipped to another location.

Staffing for DR Testing

The business and functional aspects of executing and testing a disaster recovery plan are just as important as the underlying hardware technologies. Successfully staffing the recovery process is essential to its success. The DR plan is always role-based versus individual-based. The plan should be detailed enough so that people with iSeries technical competencies can perform the required recovery activities. Never assume that your top iSeries technical expert will be available during recovery from a disaster. Spread the testing experience around to different members of your recovery team. Yes, this means not always assigning your best staff members to every DR test. Switch up your teams, replace a senior member with someone more junior, or try something different like delaying an entire team during your next DR test, and see what effect this has on the execution of the test.

Here are key rules for staffing your DR testing:

- The nontechnical aspects are just as important as the technical.
- Every staff activity should be role-based.
- The most important people might not be there in a real disaster, so don't include them in every test.
- It's not just IT that's involved—include all key staff.
- Don't assume key services and utilities are available, including air travel, power, cell phones, and so forth.
- Overly aggressive recovery time objectives and recovery point objectives usually aren't realistic. Can you fully recover from a disaster in 12 hours? Can your staff handle this commitment?

As a general guideline, DR team members should conduct recovery tests as follows:

- At least once a year, the technical recovery teams will conduct an incident-based walkthrough of the disaster recovery plan. This test will verify that the plan is consistent with team members' expectations and that it can work regardless of the type of disaster.
- Twice a year, the technical recovery teams will need to test their ability to recover at a commercial hotsite or redundant internal data center, with an active technical test. In the second annual test, they should test the recovery of the network infrastructure as well.

Passive Testing

Passive testing, also known as a *tabletop exercise,* is a scheduled exercise when recovery team members meet in an open forum to discuss required actions for response to a specific business-interruption scenario. Every member listed in the DR plan must be present. If your name and role is referenced in the plan, you should be in attendance. Although the tabletop exercise is intended to be informal, it should be structured to ensure discussion. Explore the procedures, recovery plan detail, information flow, and personnel resources assigned to recover critical IT functions. This exercise will validate the completeness and accuracy of the plan.

A tabletop exercise will accomplish the following:

- Enable recovery teams to rehearse action to be taken during an actual disaster.
- Determine the overall readiness of the teams.
- Reinforce roles and responsibilities.
- Confirm the recovery strategy.
- Confirm that documentation is complete for an obtainable recovery.
- Enhance team organization.

Passive testing does not exercise the technical procedures or technical actions of the plan. A passive test is a walkthrough of the procedures, typically with all the disaster recovery team members jointly reading and reviewing them, literally page by page. A dry run of a procedure will verify the completeness of the steps in the procedure.

Passive Testing Format

This type of test is conducted in a conference room with a very large table, a whiteboard, a flipchart, a note taker, and above all, *no* disruptions. Turn off those cell phones and prohibit people from constantly checking their email. The length of this test is generally two to three hours. Ensure you provide breaks for people to check the pulse of their business for any urgent situations that might arise.

Include everyone listed in the DR plan, and have participants bring their copies of the plan. Then, conduct the test as follows:

1. The DR plan coordinator reviews the objectives of the test, and starts the test.
2. The recovery teams discuss the scenario.
3. Updates to the scenario are managed.
4. Progress is monitored and recorded.
5. The recovery teams execute the recovery tasks.
6. All actions are exercised as written.
7. Gaps are identified and actions items identified.

During a tabletop exercise, be sure to care for the body as well as the mind. Provide participants a comfortable work environment, if possible. Conducting tabletop exercises in rooms that are too hot, too cold, have improper lighting, or are too small, will hinder discussion and success. While such conditions might simulate actual recovery conditions, the purpose at this time is to stimulate discussion and ideas, not test participants' nerves. As mentioned earlier, the exercise typically runs two to three hours, so refreshments should be provided. An additional consideration for early morning sessions is to offer cold drinks as well as coffee and tea. Snacks or lunch should be provided if the exercise runs into lunch time. Let everyone know in advance that refreshments will be supplied.

Prior to scheduling the first desktop exercise, create a realistic disaster scenario. Use PowerPoint and review the scenario in slide form. Ensure you have a realistic scenario. Do your homework on potential disasters for the location involved. Become aware of the type of incidents occurring in your region of the country.

The role of the disaster recovery coordinator during a technical test is to:

- Manage the conduct of the test.
- Develop tabletop scenarios.
- Ensure that each objective is fully realized.
- Ensure that each test participant follows the procedures.
- Record problems and their resolutions as they arise.
- Summarize all the changes to the disaster recovery plan.

As the disaster recovery owner, you are the chairperson for a controlled walkthrough of the DR plan's procedures. One of your responsibilities is to develop a realistic scenario that will be used during the exercise. Create an outline with enough details to give it local impact and credibility. I recommend using short videotape segments about a real disaster typical in the area, such as hurricane coverage from the local news. The video helps participants mentally disengage from their daily tasks to focus on the exercise. Do not shock the members with a horrific scene to set the stage, however; just supply enough background to get the message across. You must both communicate this scenario to the team and formally document it.

Once the disaster scenario is defined, develop a basic timeline of events that could easily be modified to add additional realism. Typically, you achieve this via a series of handouts for the participants. The first handout describes the disaster, its timing, and its impact. As the walkthrough progresses, additional handouts describe how the events of the disaster have progressed. For example, in a hurricane scenario, the first handout would be quite vague on the extent of the damage and potential evacuation. The second handout would offer more information outlining the extent of the damage. The third handout might introduce a complicating factor; for example, the fire department might have concerns for the safety of the physical structure of the building, and prohibit you from accessing the computer room for an extended period of time.

The exercise should include the following:

- State the objectives of the walk through.
- List the participants.
- Select a scenario relative to your company.
- Include the scenario in definition handouts.
- Summarize the changes for the DR plan and provide a schedule for their completion.

At the beginning of the tabletop exercise, the disaster scenario is presented to the participants. The participants then verbally walk through their plan, from call procedures and first response steps to recovery of critical IT functions.

Helps your team members do the following:

- Determine if they could realistically talk through the recovery of their IT infrastructure.
- Become more aware of plan dependencies on specific people or providers.
- Acquaint themselves more thoroughly with their plan contents, as well as what needs to be added.

The rules for the walkthrough are simple. Using only the disaster recovery plan and the formal scenario descriptions, decide which specific tasks should be executed and their timing. Have the team leader and members verbalize how they would execute the procedures using the scenario and the required information. After the discussion, jointly approve or modify each task and procedure as executed.

A common mistake made is not giving sufficient attention to the call notification lists. Whenever a telephone number is found missing or has changed, we automatically flip over to our cell phone directories. We click feverishly on our cell phones' keypads . . . OK, found it! That's great, but you must also ensure that the issues with the changed phone number is immediately reflected in the DR plan. What if you have no access to your cell phone during a disaster?

Here are a few more example scenarios:

- A fire denies the use (either completely or temporarily) of the central computing facility, immediately affecting all 35 remote offices.
- The local telephone exchange office has an extended power failure. The external network is down and will be down for the next two days. Voice service is completely disabled. All equipment in the computer room is still functional.
- A pipe bursts in one of the washrooms over the weekend. The computer room has two feet of water under the raised floor.

As mentioned earlier, conduct passive testing with all recovery team participants. You might wish to invite additional participants, depending on the scenario and the components of the plan to be tested. For example, you should probably include building services if you are testing a water-related scenario. Participants should bring their current copies of the DR plan with them.

Each participant is assigned a specific role (or set of roles) to play in the disaster scenario testing. This should align with the role he or she would play in a real disaster, although sometimes, you might have participants switch roles for cross-training purposes. Rotate the primary and alternates. This becomes a meaningful exercise when someone who typically is not in charge now needs to be. Remember to test everything, and that includes the obvious. It's the items you take for granted that will cause you issues in a real disaster. Every test exercise is a fresh start, and should include the following:

- Actually call staff members on the DR plan to validate their contact numbers.

- Call vendors after normal business hours to ensure that their hotline and service numbers are correct and staffed as stated.

- Execute the full notification process, escalation tree, and assembly tasks on a non-business day.

- Verify all your vendors' published call procedures. Ensure that you can make contact with critical vendors and staff after hours, even on a long weekend. How many of us have been faced with a message like, "Hello, you have reached the office of your Primary Services Supplier. We are away for the long weekend. You can reach us on Tuesday"? Alternate numbers can be really useful in a time of need.

Sometimes, the scenario does not unfold as you expect, so as the walkthrough progresses, you might find it necessary to make some changes and clarifications to achieve the walkthrough objectives. Conduct a post-walkthrough debriefing to recap the action points noted during the exercise, and make sure each participant leaves with a copy of the list of action points.

The summary report should contain the following:

- The objectives of the walkthrough and completion status
- A list of the participants in attendance
- The scenario summary
- The scenario definition handouts
- A summary of changes required to the DR plan
- A determination of whether the changes are procedural only or require changes in the technology or solution at the data center
- A schedule for the completion of these changes

- The date to distribute all changes to plan holders
- A date for the next test

The purpose of this exercise is to demonstrate to management and to the recovery team members that your organization has the ability to resume critical server functions as documented. This familiarization exercise has many positive effects on the recovery teams. There is very little stress to deal with, which makes it a learning environment. The exercise is non-threatening, as the format is relaxed, which leads to open discussion. Participants are not required to race against the clock, make immediate decisions, or memorize their recovery actions. This is not intended to be a pressure-cooker boardroom meeting. Instead, participants are encouraged to draw upon their collective knowledge and IT expertise to find creative solutions that can be identified and noted prior to a disaster event. Many recovery solutions are just expanded versions of what is used daily to resolve operational problems. Various recovery options can be considered; time can be taken to discuss questions, and participants can identify any new concerns and solutions as they come to mind.

Remember, the goal of the exercise is not to "ambush" recovery team members, but rather to let them discover that when it comes to disaster-recovery testing exercises, a discovered failure can mean future recovery success. You want recovery tem members to identify any and all plan weaknesses today, rather than during a real disaster.

Reduce the Team

In any disaster situation, you cannot count on 100% of your recovery team members being available. This holds particularly true in a regional disaster. One way to simulate some form of realism in a desktop exercise is to reduce the teams. Typically, I recommend placing all participants' names in a box, and then randomly withdrawing 20-30% of the names. This always gets a few laughs as people get " eliminated." They stand up, wish everyone success, and start to leave the room.

Hold on now. This is not an invitation for recovery team members to have a day off. These people must remain present, but as quiet observers. In fact, their role actually becomes more important, as you want them to identify any deficiencies in the plan execution. Are the remaining team members missing any critical steps? Many times, the point of failure is that there is too much dependence on a few specific individuals. This is an opportunity for the disaster recovery coordinator to request additional documentation or to spread duties across several team members.

Tabletop Walkthrough Test Checklist

The walkthrough in Table 16.1 would be conducted by the disaster recovery coordinator.

Table 16.1: Checklist for a Tabletop Exercise		
#	**ACTION**	**NOTES**
1.	Welcome participants.	
2.	Explain test objectives and disaster scenario.	The disaster scenario should reflect a real potential risk to the organization and be able to test the supporting DR plan documentation.
3.	Conduct participant walkthrough introductions.	Who is the team leader? Who are the alternates? Who are the members of each team?
4.	Distribute copies of the DR plan. Copies must be complete print-outs, with all sections included. If CDs are used, ensure staff bring their laptops.	All participants need a copy. No sharing! Note any issues with the plan.
5.	Review the recovery organization, including the structure of the recovery teams. (How does it relate to the structure of the organization?) Review team roles and responsibilities.	Are the team descriptions and responsibilities complete and clear? Do all team members understand and accept their roles and responsibilities? Are there any assumptions? Note any issues.
	Recovery team members Vendors Hotsite	Are phone numbers and street addresses included? Note any required changes.
	Activation call lists	Are the call lists complete? Note any required changes.

#	ACTION	NOTES
	Table 16.1: Checklist for a Tabletop Exercise (continued)	
6.	Review the recovery process overview, the recovery timeframe objective (RTO), recovery point objective (RPO), and recovery strategy.	Are the processes, RTOs, and strategies complete and clear? Has the DR coordinator and the business approved the RTOs, RPOs, and strategies? Note any issues.
	Review the plan assumptions.	Are the assumptions consistent with the DR initiatives? Note any issues.
7.	Review the recovery tasks checklists. Team Leader Tasks: - Declare disaster - Activate teams - Hold team kick-off meeting - Make team assignments	Look for the following: - Complete action sequences. - Clear and easy-to-understand tasks. - A logical sequence of tasks. Note any issues or required changes.
	Team Member Tasks: - Notify contacts - Obtain resources - Offsite records/data - Restart minimum ops - Damage Assessment	Ensure that the tasks speak to actions. Note any issues or required changes.
8.	Review the critical recovery resources: - Critical sever equipment and software - Telecommunications - Special equipment and materials - Vital records - Travel	Ensure that the teams have identified all of the critical resources they require, including complete descriptions and 24 hour staffing. All of these resources need to be included in this section of the plan. If you find inconsistencies, make a note to contact the technical team leader for guidance.

#	ACTION	NOTES
	Table 16.1: Checklist for a Tabletop Exercise (continued)	
9.	Review the critical contacts (customers and vendors).	Contacts should include names, addresses, and phone numbers of customers and vendors (or other support organizations) that the team will have to inform about the disruption. If the contact is a vendor, check for an account and/or contract number.
10.	Review the critical locations: - Recovery location - Location of vital records - Location of backup copies of IT records - Other	Locations should include names, addresses, and phone numbers of the appropriate contacts. Note any required changes.
11.	Review the appendices.	Check for recommended policy guidelines for pay, travel, and expenses. Note any required changes.
12.	Review the general overview.	This section should include the standard material provided by the DR coordinator. Note any issues.
13.	Review the notification and activation procedures: - Interfaces chart - Responsibilities - Declarations - Recovery progression	This section should include the standard material provided by the DR Coordinator. Note any issues.
14.	Review the test and review procedures.	Make sure the teams understand their responsibilities for testing the plan and for updating it to reflect changes. Note any issues.

#	ACTION	NOTES
15.	Review the results and lessons learned from this exercise.	The team leader should facilitate a discussion of the following points: - Was the disaster scenario followed? - Do the team structures and responsibilities make sense? - Was the team plan properly invoked? - Were the tasks completed? - Were the proper recovery resources identified? - Is the overall recovery plan viable? - What overall results were attained? - What findings should be documented? Required changes? - What strengths/weaknesses were observed? (Plan and team.) - How might walkthrough tests be improved? Make sure that each participant has a chance to identify lessons learned and ways to improve future tests. The team leader should ensure that all action items have been identified.
16.	Assign action items	The team leader should assign responsibilities and due dates for completing all of the required action items. The team leader must take responsibility for providing the test and plan updates to the DR coordinator via e-mail. The DR coordinator must take responsibility for making all of the required changes to the DR plan and distributing the new version.
17.	Review the anticipated contents of the report with business and senior management.	The team leader should summarize the overall results of the exercise and the intended content of the report for senior management.
18.	Schedule the next required walkthrough test.	The team leader should select a date for the next walkthrough test.
19.	Close the test session.	The team leader closes the session.

Table 16.1: Checklist for a Tabletop Exercise (continued)

Active Testing

A wise man once said, "Testing disaster recovery is really pretending that you have had a disaster. Testing must be pretending reality!"

Hotsite (active) tests not only demonstrate that your DR plans work, but they also provide your organization with the opportunity to improve the process and eliminate wasted hours in poor execution. When recovering the business-critical applications as defined in the critical server definitions, time is always of the essence. Minimizing restore times per server is crucial because every hour reduced from the restoration process time (RTO) can translate into thousands of dollars saved. This was clearly stated in the business impact analysis.

Active testing validates the recovery plan in the following terms:

- Recovery capability
- Completeness
- Restoration timeline commitments
- Alternate-site configuration
- Network recovery
- Offsite records
- Weaknesses in the plan
- Training

The 3-Step Special

Your active test will start with a three-step questionnaire that serves as a guideline to getting you started in your initial testing of the DR plan. Use this as a baseline success criteria for disaster recovery testing.

1. Your initial test:
    - » Did you successfully recover at least 60% of your server applications?

» Were you able to correct or update your disaster recovery plan based on initial results?

» Did you achieve your recovery time objectives (RTOs) and recovery point objectives (RPOs)? Why or why not?

2. Your second test:

» Did you successfully recover at least 80% of your server applications?

» Was your disaster recovery plan 95% accurate?

» Did you successfully recover servers and cross-platform server interdependencies?

» Did you meet your RTOs and RPOs?

3. Your third test:

» Did you successfully recover all of your server applications, including cross-platform servers ?

» Did you perform successful backups of your data recovery site to simulate recovery back to the primary site?

» Did you include fail-back to the primary data center in your tests?

» Did you benchmark performance of your applications at the recovery site?

» Did you identify opportunities to improve on your RTOs or RPOs?

Proper active testing mandates that the procedures under review be executed exactly as written. Using your memory or doing it "cold" is not an acceptable practice. Your recovery team should test the procedure for declaring a disaster with your hotsite vendor. Test the procedure and the ability of your offsite tape storage provider to deliver backup tape media to the hotsite in a timely manner. Finally, test your recovery methodology for restoring your systems. Each step must be executed completely, and the data must be tested thoroughly by end-user departments to validate recovery.

A wide variety of active tests should be performed, including the following:

• A full technical test of restoration of production application systems on the servers and other mission-critical hardware

- A technical test of the LAN and WAN, including any existing WAN failover mechanisms
- A test of the high-availability solution that switches your users to the alternate facility, then checks the validity of the data

A technical test demonstrates your ability to move processing into the recovery facility within the required time. In advance of the test (preferably 45 days out), ensure the disaster recovery coordinator has had a chance to explain the format, structure, and testing objectives. At this time, participants will have time to ask questions and voice any concerns. Sometimes, participants had never taken part in any type of actual recovery exercise. Fear of the unknown naturally creates anxiety. The briefing is helpful to defuse that anxiety. This also allows the facilitator to establish a relationship with participants prior to the exercise. In a large organization, these meetings can serve as introductions. Never be strangers, as this adds stress to the process. If the exercise is out of town, a conference call can substitute for the meeting. A concise handout is provided with the objectives of the exercise and a description of the various roles and exercise logistics (time, date, place, and participant list). Planning for the test should proceed as follows:

1. At least 90 days in advance, schedule the test with your hotsite provider. Notify plan participants of your selected date and time.

2. Meet with your IT recovery team to establish final test objectives 45 days before the test date. This will determine the participants' requirements for the test and let you develop a suitable test schedule.

3. Two weeks before the test, publish the test plan to participants and confirm your test date.

4. Initiate the transfer of tapes from the offsite tape storage facility to the recovery services facility.

Ensure Your Objectives Are Realistic

Your objectives should not exceed your technical or staff resource capabilities. I always say that it's better to underestimate and achieve all of your stated objectives than to state something like, "We will recover everything on the first go-round." Credibility is very tough to recover . . . much tougher than any system. Do not create doubt in your team members or senior management right out of the gate. Walk before you run. Figure 16.1 shows sample test objectives.

Date of test:_____

Test participants' names: _____

Site location:_____

Intel
  ❑ Recover Active Directory.
  ❑ Recover Citrix server farm.
  ❑ Recover File and Print.

iSeries
  ❑ Recover production ERP partition, and Lotus Notes partition from backups.
  ❑ Validate recent BRMS implementation changes.
  ❑ Validate written recovery procedures.
  ❑ Obtain and install license codes from various application vendors using information from the disaster recovery plan.
  ❑ Verify critical applications.
  ❑ Train alternate staff.

Miscellaneous
  ❑ Verify tape shipment procedures.
  ❑ Verify the communication plan.
  ❑ Establish time lines for recovery of segments and recovery rates.
  ❑ Verify completeness of the hotbox contents.
  ❑ Verify the tape-retrieval process.
  ❑ Assess the completeness of the DRP manual.

High-availability-related objectives
  ❑ Access role swap readiness:
    ✓ Backup copy must be identical.
    ✓ Object authority must be identical.
    ✓ Referential integrity constraints must be applied and enabled.
    ✓ Triggers must be enabled and operative.
    ✓ Verify schedule entries are in sync.
    ✓ Verify users and applications correctly stopped on primary and started on backup.

  ❑ High-availability auditing capabilities exist for the following:
    ✓ Out of sync files by attributes
    ✓ Out of sync objects by existence
    ✓ Out of sync data areas by content
    ✓ Suspended objects
    ✓ Object integrity
    ✓ Automation to resolve these issues
    ✓ The event log for error messages
    ✓ Message queues

Figure 16.1: Sample test objectives.

Disaster Recovery Coordinator Testing Duties

Testing will be coordinated by the disaster recovery coordinator, but all the recovery actions will actually be performed by the management and technical recovery team members. All testing objectives will be coordinated through the disaster recovery coordinator well in advance of any testing taking place.

Booking and coordinating access to the hotsite, scheduling, arranging travel and accommodations for staff, and auditing the testing will all be coordinated.

The role of the disaster recovery coordinator during an active (technical) test is to do the following:

- Schedule test time with the hotsite.
- Define the type of test and the testing objectives.
- Facilitate internal technical meetings to review objectives for the technical solution.
- Identify technical staff responsible for testing with the team lead of the technical recovery team.
- Document testing requirements and prepare all required components.
- Arrange for travel, if required.
- Conduct the final pre-test meeting with staff and hotsite personnel.
- Communicate results and any required changes to the recovery team management leader.
- Manage the conduct of the test.
- Ensure that each objective is fully realized.
- Ensure that each test participant follows the procedures from the disaster recovery plan as precisely as possible.
- Document changes necessary to make the procedures of the plan work.
- Record problems and their resolutions as they arise.
- Record the time for each of the procedures.
- Liaise with the hotsite staff.

The disaster recovery coordinator is also responsible for writing the summary report for both the tabletop and active test. The summary report should include the following:

- The objectives of the test
- The participants
- The changes to the plan
- Any recommendations resulting from the test
- The schedule for the next test

Introducing Murphy's Law

Many people tend to take shortcuts in disaster recovery testing because they want to make the conditions for success a little more obtainable. Here are a few popular "no- no's":

- Testing is always done from full system save backups (Option 21).
- Only a mid-week recovery is tested, using incremental tapes.
- Special backups are performed in advance of the test to ensure success. An Option 21 full save is specially scheduled for the test.
- Backup tapes are pre-shipped, or the offsite carrier is told to ship tapes early.
- Files are FTP-ed to facilitate a successful test.
- The same staff members perform recovery steps for every test, while the alternates stay at home to run the shop. (After all, the hotsite is in sunny Phoenix, next to the golf course!)
- The whole IT structure is never tested (communications and all servers in the enterprise) because:
  - » There's not enough test time in the contract.
  - » It's impossible for staff to rebuild all servers identified as critical. There's not enough head count, or not enough distributed skill.

Evaluation of Test Results

All data must be validated during any active data recovery test. If you cannot validate your data during the test without using information obtained from the primary data center, then you have to get creative. There must be some means of verifying the validity of the test as it progresses, so if there are problems with the process, they can be corrected and documented immediately. Daily transmissions of inventory totals, critical query reports, or key balance statements to an offsite server or secure mail account are two creative ways of validating data in the recovery test and during an actual recovery. Programmers typically have application test scripts, which can also prove useful. All data selection criteria or testing methodology must be agreed upon by your management, allowing the testing to be performed within time constraints.

All team personnel should log events during the test that will help evaluate the results. The testing process should provide feedback to the disaster recovery team to ensure that the plan is adequate. The recovery team, which normally consists of key IT personnel, should assess test results and analyze recommendations from various team leaders regarding improvements or modifications to the plan. It is essential to measure the test results, including the following:

- Ensure that each objective is fully realized.
- Did each test participant follow the procedures from the plan as stated?
- Were required changes documented?
- Did recovery team members record problems and their resolutions as they arose?
- Record the elapsed time to perform various activities.
- Did the total restoration time meet the business objectives?
- Summarize all the changes and provide them to the DR coordinator.

The results of the tests will most likely lead to changes in the plan. These changes should enhance the plan and provide a more workable recovery process. Post-test activities include careful review of the logs, action-item execution, and routine maintenance. Without this last step, the plan will not progress to a level of efficiency that will meet longer-term audit expectations.

Be a Survivor

Testing exercises will help change senior management's perception, and maybe even yours. Many times, testing will reveal non-technical issues. We in the IT industry are generally technically sound in our work, but the "procedural stuff" will bite us every time. A common problem I find is that management recovery personnel are unable to declare a disaster properly because they are unfamiliar with crucial procedures. Testing creates a safe "make-believe" situation that is free of embarrassment. Everyone can demonstrate their abilities and understand the relative importance of these procedures without suffering damage or great costs.

The timeline is important. One major facilitator challenge is directing the exercise to assure important issues are addressed, while encouraging spontaneity, creativity, and flexibility. The goal of recovery plans is recovery, not adhering strictly to written documentation. The DR plan is only a tool. The result is what counts. In a disaster, the only valid result is recovery. In a test, the only valid result is enhanced recovery capability.

Making a management commitment to regularly testing, validating, and refreshing your disaster recovery plan will protect your company from the greatest risk of all: complacency. Today's computing environments face rapid business and technological changes; the smallest alteration to a critical application or system can cause an unanticipated failure that you might not be able to recover from if you do not test. Recovering from a disaster can be overwhelming. This can lead to frustration and loss of motivation.

Frequent testing results in the following:

- Recovery team members are comfortable in familiar situations.
- Recovery team members can actually see the recovery goal and efforts.
- Confidence is already in place because this is not their maiden voyage.

Be a survivor. It's true that disasters, even simulated ones, do not happen very often. However, it is also true that without disaster recovery testing, you will never know whether your plan will work when "the big one" hits. A disaster will not be a scheduled event. You must always remain prepared. Companies have experienced and survived disasters, but only when they have properly tested.

Real-World Example: The Surprise Fire Drill

I had a large customer in the pharmaceutical industry that actively participated in disaster recovery testing twice each year. They were always successful and found these tests productive, as they always enhanced their written disaster recovery plans. We had staged many tests in the past, but the knock against the organization was whether they could respond in a true disaster, without warning. IT was prepared, but the business was not convinced. The business units felt that IT was always getting ready in advance, and that was not realistic. There was no element of surprise. So, we decided to change that perception, proving IT was, in fact, ready should the need arise.

The emergency evacuation drill is something familiar to everyone. It has been embedded in our minds since grade school, when we followed the teacher outside and lined up on the playground. In the adult world, most organizations conduct at least one emergency evacuation drill every year. I decided to use a surprise fire drill as the start for the next disaster recovery test. In order to pull this off, we got approval in advance from the CIO. We wanted to prove that the IT staff were indeed ready in a disaster. The emergency evacuation drill offers this unique opportunity. When everyone came out of the building in a somewhat orderly fashion, we had a mini-bus waiting in the parking lot. The IT folks quickly noticed the bus and joked that it was a party bus or a free ride to the local golf course. When the CIO announced that we were declaring a disaster, the party talk quickly turned to nervous anticipation and comments like, "You have got to be kidding!" The event was all about capturing the IT staff's knowledge of what to do next. In mature organizations, an evacuation drill is a real-time way to judge the assessment, activation, and execution of the plan.

As the bus left for the hotsite facility, I informed everyone of the details surrounding this surprise drill. The scope of the drill was to be an IT event only; we were recovering several critical iSeries partitions and switching only part of the network. The rest of the business needed to function normally. We were now off to the hotsite, so I passed the management duties over to the team leaders. The first few questions raised were "Where is the disaster recovery plan?" and "What about our backups?" One of the team leaders quickly replied, "The backups are all stored offsite and the tapes were already picked up this morning. I will give them a call from my cell phone. I have the number programmed in." We were off to a good start.

Several lessons were learned from this surprise test that we could never simulate. There had been many tests and everyone believed the plan was complete. Everyone now understood the true level of commitment needed to maintain the disaster recovery plan and to ensure the recoverability of the data center. The new measure of success was if you're not finding something in your plan that can be improved, then you're not exercising strenuously enough.

Summary

Testing the disaster recovery plan should be efficient and cost-effective. It provides a means of continually increasing the level of education, awareness, and quality of the plan and the people who execute it.

A carefully tested plan provides the organization with the confidence and experience necessary to respond to a real emergency. Disaster recovery plan testing should consider scheduled and unscheduled tests for both partial and total disasters.

17

Plan Maintenance

Prevention costs less than recovery. Similarly, maintaining a DR plan takes much less time than writing a complete and comprehensive plan. By now, you know that having a disaster recovery plan is vital to the health of your business. But has your plan had a recent checkup? Book a meeting with your plan. Yes, I am serious. Create a calendar entry, book a meeting room, attend the meeting, and open your DR plan and read it.

You must consider that maintaining a disaster recovery plan is a process. Building a complete plan is a project. Allowing it to become outdated due to lack of maintenance turns it into a big project all over again, versus a regularly scheduled maintenance process.

No matter how well-designed or well-written your DR plan is, it is subject to complete failure (well before an actual disaster) if it is not maintained. Your computing systems are subject to frequent enhancements, and the system documentation will quickly become obsolete if it is not maintained regularly. Consider how many changes have been implemented in your IT department in the past year. The numbers are quite revealing. If you were to discover the disaster recovery plan was out of date, you would simply not trust it, and might stop using it altogether. That's an even bigger issue.

From a management perspective, I have heard IT support staff openly state, "The disaster recovery planning project is finally complete. We've spent months and months determining our needs, examining acceptable levels of risk, and aligning business priorities with IT deliverables. We delivered a 400-page plan. Heck, we even tested it! We are happy to report that the project is now closed."

Successful management of a DR planning project, like any other complex, large-scale project, is not an easy undertaking. Project delivery complications are always inevitable, and the IT recovery planning team must react quickly and decisively. The success factor of this team is their ability to be proactive, anticipate obstacles, and deliver timely, corrective actions.

"An ounce of prevention is worth a pound of cure." My grandmother has preached this for years, and it holds true even in today's IT world. The first question always asked after the smoke clears is how the disaster could have been avoided. How could we have been more prepared? Too often, the answer is, "Had we kept our disaster recovery plan up-to-date, things would have been better!"

There are many reasons why DR plans become out-of-sync with the production IT infrastructure. Here are some of the most common:

- The plan was developed only to meet an audit requirement and is now collecting dust.
- The plan is not tested or maintained on a regular basis.
- The plan is maintained on a fixed schedule only (i.e., once a year or only after a test).
- Change control (or change management) does not take disaster recovery into consideration.
- A formal change-control process is absent.

Many organizations can attest that they've spent significant time and effort developing their disaster recovery plans, only to see them lapse once they're in place. How does a DR plan lapse? A plan simply lapses when it does not keep pace with the technological enhancements of your organization. Having a nice, leather-bound plan located in your CIO's office, reading "Last revision date 2001" is like having no plan at all. You are delivering a false message that this plan will work when you need it most.

Maintenance plans can help organizations guard against this because they help simplify the maintenance process. You must ensure your DR plan remains current. In the changing environment of the computer industry, your DR plan will inevitably become outdated and unusable unless someone keeps it up-to-date. That means those systems administrators you brought on board to write the initial plan must remain onboard. No one ever leaves the ship!

Every day, businesses are confronted with disasters of varying degrees. Those that have adequately developed, maintained, and exercised their disaster recovery plans will survive, yet many corporate executives continue to take the their companies' DR plans for granted. They remain complacent, assuming that they have done enough by writing the plan, and the project is now complete. The disaster recovery plan is the lifeblood of corporate survival. However, it is only as good as the foundation upon which it was built. The foundation is, of course, the deliverable in a disaster. Once the concept is developed throughout the IT organization, and is accepted by both IT management and the business, it must be maintained and always in a ready state for execution if called upon. The role of the disaster recovery coordinator is to strategically and relentlessly manage the process—every day, if necessary. In doing so, he or she must rely on complete cooperation from the entire disaster recovery team.

Your Plan Design

Probably the main reason for lack of maintenance (besides lack of discipline or desire) is that the disaster recovery plan is not easily maintainable. There are several schools of thought on how DR plans should be designed, and no two companies will agree on the same standard. There is no "one size fits all" design. As a result, many well-intentioned DR planning projects develop plans that simply are not organized in a maintainable way. They might not appear to be logical, or information is just not easily accessible.

If finding a piece of information or procedure is like finding a needle in a haystack, your plan is not easily maintainable. Flipping through hundreds of pages every time you need to locate something is far from desirable. I laugh sometimes when I see literally hundreds of pages all over a desk during a recovery test, as nothing in the DR plan is where a logical, thinking person would look for it. It is important to construct your disaster recovery plan in a modular fashion. The table of contents and index must be well-organized and bookmarked. The section headings and instructions must be concise and relative to supporting material.

Effective documentation and procedures are extremely important in a business continuity plan. Poorly written procedures can be extremely frustrating and difficult to use and maintain. Well-written plans can significantly reduce maintenance time and effort.

Implementing a Maintenance Philosophy

It is a commonplace error to schedule maintenance for your DR plan at some random interval, or when an auditor has announced a visit. You might simply schedule the complete disaster recovery plan to be reviewed and updated annually. Then the plan sits unattended until the next yearly maintenance date comes around or simply slips by. You might even take the extreme approach that it is wasteful to spend time or effort on *any* DR plan maintenance unless a major changes take place. Do any of these maintenance solutions have merit? The answer is no, yes, and maybe! Using any of these approaches alone is almost sure to lead to an improperly maintained plan, which in turn leads to a new project: writing a new disaster recovery plan.

Waiting for only major changes to occur in your company or technical infrastructure will lead to a disaster. This is because the small changes that no one considers important enough to consider for documentation will be the cause of your plan's failure. A recent DR planning survey showed that approximately 58% of respondents made changes to their plans on a predetermined maintenance cycle, while only 23% relied on a change-management process. Both of these numbers are alarming. The first implies that over 40% of organizations do not perform regular maintenance in their plans. Yikes! Worse, DR plans were not integrated into the company's change-control process over 75% of the time. Double yikes!

I recommend a combination of regularly scheduled plan maintenance as well as an internal change-control process. Having your disaster recovery coordinator schedule semi-annual review meetings for a complete tabletop read-through of the plan will help ensure nothing is missed. This get-together also familiarizes your disaster recovery team with the plan exercise. When it comes to change control, consider implementing a methodology within the IT department specifically for disaster recovery. I do not mean RPG application-programming change control; rather, a change control process to manage, monitor, and record all activities performed by system administrators. Many disaster recovery plans fail due to bad or nonexistent change-control procedures within the computer room.

A formal change-request procedure mandates your iSeries and system i5 administrators to first obtain a formal level of authorization before they perform any server maintenance or upgrades on the iSeries servers. This process ensures that more than one individual has considered the impact of the change in question as it relates to data protection and system uptime, which have an impact on DR planning. Secondly, it informs all recovery team members who need to know that there will be a change on the servers. In a best-case scenario, an organization will have clearly defined procedures for requesting and obtaining the necessary authorizations, scheduling the upgrade, and performing the work activities.

This clearly defined change process is critical in high-availability systems. With a redundant server, change-management procedures are mandatory to ensure that the production systems and the DR target systems match. Only this process will ensure success if a system failover is required. Typically, without a formal change system in place, a planned or unplanned failover will fail because the DR recovery team members will be unaware of critical patches and software updates.

Any company can establish change-request procedures with little aggravation. The biggest challenge is ensuring everyone on the DR team is fully aware of all changes that might effect DR procedures or recoverability. Here are some things to keep in mind about change control of the plan:

- Implement a change-control process to align IT infrastructure changes with any required DR plan updates, as shown in Figure 17.1.
- Ensure change control takes into consideration the disaster recovery environment and/or plan documentation when evaluating the impact of a change.
- Disaster recovery must be part of the systems development lifecycle.
- Disaster recovery planning must become an ongoing process, rather than being considered a project with an end.
- The disaster recovery coordinator should be a party in the change-review process. Waiting until the next disaster recovery test to update the disaster recovery plan is too late.

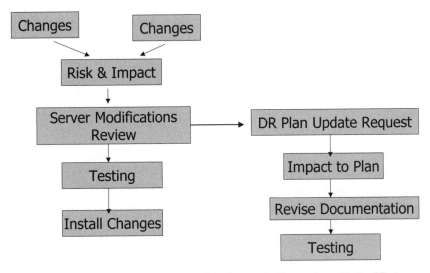

Figure 17.1: A change-control process ensures that changes to IT are reflected in the DR plan.

Changes made to any server will go through the change-management process. The documentation-update process is an extension of the change-management approach. An action item is tabled when a server update has been reviewed and approved in the hardware and software infrastructure change cycle. The DR plan coordinator initiates all required changes through this approach. Impacts are still considered, as there can be situations where a change to the infrastructure would cause the plan to not be recoverable, such as a server upgrade not supported at the hotsite.

Revisit Your Plan—Get into Maintenance Mode

Once the DR planning team has finished developing the disaster recovery plan, you should transition the project into a maintenance mode to ensure complete disaster recovery capabilities. The DR planning team should develop methods to manage the ongoing planning process. The disaster recovery coordinator and the supporting team must establish a monitoring process to determine when procedural changes are required and then test to support those changes.

There are two primary ways to ensure that the plan is current. One way is periodic testing. This means more then just the annual "satisfy the auditor" drill. It involves detailed testing that includes passive and active exercises, as discussed in the previous chapter. Testing will help identify your plan's deficiencies. It is especially useful to spot these deficiencies that have been brought forward by infrastructure changes or in the way your organization might conduct new business. Another way of ensuring that the plan remains current is through a formal change-management process.

Your IT staff will continually evaluate new technologies to enhance the business. They might also introduce technology to make the recovery process easier, by introducing a faster backup solution, for example. But just as quickly as technology changes, so does an organization's business conditions and delivery challenges. Changes within the organization or external changes might dictate the need for procedural changes to the disaster recovery plan. To ensure these changes are accommodated on a timely basis, the DR coordinator must establish a regularly scheduled review of all DR plan elements. Documentation must be updated. Testing and cross-training exercises must also remain current.

In maintenance mode, the recovery team, led by the DR coordinator, monitors, tests, and modifies the disaster recovery plan to keep it current with changes made within the organization. Keep in mind that activities in maintenance mode are not nearly as intense nor time-consuming as writing the initial DR plan. However, they are equally important. You must count on the fact that changes within the organization will occur—frequently. Examine one of your company's organization charts. How many times has it changed in the past five years? What about positive changes, such as new business your company has taken on? The disaster recovery team must ensure that such changes do not make the plan obsolete. New procedures to support any changes must be developed in the same manner as original procedures, but modifying existing procedures is far less complex.

It is important that the plan be continually maintained and updated. Disaster recovery plans should include specific maintenance responsibilities and procedures. The major considerations in this process include the following:

- Maintenance frequency
- Change factors
- Maintenance responsibilities
- Distribution considerations

Maintenance Frequency and Reasons for Change

The recovery procedures for each team should be updated at least yearly and following major organizational changes. Telephone lists and other inventories should be updated at least quarterly. The plan should also be reviewed and updated when there are major changes in technology. A plan-maintenance form can be used to record and control all maintenance changes, additions, or modifications to the plan. Consider the change itself and the source of information for determining the change, as listed in Table 17.1.

Table 17.1: Reasons and Sources for Changes	
Type of Change	**Source of Information**
Staff changes Contact information Privacy issues	IT department managers Your human resources department
Changes in computing facility Changes in building facility	Engineers or IT department managers Property managers
Changes in computer systems Changes in the network	IT department—hardware and software reseller Network managers—hardware reseller and communications carrier
Changes in business	Business executives, to ensure alignment between needs and IT deliverables
Changes in SLAs and contracts Compliance Changes in security	Legal counsel Compliance officer for SOX, ISO, COBIT, ITIL, or HIPAA Chief security officer

Table 17.1: Reasons and Sources for Changes (continued)	
Type of Change	**Source of Information**
Changes in public utility infrastructure	Local and state public works Public utilities, such as the power or water company
Changes in laws or regulations	Local, state, FEMA, public works, industry organizations

Scheduled and Unscheduled Maintenance

Scheduled maintenance is a result of scheduled plan reviews. All recovery team leaders attend these reviews. It is here the maintenance needs are discussed. This is typically a passive walkthrough exercise. The review discusses changes that have occurred in each team's area of operations and concludes whether or not formal maintenance changes are required. The DR plan coordinator schedules these reviews and is also responsible for subsequent updates to the plan based on them.

Maintenance changes that are unpredictable and cannot be scheduled fall under unscheduled maintenance. The following events might trigger unscheduled maintenance activities:

- Changes in operating systems
- Changes in ERP software
- Changes in the flow of information between systems
- Changes in communications network design, such as new routers to support Gigabit
- Changes to the data center structure
- New systems added to DR planning and recovery scope

Change Management

Change management is the process of tracking and managing all changes within your organization so that the disaster recovery plan can be kept current at all times. The absence of change control is, by far, your DR plan's worst enemy. In fact, nonexistent or insufficient change management can be the cause of a disaster in the first place. No organization would want a disaster to occur to point out the recovery deficiencies or inadequacies in its disaster recovery plan. Consider the scenario where you have a disaster, and you are a contracted hotsite subscriber. The people who are authorized to declare a disaster have long since left the organization . . . strike one. The equipment in the hotsite contract no longer matches your requirements because major system upgrades have taken place . . . strike two. The backup's program design is incomplete, forcing you to rebuild your iSeries from scratch . . . strike three. This situation arose because the organization failed to implement proper and ongoing change management. All of these failures are completely avoidable, no matter how busy you may be.

Even if you do not take the worst-case scenario, the simple nonexistence of formal plan management equals failure sooner or later. Wait until the media gets a hold of the information, for example. You must make sure that your disaster recovery plan remains a living document. Revisit the content of your plan regularly basis so that, as your business evolves, your plan will be updated accordingly. Something as simple as a personnel change in a key recovery team can undermine the plan's viability. A formal change-management procedure must be instituted by the disaster recovery planning project team. prior to project completion, to ensure that the current capability for disaster recovery remains intact.

Cha-Cha-Changes

Change management begins by identifying those dynamic entries that are responsible for changes to your disaster recovery plan. These changes will probably fall into several categories:

- Hardware
- Software
- Other technology
- Data
- Backup or recovery program design
- Facilities
- Procedures
- Personnel
- Organizational structure
- Recovery requirements (RTO or RPO)
- Disaster recovery testing

As changes occur in any of these areas, the change-management process must ensure they are incorporated into the body of the disaster recovery plan and distributed as required.

Hardware

Hardware changes can have a definitive impact on your disaster recovery plan. All hardware infrastructure changes for critical servers must be reflected in the plan. Via the proposed change control methods, the plan coordinator should coordinate the tracking of all new computer equipment that is purchased and installed. He or she must also reflect these needs in any agreements that the company has with external suppliers, such as vendors providing hotsite subscription services.

It is important to update these agreements with the current requirements in order for the disaster recovery plan to remain effective. Consider that any significant hardware changes could quickly invalidate the current hotsite subscription agreement because the solution vendor might not be able to support, say, the increased backup requirements. Secondly, a new contract revision needs to be established with the increased requirements. After all, the vendor will like to be paid for this, and you want to ensure you are legally covered. Ultimately, it might also be necessary to look for another hotsite vendor if you have exceeded the capabilities of your current provider.

Hardware changes can also include modifications to the network infrastructure or the physical communications systems, such as routers, firewalls, or switches. These might have their own implications. Even traffic rerouting strategies might have to be revised. Planners need to be sure to monitor changes in network hardware and configurations. Network changes are often overlooked, but people observe that network recovery is often the most time-consuming aspect of disaster recovery. When substantial changes are made, the network must be tested immediately. It's worthless to have systems up with no means of connecting to them.

When CPU, DASD, or other important hardware components are changed, either at the host site or backup facility, DR coordinators will need to schedule a test of their backup and recovery plan. Organizations subscribed to commercial hotsites need to consult their service contracts to determine how much advance notice they will receive regarding equipment changes at the vendor site. Some request as much as 60 days advance notice to ensure that their customers have time to assess the impact of the change and schedule a test.

Software

As you might guess, almost every software change will affect the disaster recovery plan in some way. Never assume that a minor version or application change does not warrant a change in backup or recovery procedures. This all needs to be properly documented in the disaster recovery plan.

Major software changes will involve complete application overhauls, like moving from JDE World to Enterprise One, or upgrading the operating system from V5R2 to V5R4. These changes might entail a lot of issues other than updating documentation. For instance, newer applications might demand significantly increased client server or interactive CPW (Commercial Processing Workload) processing requirements and certainly additional memory requirements. This will have a downstream impact on external hotsite vendors. It's not always a hardware change that affects your hotsite agreement. This is of particular note because if you come to a hotsite requiring hardware to support V5R4, and now you are on System i5 architecture, there is a gap. Conversely, staying on an old, or worse unsupported, IBM software version can bring another form of software and related hardware disaster.

Real-World Example

A client that was on V5R1 of OS/400 had a water main break in the computer room. It was quickly caught, but not quickly enough, as the equipment was damaged. IBM's hardware service deployment team decided they would simply replace the hardware with a newer iSeries server.

The issue was that this server required a minimum V5R3. This meant that the client in a disaster situation had no backup or procedures capable of systems recovery. They were required to a perform a RISC-to-RISC migration versus a standard unload/reload. This, of course, is not desired when you are up against the clock. The result was that no server was available for a total of 3.5 days, while the stated RTO in the disaster recovery plan's mission statement was 24 hours.

The moral of the story is to keep current software installed (V5R3/V5R4).

Keep the following in mind about software changes:

- OS/400 operating systems require specific generations of hardware.
- Replacement hardware from IBM will dictate the release you require.
- Whenever there is a major upgrade in the iSeries/400 operating system, a test should be scheduled.
- Within the DR plan, during the business impact analysis, your business functions and software applications are classified as critical

or non-critical. When a new application is added, existing software is upgraded, or a conversion is undertaken to move from one software vendor to another, change management should dictate that another test is needed.

Your Company's Data

The data stored on your System i5 server is your corporation's greatest asset. This is what disaster recovery is all about. Failure to protect (back up) and recover data to a known, consistent, useable state equals failure in a disaster. Data is probably the plan element that changes most often, so it requires the greatest amount of attention. Your data will grow significantly over time. Meanwhile, your backup windows will get smaller, so supporting backup technology (both software and hardware) will have to change. What about data encryption? Are the backups saved to tape with an encryption key? If so, who has the key?

You have the following choices for encrypting data on tape:

- Encryption built into the tape unit (LTO4, 3592)
- Encryption device between server and tape unit
- Encrypting sensitive data in database fields
- Encrypting using third-party middleware for selected objects
- Encrypting using IBM-supplied APIs (The price is right!)

With the growing data needs of a company, the necessity for offsite storage also expands. The disaster recovery coordinator must always update the inventory within the DR plan. The need is for the backup and storage techniques to be continually updated along with changes in the data needs of the organization. The DR plan coordinator must be aware of updated procedures for archiving and restoring data. As new disk storage technologies are deployed, along with new servers, the DR coordinator must update the data backup storage requirements and procedures in the DR plan.

Consider this hotsite experience:

- A client arrives at the hotsite and gets a 1 terabyte system ASP, set up with dual 3590 H tape drives. This was their contracted configuration.
- The client actually needs a 2 terabyte system ASP with a dual fiber channel LTO3 tape drive library.

This type of mismatch can cause unnecessary delays. Worse, there might be no way to meet the business requirements. Again, ensure that the configurations at any commercial hotsite are in alignment with your equipment needs.

When you need to buy more disk for your System i5, you probably go to the corner office and ask for some funding. After some grumbling and an approved business case, you install the disk. In this same business case, you should also request additional funding for your hotsite configuration. More disk capacity will be required at this site as well. This is always overlooked.

IT Recovery Team Personnel

The average individual remains in his or her job these days for about 3 years. You must stay on top of staff changes. A change to any of your recovery team personnel requires that the new team member be fully trained and well versed in the disaster recovery process. You must also consider the need to reassign roles in the interim to other members on the disaster recovery team. This is more than just adding a new name. Consider that the individual might be well versed in his or her i5 skillset, but has no business or application background.

It is also important to update the disaster recovery emergency notification procedures. The DR plan coordinator should distribute the call notification sheet upon placing the individual on the team and get immediate signoff. At the team level, the team leader should update the member list, job responsibilities, and expectations with the new personnel. This list helps ensures the recovery team can quickly get in touch with key staff, business partners, suppliers, and service providers. If notification lists are outdated, the recovery team cannot respond quickly, and all of the organizations involved might suffer a greater disruption of service than necessary.

The notification list details the following:

- Team member's name
- Home address (street address, not a P.O. box number)
- Home telephone number
- Pager number, if available
- Cellular telephone number, if available
- Personal email (not the corporate email address)
- Alternate telephone number (such as a cottage or neighbor)
- Blackberry or PDA

In addition, check your conference bridge numbers monthly. Ensure there are sufficient ports in the conference bridge and that the bridge has not been turned off as some cost-cutting accounting exercise.

Vital Record Management

With any changes or upgrades in hardware or software, there are always associated CDs and documents. This will affect items stored offsite. These typically get forgotten; "out of sight, out of mind." This affects your disaster recovery plan and ability to recover. The DR coordinator should ensure that the documents and software stored at the offsite storage provider are current. Secondly, correct inventory tracking should be in place. Perform a spot check. Recall the hot box or recovery box and inspect the contents.

Backup tape media rotation might change over time, as well. Ensure all the backup policies are clearly documented and that offsite rotations meet system requirements for data retention.

Updating Documentation for DR Plans

As changes are made to the disaster recovery plan and procedures, the DR plan coordinator must review the current working copy and create a new plan for distribution. Changes should be made to the documentation and then edited to ensure correctness. All hyperlinks should also be tested to ensure that the document is working properly. Updating a paper or CD-based version of the disaster recovery documents requires several more steps than updating those documents on the corporate intranet or Web server.

If paper documents are still used, employees must receive instructions for removing and inserting materials from older binders or books. I usually prefer to provide a complete replacement binder, versus swapping pages in and out. Yes, this kills trees, but the plan will work because it is the complete plan! If CD or paper versions are used, employees must receive instructions for returning or disposing of previous versions.

Here is a checklist for managing updates:

- Verify that the DR documents used to make updates are the correct versions and contact version tracking.
- Transfer documentation into the proper format.
- Use spell check, please. (Thank you!)
- Create graphics, tables, and charts. Visuals are important.
- Ensure graphics can be viewed without special software.
- Have someone edit the DR plan to ensure accuracy.
- Check all hyperlinks to ensure they work properly.
- Include procedures for returning or destroying older versions.
- Notify all users that changes have been made.

Technology to Distribute Your DR Plan

The complete disaster recover plan must be distributed to your plan holders. If your name is in the plan, then you are a plan holder. Everyone must be able to access their plans immediately when called upon. The plans must be maintained by the plan coordinator and available to everyone with minimal manual intervention.

Removable disks are reliable and available with little investment. Using the USB port on any computer, the OS will quickly recognize the USB device or rewritable CD. To plan holders, their disk is just another drive, so maintenance becomes easy. I prefer automation to keep my plans current by installing software with auto-run capabilities. Simply by inserting the disk device, the synchronization process begins, and a log entry is immediately made. This provides an excellent audit trail as to who has updated their plans recently. A less-automated approach will force your plan holder to click an icon to initiate a batch file on the device for the upload to take place.

Encryption keys are important to ensure the confidentiality and privacy of the disaster recovery plan. Paper-based plans pose significant challenges; a little technology can go a long way here.

To facilitate maintenance, it is important to monitor and track each copy of the plan. A distribution log can be used to record and control all copies. All plan holders should be recorded in this log sheet. The DR plan coordinator is responsible for the authorized distribution of the DR plan and should maintain a master distribution list. Each authorized copy of the plan should contain a version identification number and the DR plan recipient should be recorded on this distribution list.

Again, remind everyone when a new copy of the disaster recovery plan is distributed, that the DR plan contains information that is confidential to the organization. Recovery personnel's private information is also in this document. Accordingly, the disaster recovery plan must continue to be a restricted document and classified as confidential. Each individual holding a working copy of the DR plan is responsible for security and control of the document in accordance with the policies of your organization.

The Disaster Recovery Coordinator's Maintenance Duties

The DR coordinator will schedule planning, and create testing objectives and implementation for the overall recovery of the organization. He or she will coordinate disaster recovery activities and track recovery progress.

Publishing updated documentation is also the responsibility of the disaster recovery coordinator. Maintenance and creation of technical documentation is the responsibility of the technical recovery manager. In order for all the diverse technical responsibilities to continue to be fulfilled on an ongoing basis, the approach employed here is one where each technical and management function will coordinate activities through the disaster recovery coordinator, who has overall maintenance-coordination responsibility.

The disaster recovery coordinator's duties include the following:

- Coordination and administration of testing activities
- Determination of testing objectives and summary reporting
- Maintenance and update of documentation
- Distribution of the disaster recovery plan
- Review and approval of changes to the DR plan
- Interfacing with management objectives
- Acting as liaison with the hotsite facility for scheduling and changes

The disaster recovery coordinator is the key individual in the maintenance and testing process of your DR plan. He or she acts as the focal point and coordinator for all maintenance and testing activities. The following must be accomplished yearly:

- Budget annually for disaster recovery capability (hotsite).
- Review changes required to the hotsite configuration.
- Update the disaster recovery plan semi-annually.
- Update the critical server listing.
- Schedule two tests per year.

The disaster recovery coordinator is also responsible for maintaining a continuing awareness of the disaster recovery capability. This is done through periodic communications regarding events relevant to the capability and process involved in its maintenance. Communications typically are through chaired meetings.

The disaster recovery coordinator should publish a report semi-annually that highlights the events of the past six months related to the capabilities, gaps, testing results, documentation updates, and projects pending. This report should be circulated to all individuals who are in the distribution list for the disaster recovery, plan as well as other appropriate individuals.

All changes to documentation will be coordinated through the disaster recovery coordinator, who will receive and approve or disapprove each change request. Disapproved change requests will be returned to the originator for revisions, and resubmitted. Approved changes will be accumulated and maintained in the secure offsite storage facility. On a semi-annual basis, the disaster recovery coordinator will retrieve all changes and circulate them on new CDs, removable disks, or paper, and obtain the old items distributed previously. This occurrence can be scheduled more frequently when major changes occur.

Revision Tracking

It is important to keep track of all revisions made to the disaster recovery plan. This can be done in one of two ways. An overall revision schedule can be placed in the plan appendix, or a revision schedule can be part of every section of the disaster recovery plan. This is a matter of personal preference. Many organizations prefer to have a revision schedule as part of every section because of its proximity to the information at hand. A sample revision-schedule template is shown in Table 17.2

Table 17.2: Appendix of Chapter Revisions Schedule					
REV #	Revision Made	Revision By	Date	Section	Page #

Summary

The key to change management is proper communications within the IT department and with the DR plan coordinator. Keeping an inside track on all changes taking place in the organization is a recipe for success. For this, the DR plan coordinator needs to be in constant touch with the team leaders, department heads, change control committee, and the business.

Don't leave your plan gathering dust on the shelf. It needs to be a living document to remain viable. Revisit the content on a regular basis, as shown in Table 17.3. This way, as your business evolves, your plan can be updated accordingly. Change management depends on communications and a commitment to document change. This equals the successful execution of the disaster recovery plan.

Table 17.3: Timeframe for Maintaining the DR Plan	
Deliverable	**Due Date**
Emergency notification list	Every 3 months
Business functions spreadsheet/resource requirements	Semi-annually
Complete disaster recovery	Annually
Training and awareness	Semi-annually
Technology reviews of critical servers	Annually
Walkthrough tabletop exercise	Annually
Testing at a hotsite (simulated or actual exercise)	Semi-annually

18

Selecting a Commercial Hotsite Provider

In today's very competitive business world, a heavy reliance is placed on information systems and the availability of corporate data. IT in the past was thought of as strictly "that big expenditure" that drained all the company profits. IT had its own large, secured silo, and IT folks rarely met anyone in the business. They worked best by themselves in the computer room, for they had no business knowledge or business skills. Nobody knew what they really did.

While the IT department once acted just as an aid to the business, it has now become very much intertwined in the business. IT drives the business as much as the business continues to drive IT. When a company goes to business with just about any product, IT becomes part of the expected service delivery. As companies become more reliant on critical information technology, any potential disruption to the business due to a loss of critical server access and data becomes even more disastrous.

Organizations face many threats today when it comes to the reliability and viability of their data. As businesses rely more heavily on electronically stored data, and as regulatory pressures force companies to protect data for longer periods of time, disaster recovery plans have an ever greater impact on corporations large and small. During an unpredictable disruption or catastrophic disaster, businesses risk losing their competitive advantage by not having taken the appropriate measures to prevent loss of information availability. The protection of this data is mandated by a solid backup and recovery program design.

Regularly scheduled backups of your company's data and server infrastructure will help protect against incident-level disasters and other more serious threats. To ensure true continued continuity for the core business functions, however, companies need to take a more proactive approach to IT. This is only feasible with a commitment to DR planning and a solid recovery strategy in place well in advance of any disaster-related event.

Advance Planning = Hotsite

Information technology continues to be part of the success of every organization. Business executives must carefully evaluate their investments in recovery sites and related strategies, so that their organizations do not go down with the disaster. The best form of "insurance" or "guaranteed recoverability " from any disaster scenario is to plan for disaster recovery in advance. However, a DR plan is incomplete without a place to go and recover your critical systems. Today, one of the most common approaches for recovery of critical IT infrastructure is engaging a trusted commercial hotsite service provider. A hotsite provider offers guaranteed emergency services in the event of a fire, weather-related event, or other disaster to a building or facility. Corporations contractually signed up for these programs receive immediate priority for emergency sever-restoration services.

The concept of a recovery location, or a commercial hotsite, was initially based on the idea that most organizations have a relatively similar set of IT infrastructure needs. In the event of a disaster, organizations would transport staff, ship their backup tapes to the hotsite, get the operating system up and running, restore the servers, and continue to run the business. (This is very simplified, of course.)

Hotsites can be commercially or internally owned and operated. Commercial hotsite services are purchased by organizations that process critical business applications on the iSeries or System i5 and other supporting hardware platforms. A hotsite supports the restoration of critical business functions within the predetermined time limits and is backed by a Service Level Agreement (SLA). A hotsite maintains a facility ready to assume processing responsibility immediately after an outage of a client's server functions.

Hotsites comprise all of the required servers, data communication infrastructure, and staff necessary to meet your business requirements in the wake of a disaster. Some hotsites are also fully equipped with office services that include desktop recovery, telephony, fax machines, and printing capabilities, all set up and waiting for you and your primary business users. The servers at the hot site are powered up in advance with software pre-loaded, and network infrastructure is already pre-installed and connected to the supporting telecommunications carriers. Typically, hotsite solutions service critical business restoration, supporting Recovery Time Objectives of 24 hours to 5 days.

When a disaster disrupts or destroys a data center, the client's responsibility is to obtain the backup tapes and media from its secure offsite storage provider and deliver them to the hotsite. Once delivered, the client's IT recovery team personnel, assisted by the hotsite technicians, load the software onto the servers and restore the backup tape data to the hotsite's computer systems, and commence operations. Typically, commercial hotsite vendors allow clients to use their facilities for up to eight weeks after a declared disaster. During this time, the client must either restore back to the failed server, rebuild its data center, or make alternative arrangements. When clients are not using a hotsite to restore a data center in a declared disaster, the hotsite is used, almost continuously, to rehearse and test other customer's DR plans. Comprehensive testing is critical to effective disaster recovery, and customers contend to schedule their rehearsals or testing.

Internal or External Hotsite?

A commercial hotsite solution is available on a first-come, first-served basis for a tape recovery solution. The recovery service is always subject to availability. When your primary site is not available, your company will be expected to travel to a secondary location, at your expense. If an organization owns a facility and manages all the IT resources at the hotsite, the facility is known as an *internal hotsite*. Such an arrangement ensures that the hotsite has all the resources required to ensure business continuity and is not shared with any other company. In addition, the hardware and software at the internal hotsite will be consistent with those at the primary site.

While operational continuity of critical systems has never been simple nor inexpensive, disaster recovery is more achievable and economical when engaging a commercial hotsite provider. Many IT executives have realized that buying and managing all the required critical disaster recovery equipment and building a facility in-house is significantly more expensive than outsourcing disaster recovery to a commercial hotsite. The bigger issue is that many IT managers lack the hotsite management skills required of an internal solution. This is just not their field of expertise. Also, smaller companies are usually just not large enough to handle an internal recovery solution. The opposite can be true: a large organization's IT infrastructure can be too big to concentrate the recovery capability in-house. The reality is that becoming self-reliant is a management decision. Commercial hotsite vendors distribute the high costs of technology and space among their many customers. The internally owned and operated solution's costs is shared by one . . . your company. Table 18.1 provides more details on the costs and benefits of these two solutions.

Table 18.1: External vs. Internal Hotsite	
External, Commercial Hotsite	**Internal, Owned Hotsite**
Lower total cost of ownership Costs shared among numerous clients	Must own second, complete IT infrastructure Total cost burden—capital
Technology upgrades supported	Upgraded technology must be purchased and aligned with current production servers

Table 18.1: External vs. Internal Hotsite (continued)	
External, Commercial Hotsite	**Internal, Owned Hotsite**
Vendor's knowledge and expertise can be leveraged	Special training required
Risk of equipment access in a disaster	Risks related to the use of shared equipment no longer exist
Test time delay can be months	Available all the time
Declaration fees	No disaster-declaration fees
Top-notch security, power, and telecommunications capabilities	Second computer room many times an after-thought, or not enough budget
Vendors provide logistics assistance when disaster is declared	You're on your own
Multiple locations	Eggs in one basket
Available technical staff support	You're on your own
Staff dedicated to disaster recovery	Staff dedicated to regular IT functions
Offers disaster recover experience	Limited skill
Higher-evel availability at additional cost	Can increase footprint or systems availability solution
Strong relationships with telco and hardware providers	Telco and hardware relationships limited to your company's buying power

A balanced evaluation must relate directly to your organization's business needs. It may cost more to establish an internal hotsite, due to site building expenditures, equipment, staffing, etc. However, the benefits and risk reduction derived from this solution may outweigh the additional cost.

What to Look for in a Hotsite Provider

Organizations frequently commit to costly, long-term mistakes with their commercial hotsite selection process. Before signing a contractual agreement with an external provider, the IT recovery team and the business should scrutinize the vendor, location, site access, and legal wording laid out in the contract. Too many organizations neglect contractual language that governs accessibility, à la carte fees, test procedures, site fees, fee schedules, automatic triggers, and the scope of the equipment and related services that the agreement may include or possibly exclude altogether.

It is very easy to sign a contract, and then be surprised by lots of fine print and additional billing when you need the recovery provider the most . . . in a disaster. Remember the oldest adage out there: You get what you pay for. Also, remember its corollary: If it sounds to good to be true, it is! In the following sections, you will find a list of things to consider when looking for a commercial hotsite provider.

Building Infrastructure

Look for a dedicated building and a state-of-the-art facility constructed specifically for disaster recovery. The hotsite should have 24/7 surveillance and be administered locally, with onsite support staff. Examine the hotsite's facility to ensure it controls and manages restricted access areas. Door management should include the appropriate cardkey, swipe, or even biometrics to gain entry into the computer rooms.

Make sure the air conditioning is maintained by separate climate controls, and that a fully redundant A/C unit is available and tested. All server infrastructure should be protected from power spikes, power surges, and loss of power by redundant power supply systems with an uninterrupted power supply (UPS). In the event of a major power outage, auxiliary power should be routed through an automatic transfer switch and provided via an external natural-gas-powered generator. This is the preferred choice over a diesel generator because of the need to refill the fuel tanks. In a regional disaster, fuel can become scarce very quickly.

The hotsite center should also be equipped for fire suppression with an FM-200 fire suppression mechanism. Make sure the staff have been trained to act upon a disaster in a professional and timely manner.

Here are some elements to look for at the hotsite's physical plant:

- Surveillance
- Biometrics
- Cardkey entry
- Alarm systems
- Force-proof entry
- Fireproof construction
- Brick construction versus windows
- Dedicated facility versus shared
- Natural gas generators
- Redundant HVAC

Here are some logical elements the hotsite should have in place:

- Intrusion detection systems
- Intrusion prevention systems
- Physical security
- Firewalls
- Anti-spy software
- Antivirus software
- Access control mechanisms
- Authentications
- Network security scanners
- VPN
- SSL

Tour the Facilities

To prevent surprises, it is always best to request a tour of the disaster recovery provider's facility before signing a contract. Bring several people to discuss your findings. You should also request a pretest to insure you are getting exactly what you are paying for. The pretest is based on validating the vendor, *not* your data recovery abilities. Check out the following items during the pretest:

- Effective communication with the vendor
- All equipment (not a subset) available as stated in the agreement
- Site technical support available and knowledgeable
- Security in place
- Facilities review
- Tape handling and other logistics
- Compliance controls for scratching the system post-test

With a pretest, there are no surprises after an account is established. Investing into a hotsite blindly because the vendor produces a long list of clients is not doing your homework. Are the references local, or from other cities that do not even use the facility you are looking to sign up with?

Equipment

Does the hotsite support a broad range of computer equipment and communications infrastructure to recover critical business applications? The site must have enterprise solutions that will run your critical server processing and communications capabilities until the systems are restored or rebuilt, or another recovery solution is put into place. Will the site be able to support your technology with your current and future operating system requirements? Keep in mind there are hardware restrictions linked directly to the operating system of the hardware. Here are some other issues to consider:

- What is the equipment availability and time allocation?
- Is there availability at other, secondary sites?
- What is the type of equipment? How often is it upgraded?

- Does the hardware profile match your needs today and tomorrow?
- How is growth supported in the customer base?
- What is the networking capability/capacity?

Ensure absolute standards for compatibility of operating systems, applications, and communications.

Access in a Disaster

Shared hotsite services are operated on a subscription basis. If multiple, simultaneous disasters occur, hotsite vendors typically make their facilities available on a first-come, first-served basis, or allocate capacity among customers contending for the same computer systems. This becomes very important when considering the effects of a regional disaster. Keep in mind that you might not be the only one affected in a disaster. First-come, first-served means you need to be aggressive in declaring your disaster. If you wait too long, you will very likely be shut out of the regional recovery center.

Consider 9/11 for a minute. All the major commercial hotsite providers in the area were "sold out" in less than 45 minutes after the event. Their customers were very fast to declare. Everyone else waited and watched things unfold.

If your primary hotsite is occupied, you may be diverted to an alternate hotsite owned by the vendor. That means you might have some travel considerations. In the past, you might have had to simply drive across town or travel an hour by plane. You might have pre-bought full-fare air tickets so your staff could simply show up and use the tickets on the next available flight. With a need to go to an alternate site, however, all your travel tickets might not accommodate the new itinerary. Now you are faced with a four-hour plane ride and no option for driving because it is simply too far away. Does your disaster recovery plan account for the travel considerations, as well as distance factors? Now think about how you will get your tapes there.

Here are some considerations about access:

- Does your provider have a second site if the primary site is not available in a disaster for whatever the reason?
- What guarantees to access to subscribed equipment do you have upon declaration?
- What guarantees do you have for access to a selected recovery facility?
- What contractual guarantees are there that contention for resources won't increase over the life of the contract?
- Will your recovery operations be split among two or more sites?
- What are your disaster declaration procedures?
- What are your disaster declaration standby procedures?

Number of Customers

It is always impressive to read, "We have over 1,200 happy customers." Consider this statement carefully, however. Yes, it indicates success, but those 1,200 customers are your competition. They have the same right to the equipment that you do. Remember, equipment access is shared by all subscribers. A regional interruption might set off a mad scramble among hotsite clients for access, whether they are directly in the affected area or not. To ensure your ability to access the facilities, server infrastructure, and networks that you have subscribed to, you should determine in advance what you are up against. Ask the following questions:

- How many subscribers exist in the primary hotsite recovery facility?
- How many subscribe to the same configurations that we need?
- What are the shared equipment access ratios? 10:1? 50:1? 100:1 or unlimited?
- Would any of these other companies enjoy priority status above my company? If so, why?

- How many customers can you simultaneously support? In multiple disasters?
- What customers are nearest to my facility location? How many?
- What is the geographic separation of customers in your subscription base?
- What are my specific rights to computer access?

Testing Access

Testing your disaster recovery plan is the only way you can validate its effectiveness. In addition, testing provides the IT recovery team the all-important opportunity for hands-on training. The issue becomes access to the hotsite to facilitate testing. How long do you have to wait? Large, commercial hotsite providers have thousands of customers, each of whom needs to test its recovery capabilities regularly. Many customers discover that they cannot conduct those tests with their providers when they need to, or they can only get one test per year instead of the two they had planned for. Suppose a vendor states something like this:

- Ensured availability for testing. (We guarantee 60-day availability for a test.)

Make sure the vendor can truly deliver on this, and have a penalty clause in the contract to ensure the agreed-upon time period is met regularly. Believe me, you *will* need to test. Consider that every year you will have significant changes in your IT infrastructure, which in turn will change or modify your company's recovery needs. Most IT environments change regularly, and sometimes radically. It is important that your plan testing keeps pace with those changes throughout the year.

Experience

Everyone says they have experience, but do they really? Ask them questions. What type of experience do they have? What type of iSeries or System i5 certifications do they have? A large vendor might have experience as an organization, but what about the local site you are specifically working with? Knowing that Vendor A has supported numerous disasters in the Hurricane Belt sounds impressive, but doesn't necessarily matter if your organization is in the Midwest.

Be sure you know exactly how much experience the vendor has on staff. These are the people you will lean on during a test, as well as during a disaster. Break down the staff experience levels to hardware-related and network-related, and ask for any certifications related to specific hardware, such as the IBM V5R4 OS certification and Backup and Recovery.

Consider the following questions:

- Does the vendor have experience/qualifications specific to my industry?
- How many actual disasters have been declared at the hotsite? Results?
- How are multiple disaster declarations handled by the staff?
- What is the test time availability?
- What other services does the staff provide?
- What references are available?
- How many staff members are made available during a test and during a disaster?
- How many years of experience does the hotsite company have?
- Can the vendor detail transportation access to the hotsite facility?
- What are the details regarding geographic separation, power grid separation, and the communications center?

Tender the Hotsite

A formal bid process could be tendered to several commercial hotsite providers. This will help your organization obtain a competitive price quotation to help IT meet your disaster recovery requirements.

It is important to provide the vendors with the appropriate information to help them help you in this process. The commercial hotsite vendors will need to know the following:

- What is the anticipated timeframe for recovery?
- How much test time is required?
- How much site access time is required in a disaster?
- What are the hardware requirements, including brand name, model number, CPU, memory, disk size, and partition details?
- How many systems are required?
- Can you provide a complete, itemized list of software, including computer operating system versions?
- What are your data communications needs (frame relay, VPN tunnels, firewalls, etc.)?
- What are your network configuration requirements, including all ports, connectors, cables, interfaces, and switches, with manufacturer name, model number, nomenclature, and number of units in use?
- What are your work area recovery needs—number of workstations, standard desktop configuration details, and any telephony requirements?
- What is your need for staff technical assistance?
- Do you need start-up assistance (i.e. operating system pre-loads)?
- Do you have a location preference when multiple sites are available?
- How should an organization sign up with the hotsite company?
- Do they have multiple sites? If so, where are they?

Here are the next steps after you review tenders:

- After pre-qualifying all vendor candidates, request a presentation at your facility.
- Request written replies to follow-up questions not answered during vendor presentations.

- Visit actual sites of vendor finalists, involving your disaster recovery or security specialist to conduct site surveys.

Cost Considerations

When looking at the price model with a commercial hotsite, a detailed cost analysis will often reveal many not-so-hidden expenses in addition to the basic hotsite fees. There is a lot more to consider than just the monthly fee schedule. Sometimes, the monthly fees are purposely set low, as everything is considered a pay-as-you-play approach. When you fully use the hotsite-related services, your monthly statement price increase might cause you to fall off your office chair!

Monthly subscription rates are rarely the total cost of hotsite access. Budget-breaking hidden costs will come up. To be prepared, ask the vendor about the following:

- Your monthly fee schedule
- Additional testing costs
- Additional third-party service costs
- Disaster declaration fees
- Alert fees
- Penalties for premature disaster declaration and subsequent cancellation
- Daily site-usage fees
- Long-distance and network usage charges
- Technical support fees
- Logistical tape-handling fees
- Change of equipment fees

Hotsite Benefit Analysis Example

When breaking out the cost structure, ensure that you include adequate testing time to fully validate all your recovery planning procedures. A shortfall of test time keeps many DR coordinators from booking that extra needed test because of a lack of funding. Access time to the hotsite facility in a disaster is equally important.

Your organization can count on running your business from the hotsite for at least one week in a declared disaster. With most disasters, even small ones like a major hardware failure, count on staying at a hotsite facility until you can schedule downtime with your business to restore your servers back to the primary computer room—which implies a weekend. You might even miss the first weekend if things back home are not ready. Then you'll need to stay at the hotsite for an extra week. Most of the disasters I have covered required five to ten days of hotsite access.

Keep the following in mind when evaluating costs:

- Check for a minimum usage charge in a disaster (usually seven days) or a minimum charge.
- Ensure there are no alert costs.
- Ensure that preloading the system is available.

Consider a sample of company ABC's non-technical hotsite requirements:

- Four, 24-hour days of test time
- Ten days of access to facility and equipment in a disaster
- OS/400 preloaded at no charge at the hotsite

The cost of company ABC declaring a disaster at two different hotsites is shown in Table 18.2.

Table 18.2: Cost of Declaring a Disaster		
	Vendor 1	**Vendor 2**
Travel costs	Local—drive to site	Flight, hotel, car $8,000 for 3 staff
Declaration fee	$7,000	Included
Site setup fee	$2,000	Included
Site available for use	6 hours	4 hours
Network access available	8 hours	6 hours
Site access for 10 days	2 x 24 hours included $3,800 per day	0 x 24 hours included $2,000 per day
Technical support fee	First 48 hours included $250/hour additional time	First 48 hours included $250/hour additional time
Total cost in a disaster	**$39,400**	**$28,000**

Suppose company ABC conducts two tests per year to verify data and network connectivity, totaling four 24-hour days, or 12 8-hour segments. Assume eight hours of technical support assistance. The cost of testing at the two different hotsites is shown in Table 18.3.

Table 18.3: Cost of Testing at Hotsite		
	Vendor 1	**Vendor 2**
Travel costs	Local—drive to site	Flight, hotel, car $4,000 for 3 staff
Test time included	3 x 8 hours Additional 8-hour shift $1,500	8 x 8 hour segments Additional 8-hour segment $1,800
Site setup fee	$2,000	Included
Technical support	First 3 x 8 hours included $250/hour additional time	First 1 x 8 hours included $ 250/hour additional time
Total cost of test	**$13,500**	**$9,400**

A lot more goes into the ongoing operational costs of a hotsite contract. The total cost of ownership requires that you understand every service-delivery item and associated cost elements that makes up the contract. In Table 18.3, you can see that the cost to use vendor 1 is far more than vendor 2. Vendor 1 is local, but its costs compared to vendor 2 far outweigh that perceived benefit.

Contract Cost Considerations for Inclusion and Renewals

Always balance acceptable risk with economies of scale. Hotsite providers traditionally make their money from investing in equipment, and then syndicating the hardware infrastructure and support staff to as many clients as possible. The key is for them to do this without compromising risk or service. Your organization must fully understand the subscription level to which you intend to contractually agree. Remember, if it sounds too good to be true, it is!

Be extremely careful in evaluating what is and what is not included in the monthly subscription fee. Ensure there is a detailed schedule of additional costs attached in the contract. The extra billings must be very clear.

What is a fair contract renewal period? Many vendors will try to sign up a prospective client for a five-year term because it makes sense for the vendor. However, I believe this length of contract time is a bad business decision. Consider that your iSeries/400 is probably on a three-year lease. At the end of your lease, your IBM hardware will be no doubt be upgraded to a new, faster technology like a System i5. This will include a new CPU, more memory, additional disk storage, and probably faster tape drives. This causes a technical gap in the hotsite contract. Many vendors will suggest that this is not an issue, and your organization can easily make hardware amendments to reflect your new needs. This is where you can expect significant additional pricing, with contract coterminous terms, as the vendor now has control. The new monthly rate can make the solution no longer feasible. Before signing a hotsite contract, agree to a hardware upgrade fee schedule. How much will it cost your organization for additional CPU, additional giga-bytes of disk, etc.? Can you get out of the contract because of a gap or because you no longer need the service? (The answer is typically no.)

579

Consider these additional contract items and issues:

- Determine whether there are yearly increases linked to inflation.
- Always use a competitive tendering process, even at contract renewal time.
- Understand hardware upgrade costs.
- Specify test time and any additional à la carte fees.
- Specify site occupancy costs.
- Specify data communications costs for hookup and utilization, and testing.
- Remember that declaration fees are always negotiable.
- Check for unbundled contract costs.
- Fully understand the vendor's right of access: first-come, first-served.
- Determine whether the vendor supplies shared access for multiple declarations.
- Check the right of access if the vendor receives multiple disaster invocations.
- Check whether you can visit the hotsite recovery center and actually touch the equipment you will work with, versus being told, "It resides somewhere else."

In the contract terms, try to negotiate the following:

- Include early termination conditions.
- Include a buy-out schedule.
- Keep the length of the contract to three years.
- Set compensatory damages if the vendor cannot completely fulfill contractual service obligations.
- Eliminate any automatic renewal clause.

Summary

Highly successful companies recognize the value of a commercial hotsite provider to help plan, educate, test recovery, and most importantly provide disaster recovery support if an event causes great disruption to your company. Ensure that the hotsite you choose has all the resources required to enable business continuity in a disaster. In addition, the hardware and software at the hotsite must be consistent with those in use at the primary location. Engaging a commercial vendor enables your organization to do the following:

- Leverage the provider's extensive investments in the latest technology, continuous improvements to methodologies, and skilled people.
- Benefit from the expertise gained in solving problems for a variety of clients with similar requirements.
- Remove expensive, redundant technology assets from the balance sheet.
- Use the provider's backup facilities and staff resources.
- Take advantage of the provider's economies of scale on assets, resources, and procurement to help enable a lower cost of operation and significantly less risk.

Remember, commercial hotsite vendors are in the business of disasters, and you are not. Leverage the hotsite's technical and disaster experience to help you recover your business when you need it most . . . in a disaster. After all, isn't that what you are paying for?

19

A Family DR Plan

A family DR plan should be part of every IT disaster recovery plan. All of your disaster recovery strategies depend on the actions of your recovery teams. However, what happens if the scope and effects of the disaster include the recovery team members' families? Recovery plans must provide for family needs, as well as staff members.

In a disaster, particularly a regional disaster, the recovery team member's first and only natural reaction will be to try to look after his or her home and family. Your company, understandably, will lose the services of those employees who might be critical participants in the DR plan. Therefore, consideration should be given to helping your recovery team members develop a family DR plan to ensure they, too, are prepared.

Should a family have a disaster recovery plan? Of course. In everyday life, a large-scale emergency or disaster might seem like a remote possibility, but experience tells us otherwise. The last few years have been particularly tough on families in both the U.S. and Canada. Obviously, this type of DR plan would not support a technological response, but the all-important human response.

In the business world, the biggest mistake that a company can make in its DR planning is to focus exclusively on computer systems and infrastructure, and ignore the personnel needs of the staff. Remember that there is no disaster recovery without recovery team members available and onsite. Employees faced with conflicting obligations between the home and the workplace are less likely to cooperate during an emergency. Every company should actively promote family preparedness as part of the organizational disaster planning effort. You can support this critical issue by incorporating the provisions of preparedness in the following pages into a family DR plan for your disaster planning methodology.

Disaster Recovery Begins at Home

A disaster can happen quickly and without warning. Knowing what to do when a disaster strikes will help you better control the situation. It will put you and your family in a position to recover more quickly. Your family could be scattered and separated, the children at schools, parents working or gridlocked in a traffic jam. How will you find each other? How will you determine if everyone is safe? Do you know what to do if services such as gas, water, electricity, or telephones are unavailable? Being prepared and understanding what to do when faced with an emergency will reduce fear, anxiety, and potential losses. Emergency relief workers will be on the scene sooner or later following a disaster. However, keep in mind that in the interim, you will have to support your family without emergency services.

As a family, you can survive a disaster by preparing in advance. Meet with your family and discuss why you need to prepare for a disaster. Explain the dangers of disasters such as fire, severe weather, or an extended power outage, and how your family would respond. Explain the need to share responsibilities and safety in a disaster. Discuss the types of disasters that are most likely to happen in your community, and explain what to do in each case.

Cover the following issues in your family DR planning:

- Pick two places to meet, such as right outside your home (at the end of the driveway) in case of a sudden emergency, and somewhere outside your neighborhood in case you can't return to your home. Make this second place a central, commonly known location.

- Select an out-of-state family member or friend to be your "contact." After a disaster, it's often easier to call long-distance (collect). All family members should know to call this person and tell him or her the family member's location. Ensure everyone has memorized the contact's phone number.

- Complete the checklist in your family's plan for food, water, supplies, documents, etc.

- Teach your children how and when to call 911 for emergency help.

- Show each family member how and when to turn off the water, gas, and electricity in your home.

- Teach all family members how to use the fire extinguisher and show them where the units are kept.

- Keep a small amount of cash in a safe place where you can quickly gain access to it in the event of an evacuation.

Emergency Supplies

Coming from an Italian family, I can safely say we have at least a 30-day food supply on hand in the mini-Costco that is our basement. You should stock six basic items in your home: water, food, first aid supplies, clothing, and bedding. Keep enough of these in your home to meet your needs for at least five days. Store them in sturdy, easy-to-carry containers, such as backpacks, duffle bags, or covered plastic moving containers.

Keeping key items like matches and money in sealable, waterproof containers and bags is always preferred. Place those supplies where you would most likely need them for an instant evacuation.

Water

Purchase and store bottled water. Rotate several cases of water in and out every three months to ensure the water does not become old. Water does expire . . . honestly. A normally active person needs to drink at least two bottles of water each day. The survival rule of thumb is to store one gallon of water per person per day (two quarts for drinking, two quarts for food preparation and sanitation).

Food

Store at least a five-day supply of nonperishable food. Select foods that require no refrigeration, preparation, or cooking, and involve little or no water. Select food items that are compact and lightweight.

Include a selection of the following foods in your disaster supplies kit:

- Ready-to-eat canned meats, fruits, and vegetables
- Canned juices and soup
- A manual can opener
- Sugar, salt, and pepper
- High-energy foods such as peanut butter, jelly, crackers, granola bars, and trail mix
- Vitamins
- Foods for infants, elderly persons, or persons on special diets
- Comfort/stress foods such as cookies, hard candy, sweetened cereals, cereal bars, Tang, Kool-Aid, instant coffee, and tea bags.

First Aid Supplies

Contact your local American Red Cross chapter to obtain a basic first aid manual. Have some nonprescription drugs on hand, like pain relievers, sunscreen, mosquito repellent, antihistamines for allergic reactions, and diarrhea medicine. Also stock toothpaste and toothbrushes, hand sanitizing gel, playing cards, duct tape, and a radio with batteries.

Important Family Documents

Keep these records in a waterproof, portable container, or better yet, in a bank safe:

- Your family estate's will, insurance policies, contracts, deeds, stocks, and bonds
- Passports, social security cards, and immunization records
- Bank account numbers
- Credit card account numbers and companies
- Inventory of valuable household goods, and important telephone numbers
- Family records (birth, marriage, and death certificates)

I recommend creating an electronic summary document with all this information. Password-protect the data and keep it at a relative's home out of the state. Just having credit card numbers available can go a long way in a crisis.

Practice and Maintain Your Plan

Be sure to periodically quiz your children so they remember what to do in a disaster. For younger children, conduct a fire and home-evacuation drill. Check your home smoke and carbon monoxide detectors every time the clocks change, in the spring and fall. Change the batteries even if they appear to be fine. It's a small price to pay for safety.

Replace stored emergency supplies (such as stored food or water) every three months, to assure freshness. Also, test and recharge your fire extinguisher(s) according to manufacturer's instructions.

Personal and Family Requirements

One crucial lesson we have learned is that until an individual's basic family needs are met, he or she will not attend to your organization's problems. If a team member's family is in jeopardy, that individual will not be able to focus on recovering computer systems.

Disaster recovery plans must, therefore, provide for the personal needs of key recovery team members so that they will attend to their recovery, support, and management roles. Not only must recovery plans provide for key staff members personal and family needs, but people must be made aware that their personal needs will be met during a recovery. This must be done upfront. Recovery team members should be made to feel that the company cares about them and their families.

In cases in which disasters affect large areas, organizations might have to offer temporary shelter and food to a number of homeless families, either by themselves or in cooperation with recovery authorities. In such situations, human resources professionals should be available to help negotiate access to medical care, housing, food, daycare, and other necessities. If recovery team members see that these measures are in place, they are more likely to concentrate on enterprise recovery.

Real-World Example: A Hurricane Rita Success Story

During Hurricane Rita, I was involved with clients in the Houston area. With advance warning, the company immediately mandated that all personnel go home. The top priority was to see to their families' needs and return when they were comfortable that their loved ones were out of danger. IT initiated family DR plans in place because of the continued efforts of the DR planning team. The plan was to move families north, to Dallas, in an evacuation. Hotel and bus transportation were provided for the families in advance of the hurricane arriving. Other families who had places of their own to go to were all accounted for as well.

> This company believed that the recovery team employees onsite when the hurricane occurred would be able to recover their computer systems more effectively, and be more clear-minded, knowing their families were out of harm's way. This decision proved to be wise. The company's High Availability systems were switched on and functional almost a full day ahead of schedule—well before Rita even showed up.

Awareness Training

Educating personnel through a Disaster Recovery Awareness Day is a creative way to distribute printed materials, show videos, and in general share information about how staff can better prepare their homes and families for disasters. This provides an opportunity to share information about the company's DR plan, family and staff communication plans, bus transportation pools, and other measures the company has taken to facilitate a safe and speedy return to work. Other methods of raising awareness of the recovery plan, and especially the human factors, involve Web sites and e-mails detailing where employees can go to learn more about specific information.

Extend your training to include help for employees' home safety and preparedness. This will establish a total mindset for your employees and provide them with a means to always be prepared, at home and at work. Help families in the testing of their home DR plans, as well.

Information on Family Disaster Plans

Both the Federal Emergency Management Agency (FEMA) and the American Red Cross have developed suggested family disaster plans. These include the development of a disaster supplies kit, designation of meeting places, and emergency contacts and telephone numbers, ability to shut off utilities, knowledge of home and area hazards, and tips on first aid and CPR. For more information, see the following Web sites:

- Federal Emergency Management Agency (FEMA): www.fema.gov
- American Red Cross: www.redcross.org

Summary

As with an IT disaster recovery plan, all facets of the family DR Plan must be tested. Be sure to periodically quiz your children so they remember what to do and where things are located. Planning for disaster recovery is the responsibility of every corporation and family. The wise planner will build plans that place people first. Taking care of the needs of employees makes good sense. Promote family and staff preparedness. If individuals and families are prepared, your company and your coworkers are better positioned in an emergency situation. Employees who know their organization and families have a plan, and have seen the DR plan in action during testing exercises, will be more confident in their organization's and family's disaster recovery preparedness.

Appendix

Sample Documents

Business Impact Analysis Questionnaire

<u>Please answer the questions with the following disaster scenario in mind:</u>

- IT has experienced a major failure in the data center and the ability to supply computing services is completely destroyed.
- All systems, applications, data, and other support systems are not available.
- Your personnel <u>will not</u> be lost.
- Your primary business processes will be affected immediately and for up to at least 7 days.
- When the systems become available there will be a data loss of 24 hours.
- The disaster occurs during a peak processing period in your business unit.

Please supply the following information about your business unit:

Business Unit Name:_____

Business Unit Owner:_____

Phone Number:_____Cell Number:_____

Email Address:_____

Business Unit Process Description

In the space below, please list the primary business processes that must be executed by your business unit on a regular basis.

1.	2.
3.	4.
5.	6.

Operational Priorities

In the event of a disaster, when must your primary processes be performed? Please mark the appropriate response:

1. They must be performed as regularly scheduled.
2. They can be performed following the disaster as time and resources become available.

Operational Impacts

A disaster can affect the company in many different ways. The company may certainly lose revenue opportunities if key processes cannot be performed during a disaster period. In addition, the company may also be affected operationally in other ways if these processes cannot be performed as scheduled.

Please respond to each of the following operational impact questions.

- What types of business impacts will be experienced by the company if your primary business processes are not performed immediately following a disaster?

- How long could your processes be idled before the company would be substantially harmed in some way? one hour, 12 hours, 1 day or longer ?

Customer Service

Identify the earliest day that customer service would be impacted in a significant negative manner because your processes could not be performed.

Examples: The following processes would have an immediate impact to Customer Service: Product Distribution, Customer Response, SLA, JIT.

Circle the earliest time or day of significant negative impact.

12 hours	< 1 day	1.5	2	2.5	3	3.5	4	4.5	5	6	7	10	15	30	>30

Cash Flow/Revenue

Identify the earliest day that cash flow or revenue would be impacted in a significant negative manner because your processes could not be performed.

Examples – The following processes would have an immediate impact to Cash Flow/Revenue: Customer Sales, Accounts Receivables, or Sales Support Teams.

Circle the earliest time or day of significant negative impact.

12 hours	< 1 day	1.5	2	2.5	3	3.5	4	4.5	5	6	7	10	15	30	>30

Regulatory (If Applicable)

Identify the earliest day that the company's regulatory compliance requirements and objectives would be impacted in a significant negative manner
because your processes could not be performed.

Examples – The following processes would have an immediate impact on our
ability to meet regulatory requirements: Regulatory Affairs (FDA Filings),
Contract Operations (Customer Contracts), or Financial Filings.

Circle the earliest day or time of significant negative impact.

12 hours	< 1 day	1.5	2	2.5	3	3.5	4	4.5	5	6	7	10	15	30	>30

Increases in Liability

Identify the earliest day that the company could face a significant increase in
liabilities because your processes could not be performed.

Examples – The following processes would have the potential to significantly
increase company liability: JIT, SLA, Penalties, Regulatory Affairs (FDA
Filings or SEC Requests for Information), or other filings.

Circle the earliest hour or day of significant negative impact.

12 hours	< 1 day	1.5	2	2.5	3	3.5	4	4.5	5	6	7	10	15	30	>30

State Financial Impact _____

Vendor Relations

Identify the earliest day that vendor relations would be impacted in a significant negative manner because your processes could not be performed.

Examples – The following processes would have the potential to significantly impact vendor relations: Accounts Payable (Payments and Inquiries), Purchasing (Purchase Orders), or Legal (Contracts). JIT, Dependent Partners.

Circle the earliest hour or day of significant negative impact.

12 hours	< 1 day	1.5	2	2.5	3	3.5	4	4.5	5	6	7	10	15	30	>30

State Financial Impact _____

Financial Control/Reporting

Identify the earliest day that financial control/reporting requirement would be impacted in a significant negative manner because your processes could not be performed.

Examples – The following processes have the potential to impede company financial control and reporting: Financial Reporting or Sales Reporting.

Circle the earliest hour or day of significant negative impact.

12 hours	< 1 day	1.5	2	2.5	3	3.5	4	4.5	5	6	7	10	15	30	>30

State Financial Impact _____

Mission Critical IT Applications

Business units may require the timely access to and use of certain key
mission critical information technology applications.

Using the table below, please identify the top mission critical applications
that your business unit must have use of in order to accomplish your critical
processes during a business recovery effort. The following information is
required for each of the applications:

- Application Name—Provide the specific name of application
- Application Priority—Using the numbers 1-6, prioritize the order in
  which the applications must be made available
- Maximum Outage—Specify the maximum number of days (Hours)
  without use of the application that can be tolerated without significant
  impact.

Mission Critical Application Name	Application Priority	Maximum Outage

Vulnerability

Some processes may be more vulnerable to a prolonged disruption or outage
than others. There could be several reasons:

- The process may involve new or complex information processing
  technology.

- The process may involve older technology that requires considerable maintenance and is susceptible to major breakdowns.

- The process is often interrupted as a result of external factors beyond your control such as suppliers or partners.

Based on your knowledge and experience, how would you rate the vulnerabilities of your processes? Select a number to rate the vulnerability using a scale of 1-7 where 1 is not vulnerable and 7 is extremely vulnerable to an outage.

1	2	3	4	5	6	7

Server Criticality Analysis

	Department and Server Function/Activity:						
1.	What deadlines does your department meet for this function? (Please circle)						
	Daily	Weekly	Monthly	Quarterly	Semiannually	Annually	Other
2.	What other business functions or departments directly depend on this function?						
3.	Is this a deferrable function?						
	If no, required resumption time:			hours			
	If yes, maximum time deferrable			hours	days	weeks	
4.	Can this function be performed manually? Yes/No						
5.	Does this function need to be done within certain hours of the day? Yes/No						

6.	Is this function supported by a specific server?				
	If yes, application name:				
7.	Is this function supported by any specialized software?				
	If yes, please describe:				
8.	Is this function supported by any specialized hardware?				
	If yes, please describe:				
9.	Is this function governed by an SLA?				
	If yes, please describe:				
10.	Reports Produced	(Circle one)	Yes/No		
	Name:		Hardcopy	Online	Critical for Recovery

598

Index